ICSEA 2023

The Eighteenth International Conference on Software Engineering Advances

November 13th – 17th, 2023

Valencia, Spain

ICSEA 2023 Editors

Herwig Mannaert, University of Antwerp, Belgium

Radek Koci, Brno University of Technology, Czech Republic

Printed from e-media with permission by:

Curran Associates, Inc.
57 Morehouse Lane
Red Hook, NY 12571

Some format issues inherent in the e-media version may also appear in this print version.

Printed with permission by Curran Associates, Inc. (2024)

International Academy, Research, and Industry Association (IARIA)
412 Derby Way
Wilmington, DE 19810

Phone: (408) 893-6407
Fax: (408) 527-6351

petre@iaria.org

Additional copies of this publication are available from:

Curran Associates, Inc.
57 Morehouse Lane
Red Hook, NY 12571 USA
Phone: 845-758-0400
Fax: 845-758-2633
Email: curran@proceedings.com
Web: www.proceedings.com

Table of Contents

ICSEA 2023

Forward

The Eighteenth International Conference on Software Engineering Advances (ICSEA 2023), held on November 13 - 17, 2023 in Valencia, Spain, continued a series of events covering a broad spectrum of software-related topics.

The conference covered fundamentals on designing, implementing, testing, validating and maintaining various kinds of software. The tracks treated the topics from theory to practice, in terms of methodologies, design, implementation, testing, use cases, tools, and lessons learnt. The conference topics covered classical and advanced methodologies, open source, agile software, as well as software deployment and software economics and education.

The conference had the following tracks:

- Advances in fundamentals for software development
- Advanced mechanisms for software development
- Advanced design tools for developing software
- Software engineering for service computing (SOA and Cloud)
- Advanced facilities for accessing software
- Software performance
- Software security, privacy, safeness
- Advances in software testing
- Specialized software advanced applications
- Web Accessibility
- Open source software
- Agile and Lean approaches in software engineering
- Software deployment and maintenance
- Software engineering techniques, metrics, and formalisms
- Software economics, adoption, and education
- Business technology
- Improving productivity in research on software engineering
- Trends and achievements

Similar to the previous edition, this event continued to be very competitive in its selection process and very well perceived by the international software engineering community. As such, it is attracting excellent contributions and active participation from all over the world. We were very pleased to receive a large amount of top quality contributions.

We take here the opportunity to warmly thank all the members of the ICSEA 2023 technical program committee as well as the numerous reviewers. The creation of such a broad and high quality conference program would not have been possible without their involvement. We also kindly thank all the authors that dedicated much of their time and efforts to contribute to the ICSEA 2023. We truly believe that thanks to all these efforts, the final conference program consists of top quality contributions.

This event could also not have been a reality without the support of many individuals, organizations and sponsors. We also gratefully thank the members of the ICSEA 2023 organizing committee for their help in handling the logistics and for their work that is making this professional meeting a success.

We hope the ICSEA 2023 was a successful international forum for the exchange of ideas and results between academia and industry and to promote further progress in software engineering research. We also hope that Valencia provided a pleasant environment during the conference and everyone saved some time for exploring this beautiful city

ICSEA 2023 Steering Committee

Herwig Manaert, University of Antwerp, Belgium
Radek Koci, Brno University of Technology, Czech Republic
Sébastien Salva, University of Clermont Auvergne | LIMOS Laboratory | CNRS, France
José Carlos Metrôlho, Polytechnic Institute of Castelo Branco, Portugal
Luigi Lavazza, Università dell'Insubria – Varese, Italy
Hironori Washizaki, Waseda University / National Institute of Informatics / SYSTEM INFORMATION, Japan
Roy Oberhauser, Aalen University, Germany

ICSEA 2023 Publicity Chair

Lorena Parra Boronat, Universitat Politecnica de Valencia, Spain
Sandra Viciano Tudela, Universitat Politecnica de Valencia, Spain
Jose Miguel Jimenez, Universitat Politecnica de Valencia, Spain

ICSEA 2023

Committee

ICSEA 2023 Steering Committee

Herwig Manaert, University of Antwerp, Belgium
Radek Koci, Brno University of Technology, Czech Republic
Sébastien Salva, University of Clermont Auvergne | LIMOS Laboratory | CNRS, France
José Carlos Metrôlho, Polytechnic Institute of Castelo Branco, Portugal
Luigi Lavazza, Università dell'Insubria – Varese, Italy
Hironori Washizaki, Waseda University / National Institute of Informatics / SYSTEM INFORMATION, Japan
Roy Oberhauser, Aalen University, Germany

ICSEA 2023 Publicity Chair

Lorena Parra Boronat, Universitat Politecnica de Valencia, Spain
Sandra Viciano Tudela, Universitat Politecnica de Valencia, Spain
Jose Miguel Jimenez, Universitat Politecnica de Valencia, Spain

ICSEA 2023 Technical Program Committee

Tamer Abdou, Ryerson University, Canada
Morayo Adedjouma, CEA Saclay Nano-INNOV - Institut CARNOT CEA LIST, France
Ammar Kareem Obayes Alazzawi, Universiti Teknologi PETRONAS, Malaysia
Washington H. C. Almeida, CESAR School, Brazil
Eman Abdullah AlOmar, Rochester Institute of Technology, USA
Sousuke Amasaki, Okayama Prefectural University, Japan
Talat Ambreen, International Islamic University, Islamabad, Pakistan
Amal Ahmed Anda, University of Ottawa, Canada
Daniel Andresen, Kansas State University, USA
Giusy Annunziata, University of Salerno, Italy
Jean-Paul Arcangeli, UPS - IRIT, France
Francesca Arcelli Fontana, University of Milano Bicocca, Italy
Héber H. Arcolezi, Inria & École Polytechnique (IPP), Palaiseau, France
Benjamin Aziz, University of Portsmouth, UK
Takuya Azumi, Saitama University, Japan
Jorge Barreiros, ISEC - Polytechnic of Coimbra / NOVA LINCS, Portugal
Marciele Bergier, Universidade do Minho | Research Center of the Justice and Governance, Portugal
Silvia Bonfanti, University of Bergamo, Italy
Mina Boström Nakicenovic, Paradox Interactive, Sweden
Khadija Bousselmi Arfaoui, University of Savoie Mont Blanc, France
José Carlos Bregieiro Ribeiro, Polytechnic Institute of Leiria, Portugal
Uwe Breitenbücher, University of Stuttgart, Germany

Silvana Togneri Mac Mahon, Dublin City University, Ireland
Frédéric Mallet, Université Cote d'Azur | Inria Sophia Antipolis Méditerranée, France
Herwig Mannaert, University of Antwerp, Belgium
Krikor Maroukian, Microsoft, Greece
Johnny Marques, Aeronautics Institute of Technology (ITA), Brazil
Célia Martinie, Université Paul Sabatier Toulouse III, France
Rohit Mehra, Accenture Labs, India
Kristof Meixner, Christian Doppler Lab CDL-SQI | Institute for Information Systems Engineering | Technische Universität Wien, Vienna, Austria
Vojtech Merunka, Czech University of Life Sciences in Prague / Czech Technical University in Prague, Czech Republic
José Carlos M. M. Metrolho, Polytechnic Institute of Castelo Branco, Portugal
Sanjay Misra, Covenant University, Nigeria
Mohammadsadegh Mohagheghi, Vali-e-Asr University of Rafsanjan, Iran
Miguel P. Monteiro, Universidade NOVA de Lisboa, Portugal
Fernando Moreira, Universidade Portucalense, Portugal
Óscar Mortágua Pereira, University of Aveiro, Portugal
Ines Mouakher, University of Tunis El Manar, Tunisia
Kmimech Mourad, Higher Institute for Computer Science and Mathematics of Monastir, Tunisia
Lucilene F. Mouzinho da Silva, Federal Institute of Maranhão, Brazil
Sana Ben Hamida Mrabet, Paris Nanterre University / LAMSADE - Paris Dauphine University, France
Kazi Muheymin-Us-Sakib, Institute of Information Technology (IIT) | University of Dhaka, Bangladesh
Marcellin Nkenlifack, University of Dschang, Cameroon
Marc Novakouski, Carnegie Mellon Software Engineering Institute, USA
Roy Oberhauser, Aalen University, Germany
Shinpei Ogata, Shinshu University, Japan
Flavio Oquendo, IRISA (UMR CNRS) - University of South Brittany, France
Marcos Palacios, University of Oviedo, Spain
Beatriz Pérez Valle, University of La Rioja, Spain
Quentin Perez, IMT Mines Alès, France
Michalis Pingos, Cyprus University of Technology, Cyprus
Monica Pinto, University of Málaga, Spain
Blaž Podgorelec, Graz University of Technology / Secure Information Technology Center Austria (A-SIT), Austria
Aneta Poniszewska-Maranda, Institute of Information Technology | Lodz University of Technology, Poland
Pasqualina Potena, RISE Research Institutes of Sweden AB, Sweden
Evgeny Pyshkin, University of Aizu, Japan
Claudia Raibulet, University of Milano-Bicocca, Italy
Aurora Ramírez, University of Córdoba, Spain
Raman Ramsin, Sharif University of Technology, Iran
Gilberto Recupito, University of Salerno, Italy
Stephan Reiff-Marganiec, University of Derby, UK
Fernando Reinaldo Ribeiro, Polytechnic Institute of Castelo Branco, Portugal
Catarina I. Reis, ciTechCare - Center for Innovative Care and Health Technology | Polytechnic of Leiria, Portugal
Wolfgang Reisig, Humboldt University, Berlin, Germany
Michele Risi, University of Salerno, Italy

Simona Mirela Riurean, University of Petrosani, Romania
Nelson Rocha, University of Aveiro, Portugal
José Raúl Romero, Universidad de Córdoba, Spain
António Miguel Rosado da Cruz, Polytechnic Institute of Viana do Castelo, Portugal
Adrian Rutle, Western Norway University of Applied Sciences, Norway
Ines Bayoudh Saadi, ENSIT - Tunis University, Tunisia
Gunter Saake, Otto von Guericke University of Magdeburg, Germany
Nyyti Saarimäki, Tampere University, Finland
Mohamed Aymen Saied, Laval University, Canada
Khayyam Salehi, Shahrekord University, Iran
Bilal Abu Salih, The University of Jordan, Jordan
Sébastien Salva, University of Clermont Auvergne | LIMOS Laboratory | CNRS, France
Hiroyuki Sato, University of Tokyo, Japan
Wieland Schwinger, Johannes Kepler University Linz (JKU) | Inst. f. Telekooperation (TK), Austria
Vesna Šešum-Čavić, TU Wien, Austria
István Siket, University of Szeged, Hungary
Karolj Skala, Hungarian Academy of Sciences, Hungary / Ruđer Bošković Institute Zagreb, Croatia
Juan Jesús Soria Quijaite, Universidad Peruana Unión, Lima, Peru
Nissrine Souissi, MINES-RABAT School (ENSMR), Morocco
Maria Spichkova, RMIT University, Australia
Alin Stefanescu, University of Bucharest, Romania
Sidra Sultana, National University of Sciences and Technology, Pakistan
Yingcheng Sun, Columbia University in New York City, USA
Jose Manuel Torres, Universidade Fernando Pessoa, Porto, Portugal
Christos Troussas, University of West Attica, Greece
Mariusz Trzaska, Polish-Japanese Academy of Information Technology, Poland
Masateru Tsunoda, Kindai University, Japan
Simona Vasilache, University of Tsukuba, Japan
Sylvain Vauttier, LGI2P - Ecole des Mines d'Alès, France
Rohith Yanambaka Venkata, Nokia Bell Labs, USA
Colin Venters, University of Huddersfield, UK
Laszlo Vidacs, Hungarian Academy of Sciences / University of Szeged, Hungary
Hironori Washizaki, Waseda University / National Institute of Informatics / SYSTEM INFORMATION, Japan
Bingyang Wei, Texas Christian University, USA
Mohamed Wiem Mkaouer, Rochester Institute of Technology, USA
Dietmar Winkler, Institute for Information Systems Engineering | TU Wien, Austria
Krzysztof Wnuk, Blekinge Institute of Technology, Sweden
Heitor Augustus Xavier Costa, Federal University of Lavras, Brazil
Simon Xu, Algoma University, Canada
Rihito Yaegashi, Kagawa University, Japan
Guowei Yang, The University of Queensland, Australia
Yilong Yang, University of Macau, Macau
Haibo Yu, Kyushu Sangyo University, Japan
Zifan Yu, Arizona State University, USA
Mário Zenha-Rela, University of Coimbra, Portugal
Qiang Zhu, University of Michigan - Dearborn, USA

Martin Zinner, Technische Universität Dresden, Germany
Kamil Żyła, Lublin University of Technology, Poland

Copyright Information

Resolution to Educational Group Formation Problem Based on Improved Particle Swarm Optimization Using Fuzzy Knowledge

Hasan Bikhtiyar
Higher Institute of Computer Science and Communication Technologies
University of Sousse
Sousse, Tunisia
bikhtiyar.hasan85@gmail.com

Amine Boufaied
Higher Institute of Computer Science and Communication Technologies
University of Sousse
Sousse, Tunisia
Boufaied.amine@gmail.com

Abstract— **In the educational context, instructors usually partition students into collaborative learning teams to perform collaborative learning tasks. Indeed, one of the grouping criteria most utilized by instructors is based on the students' roles and on forming similar teams according to the roles of their members, which is costly and complex. This paper addresses the optimization problem of forming automatic learning teams by minimizing the knowledge-difference cost among formed teams. The knowledge index of each group depends on the Belbin roles of their students' members in the form of a sum of students' fuzzy rating indexes. The proposed algorithm is called improved particle swarm optimization with multi-parent order crossover (IPSOMPOX). The multi-parent order crossover is used in IPSOMPOX in order to investigate new solutions in the search space and to accelerate the convergence of the proposed algorithm to the best global solution. To evaluate the performance of the proposed algorithm, we apply it to several different experiments with different numbers of teams and students. The results demonstrate the superiority of our proposed performance over the standard PSO.**

Keywords— Particle Swarm Optimization; Learning group formation problem; Belbin roles; Multi-Parent Order Crossover; Fuzzy Classification.

I. Introduction

Nowadays, there is an increasing interest in developing teamwork skills [1] [2]. This growing interest is motivated by its effectiveness and the fact that, in labor contexts, enterprises organize their employees in teams to carry out complex projects [3]. In fact, problems relating to team formation are common across many industrial sectors, including education, sport and general business. It is beyond manual implementation to build near-optimal teams as pools of candidates grow [4]. The team is comparable to the human body, like various organs collaborate to make things happen, and the various individuals collaborate daily to bring success to the project [5].

Recently, an appreciable number of researchers have attempted to solve the problem of team formation without leaders. In 1995, Kennedy and Eberhart designed the particle swarm optimization (PSO) in observations modeling the "social behavior" of schools of birds or fish searching for their nest or food. Kennedy and Eberhart expressed interest in Frank Heppner's model (among the various available models). In [6], a modified PSO algorithm is proposed for solving a team formation optimization problem by minimizing the communication cost among experts. The proposed algorithm is called Improved Particle Swarm Optimization with New Swap Operator (IPSONSO). In IPSONSO, a new swap operator is applied within particle swarm optimization to ensure the consistency of the capabilities and the skills to perform the required project.

In the educational context, one of the grouping criteria most utilized by instructors is based on taking into account the students' roles and forming teams according to the roles of their members [7]. A role is how a person tends to behave, contribute and interrelate with others throughout a collaborative task. Several team role models proposed in the literature recommend this grouping criterion [8]. Students belonging to Belbin teams acknowledge that they attend classes more regularly, need less time to study outside the classes and show a higher interest in the subject at the end of the course. This team forming method allows students to identify their own strengths and weaknesses and understand the roles (behaviors) of their teammates and their strengths and weaknesses [9].

In this paper, we propose a new method addressing the optimization problem of forming automatically working teams and making the teams as similar as possible to each other across the knowledge indexes to get a homogenous working rate. These knowledge indexes depend on the skills of their members in the form of a sum of fuzzy rating indexes. The proposed algorithm is named Improved Particle Swarm Optimization with Multi-Parent Order Crossover (IPSOMPOX). The multi-parent order crossover is used in IPSOMPOX in order to investigate new solutions in the search space and to accelerate the convergence of the proposed algorithm to the best global solution.

The rest of this paper is structured as follows. Section II presents the problem statement. Section III provides important details about the optimization algorithm. Our proposed algorithm (IPSOMPOX) is described in Section IV. Section V evaluates the proposal and compares it with traditional PSO. Section VI concludes this paper.

II. Problem Statement

Let set S comprise n collaborators, $S = \{s_1, s_2, \ldots, s_n\}$. We have to partition the n collaborators into a set GP_k of g teams, $GP_k = \{G_1, G_2, \ldots, G_g\}$, k is a positive integer. Each team G_i, i=1…g, is made up of a z_i number of member collaborators, and each collaborator can only belong to one team.

Regarding team size, collaborators must be divided so that the g teams have a similar number of collaborators each. Specifically, the difference between a team's size and the other teams' size must not exceed one. The values of the terms n and g are known.

Each team G_i has to accomplish a given task (i.e., a project or a part of the same global project), and a set of m skills $R = \{r_1, r_2, \ldots, r_m\}$ represents the abilities of the collaborators to a given task.

The pair (F, R) is called a Fuzzy Soft Set over S, where F: R → P(S) and where P(S) is the set of all fuzzy subsets of a universal set S relative to a $r_i \in R$ [5] [10].

Every skill in this problem is not in crisp nature. Skills are all in a fuzzy nature and are called linguistic variables. The linguistic variables do not receive any numerical values but some words or sentences of information. The linguistic variables of the fuzzy system for project team selection can be classified into four categories: VG (very good), GD (good), FR (fair), and PR (poor) [11].

Here, we consider that each collaborator has an evaluation for each skill. In this sense, we define four evaluations: VG (very good), GD (good), FR (fair), and PR (poor). The evaluation determines the degree to which a collaborator possesses a particular skill naturally. Therefore, the membership value (MV) of a collaborator to a skill can be calculated as follows.

$$MV = [LB + (UB - LB) * (AV/100)] \quad (1)$$

where LB: Lower Bound, UB: Upper Bound and AV: Actual Value.

Let us define $x_1, x_2 \ldots x_j$ as the membership values of each evaluation. Additionally, let $w_1, w_2 \ldots, w_j$ are the weights of the required skills for a given project respectively, $\sum_{i=1}^{j} w_i = 1$, then the fuzzy rating indexes (FRI) are:

$$(FRI)s_i = \Sigma[x_i * w_i],\ i=1 \text{ to } j \quad (2)$$

$$(DFRI)s_i = (FRI)s_i * 100 \quad (3)$$

Where $(DFRI)_{si}$ is the defuzzified or crisp value of $(FRI)_{si}$ of the collaborator s_i. The output can be interpreted based on a fuzzy rating index or its defuzzified value (crisp value).

For each group $G_i \in GP_k$, i=1...g, we calculate the Knowledge Index (KI), which is the sum of the fuzzy rating index of its collaborators.

$$KI(G_i) = \sum_{k=1}^{/G_i/} FRI_{S_k} \quad (4)$$

From equation (4), we calculate the average AV of the different KIs.

$$AV(GP_k) = \frac{\sum_{i=1}^{g} KI(G_i)}{g} \quad (5)$$

Then, we calculate the squared difference between each KI and the average. For instance, for the first KI:

$$(KI(G_1) - AV)^2 \quad (6)$$

The squared deviations of each value are then added:

$$\sum_{i=1}^{g} (KI(G_i) - AV)^2 \quad (7)$$

This sum is then divided by the number of KIs to get the variance, i.e.,

$$\frac{\sum_{i=1}^{g} (KI(G_i) - AV)^2}{g} \quad (8)$$

The standard deviation ST of a team's partition GP_k is given with:

$$ST(GP_k) = \sqrt{\frac{\sum_{i=1}^{g} (KI(G_i) - AV)^2}{g}} \quad (9)$$

$ST(GP_k)$ is zero if all the Knowledge Indexes (KI) of teams in the partition GP_k are the same (because each value is equal to the average).

A set of weighted skills forms a given project P. Each collaborator $s_i \in S$ is associated with a fuzzy rating index FRI_{si} relatively to the given project. A set of possible collaborators' partitions achieving P is denoted GP, GP = $GP_1, GP_2, \ldots, GP_m$, where m is a positive integer. The goal is to find a partition with the least knowledge difference cost among teams of collaborators $ST(GP_k)$, $k \in \{1..m\}$ realizing the same given project according to (9).

The team formation problem can be considered as an optimization problem by forming a feasible partition GP* among a set of possible collaborators' partitions with minimum knowledge difference cost among formed teams, and GP* can be obtained by the following:

$$Min_{(GP_k \in GP)}\ ST(GP_k) = \sqrt{\frac{\sum_{i=1}^{g} (KI(G_i) - AV)^2}{g}} \quad (10)$$

subject to

$$\forall s_j \in S, \sum_{i=1}^{g} P_{ij} = 1 \quad (11)$$

Where P_{ij} is a binary variable, $P_{ij} = 1$ if collaborator s_j belongs to the team G_i and 0 otherwise. A collaborator belongs to one team among a partition GP_k.

The notations of the team formation problem are summarized in Table 1.

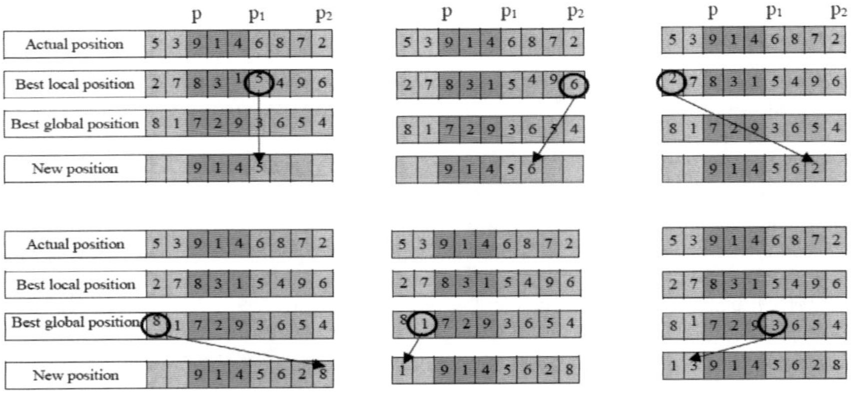

Figure. 1. An example of the implementation of the 3-POX.

TABLE I. NOTATIONS OF TEAM FORMATION PROBLEM

Notation	Definition
S	A set of collaborators
GP_k	A partition of collaborators into g teams
P	A project with weighted skills
R	A set of skills
G_i	collaborators' team
$(FRI)_{si}$	The fuzzy rating index of a collaborator s_i
$KI(G_i)$	Knowledge index of a team G_i

III. OPTIMIZATION ALGORITHM

Each solution in the optimization algorithm population represents a set GP_k of g teams (g is the number of teams), which may be built when the n collaborators in the class are partitioned. Each solution is represented as a list with a length equal to n (i.e., a list with as many positions as students in the class). Specifically, each position p (p = 1..., n) on this list contains a different collaborator (i.e., repeated collaborators are not admitted) (n is the number of collaborators). Besides, each collaborator s_j (j = 1..., n) may be in any position on the list. In short, the list is a permutation of the n collaborators [8].

In this process, the g teams are built, considering the two restrictions as part of the problem. The first restriction is that each student may belong to only one team. While the second restriction holds that the difference between the size of a team and the size of the rest of the teams must not exceed one. The size of the teams is considered to depend on the relationship between the values n and g.

When n>2, there are so many possible permutations to realize from a functional point of view. Therefore, designing an intelligent mechanism to realize a minimum number of permutations is necessary to finally get a collaborator's partition with minimum difference knowledge between its teams. We propose to use a new, improved Particle Swarm Optimization (PSO) method to solve such an optimization problem.

In fact, to solve the stated working group formation problem, we used the Multi-Parent Order Crossover (MPOX). We developed a new, Improved Particle Swarm Optimization with Multi-Parent Order Crossover (IPSOMPOX).

IV. THE IMPROVED PARTICLE SWARM OPTIMIZATION WITH MULTI-PARENT ORDER CROSSOVER (IPSOMPOX)

IPSOMPOX starts with an initial population containing a specific number of feasible particles. Each particle consists of a permutation of the n collaborators and is a list. A random method has been designed to generate each of the particles of this population. This kind of method guarantees a good level of diversity in the initial population and, therefore, helps prevent the premature convergence of the algorithm. Then, *itmax* iterations are executed to define the content of the positions of the particles. All the swarm particles are updated in each iteration m (m =1..., itmax). The position of a particle is updated using the multi-parent order crossover (MPOX) [12]. In our resolution method, we used three parents: the actual position, the best local position and the best global position.

The following algorithm 1 presents the pseudocode of the 3-POX. Notice that moving through the actual position, the best local position, the best global position, or the new position can be circular) (see Figure 1).

Algorithm 1 (3-parent order crossover (3-POX)):

1. ***Parents selection:*** select the actual position, the best local and global positions.
   // Three segments selection
2. ***Crossover points generation:*** randomly generate the first crossover points p and calculate p_1 and p_2 to divide the actual position into almost equal three segments' widths. The three segments' widths are equal if the actual position width is divisible by 3.
   // Segment copy
3. For i = p to p_1
   Copy the elements from actual_position[i] into the new position[i].

// Elements' selection

4. Pick up the elements from the best local position, starting at p_1, which do not exist in the new position, and copy them into the new position starting at p_1 until reaching p_2.
5. Pick up the elements from the best global position, starting at p_2, which does not exist in the new position, and copy them into the new position starting at p_2 until reaching p.

V. Simulations and Performance Evaluation

In this section, we study the performance of the IPSOMPOX algorithm using a numerical simulation of several student's permutations in order to verify the effectiveness of our team formation approach. In fact, we conducted a series of experiments to evaluate the performance of our proposed algorithm.

A. Preliminaries

We started by creating a collaborator's vector noted *collaborators* whose size is the number of collaborators noted *nCollaborators*. The value of *nCollaborators* is initialized at the start of the simulation execution. Each component of the collaborator's vector is a student defined by rank and fuzzy rating index (FRI).

Knowing the number of groups *g*, we calculate the number of collaborators per group and create a group vector noted *groups*. The *groups* vector, whose size is the number of collaborators, contains the instances of groups.

The MPSO (3-POX) is applied when the number of collaborators exceeds 2. It is noted that the variable containing the maximum number of iterations of *MaxIt*. We also chose the population number of the swarm equal to *nPop*. Thus, a random population of *nPop* particles is created (These are particles collaborator's permutations). Each particle has a position whose size is *nCollaborators*, where a particle is a possible solution for our optimization problem. The cost of its position is the best position. The cost function returns the standard deviation of the knowledge indexes of all teams, Equation (12).

$$Cost(particle_i.position) = ST(KI(GP_k), k=1..g, \text{ in } particle_i)$$
$$i = 1..\ nPop \quad (12)$$

When IPSOMPSO is launched, the positions of the different particles are updated, and their costs are calculated, as shown previously. Also, the best personal solution and the best global solution are updated. The particles are moving and approaching the optimal solution from iteration to iteration. Once the stop condition is verified, execution stops, and we get a student's partition into g groups with the minimum standard deviation between the group's knowledge indexes.

B. Evaluation

We conducted a series of experiments to evaluate the performance of our proposed algorithm.

In the first simulation, we considered 50 students to partition into nine learning groups. We got the nine weights w_i of the Belbin roles relatively to the project P to accomplish from the instructor (i.e., P = {w_1*PL, w_2*RI, w_3*CO, w_4*SH, w_5*ME, w_6*TW, w_7*IM, w_8*FI, w_9*SP}), $\sum_{i=1}^{9} w_i = 1$. With the results of the Belbin Team Role Self-Perception Inventory (BTRSPI), we obtain Table II, showing the FRI of each student.

TABLE II. The FRI of each student

Student	FRI	Student	FRI	Student	FRI
1	0.0966	18	0.4769	35	0.8325
2	0.2654	19	0.1296	36	0.1751
3	0.7919	20	0.2281	37	0.8798
4	0.9369	21	0.1811	38	0.2796
5	0.5683	22	0.6720	39	0.8495
6	0.9380	23	0.3258	40	0.8067
7	0.5972	24	0.7906	41	0.1891
8	0.9880	25	0.5460	42	0.9786
9	0.7623	26	0.2306	43	0.2537
10	0.1856	27	0.6868	44	0.7785
11	0.5168	28	0.0491	45	0.8108
12	0.6402	29	0.5726	46	0.4980
13	0.8690	30	0.9938	47	0.9157
14	0.6001	31	0.3630	48	0.1010
15	0.9997	32	0.5587	49	0.1358
16	0.1292	33	0.9273	50	0.8583
17	0.2934	34	0.2599		

Table III shows le number of students in each group.

TABLE III. Number of students in each group

Group 1	Group 2	Group 3	Group 4	Group 5	Group 6	Group 7	Group 8	Group 9
6	6	6	6	6	5	5	5	5

Once the execution of the IPSOMPOX is finished, it is possible to calculate the partition of the students (as listed in Table IV). Partition of students into groups.

TABLE IV. PARTITION OF STUDENTS IN EACH GROUP

Group 1	Group 2	Group 3	Group 4	Group 5	Group 6	Group 7	Group 8	Group 9
36	4	42	46	9	50	47	6	5
29	48	28	26	41	8	44	25	15
2	22	37	17	33	12	11	21	49
40	16	19	10	1	18	43	3	20
32	35	24	30	13	38	27	14	45
7	34	23	39	31				

Accordingly, as listed in Table V, we calculate the KI of each group G_k.

TABLE V. Knowledge index of each group

$KI(G_1)$	$KI(G_2)$	$KI(G_3)$	$KI(G_4)$	$KI(G_5)$	$KI(G_6)$	$KI(G_7)$	$KI(G_8)$	$KI(G_9)$
2.9758	2.9314	3.1534	3.0507	3.2073	3.2429	3.1515	3.0572	2.7427

The minimal standard deviation we got is equal to 0,1478, Figure 2.

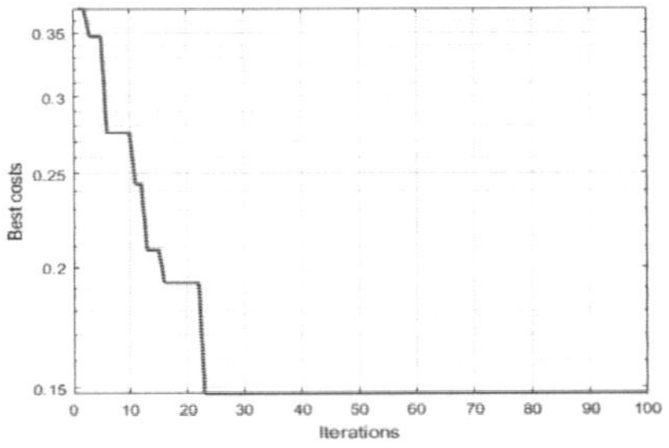

Figure 2. The Best Costs of the example of Table II.

Table VII presents the costing intervals of the knowledge difference costs for three experiments on randomly generated data. The results of IPSOMPOX decrease iteratively to the number of iterations than PSO, achieving better performance ranging from 31% in the fourth iteration to 14% in the last iteration for experiment 1. In comparison, the percentage of the improved results ranged from 2.4% in the second iteration to 16.7% in the fourth iteration when compared with PSO in experiment 2. Also, the results of IPSOMPOX are better and more efficient than PSO, with knowledge difference cost going down from 8.3% better performance in the tenth iteration to 56.4% in the third

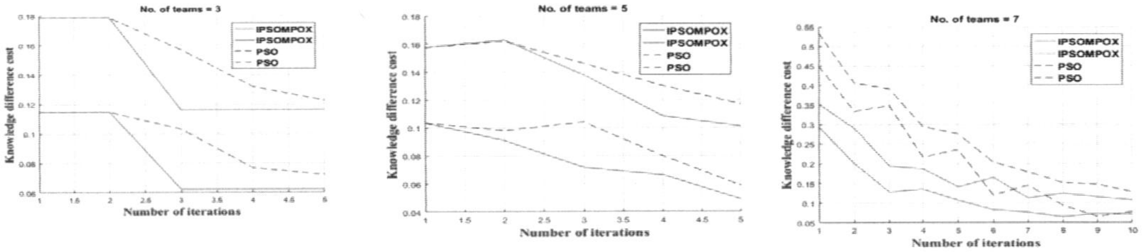

Figure.3. Comparison between PSO and IPSOMPOX on random data.

iteration of experiment 3. In Figure 3, the costing intervals of the proposed algorithm are presented against the standard PSO for different team numbers by plotting the number of iterations against the costing intervals on knowledge difference costs. The results in Figure 3 show that the proposed algorithm is better than the standard PSO.

In a second simulation, three experiments are performed on the random dataset with different teams and student numbers to evaluate the performance of the proposed algorithm that focuses on iteratively minimizing the knowledge difference cost among teams. The average results are taken over 50 runs. The parameters are reported in Table VI. The proposed algorithm is compared with the standard PSO to verify its efficiency.

TABLE VI. PARAMETER SETTING

Exp. No.	No. of iterations	No. of the initial population	No. of teams	No. of students
1	5	5	3	10
2	5	10	5	20
3	10	20	7	30

In Table VII, the average ($\bar{x}$), the standard deviation (s) and the mean (μ) of the results sample are reported over 50 random runs. The mean μ is also reported with a confidence level of 95%.

The performance (%) between the compared algorithms can be computed in Eq. (13).

$$\text{Performance}(\%) = \frac{(\mu_{(PSO)} - \mu_{(IPSOMPOX)})}{\mu_{(PSO)}} * 100 \qquad (13)$$

where $\mu_{(PSO)}$ and $\mu_{(IPSOMPOX)}$ are the mean results obtained from SPSO and IPSOMPOX algorithms, respectively.

TABLE VII. COMPARISON BETWEEN PSO AND IPSOMPOX ON RANDOM DATA

Exp. No.	Iteration no.		PSO	IPSOMPOX
1	1	$\bar{x}$	0,1488	0,1488
		s	0,0125	0,0125
		μ ± 2,5*σ	0,1466±0,032	0,1466±0,032
	2	$\bar{x}$	0,1488	0,1488
		s	0,0125	0,0125
		μ ± 2,5*σ	0,1466±0,032	0,1466±0,032
	3	$\bar{x}$	0,1321	0,0815
		s	0,0114	0,0109
		μ ± 2,5*σ	0,1301±0,027	0,0893±0,0269
	4	$\bar{x}$	0,1190	0,0815
		s	0,0108	0,0109
		μ ± 2,5*σ	0,1043±0,0275	0,0893±0,0269
	5	$\bar{x}$	0,0935	0,0815
		s	0,0099	0,0109
		μ ± 2,5*σ	0,0973±0,0251	0,0893±0,0269
2	1	μ ± 2,5*σ	0,1307±0,027	0,1307±0,027
	2	μ ± 2,5*σ	0,1301±0,032	0,1270±0,036
	3	μ ± 2,5*σ	0,1251±0,021	0,1048±0,033
	4	μ ± 2,5*σ	0,1048±0,025	0,0873±0,021
	5	μ ± 2,5*σ	0,0879±0,029	0,0751±0,026

3	1	μ ± 2,5*σ	0,4923±0,042	0,3235±0,029
	2	μ ± 2,5*σ	0,3693±0,036	0,2453±0,045
	3	μ ± 2,5*σ	0,3693±0,021	0,1610±0,033
	4	μ ± 2,5*σ	0,2557±0,039	0,1610±0,026
	5	μ ± 2,5*σ	0,2557±0,02	0,1239±0,017
	6	μ ± 2,5*σ	0,1619±0,042	0,1239±0,041
	7	μ ± 2,5*σ	0,1619±0,017	0,0945±0,018
	8	μ ± 2,5*σ	0,1224±0,029	0,0945±0,030
	9	μ ± 2,5*σ	0,1067±0,041	0,0945±0,021
	10	μ ± 2,5*σ	0,1031±0,025	0,0945±0,023

Finally, based on [13], the average processing times (in seconds) reported in Figure 4 over 50 runs for each experiment. We consider the 90 students and vary the number of working groups (10 experiments): 3, 5, 7, 9, 11, 15, 19, 21, 25, 30.

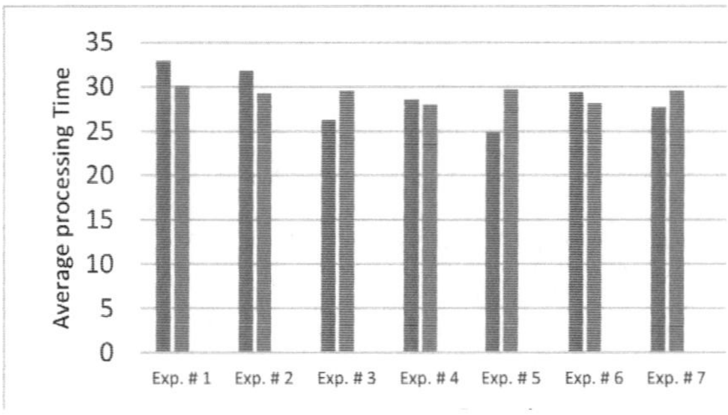

Figure 4. The average processing times (in seconds) of the PSO and IPSOMPOX

As shown in Figure 4, the time for forming a working group using the proposed algorithm IPSOMPOX varies slightly from one experiment to another and is around a mean of 29,4s. Also, the average processing time of PSO has a mean of 28,9s. Thus, the average processing time of PSO is better than that of IPSOMOX with 1,8%. This is due to additional processing time using the multi parent order crossover (MPOX).

VI. Conclusion and futur works

This study investigates a new particle swarm optimization algorithm to solve the team formation problem. The proposed algorithm is called Improved Particle Swarm Optimization with Multi-Parent Order Crossover (IPSOMPOX). In the IPSOMPOX algorithm, exploiting the multi-parent order crossover in the proposed algorithm has accelerated its convergence to the global best solution. The performance of the proposed algorithm is investigated in five experiments with different numbers of teams and students. The results of the proposed algorithm show that it can obtain a promising result in a reasonable time compared to the standard PSO.

As a future work, we propose to compare our method's performance when using the adjacency-based crossover (ABC) or the multi-parent partially mapped crossover (MPPMX) instead of the 3-POX. Also, it is worthwhile to test our proposed algorithm over various benchmark problems of nonlinear mixed integer programming problems.

References

[1] D. Mburasek, and M. Odon, «Development of a tool for team formation in engineering education,» *International Journal Of Engineering And Management Research,* vol. 11, n°16, pp. 62-69, 2021.

[2] O. Zvereva, and E. Milovidova, «Engineering Effective Teams: An Example From Educational Domain,» Chez *International Conference on Applied Mathematics & Computational Science (ICAMCS. NET)*, 2018.

[3] J. Alberola, E. Del Val, V. Sanchez-Anguix, A. Palomares and M. Dolores Teruel «An artificial intelligence tool for heterogeneous team formation in the classroom,» *Knowledge-Based Systems,* vol. 101, pp. 1-14, 2016.

[4] J. Flores-Parra, M. Castañón-Puga, R. Evans, R. Rosales-Cisneros and C. Gaxiola-Pacheco «Towards team formation using Belbin role types and a social networks analysis approach,» chez *IEEE Technology and Engineering Management Conference (TEMSCON)*, 2018.

[5] S. Kalayathankal, J. Kureethara and S. Narayanamoorthy, «A modified fuzzy approach to project team selection,» *Soft Computing Letters 3,* vol. 3, p. 100012, 2021.

[6] W. El-Ashmawi, A. Ali and M. Tawhid, «An improved particle swarm optimization with a new swap operator for team formation problem,» *J Ind Eng Int,* vol. 15, p. 53–71, 2019.

[7] M. Winter, Developing a group model for student software, Master's thesis, University of Saskatchewan, 2004.

[8] V. Yannibelli and A. Amandi, «Forming well-balanced collaborative learning teams according to the roles of their members: An evolutionary approach,» Chez *12th International Symposium on Computational Intelligence and Informatics (CINTI)*, 2011.

[9] A. Aranzabal, E. Epelde and M. Artetxe, «Team formation on the basis of Belbin's roles to enhance students' performance in project based learning,» *Education for Chemical Engineers,* vol. 38, pp. 22-37, 2022.

[10] Z. Chen, S. Kosari, S. Kaarmukilan, C. Yuvapriya. «A video processing algorithm using temporal intuitionistic fuzzy sets,» *Journal of Intelligent & Fuzzy Systems,* vol. 43, pp. 8057-8072, 2022.

[11] L. Zhou, Y. Wang and Y. Jiang, «Investment Project Assessment by a MAGDM Method Based on the Ranking of Interval Type-2 Fuzzy Sets,» *Journal of Intelligent & Fuzzy Systems,* vol. 35, n° 12, p. 1875 – 1888, 2018.

[12] A. Arram and M. Ayob, «A novel multi-parent order crossover in genetic algorithm for combinatorial optimization problems,» *Computers & Industrial Engineering,* vol. 133, pp. 267-274, 2019.

[13] A. Boufaied, «A Diagnostic Approach for Advanced Tracking of Commercial Vehicles With Time Window Constraints,» *IEEE Transactions on Intelligent Transportation Systems,* vol. 14, n° 13, pp. 1470-1479, 2013.

What Do Critical Success Factors of Collaboration Really Mean in the Context of DevOps?

Michiel van Belzen, Jos Trienekens, Rob Kusters
Faculty of Science
Open University
Heerlen, The Netherlands
email: michiel.vanbelzen@ou.nl, jos.trienekens@ou.nl, rob.kusters@ou.nl

Abstract—**Collaboration is an important aspect of DevOps. However, researchers continue to report problems with collaboration between development and operations. Critical Success Factors (CSFs) may contribute to solve these problems. Prior research found CSFs of collaboration. Yet we did not find any comprehensive list of CSFs of collaboration grounded in DevOps practice by real-life examples making them meaningful in that context. Therefore, we aim to show that CSFs of collaboration found in other contexts are also recognized in a DevOps context and what previously validated generally applicable CSFs of collaboration really mean in a DevOps context. The research method comprises of a systematic literature review to find a comprehensive list of generally applicable CSFs of collaboration, a multiple case study to find on the one hand which of these CSFs were recognized in a DevOps context and on the other hand to find real-life examples, which substantiated the CSFs recognized. Finally, the aim is to develop a classification of the CSFs. Our main contribution to theory is a well-founded and structured list of CSFs meaningful for the DevOps profession. The list of CSFs can aid practitioners to have a necessarily impact on the success of collaboration.**

Keywords – adoption; classification; collaboration; critical success factors; DevOps.

I. INTRODUCTION

DevOps is a compound of development and operations [1]. Adopting DevOps improves cycle times, software processes and quality [2].

Collaboration is seen as an important aspect of DevOps. DevOps is considered as an interaction between development and operations [3] and a set of practices and mechanisms supporting their integration [4][5][6][7]. However, literature reports problems with collaboration between both. For example, Iden, Tessem, and Paivarinta [8] and Lwakatare, Kuvaja, and Oivo [9] found poor communication, Wettinger, Breitenbücher, Falkenthal, and Leymann [10] found cultural gaps, and Colomo-Palacios, Fernandes, Soto-Acosta, and Larrucea [2] and Nielsen, Winkler, and Norbjerg [11] found knowledge boundaries.

Critical Success Factors (CSFs) may contribute to solve problems with collaboration between development and operations. However, to the best of our knowledge we did not find any comprehensive list of CSFs of collaboration in a DevOps context. Yet earlier research found CSFs of collaboration validated in other contexts. However, these CSFs can be improved in terms of specializing by context, comprehensiveness and timeliness. For example, Mattessich and Monsey [12] found nineteen factors influencing the success of collaboration and Kolfschoten, De Vreede, Briggs, and Sol [13] derived three factors in an attempt to define the concept of collaboration. As these CSFs are valid in different contexts, they may also be applicable in a DevOps context. For example, Lwakatare, Kuvaja, and Oivo [9] mentioned information sharing and skill sets and Erich, Amrit, and Daneva [3] reports culture and automation. Therefore, our research goal is to show that CSFs of collaboration found in other contexts are also recognized in a DevOps context. And we will also clarify what previously validated generally applicable CSFs of collaboration really mean in a DevOps context. Clarification of these CSFs by formulating them in terms of the DevOps profession is important as it makes CSFs meaningful in that context. Meaningful CSFs of collaboration can be addressed more easily leading to performance improvements in collaboration. Prior research present CSFs often in an abstract way and expressed in general terms. That makes these CSFs difficult to interpret, apply and measure in the context of DevOps.

This research goal brings us to our research question: Which generally applicable CSFs of collaboration are recognized in the context of DevOps and how to make them meaningful in the context of DevOps? To answer the main research question, we divide it into the following three sub questions (SQs): (SQ1) What are generally applicable CSFs of collaboration? (SQ2) Which generally applicable CSFs of collaboration are recognized in the context of DevOps? SQ3: How to make the recognized generally applicable CSFs of collaboration meaningful in the context of DevOps?

We will contribute to the existing literature by adding another research context, namely the context of DevOps. This is important, because literature has given little notice to different contexts of collaboration [14], such as the DevOps context. Second, CSFs vary in terms of abstraction and explanation as we will explain in Section 2.

The outline of this article is as follows. In Section 2, we present previous research on CSFs of collaboration. Subsequently, in Section 3, we describe the research method. In Section 4, we present the results of the case study. In Section 5, we discuss the implications and limitations, and present suggestions for future research. Finally, we reflect on our research question and research goal in Section 6.

II. THEORETICAL BACKGROUND

Considering the research question, we explored related work to find a comprehensive list of CSFs of collaboration which can be used in a case study to verify whether generally applicable CSFs are recognized in a DevOps context. To support this, we used the definition of collaboration defined by [15] as "An evolving process whereby two or more social entities actively and reciprocally engage in joint activities aimed at achieving at least one shared goal". In addition, we defined a CSF as a factor leading to successful outcome, which is in line with [12][16].

Although prior research views collaboration from different perspectives, reflection on CSFs found earlier is limited. In the early stages of research on collaboration in general, [12] reviews and summarizes existing research literature on CSFs which influence the success of collaboration. The researchers found nineteen CSFs of collaboration validated in health science and social science, and also in education and public affairs domains. In 2001 these nineteen CSFs were confirmed and an additional CSF was added: "an appropriate pace of development" [17]. Reference [18] studied a partnership between two organizations and found the factors of successful collaboration to be: partnership attributes of commitment, coordination, trust, communication quality, participation, and the conflict resolution technique of a joint problem. Collaboration between team members was studied by [19]. They mentioned human-related factors, such as social ties and knowledge sharing as important for collaborative work. The authors report in particular the importance of rapport and transactive memory, and organizational mechanisms creating and maintaining social ties between distributed team members. Reference [13] conceived collaboration as a process and a system. According to [13], collaborative success depends on willingness of its participants, which makes it a complex activity. The authors explained that collaboration involves individuals working together to achieve a group goal. Reference [15] focused on a multidisciplinary conceptualization of collaboration. According to [15] effective collaboration needs coordination. This was confirmed by [20][21] who consider coordination and cooperation as the most important problems that must be solved when individuals from diverse backgrounds and different organizations have to collaborate. Reference [22] studied collaboration among supply chain partners and identified the CSFs trust, commitment, mutuality and reciprocity.

Prior research not just identified CSFs but attempted to classify CSFs found as well. However, they classify CSFs differently based on various perspectives. For example, Mattessich and Monsey [12] classified the CSFs found into six groups: environment, membership, process/structure, communications, purpose and resources. Reference [15] applied an abstract classification and distinguished different characteristics. Reference [23] deduced the classification from their description of collaborative work. According to [23] aspects of collaborative work can be classified into seven main factor groups: context, support, tasks, interaction processes, teams, individuals and overarching factors. Finally, differences in grouping CSFs were also noticed by [14] who elaborated "Many studies have attempted to assess the CSFs for collaboration. In these studies, CSFs can be classified into CSFs influencing the likelihood of collaboration, CSFs influencing the performance of collaboration, and those influencing the collaboration type". However, [14] does not explain how CSFs can be classified.

Research on collaboration in a DevOps context has limitations as well. Prior research presents CSFs which are broad and not only focused on collaboration, and are limited in terms of comprehensiveness [24]. For example, Lwakatare, Kuvaja, and Oivo [9] mentioned information sharing and broadening of skill sets and relates them to the intended outcome, which is taking full responsibility for developing and operating an entire service. Reference [3] reports core parts of DevOps adoption, such as culture and a high degree of automation. According to the authors, organizations attempt to remove the cultural barrier between development and operations personnel and create a culture of empowerment. For example, by assigning more responsibilities to the DevOps team and giving team members the freedom to share what is on their mind. Reference [25] noticed in a study on DevOps maturity that the organization itself should be ready to execute work. They explain that DevOps team members should communicate, share knowledge, have trust and respect for each other, and align between internal and external dependencies to timely deploy software.

Grounding CSFs in DevOps practice makes CSFs better useful in the context of DevOps. The CSFs found were grounded in practice containing terminology common in the professional field. For example, Lwakatare, Kuvaja, and Oivo [9] mentioned monitoring information to illustrate knowledge sharing and Erich, Amrit, and Daneva [3], who noted automating the software release process, which can be considered as a form of clear rules and procedures. Therefore, a comprehensive list of CSFs grounded in a DevOps practice is needed.

In summary, research on CSFs of collaboration and research on collaboration in a DevOps context has limitations. In the first place, the lists found are limited build upon evolving literature of collaboration. Second, CSFs should be more generic in order to be useful in different contexts. Third, prior research has not resulted in a comprehensive list of CSFs grounded in DevOps practice. Therefore, a systematic literature review is needed first to find a more comprehensive and general list of CSFs, which can be made meaningful in the DevOps context.

III. RESEARCH METHODOLOGY

To obtain a comprehensive list of CSFs manageable and meaningful in a DevOps context, we followed three phases. The systematic literature review was the first phase in which we obtained a more comprehensive list of generally applicable CSFs. In the second phase a multiple case study was conducted to verify recognition of the CSFs found and to find corresponding real-life examples. The third phase concentrated on the classification of CSFs to develop a structured list of CSFs manageable and meaningful in a DevOps context. Classification was not possible until this phase because we need the real-life examples obtained in the second phase to infer what the CSFs recognized really mean in a DevOps context.

A. *Systematic literature review*

In order to pursue comprehensiveness, we conducted the systematic literature review in two steps applying two methods. In the first step, we conducted a literature review as described by [26] followed by snowballing in the second step. Access to digital library records was limited to the subscription of our institution. In the first step, we chose to search in the Web of Science digital library using two search strings. The first search string contained 'collaboration' in title and 'success AND factor' in all fields. As the second search string we used 'collaboration AND factor' in title. We started the search from 1992, the publication of [12]. The first search provided 205 papers and the second provided 210 papers. We removed duplicates and undertook an initial screening, which resulted in 58 papers found. Next, we assessed the remaining papers to identify papers that could be rejected based on the full text on the basis that they did not include CSFs or barriers of collaboration or on the basis of quality issues. For example, irrelevant papers or papers that contain drivers that may trigger collaboration. We found 44 papers, which included 374 CSFs.

After that, we continued in the second step our search for CSFs by applying backward snowballing and forward snowballing on the 44 papers in which we found CSFs [27]. During snowballing, 4314 papers were found. We removed duplicates and papers based on title, abstract and full text on the basis that they did not include CSFs or barriers of collaboration. This resulted in 21 papers found, which contained 198 CSFs. As we found a lot of duplicate CSFs, we did not expect to find additional CSFs by conducting more iterations of snowballing. Therefore, we stopped after one iteration. Thus, we found 572 CSFs so far.

In addition, we found 23 CSFs in the following six papers of which we were aware: [9][13][15][19][22][25]. This resulted in 595 CSFs found in total.

Because we did not yet know which CSFs would be recognized and what the CSFs found would mean in a DevOps context, we were not able to classify them. However, to be able to discuss the 595 CSFs found in the consecutive case study we grouped them according to the 20 factors found by the often-cited papers of [12][17], the ten additional factors found by [23] and the two additional factors (CSF 4 and CSF 11) found by [14][22][28]. We adopted the names of the CSFs from literature, and condensed the key findings and used them as clarifications. Thus, the results of the systematic literature review consist of a list of 32 generally applicable CSFs of collaboration.

We published the list of 32 CSFs in [24]. An example from this list is the CSF "Concrete attainable goals and objectives" described by the following clarification "Setting of clear goals (at the planning stage) [23], supplementary purposes [14] and feasible [12], based on key community issues, agreed upon [13][28][29]".

This list answers sub question SQ 1 and extended the CSFs found previously by Mattessich, Murray-Close, and Monsey [17]. However, prior research has limitations. For example, brief contextual information, limitations on definitions of CSFs and limitations on generalizability. Furthermore, we did not know whether these CSFs will be recognized in a DevOps context and whether there are more applicable CSFs. Therefore, we conducted a multiple case study.

B. *Multiple case study*

We consider a case study as a relevant method, because it addresses our research questions on collaboration which require to explain and describe this social phenomenon [30]. According to [23] collaboration can best be understood in terms of the context in which people are working and their interactions. Therefore, we decided to conduct a multiple case study and based the methodology on five steps proposed by [30]: (1) designing the case study, (2) preparing to collect evidence, (3) collecting evidence, (4) analyzing evidence, and (5) reporting results.

In the first step, we designed the case study to assure the data to be collected relates to our research question [30]. To validate our list of CSFs in a DevOps context we used an inductive approach. We carry out cross-sectional semi-structured interviews, which allowed us exploration of the CSFs and improvisation [31].

In the second step, we prepared the collection of evidence. We choose to collect data in organizations which experienced DevOps for several years, because we needed real-life examples to substantiate the CSFs found. Thus, we contacted gatekeepers of organizations that appear to comply to our requirement regarding DevOps experience and explain our study. We found two governmental ISPs which wanted to participate in this study, which met our criterion and experienced DevOps for several years. Both organizations studied were professional and large organizations which exist for a long time. The gatekeepers had a central role with a good overview of DevOps developments in the organization for a number of years.

We asked the gatekeepers for permission to interview employees who met our criteria of at least two years of practical and broad experience with DevOps to be able to mention and elaborate on examples.

Together with the gatekeepers we selected interviewees who had a coordinating role or advisory role or developer role. Each organization provided five interviewees originating from different teams. We contacted the potential interviewees, explained our study and verified whether they were available and willing to participate.

We were able to select interviewees who had at least two years of practical experience as an advisor, developer, scrum master or manager with the application of aspects (in a broad sense) of DevOps.

In order to assure reliability, we prepared an interview protocol, which contained information on the research project, procedures for data collection and analysis, and three main interview questions. We asked: (1) whether and to what extent the interviewees recognized the definition of collaboration according to [15]; (2) whether they recognized each CSF and if they knew any additional CSFs; (3) per CSF for real-life examples and facts based on their own experiences. The first question was intended to introduce the concept of collaboration and to verify whether the interviewee had the same interpretation of this concept in the context of DevOps. We stored the protocol as well as the results into a database. We started the interviews with a pilot interview. According to the interview protocol, we sent the interviewee the interview questions and the appendices. Afterwards, we applied the interview questions during the pilot interview. By applying the interview protocol and interview questions in a real-life setting we learned that no improvements to our interview protocol or interview questions were necessary. Thus, we proceeded to the third step.

In the third step, we collected the evidence by conducting the other interviews. Each interview took place face-to-face. The researcher conducting the interview also took notes during the interviews, recorded each interview and transcribed each interview afterwards. Subsequently, we sent a transcription to the corresponding interviewee, which enabled the interviewee to amend the transcription.

In the fourth step, we analyzed the content. Therefore, we familiarized ourself with the content, divided the text up into meaning units and condensed these units if appropriate and formulated codes [32]. We coded our data using ATLAS.ti by reading the transcripts and adding codes to meaning units, such as feedback on the definition of collaboration, recognized CSFs, mentioned additional CSFs and real-life examples. In that way we were able to export tables of the results. Next, we condensed the meaning units if appropriate to support the classification of the results, which was particularly appropriate in the case of the real-life examples to make them more concise.

The real-life examples illustrate the recognition of experts regarding all 32 CSFs found. For example, the development of a unique product as an example of a goal, or reviewing new code before merging as an example of a rule. They also contain specific, concrete and 'richer' experience-based information on what the CSFs really mean in a DevOps context. This enabled us to refine the initial names and clarifications of the CSFs to reflect the DevOps context. Therefore, we replaced the more general concepts by concepts and descriptions based on the supporting evidence. Some parts of initial clarifications were neglected due to irrelevance or lack of evidence.

In the fifth and last step, we put the recognized CSFs, the corresponding refined clarifications and the condensed real-life examples in one table.

C. *Classification of the 32 CSFs recognized*

In the third phase we developed categories of CSFs by classification of the 32 CSFs recognized. Until this phase classification was not possible because we need the real-life examples obtained in the previous phase to infer what the CSFs recognized really mean in a DevOps context.

We based the classification on the metaplan-method [33]. The identification and classification of similar CSFs make the list of CSFs more manageable and provides the basis for making the CSFs measurable. As part of the classification, we could infer clarifications meaningful in the DevOps context.

During the metaplan session we stated and discussed the rationale for sorting each card, determined the name of each emerged CSF and derived the clarifications of the fourteen new emerged CSFs from the grouped CSFs. For example, we grouped CSF "Roles and responsibilities" with CSF "Rules and procedures" into CSF "Procedures and responsibilities" based on examples mentioned, such as "Members determine their own way of work" and "The whole team is responsible for everything they deliver". In the following three cases, we adopted clarifications from literature: Knowledge Management, Communication and Leadership. With the resulting fourteen CSFs, corresponding clarifications and condensed real-life examples we were able to answer the sub research questions in Section 4.

IV. RESULTS OF THE MULTIPLE CASE STUDY

In Section 3, we have found that all generally applicable CSFs found in literature were recognized, which answers sub question 2. Furthermore, we did not find additional CSFs. We also showed how recognized generally applicable CSFs of collaboration could be made meaningful in the context of DevOps, which answers sub question 3. Thus, we are now able to prove that we obtained the research goal by showing what previously validated generally applicable CSFs of collaboration really mean in a DevOps context. Therefore, we present the fourteen CSFs of collaboration in a DevOps context in Table I together with clarifications which makes the CSFs meaningful for the DevOps profession.

TABLE I. CSFS OF COLLABORATION IN A DEVOPS CONTEXT

CSF	**Clarification to make the CSF meaningful in a DevOps context**
Goals and vision	Concrete, attainable and unique goals derived from a shared vision, which are mutual understood and agreed by the whole team and supported by stakeholders.
Procedures and responsibilities	Clear procedures, rules and responsibilities to structure collaboration.
Performance measurement	The performance of collaboration is measured by quantitative and qualitative measurement methods.
History	The length of time for which team members have known each other.
Workload	Feasible balance between available resources, time and required output.
Knowledge Management	Distinct but interdependent processes of knowledge creation, knowledge storage and retrieval, knowledge transfer, and knowledge application [34].
Communication	A synthesis of a selection of information, the utterance of this information and a selective understanding or misunderstanding of this utterance and its information [35].
Leadership	The ability to build and maintain a group that performs well relative to its competition [36].
Tools	Technological support for collaboration and communication.

CSF	Clarification to make the CSF meaningful in a DevOps context
Task characteristics	Recognizing relevant task characteristics.
Perceived benefits of collaboration	Collaboration is seen as valuable for the individual, team and the organization.
Team recognition	The team is perceived as a leader, at least related to the goals and activities it intends to accomplish.
Resilience	The ability to deal with changing conditions.
Team composition	Make-up of team membership.

Based on the results, we are able to discuss the implications in Section 5.

V. DISCUSSION

Our findings have several theoretical implications. First, our findings confirm that generally applicable CSFs of collaboration found in literature can be recognized in a DevOps context. These implications extent theory on CSFs of collaboration at large. It supports the statement of [17] that the CSFs they found are applicable to many different collaborative situations. It is also in line with the findings of [9][25] who studied the DevOps phenomenon. Second, we developed and validated an approach that generally applicable CSFs can be made meaningful in a DevOps context. This approach enables the operationalization of the CSFs in a DevOps context and may be useful to other contexts as well. Third, the real-life examples illustrate how the CSFs are anchored in the way team members work together. This shows that collaboration is indeed an important aspect of the adoption of DevOps. Researchers could build on these insights for future research into the DevOps phenomenon. Fourth, the findings discover additional evidence to confirm the importance of each factor previously found by [17].

The findings of our study also have implications for practitioners. First, the CSFs could aid practitioners to better understand the concept of collaboration in a DevOps context in order to have a necessarily impact on the success of collaboration. Second, the implications from this study of CSFs challenge the general view on DevOps as just an interaction between development and operations personnel [3][5][7]. As shown in the results, organizations should take into account many CSFs of collaboration. The number of CSFs requires adequate attention to let the collaboration be successful. In line with the suggestion of [17], organizations can use the list of CSFs to assess the readiness of team members to collaborate in a DevOps context or to find aspects to improve the collaboration within an existing team.

Even though our initial list of CSFs based on literature and used in our multiple case study would appear to be a strong basis, we have to mention some remarks. The CSFs found were based on earlier research conducted in different contexts and studied from different perspectives. For example, Marek, Brock, and Savla [29] studied individual coalitions and initiatives across state, regional and nationwide. Reference [13] studied collaboration from social and technical perspectives. Other examples are Yoon, Lee, Yoon, and Toulan [14], Mattessich, Murray-Close, and Monsey [17], Mohr and Spekman [18], Tsanos, Zografos, and Harrison [22], and Patel, Pettitt, and Wilson [23], who concentrate on interorganizational collaboration, which could be in the form of collaboration between team members. In short, the CSFs used in our multiple case study differ in terms of operationalization, abstraction level, validation context and research area. This could have influenced the results of this study.

Although it took some time before we could publish the results of our study, we could not find publications which present a similar list of CSFs of collaboration in a DevOps context in the meantime.

Our findings appear to be more widely useable due to the fact that the findings are based on two case organizations. However, the list of CSFs should be adapted to the local context.

According to the chosen definition, a CSF must have an impact on the success of collaboration. A study into measuring the impact may be an interesting topic. Careful and explicit research is needed to verify that the resulting model of CSFs is actually adequate. Research could validate whether a certain CSF aided in the improvement of collaboration.

When we discussed CSFs during the interviews, interviewees made some remarks on relations between CSFs confirmed. Although we did not research this aspect, we think it may contain interesting topics for future research as they may aid in understanding collaboration in a DevOps context.

Classification of CSFs into CSFs of collaboration in a DevOps context influencing the likelihood of collaboration and CSFs influencing the performance of collaboration may be a topic for further research. Knowing which CSFs play a role during the beginning of a collaboration could ease decision-making by management [37].

Although we conducted two case studies, we recommend more case studies conducted in a DevOps context, which will enrich the list further. Future research could focus on the validation of certain CSFs with more concrete real-life examples.

Finally, future research could apply the developed approach to make generally applicable CSFs meaningful in specific context.

VI. CONCLUSIONS

Research into the effectiveness of integrated corporate functions is relevant, such as research on DevOps. Collaboration is an important aspect of DevOps, which should contribute to the effectiveness of DevOps. Therefore, reported problems with collaboration should be solved. CSFs of collaboration may contribute to solve problems with collaboration. This study found generally applicable CSFs of collaboration and provides insight into the way two case organizations addressed these CSFs in a DevOps context. We used this insight and made the generally applicable CSFs meaningful in a DevOps context.

This knowledge adds to existing theory on collaboration by providing a comprehensive list of CSFs meaningful in a DevOps context. Furthermore, our study validated an approach by which generally applicable CSFs of collaboration could be made meaningful in a certain context. The CSFs confirmed could aid practitioners to better understand the concept of collaboration in a DevOps context in order to have a necessarily impact on the success of collaboration. Organizations could use the CSFs to assess the readiness of team members to collaborate or to find aspects to improve the collaboration within existing DevOps teams.

All data emerged during the research process are available on request.

REFERENCES

[1] I. M. Sebastian et al., "How Big Old Companies Navigate Digital Transformation," MIS Quarterly Executive, vol. 16, pp. 197–213, 2017.

[2] R. Colomo-Palacios, E. Fernandes, P. Soto-Acosta, and X. Larrucea, "A case analysis of enabling continuous software deployment through knowledge management," International Journal of Information Management, vol. 40, pp. 186–189, 2018.

[3] F. M. A. Erich, C. Amrit, and M. Daneva, "A qualitative study of DevOps usage in practice," Journal of Software: Evolution and Process, vol. 29, 2017.

[4] G. G. Claps, R. B. Svensson, and A. Aurum, "On the journey to continuous deployment: Technical and social challenges along the way," Information and Software Technology, vol. 57, pp. 21–31, 2015.

[5] C. Ebert, G. Gallardo, J. Hernantes, and N. Serrano, "DevOps," IEEE Software, vol. 33, pp. 94–100, 2016.

[6] M. Hüttermann, DevOps for developers. Apress, 2012.

[7] A. Wiedemann, "IT Governance Mechanisms for DevOps Teams - How Incumbent Companies Achieve Competitive Advantages" The 51st Hawaii International Conference on System Sciences, 2018, pp. 4931-4940, ISBN: 978-0-9981331-1-9

[8] J. Iden, B. Tessem, and T. Paivarinta, "IS development/IT operations alignment in system development projects: a multi-method research," International Journal of Business Information Systems, vol. 11, no. 3, pp. 343–359, 2012.

[9] L. E. Lwakatare, P. Kuvaja, and M. Oivo "Dimensions of devops" The 16th International Conference on Agile Processes in Software Engineering and Extreme Programming Springer International Publishing, May 2015, pp. 25-29

[10] J. Wettinger, U. Breitenbücher, M. Falkenthal, and F. Leymann, "Collaborative gathering and continuous delivery of DevOps solutions through repositories," Computer Science - Research and Development, vol. 32, pp. 281–290, 2017.

[11] P. A. Nielsen, T. J. Winkler, and J. Norbjerg, "Closing the IT Development-Operations gap: The DevOps knowledge sharing framework" The 16th International Conference on Perspectives in Business Informatics Research (CEUR), 2017

[12] P. W. Mattessich and B. R. Monsey, Collaboration--what makes it work: a review of research literature on factors influencing successful collaboration. St. Paul, Minn: Amherst H. Wilder Foundation, 1992.

[13] G. L. Kolfschoten, G. J. de Vreede, R. O. Briggs, and H. G. Sol "Collaboration 'Engineerability'," Group Decision and Negotiation, vol. 19, pp. 301–321, 2010.

[14] C. Yoon, K. Lee, B. Yoon, and O. Toulan, "Typology and Success Factors of Collaboration for Sustainable Growth in the IT Service Industry," Sustainability, vol. 9, 2017.

[15] W. L. Bedwell et al., "Collaboration at work: An integrative multilevel conceptualization," Human Resource Management Review, vol. 22, pp. 128–145, 2012.

[16] J. Ram, D. Corkindale, and M. L. Wu, "Implementation critical success factors (CSFs) for ERP: Do they contribute to implementation success and post-implementation performance?," International Journal of Production Economics, vol. 144, pp. 157–174, 2013.

[17] P. W. Mattessich, M. Murray-Close, and B. R. Monsey, Collaboration What Makes It Work. Saint Paul, MN: Fieldstone Alliance, 2001.

[18] J. Mohr and R. Spekman, "Characteristics of partnership success: Partnership attributes, communication behavior, and conflict resolution techniques," Strategic Management Journal, vol. 15, pp. 135–152, 1994.

[19] J. Kotlarsky and I. Oshri, "Social ties, knowledge sharing and successful collaboration in globally distributed system development projects," European Journal of Information Systems, vol. 14, pp. 37–48, 2005.

[20] J. Söderlund, Theoretical Foundations of Project Management. Oxford University Press, 2011.

[21] J. Iden and B. Bygstad, "The social interaction of developers and IT operations staff in software development projects," International Journal of Project Management, vol. 36, pp. 485–497, 2018.

[22] C. S. Tsanos, K. G. Zografos, and A. Harrison, "Developing a conceptual model for examining the supply chain relationships between behavioural antecedents of collaboration, integration and performance," The International Journal of Logistics Management, vol. 25, pp. 418–462, 2014.

[23] H. Patel, M. Pettitt, and J. R. Wilson, "Factors of collaborative working: A framework for a collaboration model," Applied Ergonomics, vol. 43, pp. 1–26, 2012.

[24] M. van Belzen, D. de Kruijff, and J. Trienekens, "Success Factors of Collaboration in the Context of DevOps, " The 12th International Conference Information Systems IADIS, 2019, pp. 26–34, ISBN: 978-989-8533-87-6

[25] R. de Feijter, S. Overbeek, T. van Vliet, E. Jagroep, and S. Brinkkemper, "DevOps Competences and Maturity for Software Producing Organizations," Enterprise, Business-Process and Information Systems Modeling, vol. 318, pp. 244-259, 2018.

[26] B. Kitchenham et al., "Systematic literature reviews in software engineering – A tertiary study," Information and Software Technology, vol. 52, pp. 792–805, 2010.

[27] S. Jalali and C. Wohlin, "Systematic literature studies: database searches vs. backward snowballing" The ACM-IEEE international symposium on Empirical software engineering and measurement (ESEM) ACM-IEEE, Sep. 2012, pp. 29-38, ISBN: 978-1-4503-1056-7

[28] C. A. Olson, J. T. Balmer, and G. C. Mejicano, "Factors Contributing to Successful Interorganizational Collaboration: The Case of CS2day," Journal of Continuing Education in the Health Professions, vol. 31, pp. 3–12, 2011.

[29] L. I. Marek, D. J. P. Brock, and J. Savla, "Evaluating Collaboration for Effectiveness: Conceptualization and Measurement," American Journal of Evaluation, vol. 36, pp. 67–85, 2015.

[30] R. K. Yin, Case study research and applications: design and methods. Los Angeles, CA: SAGE, 2018.

[31] P. Runeson and M. Höst, "Guidelines for conducting and reporting case study research in software engineering," Empirical Software Engineering, vol. 14, pp. 131-164, 2009.

[32] C. Erlingsson and P. Brysiewicz, "A hands-on guide to doing content analysis," African Journal of Emergency Medicine, vol. 7, pp. 93–99, 2017.

[33] E. Schnelle, The Metaplan-Method communication tools for planning and learning groups. Quickborn, Metaplan, 1979.

[34] M. Alavi and D. E. Leidner, "Review: Knowledge Management and Knowledge Management Systems:

Conceptual Foundations and Research Issues," MIS Quarterly, vol. 25, no. 1, pp. 107-136, 2001.

[35] N. Luhmann, "What is Communication?," Communication Theory, vol. 2, pp. 251–259, 1992.

[36] R. Hogan and R. B. Kaiser, "What we know about Leadership," Review of General Psychology, vol. 9, pp. 169–180, 2005.

[37] C. Bai and J. Sarkis, "A grey-based DEMATEL model for evaluating business process management critical success factors," International Journal of Production Economics, vol. 146, pp. 281–292, 2013.

Exploring the Creation and Added Value of Manufacturing Control Systems for Software Factories

Herwig Mannaert

Normalized Systems Institute
University of Antwerp, Belgium
Email: herwig.mannaert@uantwerp.be

Koen De Cock and Jeroen Faes

Research and Development
NSX bv, Belgium
Email: koen.de.cock@nsx.normalizedsystems.org

***Abstract*—Software engineers have been attempting for many decades to produce or assemble software in a more industrial way. Such an approach is currently often associated with concepts like *Software Product Lines* and *Software Factories*. The monitoring, management, and control of such factories is mainly based on a methodology called *DevOps*. Though current DevOps environments are quite advanced and highly automated, they are based on many different technologies and tools. In this contribution, it is argued that more integrated software manufacturing control systems are needed, similar to control systems in traditional manufacturing. This paper presents a scope, overall architecture and prototype implementation of such an integrated software manufacturing control system. Moreover, several detailed scenarios are elaborated that can leverage such integrated control systems to optimize the operations, and improve both the quality and output of modern software factories.**

Index Terms*—*Software Factories; Software Product Lines; DevOps; Control Systems; Evolvability.

I. INTRODUCTION

The expression *"Software is eating the world"* was formulated in 2011 by Marc Andreessen [1] to convey the trend that many industries were being disrupted and transformed by software. And indeed, more and more major businesses and industries are being run on software systems and delivered as online services. These software systems include *Enterprise Resource Planning (ERP)* systems to design and manage the business processes, *Supervisory Control and Data Acquisition (SCADA)* systems to manage and control production processes in real-time, and *Manufacturing Execution Systems (MES)* to track and document the transformation of raw materials to finished goods, enabling decision-makers to optimize conditions and improve production output. As software systems become more pervasive to manage and control the end-to-end production processes in factories, it seems logical to have or create such control systems for the software systems themselves, i.e., systems to manage and control the building and assembly of software systems in so-called software factories. In this contribution, we explore the creation of such systems to manage and control software manufacturing and assembly.

The remainder of this paper is structured as follows. In Section II, we briefly discuss software factories, the *DevOps* methodology, and situate our approach. In Section III, we describe the scope, overall architecture, and the implementation characteristics of the proposed manufacturing control system for software factories. We present various use cases and types of added value for such an integrated control system in Section IV. Finally, we present some conclusions in Section V.

II. SOFTWARE FACTORIES AND DEVOPS

A. *On Software Factories and Reusability*

The idea to produce and/or assemble software in a more industrial way, similar to automated assembly lines in manufacturing, has been pursued for many decades. Such an approach is currently often associated with concepts like *Software Product Lines (SPLs)* and *Software Factories*, but can easily be traced back as far as 1968 to the paper on *mass produced software components* from Doug McIlroy [2]. The concept of *Software Product Lines* has been extensively described by the Carnegie Mellon *Software Engineering Institute (SEI)* [3], and refers in general to software engineering methods, tools and techniques for creating a collection of similar software systems from a shared set of software assets using a common means of production. The characteristic that distinguishes software product lines from previous efforts is predictive versus opportunistic software reuse, as it stresses that software artifacts should only be created when reuse is predicted in one or more products in a well-defined product line [4]. The term *Software Factory* emphasizes the techniques and benefits of traditional manufacturing, and is for instance defined by Greenfield et al. as a software product line that configures extensive tools, processes, and content using a template based on a schema to automate the development and maintenance of variants of an archetypical product by adapting, assembling, and configuring framework-based components [5].

The reuse of software artifacts seems crucial in contemporary efforts to realize the benefits of traditional manufacturing through software factories. Nevertheless, the systematic reuse of software artifacts is not a trivial task. Saeed recently argued that software re-usability is not just facing legal issues, but methodological issues as well. Even when only reusing software to save time, and leverage off the specialization of other authors, the end-user must also have the technical expertise to search, adapt and merge these reusable assets into the larger software infrastructure [6]. We have argued in our previous work that software reuse is even more challenging, and impeded by some fundamental issues related to software evolvability [7] [8]. The sustained technological evolution leads to a continuous sequence of new versions and variants of the software artifacts that need to be reused. These new artifact versions often require changes in their usage that ripple through the entire software structure, causing an impact that is dependent on the size of the system, and limiting the evolvability of software systems [9] [7].

B. From DevOps to Integrated Control Systems

The aim of this contribution is to explore the creation of systems to manage and control the building and assembly of software systems in software factories, similar to SCADA or MES systems in traditional manufacturing. The main approach today in the software development and IT industry to control the building and assembly of software is a methodology called *DevOps*. Used as a set of practices and tools, *DevOps* integrates and automates the work of software development *(Dev)* and IT operations *(Ops)* as a means for improving and shortening the systems development life cycle [10]. It also supports consistency, reliability, and efficiency within the organization, and is usually enabled by a shared code repository or version control. As DevOps researcher Ravi Teja Yarlagadda hypothesizes, *Through DevOps, there is an assumption that all functions can be carried out, controlled, and managed in a central place using a simple code* [11].

Figure 1 presents a traditional overview diagram of a typical DevOps infrastructure environment. While the continuous integration of of the software development and IT operations is represented by the infinity symbol, the representation also contains a typical set of tools and technologies being used in such an infrastructure. We distinguish for example tools for tracking features and user stories (Jira), source control management (Git and Bitbucket), software quality control (SonarQube), automation of build pipelines (Jenkins), automated testing (Cucumber, JUnit), deployment infrastructure (Kubernetes), analytics visualization (Grafana), logging (Graylog), automated deployment (Docker, Ansible), and connecting cloud providers (AWS, Digital Ocean). While the tools in such a *DevOps* or *Continuous Integration Continuous Deployment (CICD)* infrastructure are in general numerous and versatile, there is a clear need for integrated control systems, similar to SCADA or MES systems, encompassing these processes and tools. However, software factories differ significantly from traditional industrial factories, as software is less tangible and the desired control systems need to interface with — often complex — software tools instead of physical equipment.

C. Related Work and Methodology

While academic research is available on various aspects of DevOps, like maturity assessment [12], and management challenges and practices [13], the development of integrated control systems does not seem to be one of them. DevOps platforms are considered to be based on a mix of open source and proprietary software, glued together and built into the platform by a platform team. At the same time, trade publications describe the necessity to breakdown the DevOps phases and tools to increase security and reduce technical debt [14], and acknowledge the need for solutions to scale up DevOps, as nearly a third of DevOps teams' time is spent on manual approaches that are not scalable [15].

The methodology of this paper is based on *Design Science Research* [16], where we design the integrated control system for software factories as an artifact, use a case study to evaluate it in depth in a business environment, and refine the artifact gradually as part of the design search process.

III. A Software Manufacturing Control System

In this section, we elaborate the purpose, scope, architecture, and implementation features of the software manufacturing control system, i.e., the artifact designed in this case study.

A. Purpose and Scope

To design and evaluate the integrated control system artifact, we use the case of the *NSX bv* software factory. It encompasses both the metaprogramming environment and tools to generate applications based on *Normalized Systems Theory (NST)* [7] [8], and actual *Normalized Systems (NS)* applications, i.e., multi-tier web information systems generated in that environment. The various DevOps tools and technologies of the factory correspond to a large extent to those in Figure 1. Though a rather small company, the NSX DevOps environment supports the development and operations of a wide range of heterogeneous and interlinked software artifacts.

- *Run-time libraries* providing basic software utilities to various applications and tools.
- *Expansion resources* consisting of bundles of Normalized Systems code generation modules [8].
- *Web Information Systems*, software applications based on the *Java Enterprise Edition (JEE)* standard.
- *Domain software components*, JEE components that are shared across multiple JEE applications.
- *Integrated Development Tool*, called *μRadiant*, to enable the model-driven development of NS applications.
- *Small tools and plugins* providing additional features in tools like the *μRadiant* or *IntelliJ*.

The various build pipelines, defined in the corresponding software repositories, typically contain the following steps.

- *Expanding* applications or components based on the NST metaprogramming environment.
- *Building* usable libraries, archives, or executables for components, applications, and tools.
- *Unit testing* of various software coding artifacts within the software repositories.
- *Reporting* on the repositories, such as test coverage or software quality metrics.

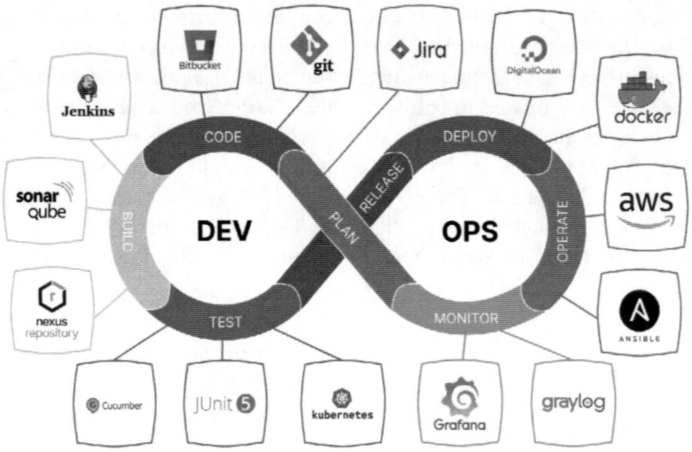

Figure 1. A traditional representation of a typical DevOps infrastructure.

- *Deploying* live instances of applications or tools.
- *Integration testing* invoking live deployments.

Consistent with the overall goal of software factories and product lines, many applications and tools in this DevOps environment are expanded and built by reusing and assembling various other software artifacts that are built in other repositories and pipelines. In order to have an idea of, for instance test coverage and code quality, in a certain version of a software application, we need an overview of these parameters across the versions of all the libraries, expansion resources and components that are being used in that application. Moreover, we need to be able to track the various deployment parameters of all the instances of that version of that application.

This type of functionality, i.e., to manage and control end-to-end the building and assembly of software systems in software factories, is indeed similar to MES systems, i.e., to track and document the transformation of raw materials to finished goods, and SCADA systems, i.e., to manage and control production processes in real-time, in manufacturing. And though almost all the required information is available somewhere in one of the DevOps tools, the integrated overviews and aggregations are not easily accessible.

B. Overall Architecture

The integrated software manufacturing system artifact or prototype for the NSX software factory is implemented itself as a *Normalized Systems (NS)* application, allowing us to take advantage of the *NST* metaprogramming environment. Moreover, as NST was proposed to provide a theoretic foundation to build information systems that provide higher levels of evolvability [9] [7], this should enable us to cope better with the rapidly changing DevOps tools and technologies. NS applications provide the main functionality of information systems through the instantiation of five detailed design patterns or so-called *element structures* [17] [7]:

- Data elements to represent a data or domain entities.
- Action elements to implement computing actions or tasks.
- Workflow elements to orchestrate flows or state machines.
- Connector elements to provide user or service interfaces.
- Trigger elements to to trigger or activate tasks or flows.

At the core of every NS information system is its data model consisting of the various domain entities. A central part of the data model of our software manufacturing control system is represented in Figure 2. As in every software factory, software artifacts are located in versioned *Repositories*. For every repository, automated *Pipelines* can be defined with different steps or *PipelineTargets*, making use of various *BuildTechnologies*. These pipelines produce various types of versioned *Resources*, like libraries, archives, and executables. We distinguish *ApplicationRepositories* corresponding to JEE *Applications* that belong to a certain *Domain*, and *ToolRepositories* for various types of *LeverTools* like plugins, command line tools, or the NS development environment.

The action or task elements serve to import, collect, and or compute various types of data for the software factory control system. Indeed, the manual entering of data in such a system would not only be extremely time consuming, it would also lead to consistency problems. More specifically, types of data that has to be collected or computed, include:

- Versions of applications and lever tools with the corresponding versions of the dependencies or building blocks.
- Aggregated information measures on source repositories, like the number of model entities, or the number and size of source code artifacts.
- Overviews of automated tasks that have been performed in build pipelines with their result status.
- Various quality measures that have been computed for the various applications and tools.
- Aggregated values for the use of different technologies, libraries and expander bundles.

C. Implementation Features

A system or artifact for the monitoring and control of software manufacturing processes should be able to track the

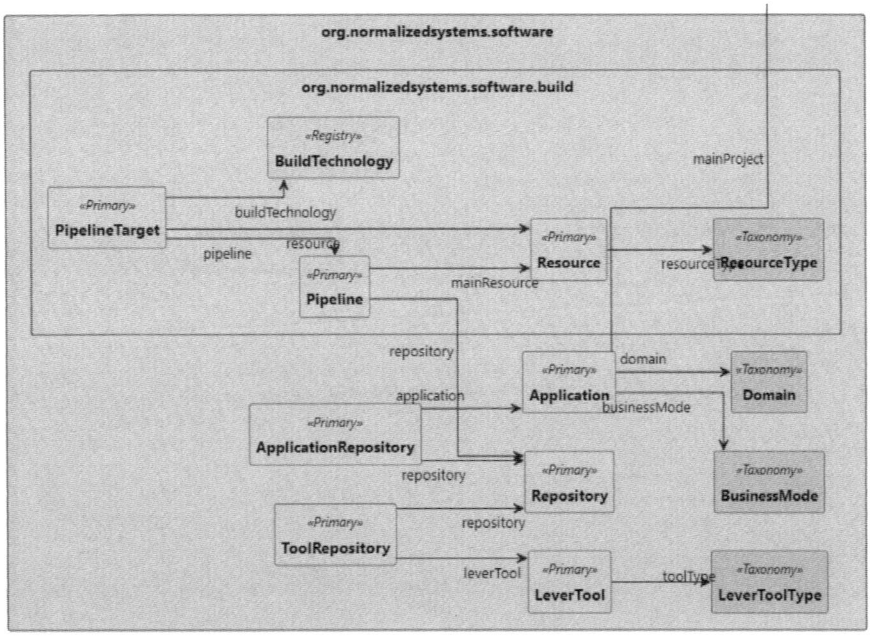

Figure 2. A representation of the data model of the integrated software manufacturng control system.

various parameters and data sets over time. This means that we need to track data over time for most data entities, like sizes of models and custom code, success rates of build processes, or software quality parameters. Therefore, so-called *history or log tables* are a crucial part of the data model. In the NS metaprogramming environment, *expanders* or code generators exist to automatically add —and even populate— an history element for every data element. These history tables can then be represented in graphs and analyzed over time, looking for possible improvements in productivity and/or output quality.

A large part of the relevant data for the software manufacturing control system is already present or computed in one of the many tools or technologies represented in Figure 1. This implies that the automated collection and or computation of software factory data in automated tasks integrates with these tools and technologies, such as *Bitbucket* repositories, *Maven* dependency declarations, *Jenkins* build engines, and *SonarQube* quality analyzers. In accordance with NST, there is a decoupling between the functionality of the data collection in the the task element, e.g., build engine results or quality measurements, and the actual implementation (class) of the task element, e.g., getting data from *Jenkins* or *SonarQube*. In this way, the software manufacturing control system is able to support additional versions or variants of these tools and technologies with limited impact.

IV. Toward a Control Layer for Software Factory Improvements

As stated in Section I, by tracking and documenting the transformation of raw materials to finished goods, *MES* enable decision-makers to optimize conditions and improve production output. In the same way, a software manufacturing control system should provide an analysis platform and control layer to improve and optimize various aspects and characteristics of the software factory operations and output. In this section, we discuss some use cases and their added value, as they are being developed as part of the iterative case-based design process.

A. Monitoring Evolutions over Time

A first avenue to optimize and improve the output and quality of the software factory, is to monitor the evolution of certain parameters over time. As explained in [8], NS information systems distinguish between software skeletons, instantiations of element structures generated by modular code generators or so-called expanders, and custom code being additional software artifacts or classes, i.e., *extensions*, or code snippets added to the generated artifacts or classes, i.e., *insertions*. From a quality and evolvability point of view, it is important to monitor the amount, size, and location of these extensions and insertions. As an example, some sample graphs are shown in Figure 3. They represent, for a specific information system, the evolution of the total amount of insertion snippets, and the total size of those insertion snippets. As done for the second graph, these values can be made relative with respect to the evolving size of the model, i.e., the number of element structures.

This type of monitoring, based on automated data collection from the *Bitbucket* repositories, has been performed for quite some time in the NSX software factory. It has provided valuable insights into the actual project phases when such custom code typically grew fast, and the software layers

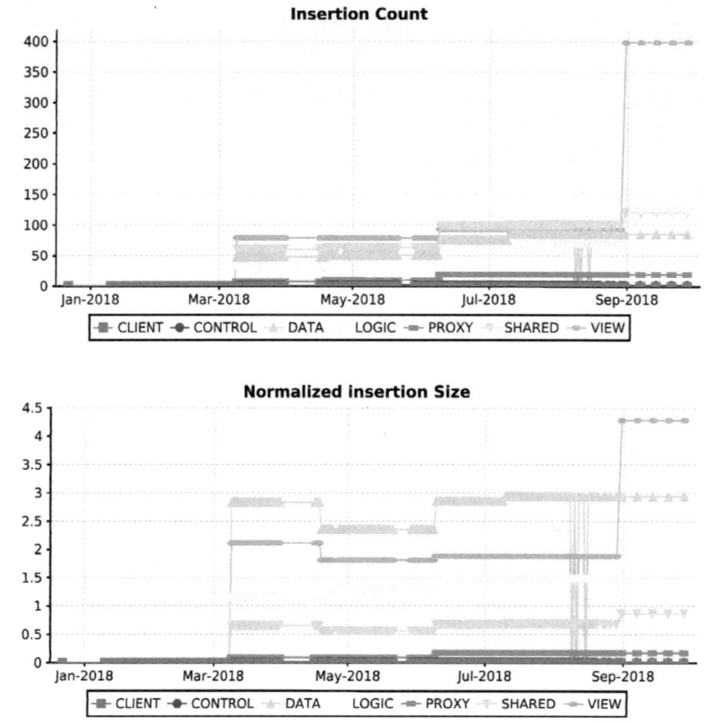

Figure 3. Sample graphs monitoring the amount of custom insertions and the normalized total size of insertions.

where such custom snippets where needed the most. This last parameter provided an indication in which layer the development of the code generators should be prioritized to provide more out of the box functionality. Of course, other types of software systems and factories, without the typical NS distinction between element structures and custom code, should monitor other structural measures to improve software structure and productivity.

While this has been integrated in the software manufacturing control system, the monitoring over time is not limited to the source code repositories. History tables are also being created for success rates of build pipelines, quality measures of the custom source code, test overage percentages and numbers of failed tests, numbers of live system deployments, etc. Of course, this implies the integration with various DevOps tools and technologies.

B. Aggregating over Manufacturing Chains

It is often considered to be a crucial characteristic of software factories and software product lines that software artifacts should only be created when their reuse is predicted in one or more products [4]. And for instance in the NSX software factory, a typical JEE application uses various other software artifacts produced by the factory, such as:

- Several *runtime libraries* providing various utilities like file handling or protocol adapters.
- Several *reusable components* supporting more generic functionality like workflows or notifications, and/or providing more domain-specific building blocks such as project planning or human resource benefits.
- Several *expander bundles* that are used during the expansion of the application, such as the expanders to generate the instances of the NST element structures, or extensions such as the *Relational State Transfer (REST)* interfaces.

These artifacts are in general stored in other repositories and built in other CICD pipelines. And while the dependency on the code generation modules may be specific to NS applications, the dependencies on various runtime libraries and domain components is valid for nearly every software factory.

While parameters related to, for instance test coverage and code quality, can be monitored for every individual software artifact that is created in the factory, it seems quite relevant to offer instant overviews and aggregations of these parameters for all artifacts that are part of a specific aggregated artifact, such as a JEE application. While obviously being relevant to the customers using or licensing such an application, this also enables the optimization and improvement of the overall quality of the factory itself. Indeed, it allows to quickly identify the weak links in such aggregated artifacts, and to prioritize these software artifacts for improvements.

C. Tracking Technology Use Across Projects

Software applications are in general dependent on multiple external artifacts and technologies, e.g., libraries and plugins, that are build outside the software factory by commercial software vendors or in open source projects. While these dependencies are available in configuration files, it is important to surface overviews and aggregations of these dependencies. Such overviews and their added value include:

- immediate overviews of the impacted applications when a vulnerability is detected in a library or technology.
- straightforward assessments of the impact when retiring a certain (version of a) technology.
- regular evaluations of the usage and adoption rate of libraries or expander bundles from the factory itself.

Obviously, such integrated information would also support decisions concerning internal resource allocation, both for supporting both internal and external technologies.

V. Discussion and Conclusion

For many years, software engineers have strived to produce and/or assemble software in a more industrial way. In today's software factories, building and assembling software systems is mainly controlled using a methodology called *DevOps*. These *DevOps* environments are quite advanced and highly automated, but are in general based on many different technologies and tools. As previously experienced in the automation of business processes and traditional manufacturing, this often leads to a need for more integrated systems. In this contribution, we have explored the creation of an integrated software manufacturing control system, similar to SCADA or MES systems in traditional manufacturing.

As part of a case-based design science approach, we have presented a functional scope and overall architecture for such a software manufacturing control system, and have described the design and prototype implementation of the artifact for the software factory case. This software manufacturing control system prototype does not provide fundamentally new information, but collects, aggregates and integrates information over time, across various repositories and build pipelines, and from different DevOps tools and technologies. Therefore, this control system does not provide new possibilities per se to optimize processes and improve output in software factories, as this can be done today by analyzing in detail the data produced by the various tools. However, aggregating and providing this information in nearly real-time, offers the opportunity to fundamentally reduce the lag times for such optimizations and improvements. Though the design as a search process is still ongoing, we have presented some use cases where the added value was validated in the case study.

Exploring the creation of such a software manufacturing control system is believed to make some contributions. First, we have identified and validated a need for integrated control in today's state of the art automated DevOps environments. Second, we have designed an architecture that enables the rather straightforward creation of such integrated software manufacturing control systems in most contemporary software factories. Third, we have described and validated a number of detailed scenarios that can leverage such an integrated control system to improve the output of such software factories.

Next to these contributions, it is clear that this explorative paper is also subject to a number of limitations. First, the case-based approach means that the integrated system has been created for a single software factory, though this factory does include for instance code generators. Second, the major part of the added value through optimizations and improvements, enabled by the drastic reduction of the lag times in the control processes, has yet to be confirmed empirically. However, its design has been validated by actors in our case study, and we are planning the empirical validation in the near future.

References

[1] A. Marc, "Why Software Is Eating the World," URL: https://a16z.com/2011/08/20/why-software-is-eating-the-world/, 2011, [accessed: 2023-07-27].

[2] M. D. McIlroy, "Mass produced software components," in Proceedings of NATO Software Engineering Conference, Garmisch, Germany, October 1968, pp. 138–155.

[3] S. E. Institute, "Software Product Lines Collection," URL: https://resources.sei.cmu.edu/library/asset-view.cfm?assetid=513819, 2023, [accessed: 2023-07-27].

[4] C. Krueger, "Introduction to the emerging practice software product line development," Methods and Tools, vol. 14, no. 3, 2006, pp. 3–15.

[5] J. Greenfield, K. Short, and S. Cook, Steve; Kent, Software Factories: Assembling Applications with Patterns, Models, Frameworks, and Tools. Wiley, 2004.

[6] T. Saeed, "Current issues in software re-usability: A critical review of the methodological & legal issues," Journal of Software Engineering and Applications, vol. 13, no. 9, 2020, pp. 206–217.

[7] H. Mannaert, J. Verelst, and P. De Bruyn, Normalized Systems Theory: From Foundations for Evolvable Software Toward a General Theory for Evolvable Design. Koppa, 2016.

[8] H. Mannaert, K. De Cock, P. Uhnak, and J. Verelst, "On the realization of meta-circular code generation and two-sided collaborative metaprogramming," International Journal on Advances in Software, no. 13, 2020, pp. 149–159.

[9] H. Mannaert, J. Verelst, and K. Ven, "The transformation of requirements into software primitives: Studying evolvability based on systems theoretic stability," Science of Computer Programming, vol. 76, no. 12, 2011, pp. 1210–1222, special Issue on Software Evolution, Adaptability and Variability.

[10] M. Courtemanche, E. Mell, and A. S. Gills, "What Is DevOps? The Ultimate Guide," URL: https://www.techtarget.com/searchitoperations/definition/DevOps, 2023, [accessed: 2023-07-27].

[11] R. T. Yarlagadda, "Devops and its practices," International Journal of Creative Research Thoughts (IJCRT), vol. 9, no. 3, 2021, pp. 111–119.

[12] A. Kumar, M. Nadeem, and S. M., "Assessing the maturity of devops practices in software industry: An empirical study of helena2 dataset," in Proceedings of the 26th International Conference on Evaluation and Assessment in Software Engineering (EASE 22), 2022, pp. 428—432.

[13] S. M. Faaiz, S. U. R. Khan, S. Hussain, W. Wang, and N. Ibrahim, "A study on management challenges and practices in devops," in Proceedings of the 27th International Conference on Evaluation and Assessment in Software Engineering (EASE 23), 2023, pp. 430—437.

[14] M. B. et al., "How to Select DevSecOps Tools for Secure Software Delivery," URL: https://www.gartner.com/en/documents/4131199, 2023, [accessed: 2023-10-10].

[15] Dynatrace, "Observability and security convergence: Enabling faster, more secure innovation in the cloud," URL: https://assets.dynatrace.com/en/docs/report/bae1393-rp-2023-global-cio-report-observability-security-convergence.pdf, 2023, [accessed: 2023-10-10].

[16] A. R. Hevner, S. T. March, J. Park, and S. Ram, "Design science in information systems research," MIS Quarterly, vol. 28, no. 1, 2004, pp. 75–105.

[17] H. Mannaert, J. Verelst, and K. Ven, "Towards evolvable software architectures based on systems theoretic stability," Software: Practice and Experience, vol. 42, no. 1, 2012, pp. 89–116.

Three-step Decision Framework for Planning Software Releases

José del Sagrado
University of Almería
Almería, Spain
email: jsagrado@ual.es

Isabel M. del Águila
University of Almería
Almería, Spain
email: imaguila@ual.es

Alfonso Bosch
University of Almería
Almería, Spain
email: abosch@ual.es

***Abstract*—We propose a framework that connects the previously solved problems, which are involved in the setting of the next release goal. A complete workflow has been defined in order to manage the need to properly set the release goal when different, conflicting stakeholders define numerous requirements. Since they cannot all be satisfied by the available resources it necessary to reach an agreement that can be supported by our framework.**

Keywords*—*stakeholder identification; next release problem; requirements negotiation.

I. INTRODUCTION

Today, systems are no longer isolated local applications; they are large and complex systems with an increasing number of connections to other similar applications. These large-scale software systems are developed worldwide, involving teams of software developers, designers, testers, project managers, and other stakeholders working together to deliver a software solution that meets specific requirements [1].

In this context, requirement engineering is not only about capturing and managing requirements but also about fostering collaboration, responding to evolving needs, and adapting to changing project circumstances in order to deliver a successful software solution [2]. It focuses on understanding and defining the needs and expectations of the software system being developed, taking into account multiple stakeholders and a wide range of functionality, expressed and modelled as requirements that may or may not be included in the product being developed.

In addition, due to the limited resources available for the next release of the current project, not all stakeholders' requests can be included in the next product to be delivered, and some will be left for later releases. At this point, software development teams need to manage and review data from multiple sources and make decisions based on the risk associated with each requirement, the cost of delivering it, the benefits the candidate will provide, or some other issues. Timelines, dependencies, resource constraints, and other factors affect this management task [3].

All these factors are estimated or assessed, usually subjectively, by a large group of stakeholders who affect or will be affected by the software under construction. We consider these stakeholders as a source of data to be managed in order to obtain the best set of requirements according to the various criteria defined for the project. However, the best solution is not always the one chosen to maximize objectives, and some kind of agreement, sometimes negotiation, is required [3]. Therefore, three questions should be considered:

- Who assesses the attributes of the requirements?
- What is the best set of requirements?
- Do we have an agreement to build the release?

In this paper, we propose a framework to answer these three questions (see Figure 1). Each of the processes involved in the workflow shown can be treated as a separate problem. The identification of stakeholders, the selection of requirement sets to be included in the next software release, and the process of reaching agreement on the release goal. The three stages are problems that have been previously studied and for which separate solutions have been proposed. Our contribution is the framework that connects all three earlier solved problems, defining a complete workflow to manage the need to properly define the release goal when different, conflicting stakeholders define numerous requirements that cannot all be covered by the available resources.

The remainder of the paper is structured as follows. Section II presents the architecture of the proposal, including the description of the three stages: stakeholder identification, elicitation of candidate requirement sets, and the next release. In Section III, these stages are applied to a case study. A discussion of the limitations and scope of the framework, including what we add to previous proposals, is included in Section IV. Finally, Section V includes the conclusion and future work,

II. SOFTWARE RELEASE PLANNING FRAMEWORK

To address the three issues raised, the framework is divided into three phases or stages (see Figure 1). The first phase (*stakeholder identification*) deals with the identification of the relevant stakeholders in the software project who will be taken into account when proposing the requirements that will be used to define the next release goal. In the second phase (*elicitation of candidate requirement sets*), the requirements proposed by the relevant stakeholders are collected and, based on their assessments, an optimization problem is defined, from which different alternatives (i.e., candidate requirement sets) for the next release are obtained. Finally, in the third phase (*next release agreement*), the aim is to reach agreement on the set of requirements that will make up the next version of the software, selecting one of the candidate sets of requirements found in the previous stage on the basis of productivity indicators and the degree to which stakeholder suggestions have been taken into account,

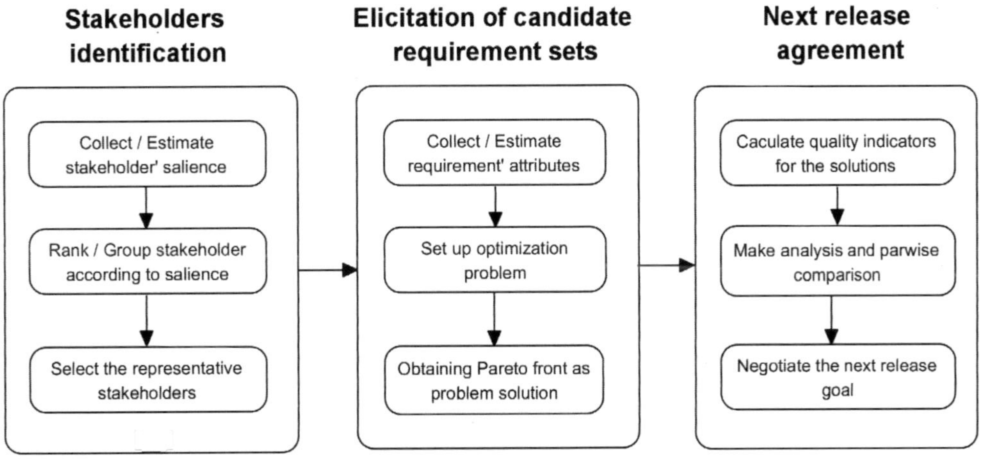

Figure. 1. Workflow defined for the framework.

A. Stakeholders Identification

Stakeholder identification ensures that all individuals, groups, or organisations with a valid interest in the project are considered, as they are the main source of requirements. This is even more evident in large projects where there is a huge community of stakeholders to consider. Their demands are likely to be diverse and conflicting.

An alternative is to reduce the number of stakeholders to manage, but maintain stakeholder coverage [4]. Identifying key stakeholders would reduce the effort required to define the release goal by focusing on the most influential stakeholder representative.

Let $\mathbf{Stk} = \{sk_1, sk_2, \ldots, sk_q\}$ be the set of stakeholders to consider. They represent candidate stakeholders who may be involved in the definition of new features for the next version of a given product.

Each stakeholder is characterised by its salience based on *power*, *legitimacy* and *urgency* as salience components [5]. These values are revealed, usually through interviews, by people involved in the project, who may or may not be stakeholders. Each interviewee could assign a value to the three salience components, but this is not necessary for all of them, and the sets of interviewees for the components can be disjoint. There are h, k and q interviewees about power, legitimacy and urgency respectively, where wp_{ij}, wl_{ij} and wu_{ij} are the values that the interviewee i gives to the stakeholder j in $\mathbf{Stk}$. The power, legitimacy and urgency of a stakeholder j could be defined by aggregating the values obtained from the interviewees.

$$\begin{aligned} p_j &= \textstyle\sum_{i=1}^{h} wp_{ij}, \\ l_j &= \textstyle\sum_{i=1}^{k} wl_{ij}, \\ u_j &= \textstyle\sum_{i=1}^{q} wu_{ij}. \end{aligned} \tag{1}$$

We can define different strategies to select the most influential stakeholders, for example, by clustering them [4] or giving them a weight according to the number of groups identified [6]. As a result, we have a set of m stakeholders who are allowed to propose the requirements that will define the next release goal.

So we can answer the first question in the affirmative, because this stage, *stakeholders identification*, certainly has the ability to define *who assesses the attributes of the requirements*.

B. Elicitation of Candidate Requirement Sets

Let $\mathbf{R} = \{r_1, r_2, \ldots, r_n\}$ be the set of requirements to be considered. These represent new functionalities of the current system suggested by a set of m stakeholders, $\mathbf{Stk} = \{sk_1, sk_2, \ldots, sk_m\}$. $\mathbf{R}$ represents the candidates for inclusion in the next software release. The stakeholders are responsible for setting the preference value of the requirements by defining a value matrix, where each v_{ij} is the subjective value that the stakeholder $sk_i \in \mathbf{Stk}$ assigns to the requirement r_j. The stakeholders to be considered are those that have been selected in the process described in the previous section, and since they do not all have the same importance to the project, it is also defined and $\mathbf{W} = \{w_1, w_2, \ldots, w_m\}$ as the set of weights representing the importance of stakeholders, these values may or may not be calculated based on the salience components. Thus, for a given requirement $r_j \in \mathbf{R}$, its satisfaction s_j is:

$$s_j = \sum_{i=1}^{m} w_i * v_{ij}. \tag{2}$$

In addition, each r_j has an associated cost e_j, which indicates the development effort required to develop it, as estimated by the developers, resulting in the set $\mathbf{E} = \{e_1, e_2, \ldots, e_n\}$. Each software release has a cost limit B, which represents the amount of available resources that cannot be exceeded.

We are able to formulate an optimization problem to be solved in order to obtain the candidate requirement sets, $\mathbf{U}$, to be included in the next release using Pareto dominance as [7]:

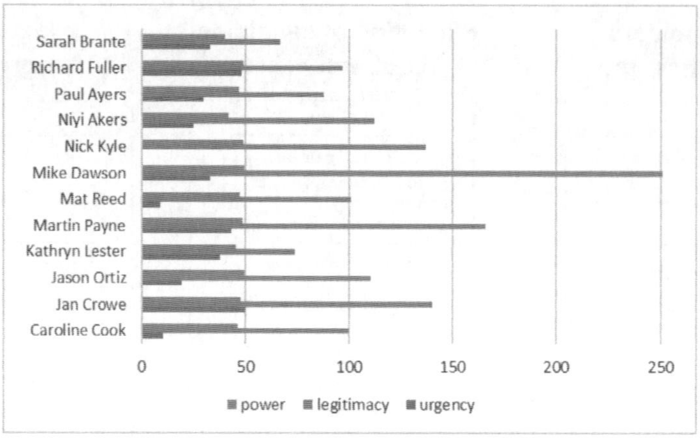

Figure. 2. 12 Stakeholders selected.

$$\begin{array}{ll} \max \sum_{j\in\mathbf{U}} \mathrm{s}_j, & \\ \min \sum_{j\in\mathbf{U}} \mathrm{e}_j, & \\ \text{subject to} & \sum_{j\in\mathbf{U}} \mathrm{e}_j \leq B. \end{array} \quad (3)$$

In addition to the effort-bound constraint (B), alternative formulations may also include constraints associated with requirement relationships or interactions. Specifically, structural interactions impose a particular implementation order, thereby downsizing the NRP feasible solution set [8]. *Implication*, *combination* and *exclusion* dependencies are the functional interactions most commonly studied in the NRP literature:

- Implication interaction, (r_i *implies* r_j), models that a requirement r_i must be implemented before the requirement r_j.
- Combination interaction, (r_i *combined with* r_j), indicates that both requirements must be developed in the same iteration.
- Exclusion interaction. The interaction (r_i *excludes* r_j) reveals that both requirements are incompatible. That is, they could not be developed in the same product.

Next, an optimization algorithm is used to obtain the set of Pareto optimal solutions, which we call candidate requirement sets because all the solutions on the Pareto front are feasible to be considered as the next release goal. There are many solving techniques that have been applied in order to find this set of requirements, including algorithms based on genetic inspiration, the use of nature-inspired optimization, linear programming, clustering approaches or even exact methods for finding the entire Pareto front. A detailed study of their quality is beyond the scope of this paper [9]. Since it is possible to obtain the candidate requirement sets, we can use them to identify the best requirement set, which provides a positive answer to the second research question. Finally, after an analysis of the alternatives obtained, the one to be implemented is chosen by reaching an agreement on the release objective.

C. Next Release Agreement

The task of software release planning does not end when the Pareto front is obtained. To answer the last question, "*Do we have an agreement to build the release?*", the development team must choose which of the alternative sets of requirements (i.e., Pareto optimal solutions) will be implemented.

Due to the black-box nature of optimization algorithms [10], Human experts in charge of decision making need to be supported by additional analysis of optimization results. Although there are well known quality indicators to measure the performance of algorithms [9] and Pareto fronts (such as Hypervolume or Spread), we propose the use of quality indicators that, correctly displayed by some kind of tool, guide decision makers when comparing solutions [11] at the software level. Thus, in addition to the data resulting from the optimization algorithms (such as the number of requirements in a solution, the detailed list of requirements, and the values achieved by the solutions in the objective functions), some other useful indicators can be calculated.

The first is *Productivity*. Let $\mathbf{U} \subseteq \mathbf{R}$ be the solutions under analysis, then

$$\mathrm{prod}(\mathbf{U}) = \mathrm{sat}(\mathbf{U})/\mathrm{eff}(\mathbf{U}), \quad (4)$$

is the benefit obtained by the solution, expressed in terms of how much satisfaction is obtained per unit of effort.

Another indicator is the measure of the amount covered by a solution with respect to everything that is raised by the stakeholder (i.e., stakeholder fairness), which is called *coverage* [11]. Thus, given a stakeholder $sk_i \in \mathbf{Stk}$, this measure associated to a solution $\mathbf{U} \subseteq \mathbf{R}$ with respect to all the requirements valuated by her/him is

$$\mathrm{stcov}_i(\mathbf{U}) = \sum_{j\in\mathbf{U}} v_{ij} / \sum_{j\in\mathbf{R}} v_{ij}, \quad (5)$$

where v_{ij} is the value that the stakeholder sk_i assigns to requirement r_j.

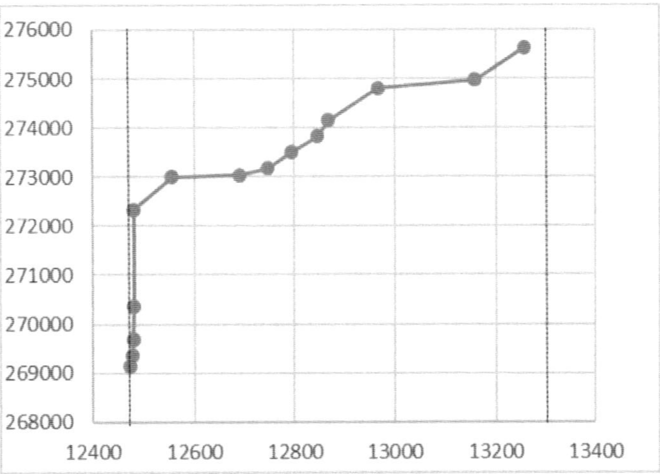

Figure. 3. Pareto front.

III. Case Study

In order to show how this framework can be used in a real-world project, we have included a case study of its application. The dataset used to investigate the validity of the research questions is the *Replacement Access, Library and ID Card project* (RALIC). This was a software project to improve the existing access control system at University College London (UCL). The project combined several UCL access control mechanisms (such as access to the library and fitness centre) into one, eliminating the need for a separate library registration process for UCL ID card holders [12]. This is a widely studied dataset within the domain of Requirements Engineering, and has been used in several works with many different approaches.

RALIC identifies stakeholders by creating a network of recommendations. Each recommender selects a set of other stakeholders, gives them a level of influence on the projec, thus defining a network. The RALIC project involves 144 stakeholders in the network, some of whom only act as recommendees. However, not all recommendees or recommenders have proposed an enhancement or new functionality to be included in the software to be built.

The project includes 138 requirements as increases to the actual access, library, and ID card system, which are arranged in three levels: objectives (10), requirements (48), and specific requirements (104); they are represented by $\mathbf{R} = \{r_1, r_2, \ldots, r_n\}$. Their effort range varies from 4 to 7000 persons-hour. Only 75 RALIC stakeholders use the 100-point method (each stakeholder receives 100 points that can be used to vote for the most important requirements) to prioritise the requirements they are interested in; points_{ij} represents the votes that the stakeholder i assigns to the requirement r_j that can be used to calculate the satisfaction of the requirements. However, stakeholders do not vote at the same level as the three defined ones. These facts translated into the reorganisation of requirements (e.g., requirements that nobody asks for are erased), obtaining for our study 83 requirements, $\mathbf{R} = \{r_1, r_2, \ldots, r_{83}\}$ and their corresponding development efforts in $\mathbf{E} = \{e_1, e_2, \ldots, e_{83}\}$, there are not defined interactions between these requirements.

A. RALIC Stakeholders Identification

The identification of relevant stakeholders can be carried out according to different strategies. In fact, it is defined as a separate problem. In this case, we have applied a clustering approach, using k-means with 4 clusters; a detailed description is beyond the scope of this paper [4]. As a result, the set of 144 stakeholders initially considered is reduced to 12 relevant stakeholders.

The result of this first stage is shown in Figure 2. It also shows the value of the components that define the stakeholder salience, so $\mathbf{Stk} = \{stk_1, stk_2, \ldots, stk_{12}\}$.

B. RALIC Elicitation of Candidate Requirement Sets

From these three sets, $\mathbf{Stk}$, $\mathbf{R}$ and $\mathbf{E}$, together with the definition of the requirement satisfaction values (Equation 2), we can define the overall next release problem for RALIC as the following optimisation problem:

$$\begin{array}{ll} \max \sum_{j \in \mathbf{U}} s_j, & \\ \min \sum_{j \in \mathbf{U}} e_j, & \\ \text{subject to} & B_1 \leq \sum_{j \in \mathbf{U}} e_j \leq B_2. \end{array} \quad (6)$$

where $\mathbf{U}$ is a solution (that is, a set of requirements that conforms to the next release). The resource / effort limits are defined in the range $[B_1, B_2]$ which, respectively, corresponds to the 20 % effort required to develop all the requirements for B_1, while B_2 is 25 %. These values have been chosen taking into account the contingency value for effort, that is, an allowance made for the risk that something will not be undertaken with the planned estimated effort. We have decided to define a resource limit interval because, on the one hand, the original data set did not include an upper resource limit and, on the other hand, developers usually discard solutions

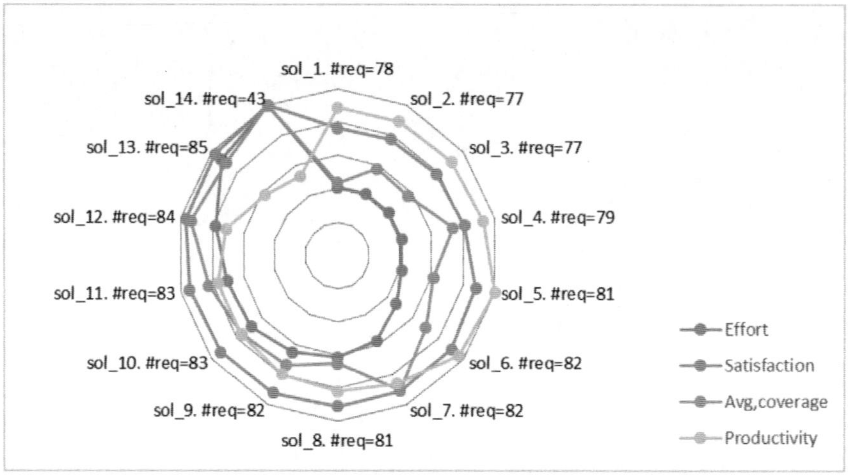

Figure. 4. Quality indicators for the Pareto front solutions.

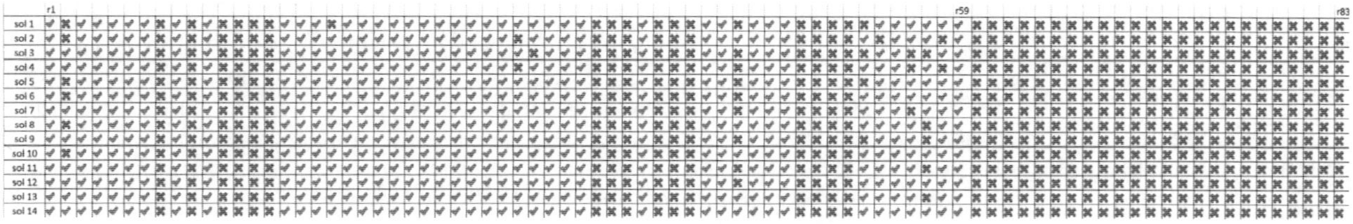

Figure. 5. Distribution of requirements in candidate solutions.

on the Pareto front with low effort value [11]. For RALIC, the values for B_1 and B_2 are 12473.3 and 13304.8, respectively.

To find the Pareto front, we have resorted to a greedy algorithm. This algorithm works as follows: for each effort value in the range $[B1, B2]$, we fill the solution with as many requirements as we can. Then, in a fixed number of attempts, we try to remove each requirement one by one in the solution, replacing it with another that is valid for that level of effort. After each change, the dominance is checked and the solution is replaced if necessary.

Although this may not be the best algorithm for finding Pareto fronts, it is at least simple and produces a Pareto front that can be used to demonstrate the application of the proposed framework. If a better algorithm were used, a more accurate and larger number of candidate solution sets would be found. Figure 3 shows the 14 sets of candidate requirements obtained using this greedy strategy.

C. RALIC Next Release Agreement

The starting point for the final decision is the set of candidate requirement sets, in our case 14 solutions. The analysis includes, on the one hand, the inspection of the values reached in the objective functions (satisfaction, effort) and, on the other hand, the quality indicators defined by the decision makers. For the RALIC case study, these are the number of requirements, productivity, and coverage. It should be noted that we have used the average for the coverage indicator instead of examining the 12 values separately. The use of too many indicators can hinder rather than help decision-making; the general rule should be the simpler the better.

The indicators are shown in Figure 4. One might think that the best candidate solutions are 13 or 14, which achieve the best satisfaction and effort values with 85 and 43 requirements, respectively, and perhaps 13 would be chosen because it covers more requirements. However, when we look at productivity, these alternatives have low values, i.e., using more effort does not result in the same increase in satisfaction.

At this point, the tacit knowledge of developers and stakeholders helps to reach an agreement between possible alternatives. As this is a human process, it is common to use pairwise comparisons of the solutions [11]. For example, let us compare solutions 12 and 7. Both have acceptable satisfaction and productivity values, with a good average stakeholder coverage. The decision in this case could be based on other factors that have not been considered in quantitative terms, such as risk; if we are dealing with higher risk requirements, it is preferable in this case to select solution 7 to have a cushion of effort in case a risky situation needs to be solved.

In some situations, it might be necessary to go down to study the problem at the level of each requirement, negotiating its status in the solution, but this is more difficult to manage ad hoc; just compare Figure 4 and Figure 5, which only show the indicators or the inclusion status for each requirement. It is always better to use quality indicators that are able to summarise the information in a more useful way, just compare the two figures.

IV. Appraisal of the Framework

Previous strategies answer the three questions proposed in this work separately; for example, the problem *"What is the best set of requirements?"* has been formulated as an optimization problem, with customer satisfaction and development cost as the basic optimization objectives, and has been the subject of much research [13]. However, the literature reviewed in this work has neglected the initial identification and prioritization of requirements sources. Similarly, stakeholder identification methods have typically relied on practitioners to manually identify stakeholders based on the use of intuition and experience [14]. Other systematic identification methods follow a set of steps or procedures to ensure consistency, precision, and completeness in achieving the desired result [15], [16]. However, these proposals were not followed by a requirements selection task. Furthermore, the final selection of a solution in the Pareto front could be solved using complex techniques such as ranking of Pareto-optimal solutions or using a mathematical preference model, but no one has connected the three stages in a unique framework, which is precisely our contribution.

V. Conclusion and Future Work

This paper shows how three complex software engineering problems, usually treated independently, are linked together to give a global view of the problem of defining the next release goal for a software product. This framework provides practitioners with a pragmatic approach to solving this complex process in a software engineering project. The three defined stages, *stakeholder identification*, *elicitation of candidate requirement sets*, and *next release agreement*, allow us to manage and improve the tools and/or algorithms defined to solve each stage separately, thus improving the whole process. The validity of our proposal has been demonstrated through its application in a real-world case study, the *Replacement Access, Library and ID Card project* (RALIC) system.

Future work includes the application of the proposed framework to other software projects where data on stakeholders and requirements have been collected. Attention should also be given to investigating the impact on the solutions that make up the NRP solution.

Acknowledgment

This research has been funded by the Spanish Ministry of Science, Innovation and Universities under project PID2019-106758GB-C32 (EML-PA), being also partially supported by the Data, Knowledge, and Software Engineering (DKSE) research group (TIC-181) of the University of Almería.

References

[1] D. Šmite, C. Wohlin, T. Gorschek, and R. Feldt, "Empirical evidence in global software engineering: a systematic review, " Empirical software engineering, vol. 15, pp. 91–118, 2010.

[2] V. Stray and N B. Moe, "Understanding coordination in global software engineering: A mixed, -methods study on the use of meetings and Slack," Journal of Systems and Software, vol. 170, p. 110717, 2020.

[3] K. Brennan (ed.)."A Guide to the Business Analysis Body of Knowledge". IIBA, International Institute of Business Analysis, 2009.

[4] I.M. del Águila and J. del Sagrado, "Salience-based stakeholder selection to maintain stakeholder coverage in solving the next release problem," Information and Software Technology, vol. 160, p. 107231, 2023.

[5] R. K. Mitchell and J. H. Lee, "Stakeholder identification and its importance in the value creating system of stakeholder work," in The cambridge handbook of stakeholer theory, J. S. Harrison, J. B. Barney, R. E. Freeman, and R. A. Phillips, Eds., Cambridge University Press Cambridge, 2019, pp. 53–73.

[6] J. A. Sierra, I. M. del Águila, and J. del Sagrado. "Importance of stakeholders in the next release problem.- Importancia de los interesados en el problema de la siguiente versión," in Actas de las XXV Jornadas de Ingeniería del Software y Bases de Datos (JISBD 2021), Abrahão, S. (Ed.), 2021.

[7] Y. Zhang, M. Harman, and S.A. Mansouri, "The multi-objective next release problem," in Proc. of the 9th annual conference companion on Genetic and evolutionary computation, 2007, pp. 1129–1137

[8] J. del Sagrado, I.M. del Águila, and F. Orellana, "Requirements interaction in the next release problem," in Proc. of the 13th annual conference companion on Genetic and evolutionary computation, 2016, pp. 241–242.

[9] J.A. Nuh, T.W. Koh, S. Baharom, M.H. Osman, and S.N. Kew, "Performance Evaluation Metrics for Multi-Objective .Evolutionary Algorithms in Search-Based Software Engineering: Systematic Literature Review", Applied Sciences, vol. 11(7), p. 3117, 2021.

[10] G. Du and R. Guenther, "Two machine-learning techniques for mining solutions of the ReleasePlanner^{tm} decision support system", Information Sciences, vol. 259, pp. 474–489, 2014.

[11] I.M. del Águila and J. del Sagrado, "Three steps multiobjective decision process for software release planning, Complexity vol 21 (S1), pp 250–262, 2016.

[12] S.L. Lim and A. Finkelstein, "Stakerare: using social networks and collaborative filtering for large-scale requirements elicitation," IEEE T Software Eng, vol. 38, pp. 707–735, 2011.

[13] A.M. Pitangueira, R.S.P. Maciel and M. Barros, "Software requirements selection and prioritization using SBSE approaches: A systematic review and mapping of the literature," J. Syst. Software, vol. 103, pp. 267–280, 2015.

[14] D. Häuber, K. Lauenroth, H. van Loenhoud, A. Schwarz, and P. Steiger: Handbook ireb certified professional for requirements engineering advanced level elicitation - version 1.0.3. IREB International Requirements Engineering Board, 2019.

[15] L.C. Ballejos and J.M. Montagna, " Method for stakeholder identification in interorganizational environments, Requirements engineering,", vol. 13, pp. 281–297, 2008.

[16] M.M. Rahman, M.M. Moonira and F.T. Zuhora, " A systematic methodology and guidelines for software project manager to identify key stakeholders," International Journal of Research in Computer and Communication Technology, vol. 4, no 8, pp. 509-517, 2015.

Design Elements for a Space Information Network Operating System

Anders Fongen
Norwegian Defence University College (FHS)
Lillehammer, Norway
email: anders@fongen.no

Abstract—**Space Information Networks (SIN) have quite different characteristics from ordinary distributed systems and clouds. Therefore, the middleware and operating systems governing the service provision in SIN spacecrafts must manage the resources involved, as well as the lifecycle of the components that depend on these resources. This paper goes into detail in the distinguishing characteristics and proposes a blueprint for software design.**

Keywords*—*LEO satellites; space information networks; distributed OS; mobile computing.

I. INTRODUCTION

The term *Space Information Network* (SIN) describes a set of satellites that cooperatively offer services for information processing and sharing, as well as traditional communication services. SIN is regarded as a natural evolution of satellite services, from radio mirrors in geostationary orbit and Low Earth Orbit (LEO) constellation for communication services (e.g., Iridium) [1][2]. Among expected benefits from a SIN is (1) very low end-to-end latency, as low as 3 ms, and (2) global coverage. A SIN is likely to drive new applications which require these properties.

In a series of previous publications, different aspects of SIN operation (architecture [3], security [4], cache management [5], routing [6], session state management [7]) and data sharing [8] have been addressed. Building on these studies, this position paper proposes a design blueprint of a middleware/operating systems, which offers the necessary services and defines Application Programming Interfaces (APIs) to ground based clients, service components and service containers operating in each spacecraft. Within the presented article, the term "Space Information Network Operating System" will be abbreviated "SIN-OS".

The perspective of the presented analysis is that of Distributed Computing. Technical and physical properties of satellites related to energy management, antenna design, modulation, coding, jamming resistance etc., are not taken into consideration.

The remainder of the article is organized as follows: In Section II, some of the characteristics of SIN operations are identified as premises for the analysis, and Section III presents the components and services of the proposed SIN-OS design. The specific details of the proposed API are discussed in Section IV. For future study, the software simulator to be used is briefly presented in Section V, and the article draws its conclusion in Section VI.

II. OVERARCHING DESIGN CONSIDERATIONS

Central to the efforts presented in this manuscript are architectural properties, which heavily influences the software design. A selection of these properties are listen in the following paragraphs:

A. The N-layer Structure

The N-layer structure of service producers and service consumers is a typical property of any distributed systems, which also applies to a SIN. Any entity which offers services to a client may be a client to a service at a "deeper" level, and these relations form a tree structure rooted in the spacecraft, which connects to the surface client.

Some rules are chosen to simplify the design slightly:

- A surface client can only access one single service endpoint, and therefore connects to a single tree of service providers.
- There is a distinction between *servers* and *clients* at the surface. A space client can access a surface service, but not the other way around. Surface clients will never receive service requests.

B. Handover Operations

Surface based clients are stationary, while the orbiting elements are not, which causes a series of handover operations to take place for the sake of link maintenance. While the link budget for inter-satellite links to some extent can be estimated, the link from a surface client is dependent on nearby buildings and terrain and cannot be easily calculated in advance. The general problem of handover, whether between spacecrafts or from a surface client, are approached with the following rules:

- A handover operation is always initiated from the client side
- A handover operation is prepared and conducted by the server side, subsequent to a client request.

The following steps indicate the necessary actions taken during a handover operation: (1) The client notifies the server that a handover is requested, (2) The server decides which server is the best candidate to take over, and (3) transfer the session state to this candidate, then (4) inform the client of the new endpoint to use. Finally, (5) the client establishes a connection to the new server as indicated in step (4) and resumes the dialogue.

Handover is a solved problem in satellite constellations that offer stateless communication services, e.g., Iridium. This manuscript will therefore focus on problems related to handover operations where *stateful* and *collaborate* services are offered. In that case, handover also involves the migration of all data that constitutes the session state.

A handover request are likely to create cascades of new handover requests propagating through the tree of service providers. Client-server relations between spacecrafts are assumed to take place between units orbiting in the same direction, which may cause handover operations in one link to initiate handovers in the next link of the service chain, in the worst case, through all the orbiting units involved in the service provision.

C. Stateful Migration

A stateful service component in a spacecraft needs to migrate its units of execution during a handover operation. Stateless services are easily migrated if migration takes place *between* service invocations, not during the invocation processing. Given that the components are stateful, *session objects*, familiar from web programming, should be the data unit for migration [7]. Data elements are not migrateable if they represent operating system resources like open files, sockets or locks (cf. the `serializable` interface in Java).

Migration of service components requires the implementation of callback methods for life cycle management, since only the component itself will know how to prepare its session state into a representation fit for migration.

D. Resource Needs and Load Predictability

Since the grid of spacecrafts are orbiting the Earth in a predictable manner, both the available communication links and the expected *offered load* from surface clients can be estimated in advance. The population density and technological advancement of any area of the Earth is well known, so the expected offered load can be estimated based on position and time (night/day, etc.), or subject to a machine learning algorithm.

The population density on Earth is highly concentrated within small areas, and an orbiting spacecraft will spend most of its time over uninhabited areas. Figure 1 shows the population number within the footprint of a satellite during three consecutive orbits. It has been an essential idea in the SIN study that busy satellites should be able to share their workload with idle satellites in the vicinity [5].

Due to these properties, there is less need for discovery protocols related to link or peer availability. *Service discovery* mechanisms are likely still to be necessary since the migration and activation pattern of *services* are independent from orbital elements and population density data.

E. Fail-over Arrangements

What is not predictable, however, are fail and crash of services or entire spacecrafts. A simplistic fail-over arrangement would be to redirect client requests to redundant servers, while a more elaborate approach would also deal with the recovery of atomic transactions through, e.g., checkpoints or idempotent operations. For many applications, the simplistic approach suffices. The fail detection mechanism must produce the same result for all clients, for the sake of sharing and cooperation between clients. The fail management should therefore be conducted in the system/network management plane and the necessary fail-over information distributed to all spacecrafts.

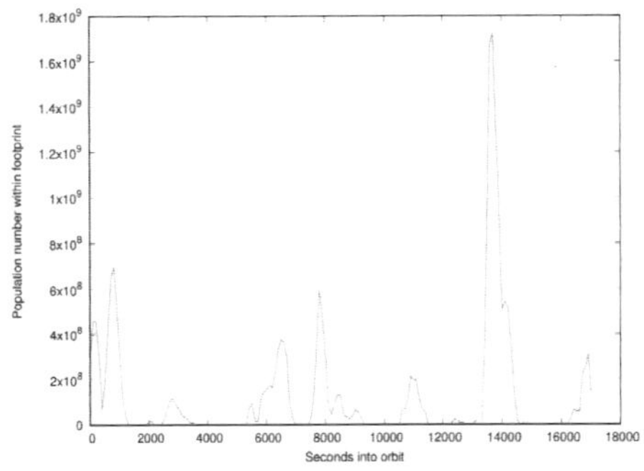

Figure 1. The population number inside the footprint of a satellite during three subsequent orbits.

F. Security and Trust Management

The SIN exposes a high number of service access points, and surface clients as well as customer code running in services inside the spacecrafts are not to be trusted. The links between spacecrafts running SIN-OS instances carry application traffic, as well as communication related to management and maintenance (cache replication, state migration, software updates, etc.). Application and administrative communication must be kept strictly separate through, e.g., Virtual Private Network (VPN) technology. VPN also contributes to relaxed IP address management for SIN customers.

With regard to trust management (a term that includes credential management and validation), the analysis published in 2021 [4] concluded that (1) the standard PKI model is not well suited due to connectivity and capacity demands, and (2) that both authentication and authorization control should happen in the same invocation, using the same set of credentials [9].

III. SIN-OS OVERVIEW

The different software components of a SIN-OS are shown in Figure 2 with their relations indicated by arrows. The executing component both on the server and the client side has been placed in *containers*, as a middleware layer for useful abstractions of the host API, as well as the control of the component's life cycle. On the client side, the management of handover operations is likely to demand a cross-layer connection to the radio hardware in order to detect when a handover is necessary. Event notifications are found in the Component API, for life cycle management purposes. No need for event notifications from the host OS to the container was identified at this stage of study.

The Connection Management and Communication Subsystem, shown in the bottom part of Figure 2, are comprehensive components which handle packet forwarding, route planning, handover planning and execution, fail-over execution, etc. For the services offered by the SIN-OS, shown on the right side of Figure 2, the following comments apply:

Non-Volatile Storage
For storage of data across the duration of client sessions. This service is more than a simple file service, since it may scatter data on several storage tiers based on their access frequency. The API for the service may employ different access semantics: Flat files, Relational Database Management System, Tuplespace, etc.

Shared data segments
Clients should be able to collaborate through shared data segments offered through a service interface, which ensures the chosen semantic properties: transactional context, update ordering, etc. The service may choose to spread the data across several spacecrafts according to their access frequencies in order to reduce the overhead of handover operations [8].

Cooperative caching
A caching service used by one or more clients for lookup on immutable data elements. The service employs a cluster of neighborhood satellites for load balancing purposes, and replication of data between cache clusters to improve cache hit-rate [5].

Session State objects
The application component may keep its session state in a separate *session object*, which must be migrated to new nodes subject to a handover operation. It is the responsibility of this service to associate a running session with a specific object to determine the migration operation. Studies have shown that, in the same manner as a shared object, the data elements can be "left behind" during handover and migrated on demand as they are being accessed from the new space location [7].

Discovery Services
Application components may need to invoke services elsewhere in the SIN. The interface of the dependent service is known at compile time and necessary stubs generated, etc., but the location of their endpoint must be determined in run time. The discovery service serves this purpose, and application services notify the discovery service about their new endpoint as they are migrated to new endpoints.

Certificate & Key store
Certificates should be kept in a safe storage after they have been validated, and private keys should not be exposed outside a trusted environment. This particular service is shown not to reference the communication subsystem, it is a local service which offers a client to sign a hash value or a secret key with the encapsulated private key. The implementation of this service has not been decided, but should employ suitable hardware based solutions (e.g., the Trusted Platform Module).

IV. API COLLECTION

The different software components involved in the SIN service will need APIs related to the specific tasks that the component is assigned to. Three distinct APIs will be briefly presented, together with a suggested set of service calls. Please observe that there is no call to establish an authenticated session, so necessary credentials and validation parameters for two-ways authentication and authorization control must be given as parameters in the service call. The reason for this design choice is to keep transactions atomic and idempotent. If either of the two parties fail to provide necessary credentials the actual service call will not be executed.

A. Client API

The client API is implemented as a container layer in the surface based client computers, it serves requests from "end" clients (clients that do not provide services to satellite based processes). The same API is used by application *owner*, who is allowed to start/stop/update the service, and application *user*, who are allowed to connect/invoke the service. The proposed service calls are:

`uploadApplication`
Deploy new and updated applications

`startApp, stopApp`
Reserved for the application owner

`connectApp, invokeService`
Used by application user

`requestHandover`
A handover is not initiated by user commands, but by the communication stack

B. Container API

The container is responsible for the creation of a runtime environment for the service application component, as well as the interface to the host resource management and the migration of components. The API offered to the container by the SIN-OS will not include calls across the interface between the container and the component. These calls will be introduced with the component API. The suggested calls are:

`loadApp, startApp, suspendApp, destroyApp`
Call to allocate resources and load code segments

`executeHandover`
Call to the host to find a new candidate service and to move the state representation there. The container must identify to the host the resources that must be migrated.

The container architecture is inspired by the Docker Swarm project [10], but its simplistic approach to load balancing, where the requests are distributed without regards to the networking costs/latency, must be replaced with a mechanism which takes the workload on intermediate nodes into consideration.

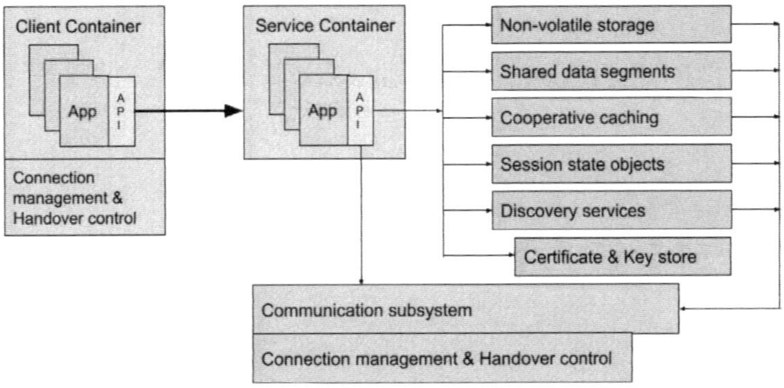

Figure 2. The components of a SIN-OS and their relations

C. Component API

The application components need access to services essential to their execution, including

`open, read, write, append, close, delete`
: Access to non-volatile memory

`open, close, read, write`
: Access to shared segments [8]

`open, lookup, add, close, delete`
: Creation/access to cooperative caches [5]

`findService, invokeService`
: Discovery/invocation of dependent services

`socket, read, write, close`
: Access to communication sockets

`init, destroy, suspend, resume`
: Life-cycle management callbacks

For service components, compile-time resources are also needed for the access to dependent services: Naming convention, stub object generations, etc.

V. The Software Model

This position paper presents a design proposition for a SIN-OS design, but the design should be subject to a closer study through a realistic software model of the satellite constellation. Previous efforts in this series of SIN studies have employed a software model programmed in Java for this purpose. A screenshot of this model is shown in Figure 3 for a constellation of 150 satellites at 500 km altitude. The colored backdrop in the figure indicates the population density inside the satellite footprint at a given location, based on gridded population data from NASA [11]. This data set has also been used to calculate the graph in Figure 1. The author prepares this model with additional logic for testing the API design as a further study.

VI. Conclusion

This article has proposed a design for a SIN-OS, based on a series of studies into a range of operational problems related to SIN-OS operation. Both a component/service map and a list of APIs have been presented. The proposed design is a part of an ongoing feasibility study on SIN development, and there are still many details in need for a further study. This will be the focus for further research effort in the field of SIN operation.

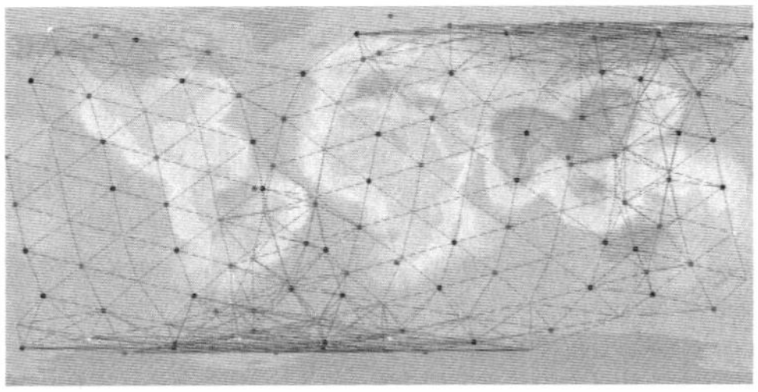

Figure 3. Screenshot from the satellite constellation model.

References

[1] S. Briatore, N. Garzaniti, and A. Golkar, "Towards the internet for space: Bringing cloud computing to space systems," in *36th International Communications Satellite Systems Conference (ICSSC 2018)*, 2018, pp. 1–5.

[2] L. Bai, T. de Cola, Q. Yu, and W. Zhang, "Space information networks," *IEEE Wireless Communications*, vol. 26, no. 2, pp. 8–9, 2019.

[3] A. Fongen, "Application services in space information networks," in *CYBER 2021*. Barcelona, Spain: IARIA, Oct 2021, pp. 113–117.

[4] A. Fongen, "Trust management in space information networks," in *SECURWARE 2021*. Athens, Greece: IARIA, Nov 2021, pp. 14–18.

[5] A. Fongen, "Cooperative caching in space information networks," in *INTERNET 2022*. Vienna, Italy: IARIA, May 2022, pp. 1–5.

[6] A. Fongen, "Population-based routing in leo satellite networks," in *MOBILITY 2022*. Porto, Portugal: IARIA, June 2022, pp. 1–4.

[7] A. Fongen, "Transfer of session state between satellites in a space information network," in *INTERNET 2023*. Barcelona, Spain: IARIA, March 2023, pp. 1–4.

[8] A. Fongen, "Data sharing services in a space information network," in *EMERGING 2023, The Fifteenth International Conference on Emerging Networks and Systems Intelligence*. Porto, Portugal: IARIA, September 2023, pp. 1–4.

[9] A. Fongen, "Optimization of a public key infrastructure," in *IEEE MILCOM*, Baltimore, MD, USA, Nov 2011, pp. 1440–1447.

[10] A. Modak, S. D. Chaudhary, P. S. Paygude, and S. R. Ldate, "Techniques to secure data on cloud: Docker swarm or kubernetes?" in *2018 Second International Conference on Inventive Communication and Computational Technologies (ICICCT)*, 2018, pp. 7–12.

[11] "Gridded population of the world v.4.11," [Online; retrieved 8-Oct-2023]. [Online]. Available: https://sedac.ciesin.columbia.edu/data/collection/gpw-v4/sets/browse

Software Pipeline for 3D Heritage Digitization - The Case of Faro Focus Scans

Kamil Żyła
Department of Computer Science
Lublin University of Technology
Nadbystrzycka 36B, 20-618 Lublin, Poland
e-mail: k.zyla@pollub.pl

Jacek Kęsik
Department of Computer Science
Lublin University of Technology
Nadbystrzycka 36B, 20-618 Lublin, Poland
e-mail: j.kesik@pollub.pl

Abstract: **Heritage 3D digitization is a research topic undertaken by a broad community of scientists and policy makers. One of the technological solutions chosen is Faro Focus laser scanners. 3D digitization is carried out according to a unified procedure using device-dedicated software. The sequential nature of this procedure and the features of the dedicated software prevent the full potential of the supported hardware from being used. Optimization is possible at the stage of process allocation for many digitization tasks. We propose a software pipeline and its simple optimization that allows at least some of these challenges to be overcome. Validation was performed on 3D scans of three Romanian wooden churches. The proposed approach allowed the production of high-quality 3D models. Optimization, despite simplicity, showed a noteworthy effect in the case of processing 3D scans of a number of objects.**

Keywords: software pipeline; 3D digitization; heritage; Faro Focus; 3D laser scanner; wooden church.

I. INTRODUCTION

Heritage 3D digitization is an emerging topic of current research [1]. We can observe efforts in terms of technology and heritage protection protocols in a variety of domains, including architecture [2], clothing [3][4], and small–medium sized objects [5], as well as intangible heritage [6]. Archiving [7], reconstruction [8], and dissemination [9][10] are considered as the typical goals of digitization.

Among technologies used, laser scanning emerged as the default technology used in the case of architecture [7][11]. One of the frequently used solutions is Faro Focus 3D laser scanner. As a result of the scanning, point clouds are produced. Then, they are transformed to a base 3D model, of reasonably high quality, that might undergo certain simplifications for the purpose of its dissemination.

We, based on our long-term experience and literature survey, see some important software challenges that occur during the transformation from point clouds from Faro Focus scanner to 3D models. The following can be mentioned [2][7]:

- Equipment performance – the time of data processing might be long (even days in the case of very large 3D models). Sometimes some of the data processing steps have to be repeated to obtain a result of proper quality.
- Software interoperability – in order to obtain a 3D model of a proper quality, many programs from different vendors have to be used. This causes the need for exporting/importing data in a compatible format, which also takes significant time.
- Workflow parallelization – in order to speed up data processing, some of the steps should be able to be executed in parallel. Usually the disk drive, processor and memory are not evenly and fully used during the sequential execution of the steps.
- Missing common software pipeline – due to the heavy and long computations, a proven and stable set of software tools is desired.
- Software pipeline dependent on requirements for the final 3D model – 3D models for the purpose of documentation focus on quality and precision, while dissemination 3D models focus on the presentation issues and performance of target devices.

This work presents a software pipeline that fits the specificity of a Faro Focus 3D scanner. Some basic optimizations are also discussed and preliminarily verified. The real-life case studies of wooden churches from Romania were chosen. We believe that this work might be valuable for readers in terms of identifying important challenges, describing the software gap that needs amelioration and automation, and providing a suggestion of what to do until better software appears. Persons involved in the hot topic of 3D heritage digitization can learn of a proven set of tools that could be applied during their activities.

In Section II, related works are investigated. In Section III, the proposed approach is introduced. In Section IV, materials and methods are described. In Section V, results regarding real-life examples, being three wooden churches, are discussed. Finally, in Section VI, conclusions are drawn.

II. RELATED WORK

Faro Laser scanners have a broad range of applications: they are used to scan the interiors [11][12] and exteriors [13][14] of buildings, as well as sculpture-size objects [15][16], or even petroglyphs [17][18]. Authors of previous works highlight the specificity of the laser light, which makes it suitable for outdoor conditions as well as for dealing well with large-sized objects (even above one hundred meters).

It was also revealed that there is no common pipeline used. Authors employed a custom and differentiated set of software tools. Sometimes sets of tools were the same, although they were used to perform different data processing steps. Among others, the following pipelines are worth highlighting:

- Faro Scene for point clouds manipulation; then Autodesk Recap Pro for registration, denoising and decimation; finally MeshLab for 3D meshing [15].
- Faro Scene for point clouds manipulation; then Autodesk Recap Pro for denoising and remaining activities [11].
- Faro Scene for point clouds manipulation; then Geomagic Studio for remaining activities [17].
- Faro Scene for all the computation steps [18].

Finally, 3D data processing steps were usually not optimized. Execution was kept sequential. The topic of parallelization was omitted. Some authors have mentioned optimizations in terms of tuning-up 3D model characteristics, either in terms of the hardware acceleration of a single step, such as by utilizing graphical processing unit computing capabilities or running data computation on dedicated highly efficient machines. Works dealing with the topic of processing 3D scans of heritage objects made using Faro Focus 3D scanner in the same way as ours were not identified.

III. Proposed Approach

In order to properly present our idea for the software pipeline designed for Faro Focus scans, some introduction is needed first. The purpose of using the pipeline is to obtain a textured 3D model of high quality (so called base model), that is based on clouds of points from 3D scanning (so called scans). To achieve this goal the following software tasks (data processing steps) have to be performed: (1) opening and colorization of individual scans, (2) registration of scans in relation to each other, (3) scans cleaning, (4) generation of a 3D mesh based on scans, (5) mesh texturing, (6) export of the final model.

Software. We recommend using the following two proven software tools within the pipeline: first Faro Scene [19] and next Reality Capture [20]. Faro Scene is the dedicated software provided together with a Faro Focus 3D scanner. In our opinion, it is well suited for tasks one to three, i.e., operation on clouds of points. Reality Capture is third-party software well suited for tasks four to six, i.e., 3D model generation and texturing.

Faro Scene has some significant disadvantages, being: 3D model size limits, making Faro Scene useless in the case of large objects, like buildings; significant loss of 3D model quality due to the necessity of simplifications; unsatisfactory 3D model generation capabilities. Thus, it is supplemented with Reality Capture, which provides very rich functionality and interface, as well as capabilities for computing extremely large 3D models (even exceeding the largest ones that could be displayed by contemporary computers).

Unfortunately, the presence of two software tools within the pipeline, although necessary, introduces some overhead related to passing scans in a proper format from one tool to the other. Thus, two additional steps occur between steps three and four, i.e., data export from Faro Scene to the so-called "ordered format" and data import to Reality Capture.

Finally, software tools proposed by us might be perceived as comparable in terms of functionality with some tools identified during the literature review. Nevertheless, the proposal's superiority lies mainly in the use of tools offering the highest level of functionality and usability (independently of the 3D digitized objects' size), and being a very affordable choice at the same time. Reality Capture licensing promotes in its way academic and non-profit usage.

Optimization. Usually, the software tasks within the pipeline are executed sequentially, which causes computer resources to be partially and unevenly utilized. For example, some of the tasks heavily utilize a processor for a longer time, while disk and memory is idling.

The above-mentioned mechanism creates room for performing some specific types of tasks in parallel, e.g., data export and data import or mesh model generation. Thus, we propose to perform in parallel the types of tasks that do not heavily utilize the same computer resources. This should noticeably speed up the time of processing, which is usually the scarcest resource. Three basic types of computer resources might be distinguished: processor, graphics, and storage.

Software tools within the pipelines (not only within the one proposed by us) are basically not adjusted to the parallelization of software tasks done for one object. It is rather possible while executing many pipelines for many objects. The real-life example will be discussed in Section V, Results.

IV. Materials and Methods

The proposed approach was tested by us among others during the 3D digitization of wooden churches in Romania. Such choice was made to promote our recent activities. The scans of facades of the following churches were used for the purpose of this work:

- (C1) The orthodox church of Creaca: 13 scans – 10,338 x 4,267 pt.
- (C2) The orthodox church of Târgușor: 10 scans – 10,342 x 4,267 pt.
- (C3) The orthodox church of Petrindu in the open-air museum of Cluj-Napoca: 15 scans – 10,172 x 4,267 pt.

They all represent a similar class of heritage object, in terms of size, building materials, and shape complexity. Due to space constraints, their further description is omitted. To see short notes describing the churches, as well as models and panoramas, please refer to [21], which is a web page reporting works on the digitization of the wooden heritage of the Carpathians. This, along with the works themselves, is run as an internal initiative by the Department of Computer Science at the Faculty of Electrical Engineering and Computer Science of the Lublin University of Technology.

All computations were performed on a laptop computer equipped with: Intel i9 processor (8 cores), 64 GB RAM, nVidia RTX 2080m graphics, SSD M2 data storage drive, and Windows 11 operating system. We took care of equal conditions for each measured computation unit.

The procedure was as follows: the eight software tasks defined in Section III were executed sequentially for scans of the three chosen wooden churches. During the execution the following was measured: operator engagement; processor, graphics and storage load; task execution times. Based on the measured computer resources loads, optimization by parallelization was planned. Then, the software tasks were run again, but utilizing the planned optimization. The same measurements were performed. All computations were assisted by the same 3D digitization expert. The execution of each task for each church was repeated three times and measurements' average values were counted.

The operator engagement can be defined as a percentage of a total task time that involved manual actions of a human. It was described in the following scale: L (low – only up to 30% of task time), M (medium – from 31% to 70% of task time), H (high – more than 71% of task time). Computer resources loads were described using a similar scale, where L means an average load of up to 30%, M means an average load of between 31% and 70%, and H means an average load of above 71%. Task execution times were measured with a precision of 6 minutes (0.1 h), which was sufficient due to the many manual human activities involved, long overall time of computations, and general character of the evaluation.

V. RESULTS

Table I presents the validation results of our approach according to the procedure described in Section IV. In Table I, the column "Task name" contains the software tasks, in a proper order, leading from clouds of points to a 3D model. The column heading "Op. eng." stands for operator engagement. "Comp. type" stands for computation type, while the "seq" row holds values for the sequential execution of the task, and "par" holds values for the parallelized (optimized) execution of the task. "CPU" stands for the processor, "GPU" for the graphics, and "SDD" for the disk drive (storage). "C1", "C2", and "C3" stand for the models of churches 1, 2, and 3 respectively. Finally, "Exec. time" means execution time.

Thus, for example, regarding software task 1: The task, when executed sequentially ("seq" row), caused low ("L") operator engagement, medium ("M") load of CPU, low ("L") load of GPU, and medium ("M") load of disk drive. Execution of the task 1, when sequential, took 1 h 30 min in the case of church 1 ("C1"), 1 h 18 min – church 2 ("C2"), and 2 h 0 min – church 3 ("C3"). The "par" row holds values for the same single software task, but executed in the parallelized setting. It means, the measured values also refer to that single task. The times (similarly other values) might be almost the same or slightly different, because parallelization causes heavier usage of the computer resources, which might slightly slow down the execution of particular tasks, despite a shorter overall computation time being needed to obtain all 3D models of the churches.

After analyzing the measurements taken during the sequential execution of the tasks, the possible parallelized setting was developed. It took into account the preservation of the order of the tasks necessary when obtaining a 3D model from scans for a single heritage object. The optimized pipeline looked as follows: (1) Tasks 1–3 for the model of "C1". (2) In parallel, task 4 for the model of "C1" and tasks 1–3 for the models of "C2" and "C3". (3) In parallel, task 4 for the model of "C2" and tasks 5–6 for the model of "C1". (4) In parallel, task 4 for the model of "C3" and tasks 5–6 for the model of "C2", followed by task 7 for the model of "C1". Subsequent tasks for the models were carried out sequentially.

"*" denotes low operator engagement, because such scans were chosen that could be registered automatically by a software tool. "**" denotes a surprising property of Faro Scene, that export takes a lot of time yet does not heavily utilize the computer resources.

TABLE I. WORKLOAD WHILE PERFORMING 3D DATA PROCESSING TASKS

No.	**Task name**	**Comp. type**	**Op. eng. [%]**	**Load of CPU/GPU /SDD [%]**	**Exec. time for C1/C2/C3 [h]**
1	Opening and colorization of individual scans	seq	L	M/L/M	1.5/ 1.3/ 2.0
		par	L	M/L/M	1.5/ 1.5 /2.0
2	Registration of scans in relation to each other	seq	L *	H/L/M	1.0/ 0.5/ 1.0
		par	L *	H/L/M	1.0/ 1.0/ 1.0
3	Scans cleaning	seq	H	L/M/L	0.3/ 0.1/ 1.0
		par	H	L/M/L	0.3/ 0.1/ 1.0
4	Data export from Faro Scene	seq	L	L/L/L**	8.0/ 5.5/ 9.0
		par	L	L/L/L**	8.0/ 5.5/ 9.0
5	Data import to Reality Capture	seq	L	H/L/H	0.5/ 0.3/ 0.5
		par	L	H/L/H	0.8/ 0.5/ 0.5
6	Generation of a 3D mesh based on scans	seq	L	H/L/M	3.3/ 3.0/ 3.5
		par	L	H/L/M	4.0/ 3.5/ 3.5
7	Mesh texturing	seq	L	M/H/M	4.0/ 4.0/ 4.0
		par	L	M/H/M	4.0/ 4.3/ 4.0
8	Export of the final model	seq	L	H/L/H	0.3/ 0.3/ 0.3
		par	L	H/L/H	0.3/ 0.3/ 0.3

It can be seen in Table 1 that when execution is sequential, the computer is fully focused on one task only, thus times are shorter. When another task is executed in parallel, the computer resources are already occupied by the first task, thus performance drop (longer times) cannot be avoided. The key result is that, when tasks are running in parallel, a longer time for the execution of a single task is in many instances observed, although the total time needed to process the data of all the 3D scanned objects is shorter.

Finally, the sequential execution of the tasks, in order to get final 3D models of all three churches exported to OBJ file format, took 54 h 45 min. After the parallelization, achieving the same goal took 42 h 15 min. The resulting models can be found at a dedicated web page [21].

VI. Conclusion and Future Work

In order to overcome challenges of postprocessing Faro Focus 3D scans, we proposed our own software pipeline (utilizing Faro Scene and Reality Capture tools), together with a simple optimization by parallelization of performed tasks. It was then verified on the example of three Romanian wooden churches. What is more, we have used it for a longer time during our digitization works involving Faro Focus scanners.

In our opinion, the pipeline proved itself useful. Among the main advantages is its being affordable, while offering functionality and quality at the highest level. Moreover, it does not heavily engage the operator. The proposed optimization allowed us to decrease noticeably the total time of acquiring all 3D models of many objects from scans. In the case of the scans here used, it was reduced by ~1/5, despite a slightly longer execution time being seen for particular tasks due to the heavier (better, fuller) usage of the computer resources. It was also revealed that optimization did not heavily affect the computer resources loads when they were observed separately for each particular single task done for a particular single model.

As a disadvantage, the use of two software tools might be mentioned. It requires an operator to learn how to use two different tools. Moreover, the list of tasks has to be extended by the resource-consuming export and import of data. Unfortunately, there is no other way, when it comes to obtaining high-quality models of large objects, due to Faro Scene's limitations. Finally, it is possible in rare cases that very heavy tasks may cause full usage of a particular computer resource, making parallelization barely possible.

References

[1] K. Żyła, J. Montusiewicz, S. Skulimowski, and R. Kayumov, "VR technologies as an extension to the museum exhibition: A case study of the Silk Road museums in Samarkand," Muzeológia a kultúrne dedičstvo, vol. 8(4), pp. 73-93, 2020, nr 4, doi: 10.46284/mkd.2020.8.4.6

[2] M. Miłosz, J. Kęsik, and J. Montusiewicz, "3D scanning and visualization of large monuments of Timurid architecture in Central Asia - A methodical approach," Journal on Computing and Cultural Heritage, vol. 14(1), pp. 1-31, 2021, doi: 10.1145/3425796

[3] J. Montusiewicz, M. Miłosz, J. Kęsik, and K. Żyła, "Structured-light 3D scanning of exhibited historical clothing - A first-ever methodical trial and its results," Heritage Science, vol. 9(1), pp. 1-20, 2021, doi: 10.1186/s40494-021-00544-x

[4] K. Żyła, J. Kęsik, F. Santos, and G. House, "Scanning of historical clothes using 3D scanners: Comparison of goals, tools, and methods," Applied Sciences, vol. 11(12), pp. 1-18, 2021, doi: 10.3390/app11125588

[5] R. Comes, et al., "Digital reconstruction of fragmented cultural heritage assets: The case study of the Dacian embossed disk from Piatra Roşie," Applied Sciences, vol. 12(16), pp. 1-30, 2022, doi: 10.3390/app12168131

[6] M. Skublewska-Paszkowska, et al., "Methodology of 3D scanning of intangible cultural heritage - The example of Lazgi dance," Applied Sciences, vol. 11(23), pp. 1-17, 2021, doi: 10.3390/app112311568

[7] J. Kęsik, M. Miłosz, J. Montusiewicz, and K. Samarov, "Documenting the geometry of large architectural monuments using 3D scanning - The case of the dome of the Golden Mosque of the Tillya-Kori Madrasah in Samarkand," Digital Applications in Archaeology and Cultural Heritage, vol. 22, pp. 1-11, 2021, doi: 10.1016/j.daach.2021.e00199

[8] M. Miłosz, E. Miłosz, and J. Montusiewicz, "Determination of ceramic tile colour surface areas on the medieval Sher-Dor Madrasah mosaic in Samarkand – Problems and solutions," Digital Applications in Archaeology and Cultural Heritage, vol. 16, pp. 1-6, 2020, doi: 10.1016/j.daach.2020.e00134

[9] R. Comes, et al., "Enhancing accessibility to cultural heritage through digital content and virtual reality: A case study of the Sarmizegetusa Regia UNESCO site," Journal of Ancient History and Archaeology, vol. 7(3), pp. 124-139, 2020.

[10] A. M. Ciekanowska, A. K. Kiszczak-Gliński, and K. Dziedzic, "Comparative analysis of Unity and Unreal Engine efficiency in creating virtual exhibitions of 3D scanned models," JCSI - Journal of Computer Sciences Institute, vol. 20, pp. 247-253, 2021, doi: 10.35784/jcsi.2698

[11] M. Campi, M. Falcone, and S. Sabbatini, "Towards continuous monitoring of architecture. Terrestrial laser scanning and mobile mapping system for the diagnostic phases of the cultural heritage," Int. Arch. Photogramm. Remote Sens. Spatial Inf. Sci., vol. XLVI-2/W1-2022, pp. 121–127, 2022, doi: 10.5194/isprs-archives-XLVI-2-W1-2022-121-2022

[12] L. Wilson, A. Rawlinson, A. Frost, and J. Hepher, "3D digital documentation for disaster management in historic buildings: Applications following fire damage at the Mackintosh building, The Glasgow School of Art," Journal of Cultural Heritage, vol. 31, pp. 24-32, 2018, doi: 10.1016/j.culher.2017.11.012

[13] J. Kęsik, M. Miłosz, and J. Montusiewicz, "Problems of acquisition and postprocessing of 3D scans of large architectural objects," MATEC Web of Conferences, vol. 252, pp. 1-6, 2019, doi: 10.1051/matecconf/201925203001

[14] D. P. Pocobelli, J. Boehm, P. Bryan, J. Still, and J. Grau-Bové, "Building information models for monitoring and simulation data in heritage buildings," Int. Arch. Photogramm. Remote Sens. Spatial Inf. Sci., vol. XLII-2, pp. 909–916, 2018, doi: 10.5194/isprs-archives-XLII-2-909-2018

[15] E. Adamopoulos, F. Rinaudo, and L. Ardissono, "A critical comparison of 3D digitization techniques for heritage objects," ISPRS International Journal of Geo-Information, vol. 10(1), pp. 1-21, 2021, doi: 10.3390/ijgi10010010

[16] G. Guidi, U. S. Malik, B. Frischer, C. Barandoni, and F. Paolucci, "The Indiana University-Uffizi project: Metrological challenges and workflow for massive 3D digitization of sculptures" 23rd International Conference on Virtual System & Multimedia (VSMM 2017), IEEE, 2017, pp. 1-8, doi: 10.1109/VSMM.2017.8346268

[17] S. Peña-Villasenín, M. Gil-Docampo, and J. Ortiz-Sanz, "Professional SfM and TLS vs a simple SfM photogrammetry for 3D modelling of rock art and radiance scaling shading in engraving detection," Journal of Cultural Heritage, vol. 37, pp. 238-246, 2019, doi: 10.1016/j.culher.2018.10.009

[18] J. Kęsik, M. Miłosz, J. Montusiewicz, and N. Israilova, "Documenting archaeological petroglyph sites with the use of 3D terrestrial laser scanners - A case study of petroglyphs in Kyrgyzstan," Applied Sciences, vol. 12(20), pp. 1-17, 2022, doi: 10.3390/app122010521

[19] "Faro Scene homepage," https://www.faro.com/en/Products/Software/SCENE-Software, retrieved: August, 2023.

[20] "Reality Capture homepage," https://www.capturingreality.com, retrieved: August, 2023.

[21] "Wooden monuments of the Carpathians in 3D," https://carpatia3d.com/en/rezultaty-modele-3d-i-panoramy/, retrieved: August, 2023.

Source Code Analysis of GitHub Projects from E-Commerce and Game Domains

Doga Babacan
Department of Computer Engineering
Izmir Institute of Technology
Izmir, Turkiye
email: dogababacan96@gmail.com

Tugkan Tuglular
Department of Computer Engineering
Izmir Institute of Technology
Izmir, Turkiye
email: tugkantuglular@iyte.edu.tr

Abstract— **The nature of domains, such as e-commerce, affects the software development process and the resulting software. Various domains may have similarities and differences with respect to each other under source code analysis. This research project examines the similarities and differences between game and e-commerce domains. With the technology now available to everyone, finding and examining public repositories is more straightforward. The domains chosen for this project are game and e-commerce since they are two of the most popular topics. In this research, inspections are made on 25 projects, 15 from the e-commerce domain and ten from the game domain. Developing a repository mining program that works with a software analysis tool and returns the results of this analysis is also validated within this research.**

Keywords-static source code analysis; repository mining; e-commerce software; game software.

I. INTRODUCTION

Static source code analysis is a way to analyze the code without running it. Nowadays, many tools help software developers to perform this process. In the literature, research was not found that utilizes these tools to inspect multiple repositories simultaneously and compares the results depending on their similarities and differences. If automation like inspection is possible for various repositories with these kinds of tools, it may be used in many types of research for many reasons. The SonarQube is utilized for this research. It measures technical debt, number of bugs, classes, functions, complexity, cognitive complexity, etc. These values may be used in many ways and inspected for relations between them. With these values in our hands, domains in software development, like e-commerce and game, can be studied, focusing on how they behave according to the results, whether they act similarly or not.

The main objective of this research project is to find out if automation applies to these kinds of tools during research with software, which clones many projects and, analyzes them, retrieves the results. Doing sample research utilizing this software will be another task to do. Each value in the results will be another attribute to compare and inspect. The sample research looks at the behavior of game and e-commerce domains, considering their results from the source code analyses tool. Each domain will be examined separately, and there will be a comparison. Public repositories of GitHub will be used for this purpose since it is one of the most popular code-storing and managing platforms.

The proposed solution uses Python language to create software that clones repositories from each domain, namely game, and e-commerce, to local with the get requests and python library for GitHub and upload them to SonarQube by utilizing the Python package SonarQube Client to analyze those repositories. After analyzing the repositories with SonarQube, the proposed solution continues by getting each project source code analysis result with the SonarQube Client package, inspecting those results with correlation matrices for each domain, and choosing specific attributes to examine the relation between them depending on the correlation matrix.

Java projects from GitHub in the e-commerce and game domains are the focus of this research. Some of the projects cannot be analyzed by SonarQube and they are excluded from research. Projects with other programming languages from the same domains will be considered in the future.

The paper is organized as follows: Section II presents the related work. Section III explains the proposed approach. Section IV presents the result and discussion, and the last section concludes the paper.

II. RELATED WORK

Sokol et al. [1] researched software mining tools, how they work, and the alternatives for this type of program. Research mainly focuses on Metric Miner's results and adds some points on Sonar.

Spadini et al. [2] developed a mining software repository program PyDriller, using Python language and put it against Python Framework GitPython. With fewer lines of code and less complexity, the results of both programs are compared.

Dabic et al. [3] developed another mining software for GitHub projects named GitHub Search. This program works in ten languages. It is a dataset that contains information about more than 700.000 public repositories in GitHub.

Dueñas et al. [4] introduced GrimoireLab, an open-source set of Python tools used in repository mining, analyzing, and visualizing. Third parties can also use the tool, designed as a modular toolset.

Koetter et al. [5] utilized SourceMeter to calculate chosen student project metrics. For each project, a Python tool developed by the article's authors was used for the benchmark calculation. With the gathered results, they made comparisons.

Jarczyk et al. [6] worked on determining two metrics that indicate the quality of GitHub projects. The initial statistic is derived from the ratings assigned to a project by other members of GitHub, while the second metric is derived through the application of survival analysis techniques to issues reported by users of the project. Following the development of the metrics, they proceeded to collect data on various attributes of many GitHub projects. Subsequently, they conducted an analysis utilizing statistical regression techniques to examine the impact of these attributes on the overall quality of the projects.

Yalçın and Tuglular [7] worked on 21 projects from GitHub with multiple versions of a tool the author created. JSoup and Selenium are utilized in the mining process. For each project, the author looked at whether the executable and test codes are increasing in sync, whether updates affect the co-evolution of test and executable data. In using GitHub software projects from different angle, AlMarzouq et al. [8] highlighted the challenges and opportunities of using GitHub as a data source in both research and programming education.

Gousios and Spinellis [9] found that the acquisition of data from GitHub is not a straightforward task, the suitability of the data for various research purposes may be limited, and the misuse of this data can potentially result in biased outcomes. Our findings match with their findings.

III. Proposed Approach

The proposed approach is composed of three steps:

1. Data Collection from GitHub
2. Source Code Analysis using SonarQube
3. Data preparation
4. Data analysis

The first three steps are explained in detail in this section. The fourth step is presented in the following section with results and discussion.

A. Data Collection from GitHub

The primary way of searching for software projects in GitHub is performed with a get request, through Python, such as "https://api.github.com/search/repositories?q=e-commerceis:featured+language:java&sort=stars&order=desc&per_page=100&page=1". The "is: featured" part of the string helps for searching topics in GitHub. If this part is not used, the result will return as a general search instead of topics. "language" filters for the asked language. "sort" lets the user choose which attribute to sort. In this research, the number of project stars is focused on finding a more reliable project on GitHub. "per_page" is the number of projects to be returned on request.

We intend to inspect the code metrics such as code smells, bugs, security hotspots, duplications, etc. We write a code that clones each release of a GitHub project and lists them as files in a folder if it did not have a release history to download; the code looks into previous tags of the project in GitHub, if it had tags, program clones each tag's repository and list as each of the version with its project name and its tag next to it. Also, it creates each version's SonarQube project under SonarQube.

By utilizing the "OS" library already included in Python, the directory for each repository can be created with a chosen name with "os. mkdir(path)". Here path is the whole path to the location, including the directory name such as "C:/Programming/RepositoryInspectionProject/3091E-c-o-Mshopizer".

When cloning from GitHub, the code "git clone {repo_url} {directory_name}" is written inside "os. system()" because it needs to be written as a console command. "repo_url" refers to the cloning URL of the repository, and "directory_name" is the name pattern that was chosen before as "3091E-c-o-Mshopizer". After cloning each project, there is a second step for them to upload these Maven projects to SonarQube for inspection. First, the creation of the project on the SonarQube is needed. This is performed through the utilization of the SonarQube Client library on Python. The package can be used by entering the username, password, and URL of the SonarQube installed on the computer. To create projects, the line "sonar.projects.create_project()" project name is placed as an argument where it is chosen as the directory name.

After creating the projects placed on SonarQube, repositories can be uploaded. This is achieved by utilizing the line, "mvn clean verify sonar : sonar -D maven.test.skip = true -D sonar.projectKey = {projectKey} -D sonar.host.url = http://localhost:9000 -D sonar. login = ************************************", here we skip tests by using "maven.test.skip = true" because tests could not be followed when trying automation on this research project.

B. Source Code Analysis using SonarQube

SonarQube is one of the best static source code analysis tools [10]–[12]. SonarQube is a Sonar Source product, and approximately seven million people utilize Sonar Source products currently [13]. SonarQube works with more than thirty languages, and one of them is Java.

The process for source code analysis starts when the cloning and uploading process is completed. To retrieve the results from SonarQube, SonarQube Client is utilized. Data for the following metrics [14] are collected:

Complexity: Complexity (cyclomatic complexity) is a metric where the number of paths in a code is calculated, and the minimum value of the function is 1. When the control flow of a piece of code diverges, the complexity increases. This calculation may differ depending on the language being used.

Cognitive Complexity: Cognitive complexity is a more detailed way of inspecting the complexity of a code. It is not a quantitative way of measuring as it is in cyclomatic complexity; it also counts in the degree of interconnectedness and abstraction or indirection in a piece of code. Cognitive complexity shows how understandable the code is and how much it is easy to maintain.

Issues: If any piece of code breaks the coding rule, it will be counted as an issue. There are three types of issues, which are bug, vulnerability, and code smell.

Violations: Any form of issue is also called a violation. Prefixes change depending on the importance of the violation; it can be blocker, critical, major, minor, and info.

Security Hotspots: A piece of code that is security sensitive; however, it is not as crucial as vulnerability; these hotspots may not impact the whole software, unlike the vulnerability.

Lines: Number of physical lines.

Lines of Code: The number of physical lines that contain at least one character. However, this character will not be counted if it is whitespace, tabular space, or part of a comment.

Functions: Number of functions.

Statements: Number of statements.

Comments: Number of comment lines in code.

Duplicated Lines: Number of duplicated lines in code.

C. *Data Preparation*

After source code analysis finished, then the data is normalized. The values for the metrics are placed in a dictionary and converted into a data frame to save as a CSV file, which are given in Table 1 and Table 3. By doing this, it becomes easier to work with the results on the Jupyter Notebook. On the Jupyter Notebook, after opening the CSV file, the data is converted to the data frame again to work on the values. All of the data (except star count and lines of code) is divided by a line of code because we want our values to be independent of the line of code of the repositories. Then, all the values are scaled to fit between 0 and 1. When the data preparation is finished, the correlation matrix is created to see the relationships among all attributes as shown in Table 2 and Table 4.

IV. Results and Discussion

The correlation matrices for the e-commerce and game domains are shown in Table 2 and Table 4. When we compare these two matrices, we see some differences between them. Positive and negative relations are different for game and e-commerce domains. The results are expected for the e-commerce domain; for instance, it is likely that with the decreasing number of classes, we expect a higher number of bugs which means there should be a negative relation between those two values. However, this does not apply to the game domain. This can be due to some outliers. The diagram lets the user see which attributes have positive and negative relations.

First, pair of attributes are selected. The first pair will be the number of comment lines and the number of code smells. It is a fact that code should explain itself without needing much of an explanation. These explanations are done with comment lines in the code. Code smells also tells us the software developer does not have much experience in writing code, most probably not following specific rules, does not apply tests, etc. A positive relationship is expected between them. The second pair is chosen as the number of bugs and the number of classes. If the number of classes increases, software may be thought to be cleaner and more organized and may be considered leading to fewer bugs.

When starting with the first pair of attributes, comment lines, and code smells, the correlation matrix in Table 2 shows a positive relation which was expected; the value of 0.61 is close to value 1, which means the relationship is strong even though it is not the strongest in the matrix. When a scatter graph is drawn, it shows each data point. There are outlier-like values on the diagram. To be sure, box plots are utilized. With the boxplots it is decided that two outliers need to be removed. After removing the outliers, the linear regression line is drawn in Figure 1 with (1). Also, the linear regression line shows us the positive relation better since the line has a visible positive slope.

$$y = 0.294\,x + 0.1 \qquad (1)$$

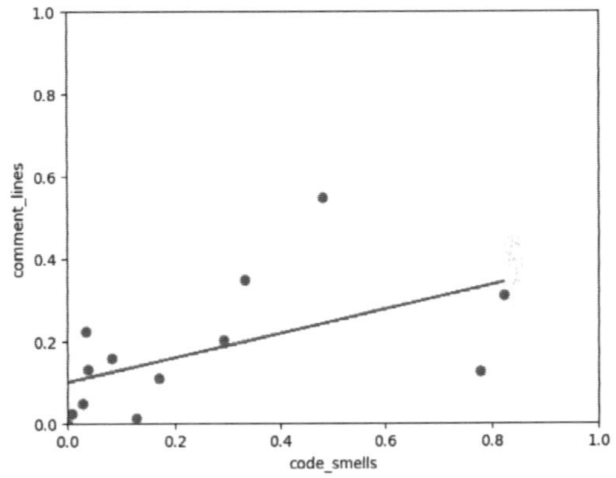

Figure 1. Linear Regression Line of Number of Comment Lines vs. Number of Code Smells of E-Commerce Domain.

The second pair of attributes, namely the number of bugs and the number of classes, are drawn on another scatter graph. Again, boxplots are utilized for each attribute to check the outliers, and it is verified that there are no outliers in this data set. The linear regression line is shown in Figure 2. The line has good visibility and a negative slope, showing a negative relation with (2).

$$y = -0.63\,x + 0.772 \qquad (2)$$

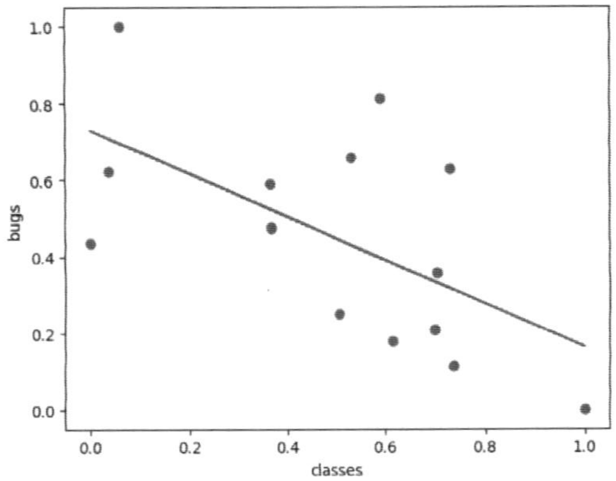

Figure 2. Linear Regression Number of Bugs vs. Number of Classes of E-Commerce Domain.

The first pair of attributes of the game domain are code smells and comment lines. Since there seems to be outliers on the scatter graph, so they are checked with the boxplots of each attribute. The boxplot showed that the two values with the number of comment lines value close to 1.0 are the outliers. After removing the outliers, a linear regression line is drawn in Figure 3 with (3).

$$y = 0.315\,x - 0.025 \quad (3)$$

The slope can be seen on the graph as positive and the equation as positive. So, as expected, if the comment lines increase, more code smells can be expected in the software.

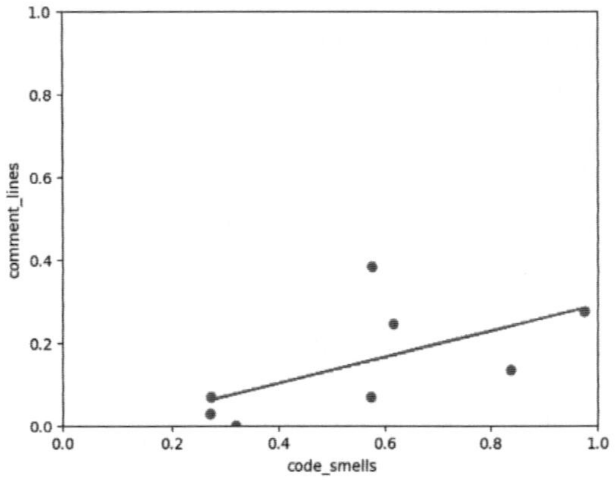

Figure 3. Linear Regression Line of Number of Comment Lines vs. Number of Code Smells of Game Domain.

The scatter graph shows how the data points are spread on the last pair of attributes set of game domain, number of classes, and number of bugs. When the outliers are checked with boxplots of each attribute, on each attribute, there is a different outlier; the number of outliers is decided as two. After removing the outliers, the scatter graph in Figure 4 is drawn with a linear regression line as in (4).

$$y = -2.586\,x + 0.755 \quad (4)$$

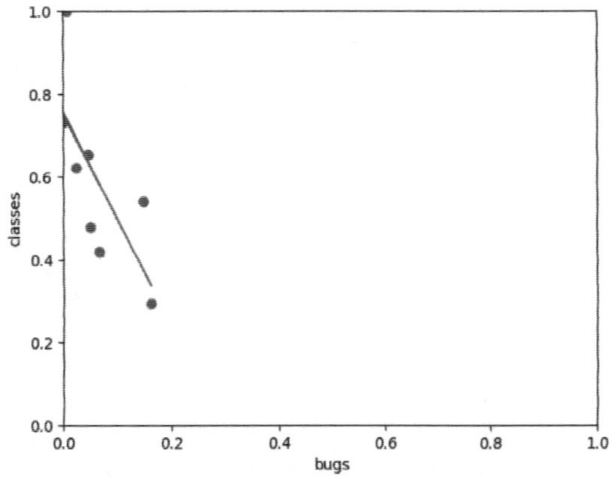

Figure 4. Linear Regression Number of Bugs vs. Number of Classes of Game Domain.

The negative slope can be seen on the graph and the equation, which means the relationship between the two attributes is negative.

There are concerns related to the generalization of results. First, all attributes should be interpreted relative to the local context; there are no absolute always correct interpretations. Second, although the projects are coded in Java, they are not necessarily object-oriented. Therefore, the results cannot be generalized to object-oriented projects. The generalizability of the research findings is limited both within the specific areas under investigation and to other domains for the following reasons. The research employs a limited sample size, and the findings lack sufficient statistical significance to generalize to the broader population. The study sample may lack representativeness in relation to the entire population. The research employs a non-random sampling technique, which has the potential to induce bias. The present study used a proprietary instrument devised by the researchers, which may potentially exhibit certain flaws or limits.

V. Conclusion

In this research, a software is developed to clone repositories and analyze them using SonarQube. Two domains, namely e-commerce and game domains, are analyzed. The correlation matrices showed that there is a difference between the two domains. The difference in the game domain can be due to structure and developers in general. However, in e-commerce, the developers follow specific rules and patterns while developing software which is common in software development. Two pairs of attributes from each domain are examined individually. The linear regression line is drawn, and the equation of the linear regression lines is shown. In conclusion, this project showed that automation could apply to repository mining, analyzing the source code, and retrieving the results of this analysis.

In this research, we first learned that the projects in GitHub are not necessarily well structured. Fetching the projects automatically was not simple and easy. Moreover, only some of the Java projects were analyzable by SonarQube. Therefore, we choose Java projects with Maven. Still, we cannot analyze all projects in the selected domains. Another source code analyzer may be used. A pluggable pipeline would be nice to have. We expected both domain projects we analyzed to be more fit to software engineering principles and best practices, but it wasn't the case.

For future work, we first plan to include more projects from the same domains and then perform cluster analysis to find the natural groups in the datasets, which can show trends, structures, or groupings that aren't obvious at first glance. This way, we plan to obtain useful insights for root causes and predictions. We also plan to figure out the dependencies between attributes.

The free version of SonarQube is employed in this research and it is limited. We would like to use the paid version for further analysis. We also plan to include other source code analysis tools such as ChatGPT and GitHub Copilot. Furthermore, some software engineering analysis tools will be included into the future research. They might give us some perspectives from software engineering point of view, such as how many people did PRs on the same part of the source code, whether there are any correlations between the design patterns or technical debt and code quality, and whether code quality is related to the organizational structure of the project team.

Moreover, we plan to expand this research to include projects from the same domains with different programming languages as well as other domains, such as IoT, Healthcare, Sports.

REFERENCES

[1] F. Z. Sokol, M. F. Aniche, and M. A. Gerosa, "MetricMiner: Supporting researchers in mining software repositories," in 2013 IEEE 13th International Working Conference on Source Code Analysis and Manipulation (SCAM), Sep. 2013, pp. 142–146. doi: 10.1109/SCAM.2013.6648195.

[2] D. Spadini, M. Aniche, and A. Bacchelli, "PyDriller: Python framework for mining software repositories," in Proceedings of the 2018 26th ACM Joint Meeting on European Software Engineering Conference and Symposium on the Foundations of Software Engineering, in ESEC/FSE 2018. New York, NY, USA: Association for Computing Machinery, Oct. 2018, pp. 908–911. doi: 10.1145/3236024.3264598.

[3] O. Dabic, E. Aghajani, and G. Bavota, "Sampling Projects in GitHub for MSR Studies," in 2021 IEEE/ACM 18th International Conference on Mining Software Repositories (MSR), May 2021, pp. 560–564. doi: 10.1109/MSR52588.2021.00074.

[4] "GrimoireLab: A toolset for software development analytics [PeerJ]," Retrieved: July, 2023 [Online]. Available from: https://peerj.com/articles/cs-601/.

[5] F. Koetter, et al., "Assessing Software Quality of Agile Student Projects by Data-mining Software Repositories:," in Proceedings of the 11th International Conference on Computer Supported Education, Heraklion, Crete, Greece: SCITEPRESS - Science and Technology Publications, 2019, pp. 244–251. doi: 10.5220/0007688602440251.

[6] O. Jarczyk, B. Gruszka, S. Jaroszewicz, L. Bukowski, and A. Wierzbicki, "Github projects. quality analysis of open-source software," in Social Informatics: 6th International Conference, SocInfo 2014, Barcelona, Spain, November 11-13, pp. 80-94. Springer International Publishing, 2014.

[7] A. G. Yalçın and T. Tuglular, "Studying the Co-Evolution of Source Code and Acceptance Tests," Int. J. Softw. Eng. Knowl. Eng., pp. 1–27, Apr. 2023, doi: 10.1142/S0218194023500237.

[8] M. AlMarzouq, A. AlZaidan, and J. AlDallal, "Mining GitHub for research and education: challenges and opportunities," International Journal of Web Information Systems 2020, 16, no. 4, pp. 451-473.

[9] G. Gousios, and D. Spinellis, "Mining software engineering data from GitHub," in 2017 IEEE/ACM 39th International Conference on Software Engineering Companion (ICSE-C), pp. 501-502. IEEE, 2017.

[10] "TOP 40 Static Code Analysis Tools (Best Source Code Analysis Tools)," Retrieved: July, 2023 [Online]. Available from: https://www.softwaretestinghelp.com/tools/top-40-static-code-analysis-tools/.

[11] "Best Static Code Analysis Tools in 2023 | Compare Reviews on 90+ | G2," Retrieved: July, 2023 [Online]. Available from: https://www.g2.com/categories/static-code-analysis.

[12] L. Zelleke, "6 Best Static Code Analysis Tools for 2023 (Paid & Free)," Comparitech, Sep. 05, 2021. Retrieved: July, 2023 [Online]. Available from: https://www.comparitech.com/net-admin/best-static-code-analysis-tools/.

[13] "Clean Code Tools for Writing Clear, Readable & Understandable Secure Quality Code," Retrieved: July, 2023 [Online]. Available from: https://www.sonarsource.com/.

[14] "Metric definition," Retrieved: July, 2023 [Online]. Available from: https://docs.sonarsource.com/sonarqube/ latest/user-guide/metric-definitions/.

TABLE I. MINED DATA FROM GITHUB FOR E-COMMERCE DOMAIN

	blocker_violations	bugs	classes	code_smells	cognitive_complexity	comment_lines	complexity	critical_violations	duplicated_lines	file_complexity	functions	lines	major_violations	ncloc	security_hotspots	stars	statements	vulnerabilities
demo-microservices	0	2	70	19	8	24	80	3	0	1,1	114	3118	12	2641	1	29	144	0
double-shop	0	3	196	49	204	263	650	5	156	3,3	636	8363	26	6211	4	34	1246	0
eCommerce-JavaBackend	1	5	37	134	50	85	207	7	92	5,6	192	1942	80	1453	4	13	356	0
spring-restapi-ecommerce	1	7	58	57	75	52	360	10	230	6,3	320	3721	24	2517	9	42	687	2
e-commerce-database	1	0	47	20	2	3	71	2	0	1,5	57	1400	10	1110	1	15	111	0
ecommerce-microservice-backend-app	11	7	237	34	8	1	389	6	1172	1,7	508	12267	8	7906	1	84	597	0
eCommerceWebsite	6	143	153	711	1776	1628	2326	269	16441	7,9	1166	67448	318	54279	103	41	6788	209
eMusicStore_eCommerce_Website	3	2	13	89	30	151	98	8	0	7,5	86	1272	48	800	15	15	271	3
ShoppingCart	0	50	44	99	122	291	378	36	161	4,9	293	13059	83	11795	31	297	572	5
open-commerce-search	5	37	298	794	2925	3420	3349	101	362	13,1	1151	26892	173	18289	4	31	6528	1
SBootApiEcomMVCHibernate	10	8	166	267	291	287	1403	35	217	8,7	1245	10293	141	7534	13	15	2246	0
shopizer	45	146	1193	4049	6911	7579	10445	1145	6205	9	7606	110936	1636	73042	35	3091	25118	525
shopping-cart	11	55	37	150	216	138	314	32	464	5,6	220	34203	121	29869	89	56	1303	60
DevOps-E-commerce-	0	4	47	60	8	99	104	14	0	2,2	149	2073	26	1506	6	17	218	14
E-Commerce-Spring-Boot	1	2	40	116	101	32	182	4	128	4,6	205	1738	69	1326	3	63	316	0

TABLE II. CORRELATION TABLE OF E-COMMERCE DOMAIN ATTRIBUTES

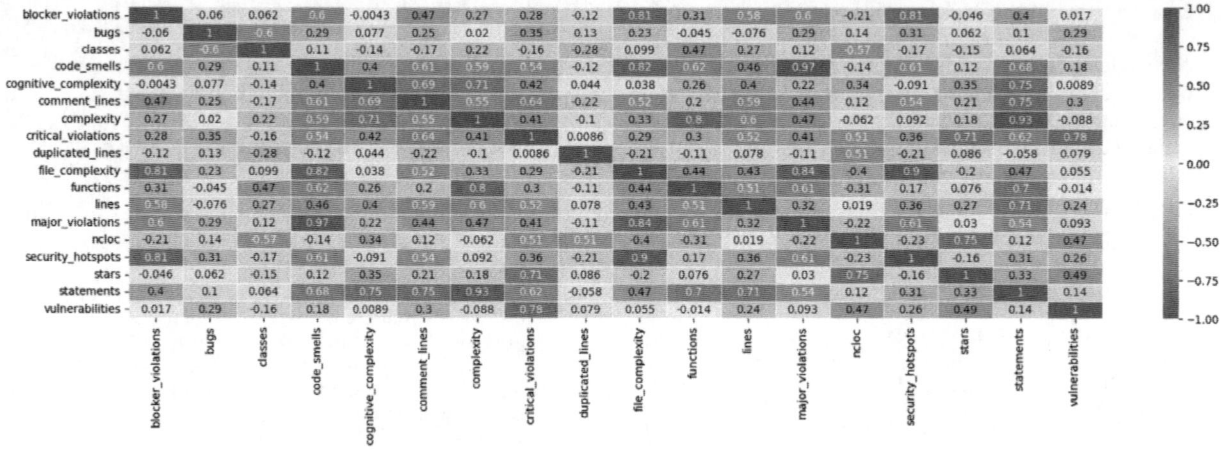

TABLE III. MINED DATA FROM GITHUB FOR GAME DOMAIN

	blocker_violations	bugs	classes	code_smells	cognitive_complexity	comment_lines	complexity	critical_violations	duplicated_lines	file_complexity	functions	lines	major_violations	ncloc	security_hotspots	stars	statements	vulnerabilities
AsciiTerminal	4	16	11	61	404	62	352	10	340	50,3	93	2247	8	1803	3	24	928	0
BatBat-Game	10	21	45	116	633	276	810	7	198	18,8	298	5271	61	3906	12	15	1999	0
gameserver	38	39	475	2126	2387	2749	4739	211	6956	11,7	3225	39201	1204	26089	71	17	10047	3
GameShardingDb	22	21	69	403	730	771	748	38	50	11,5	379	6366	250	4286	7	43	1974	0
jcards	0	0	10	49	44	286	106	0	0	11,8	66	1250	4	509	1	31	163	0
lwjglbook-leg	53	197	1748	3446	9166	5755	20724	349	130553	14,4	13388	155460	1956	116949	203	564	59028	0
OpenFighting	0	35	22	60	81	74	199	33	110	9	147	1559	11	1049	2	21	384	0
playn	43	64	398	1649	2478	6800	6168	163	2431	24,1	4412	46763	807	28753	10	239	11889	0
SypherEngine	3	3	67	233	346	622	731	27	164	9	462	5984	102	3814	4	43	1514	0
WraithEngine	0	1	101	19	307	2283	711	0	0	8,2	577	9081	19	4110	0	50	1289	0

TABLE IV. CORRELATION TABLE OF GAME DOMAIN ATTRIBUTES

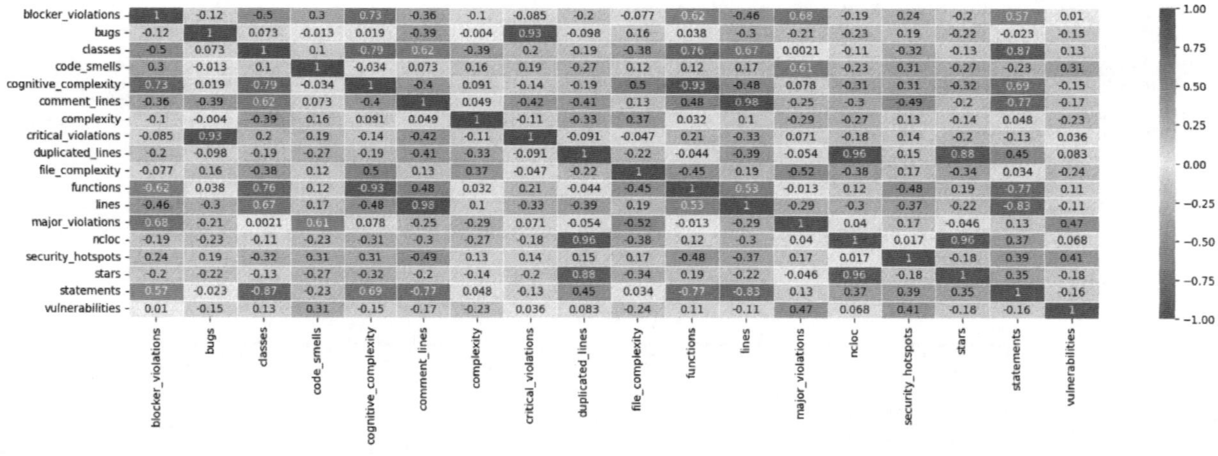

OOPS ! and Competency Questions for Evaluating the Intelligent Business Process Management Ontology

Sarra MEJRI
Laboratory RIADI-GDL, ENSI, Manouba 2010, University of Manouba, Tunisia
Higher Institute of Computer Science and Communication Techniques of Hammam Sousse, University of Sousse, Tunisia
e-mail: sarra.mejri.fsm@gmail.com

Sonia AYACHI GHANNOUCHIN
Laboratory RIADI-GDL, ENSI, Manouba 2010, University of Manouba, Tunisia
Higher Institute of Management of Sousse, University of Sousse, Tunisia
e-mail: sonia.ayachi.ghannouchi@gmail.com

Abstract— **The Intelligent Business Process Management Ontology (IBPMO) models the most important concepts in the context of both Business Process Management (BPM) and Industry 4.0. It ensures the selection of the most suitable technologies 4.0 for Business Processes (BPs). Ontologies have great promise for improving BPM and realizing the Industry 4.0 vision. Ontology Development 101 is the method of ontology modeling. A framework would be helpful to allow the involved actors benefiting from the built ontology and using it for selecting appropriate technologies 4.0 to be integrated in BPs. In this paper, an evaluation framework is proposed to evaluate our IBPM ontology for which existing evaluation methods have been combined into a single framework, dividing the methods used into two phases: verification and validation. The verification of the ontology is concerned with validating whether an ontology was correctly built. It evaluates the structure, functionality and representation of the ontology. It specifically focuses on the validation activity using OntOlogy Pitfall Scanner! (OOPS !) tools. Different metrics and common pitfalls are used to detect errors. The OOPS! tool adopts specific metrics for detecting most anomalies found in the ontology and suggests improvements. Ontology validation is achieved by using Competency Questions (CQs) and expert interviews. This evaluation, which relied on a technology-based approach, using OOPS! tool, and a prototype development, proved the validity of our IBPMO ontology.**

Keywords—ontology; Industry 4.0; Intelligent BPM; ontology evaluation; Competency Questions; OOPS!.

I. INTRODUCTION

We have proposed IBPMO, in a previous work [1], an ontology developed for intelligent BPM, divided into two modules: BPM and Industry 4.0. The use of IBPMO ensures the selection of the most suitable technologies 4.0 for BPs.

This paper aims to assess the quality and the content of the IBPM Ontology (IBPMO) to ensure that it is well built, structured and contains all important concepts and relationships for sufficient reasoning.

Ontologies consist in a formal conceptualization of the knowledge representation and provide the definitions of the concepts and relations capturing the knowledge of a domain in an interoperable way [2]. In recent years, ontology tools have been widely used for representation and reasoning in IBPM, which consists of adding smart technologies and business intelligence to BPM[2] [3].

Semantic Web technologies, especially ontologies, can be connected with logical inferences to enable a common perception of a particular specific domain. Thus, they could facilitate alignment and integration of information entities for Industry 4.0 processes, connecting people, organization of work, and application systems [4]. Ontologies are promising means to improve BPM and to realize the Industry 4.0 vision [5]. Besides, the evaluation of the modeling is an important step in the process of ontology development. This step ensures the adequacy of the ontology and reduces maintenance costs. In fact, ontology evaluation is needed to decide on the quality and content of the ontology by judging it against a reference framework and identifying what the ontology defines correctly, incorrectly or not at all. It is essential for the adoption and improvement of the ontology.

Ontology evaluation is a key ontology engineering activity that can be performed following a variety of approaches and using various tools [6]. It consists of two parts : ontology validation process and verification activity [7]. Ontology validation process checks the correctness of the built ontology and especially investigates the structure, functionality and representation of the ontology with the help of different metrics and quality criteria. Whereas, ontology verification activity checks if the right ontology is built given the suggested application of the ontology [8].

In ontology development 101 (OD 101) method [9], evaluation involves four types of references, which are CQs, application-based, modeling guidelines and expert domain. The first, third and fourth types of references are used during ontology modeling, while the second is used with the application. The Ontology Development 101 (OD 101) is used to model and evaluate ontologies effortlessly and with more flexibility. To the best of our knowledge, the existing research works for example [10] and [11] concentrate on the consideration of OD 101 for evaluating their ontologies. Thereby, in this paper, we considered the ontology evaluation during ontology modeling, which are CQs, application-based evaluation, modeling guidelines.

CQs are used as reference for verification activity. CQs play a crucial role in the ontology development lifecycle, as they represent the ontology requirements [12].

OOPS ! is used as a tool for validation activity. OOPS ! represents a tool for diagnosing (semi-) automatically in OWL ontologies and targeted at newcomers and domain experts unfamiliar with description logics and ontology implementation languages. This tool operates independently of any ontology development platform and is available online [13].

The contribution of this work is to propose an evaluation framework to evaluate the IBPMO; and thereby refine the IBPMO. The IBPMO has been evaluated using CQs. Then, IBPMO has been verified for its structure using the OOPS ! tool, which was chosen due to its ability to perform both ontology diagnosis and repair activity. The ontology is refined based on the results of this tool. The IBPMO has been validated semantically using various CQs to determine its applicability. The IBPMO has then been put to the said application and the task based evaluation has been carried out. It is found that IBPMO is able to serve its intended purpose after tuning it based on the results of evaluation. After evaluating the IBPMO, we could ensure that the procedure of selecting the most suitable technologies for BPs within the IBPMO is successfully carried out.

The goal in this paper is mainly to adopt an evaluation process in order to improve the IBPMO. For this purpose, it is worth noting that considering CQs, the OOPS ! tool and the application-based evaluation can help us to successfully evaluate our IBPMO.

The rest of this paper is structured as follows: Section 2 presents related work on ontologies evaluation. Regarding the third section, it deals with our research methodology. Section 4 briefly explains the implementation of the evaluation process in IBPMO. Section 5 concludes the findings.

II. Related Work on Ontologies Evaluation

Many researchers have worked on ontology evaluation. Jain et al. [14] proposed an evaluation framework to evaluate the Emergency Situation Ontology (ESO), in which existing evaluation methods have been combined into a single framework, dividing the methods used into two phases: verification and validation. Richard, et al. [15] proposed the LOVMI(Ontologies Validated by Interactive Method) method in order to validate ontologies and in particular their developed ontology ONTOPSYCHIA, which is an ontology for psychiatry in three modules: social and environmental factors of mental disorders, and treatments. LOVMI validation is performed in six steps: validation (1) of consistency, (2) of other structural aspects, (3) of labels, (4) of choices of label and (5) of semantic with experts and (6) of semantic in an application. On the other hand, Kalita, et al. [16] presented an evaluation of the developed ontology on traditional dances (OTD), which divides the evaluation methods into two critical steps : First, the syntactic correctness and internal consistency of the ontology were checked via the HermiT reasoner and the OOPS! tool, and, in the second step, the ontology has undergone a competency check via the CQs scenarios. In their work, Chansanam, et al. [10] presented an evaluation of The COviD-19 Ontology for Cases and Patient information (CODO) focused explicitly on the validation operation using OOPS! tools. Moreover, Yusof, et al. [11] discussed the manual approach, i.e., modeling guidelines and automatic approach, i.e., OOPS! for validating the Malaysian food composition ontology (MyFCO). In addition, Bezerra, et al. [12] proposed a mechanism to support evaluating whether the ontology follows their correspondent CQs. Pizzuti, et al. [17] validated and interrogated the MEat Supply Chain Ontology (MESCO), that is an ontology developed for supporting the management of meat traceability along the whole supply chain, through the formulation of several queries expressed in Description Logic (DL), executed using the Pellet reasoner, to deal with different scenarios and problems of traceability.

We can conclude that to the best of our knowledge rare are the approaches that have used the different types of references of the OD 101 during ontology evaluation. In our research work, we focus on CQs, application-based evaluation, modeling guidelines.

III. Presentation of our IBPMO Ontology

Semantic Web technologies, especially ontologies, are promising means to improve BPM and to realize the Industry 4.0 vision. In this scope, we presented the IBPM ontology that we have created with Protégé 5.5.0. Every IBPM ontology element is inserted as a class; the full hierarchy is shown in Figure 1 (75 classes). The IBPM ontology is an important part of our BPIGuide approach, which ensures the selection of the most suitable technologies 4.0 for BPs.

Regarding the first step, the scope of our ontology is to develop an ontology for IBPM. Basically, a number of methodologies have been used for developing ontologies, such as the methodology defined in [18], [19], [20] and [21], [22], [23]. In our research work, we have selected the methodology Ontology Development 101 defined by Noy and McGuinness's in [21] because we have exploited an existing ontology.

Concerning the second step, we have selected the existing BPM ontology presented in (von Rosing, Laurier and Polovina, 2015a), which is an empiric ontology, meaning that its roots lie in practice, as it was developed by practitioners documenting their practical knowledge of the field rather than having originated from theory and academics specialized in a restricted area of business. The selected BPM Ontology offers a set of principles, views, artefacts, and templates that have detailed metaobject relations and rules that apply to them, such as how and where can the process objects be related (and where not) (von Rosing, Laurier and Polovina, 2015a).

In order to consider the Industry 4.0 main concepts, we have been inspired from [24]. New classes were added to present the industry 4.0 concepts such as Sensor, Location, Machine, Workstation, Line, Technology4.0. The Machine has been defined with the device that performs a task by itself or by human intervention. The Workstation refers to small integrated physical groupings of machines. The Cell is a set of combined workstations for a particular complex task; and the Line is a group of cells. Consequently, new relations were added. A sensor is located in a location. A process happens in a location. A workstation contains a Machine. A machine can be an assembling machine, a testing machine and a processing machine. A business process adopts a technology 4.0.

3D printing, Augmented reality/simulation, Big data, Biomedical/digital sensor, Blockchain, Cloud computing, Collaborative robots, IoT, Machine/deep learning, Remote control or monitoring and SOA are introduced as sub-classes of Technology 4.0. A business process can be linked to a business resource through the transforms property. Besides, the hasSensor property is used to affirm that sensors are attached to a business resource. In addition, the happensIn property is used to stand for the location where a business process takes place. Moreover, the measuredBy property is used to associate a business process to the process measurement. The business process can be linked to the technology 4.0 through the adopts property.

IV. RESEARCH METHODOLOGY

This section briefly explains the activities that were carried out for ontology evaluation process. The evaluation framework is proposed to evaluate our IBPM ontology for which existing evaluation methods have been combined into a single framework, dividing the methods used into two phases: verification and validation [25].

The verification of the ontology is concerned with building an ontology correctly. It evaluates the structure, functionality and representation of the ontology. It specifically focused on the validation activity using OOPS ! tools. Different metrics and common pitfalls are used to detect errors. The validation of the ontology ensures that the right ontology for the given application is built. This is achieved by CQs and expert interviews. In particular, we focus (1) on verifying whether the developed IBPMO is correct according to three evaluation metrics [26], namely completeness, conciseness and consistency, and (2) on checking how effective the ontology is in the context of different applications. In this regard, the IBPMO is evaluated by using three approaches: CQs, technology-based, and application-based evaluations. Figure 2 shows the evaluation process of the IBPMO.

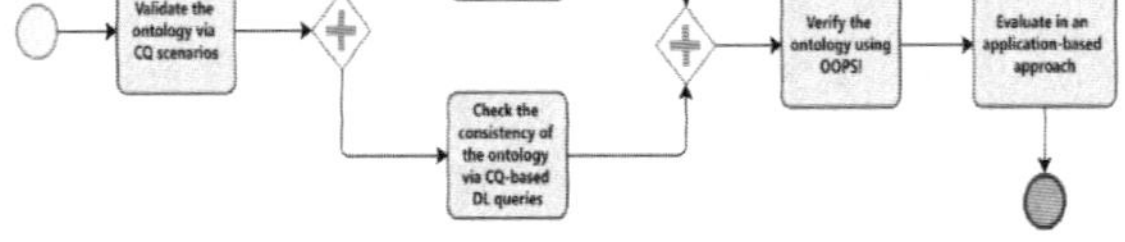

Figure 2. The proposed Evaluation Process

Figure 1. Class hierarchy of the IBPMO

V. EVALUATION OF OUR IBPMO

In this section, we represent the evaluation of our IBPMO, which focuses on the CQs, the technology-based evaluation and the application-based evaluation.

A. *Competency Questions evaluation*

For the present evaluation, CQs as a qualitative measure is the most effective and reliable way to check if all important information are included in the ontology [27]. The CQs pertain to various aspects, including class hierarchy, individuals, disjoint classes, intersections and unions of classes, equivalent classes, universal and existential quantification, as well as restrictions related to has-value and cardinality [12]. Thus, this evaluation focuses on reformulating CQs as queries to retrieve data from the ontology and to verify whether the CQs are answered or not. In this sense, queries are written in Description Logic (DL) and SPARQL language, which is a semantic query language used for describing and even worse checking the fulfillment of OWL CQs [12].

1) Consistency check via CQ-based DL: For syntactic correctness and consistency check of our IBPMO, we rely on "consistency checkers". For this task, we have used the Hermi reasoner, implemented in Protege as an external plug-in. The goal is to verify the ability of the ontology and check its consistency. The reasoner is known as a classifier and used for consistency checking as well as to compute the inferred class hierarchy (Natschläger, 2011). HermiT 1.4.3 is an OWL 2 reasoner compatible with Java. HermiT 1.4.3 provides functionalities to verify the validation, check consistency of the ontology and answer a subset of several queries expressed in DL. The evaluation process has been executed considering the monitoring of chronic disease BP, the food selection and guidance for diabetic and hypertensive patients BP and the monitoring of COVID 19 patients BP. We have considered these different BPs to elaborate our validation, but only the individuals of COVID BP will be detailed next. The monitoring of chronic disease BP concerns the continuous monitoring of patients with chronic disease to effectively manage disease. The food selection and guidance for diabetic and hypertensive patients BP concerns the Classification of Food according to patients' health. The monitoring of COVID 19 patients BP concerns the monitoring of COVID-19 patients or persons under investigation in the COVID-19 crisis unit at CHU Farhat Hached Sousse. The BP and the elaborated ontology were elaborated using various surveys and investigation. It consists of BPCOVID; Covid19CrisisCell; Physician; HealingTime; Home; IoTTech; Oximeter; Patient; QualityOfService; SensorOxygenSaturation; SensorTemprature; Thermometer; beurer HealthManager; MeasuringSpO2; RecoveringPatients; RegainingAnAcceptableTemperature; Treatment_Cost; WorkDoneByPhysician; CheckHealthStatus; CovidTreatmentProcesses; CrisisComityPerformanceIndicator; InfectiousDiseaseDepartment which are defined to represent different individuals. SensorTemperature and SensorOxygenSaturation represents the individuals of the same class Sensor. Thermometer and Oximeter are individuals of the same class ProcessingMachine. Patient and Physician are instances of the same class BusinessRole. BPCOVID is an instance of the class HumanOperation. HomeMonitoring is an individual of the class Sit-Monitoring. Covid19CrisisCell is an instance of the class ProcessOwner. We have also defined the individuals for both the monitoring of chronic disease BP and the food selection and guidance for diabetic and hypertensive patients BP. The query formulated for the identification of the BPs that have adopted the IoT Technology is showed in Fig. 2. It was applied for all the individuals of the three considered BPs.

Two examples of CQs, which cover the IBPMO, are provided along with their corresponding DL queries and results. The fact that the obtained results are conform to the expected results contributes to proving the validity of our ontology.

- CQ1 : What are the BPs that have adopted the IoT Technology ? The results of this DL query, that corresponds to this CQ1, show that it is possible to easily access to most important information related to the monitoring of chronic disease BP, the food selection and guidance for diabetic and hypertensive patients BP and the monitoring of COVID 19 patients BP in a short time, as shown in Figure 3.

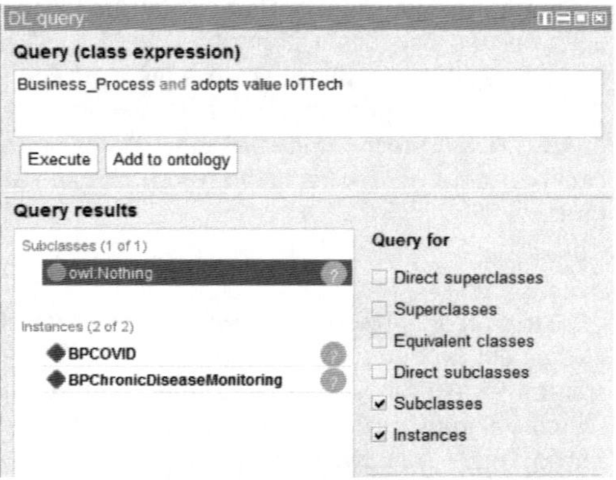

Figure 3. Query for the identification of the BPs that have adopted the IoT Technology

- CQ2: What are the BPs that have adopted the Big data Technology ? The result of this DL query, that corresponds to this CQ2, shows the instance of the BusinessProcess concept that have adopted the Big data Technology, as shown in Figure 4.

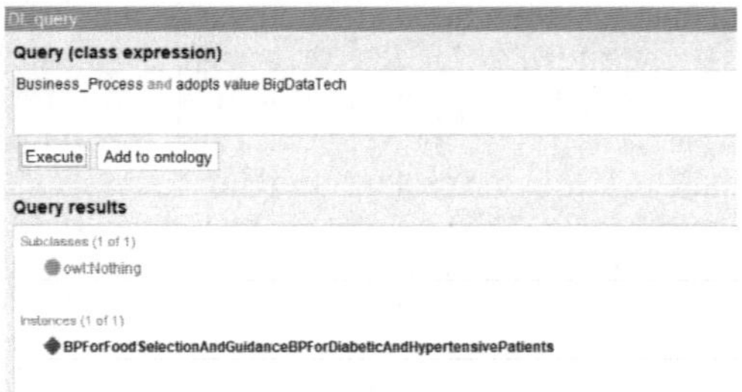

Figure 4. Query for the identification of the BPs that have adopted the Big data Technology

The phase of the internal consistence check ensures that our IBPMO does not contain any contradictory facts. In fact, The internal consistency check in ontology is performed by automated reasoners, which use formal language representation and axiomatic definitions to detect contradictions within the ontology [28].

Besides by this phase, we have checked that the model is a correct rendering of the idea we wanted to express.

2) *CQ-based SPARQL:* In this paper, each question is translated into SPARQL queries and implemented in Protégé using the SPARQL QUERY plugin.

Four examples of CQs, which cover the IBPMO, are provided along with their corresponding SPARQL queries and results.

- CQ1: What are the Business Processes contained in the ontology? The SPARQL query, that corresponds to this CQ1 to retrieve all instances of the BusinessProcess concept, is presented in Fig. 4. The result of this query, as illustrated in the Figure 5, contains the BPs modeled in the IBPM Ontology.

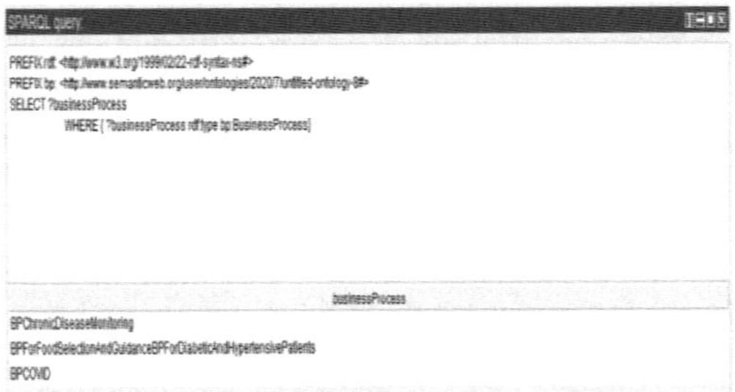

Figure 5. SPARQL query results for CQ1

- CQ2: What are the concepts represented in the ontology that model a Business Process? Figure 6 displays the formal representation of this CQ using SPARQL query. The query asks for the subclasses of the class BusinessProcess. Consequently, the result of this query as shown in the Figure 6 contains all instances of the BusinessProcess.

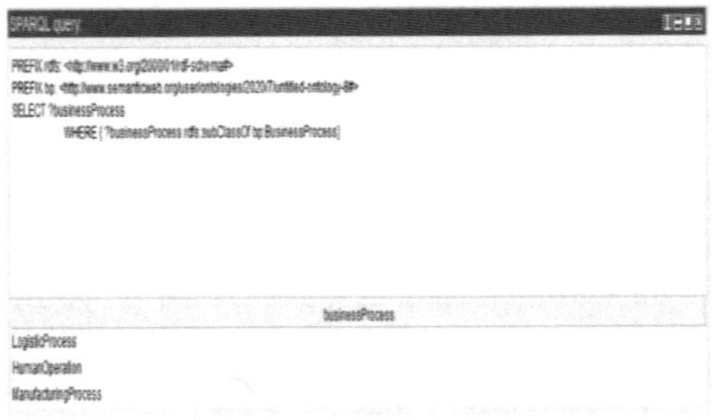

Figure 6. SPARQL query results for CQ2

- CQ3: What are the concepts modeled in the ontology that can be used to be applied to Business Processes? Fig. 6 presents the SPARQL query formalizing CQ3 to retrieve the subclasses of the class BusinessProcess that are linked to the BusinessResource/Actor class via the object property appliesTo. The result of this query, as shown in the Figure 7, contains the business resource/actor for each business process modeled in the IBPMO.

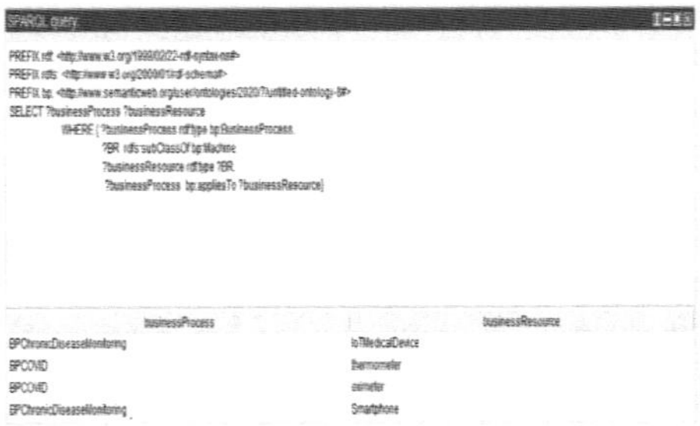

Figure 7. SPARQL query results for CQ3

- CQ4 : What are the concepts modeled in the ontology that can be used to be applied to Business Processes in a specific (particuler) domain? Figure 8 presents the SPARQL query formalizing CQ3 to retrieve the subclasses of the class BusinessProcess that are linked to the BusinessResource/Actor class via the object property appliesTo. The result of this query, as shown in the Figure 8, contains the business resource/actor and the domain for each business process modeled in the IBPMO.

By providing a set of CQs for the validation purpose, the completeness of the ontology is evaluated. Each query is run on the IBPMO to test if all requirements can be met and the correct answers can be inferred. For those queries that fail to run, the missing concepts or relations are added in the IBPMO. Nonetheless, one of the main problems that hamper the proper use of CQs lies on the completeness of the ontology that can never be proved and constant enhancement of the IBPMO needed.

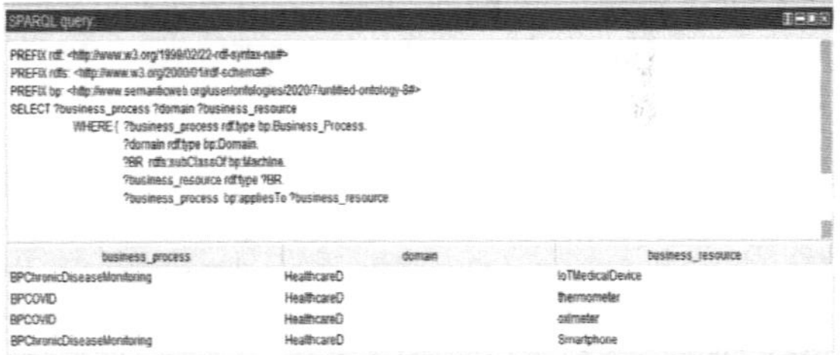

Figure 8. SPARQL query results for CQ4

B. *Technology-based evaluation*

The present evaluation is concerned with the structural characteristics of an ontology. It investigates the syntax, consistency and formal semantics and thereby aims to ensure the correctness and usability of the ontology. Different tools have been developed to support the technology-based evaluation. In this study, our IBPMO is evaluated through the OOPS ! tool, which is a web-based evaluation tool used for the detection of common pitfalls or anomalies in ontologies according to a pitfall catalogue currently containing 41 errors. This tool helps developers to improve ontology quality by automatically detecting potential errors [13].

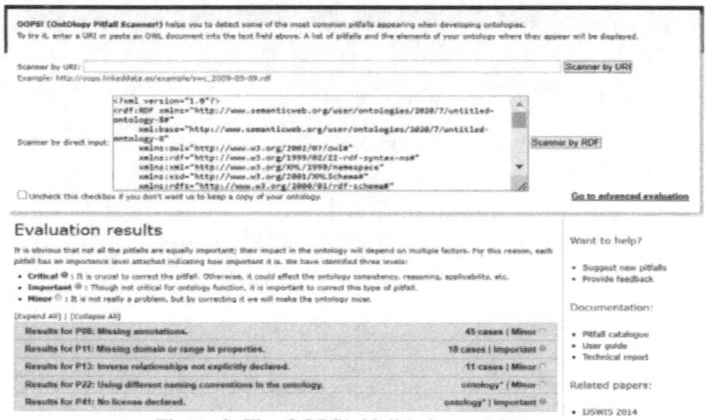

Figure 9. The OOPS! Validation results.

After executing the online tool reliably OOPS ! with the IBPMO, a summary of the pitfalls encountered is generated as shown in Figure 9. The diagnosis results obtained from OOPS! were manually revised. In fact, the OOPS! tool detects most anomalies found in the ontology and suggests improvements. Nonetheless the modifications of the ontology needs to be done manually. OOPS ! classified the results for each pitfall into three levels: critical, important, and minor levels. Priority was given for the critical level first. The minor level was not mandatory since it was not counted as a problem; however, by doing so, it will improve the IBPMO performance. Fig.8 shows the validation results for our IBPMO. It achieved two important and three minor pitfalls. It attains zero critical pitfalls. The three minor pitfalls resulted from missing annotations (P08), Inverse relationships not explicitly declared (P13) and using different naming conventions in the ontology (P22). The two important pitfalls in the opposite are caused by missing domain or range in properties (P11) and the absence of a declared license (P41). The pitfalls detected by OOPS ! can also be classified by the following evaluation criteria : consistency, completeness, and conciseness. The obtained results show that no consistency nor conciseness pitfalls are detected. Nevertheless, other pitfalls are detected (P08, P22,P41) and two of them (P11, P13) are related to the ontology completeness. Table 1 presents the five pitfalls encountered.

TABLE I. IBPMO PITFALLS DETECTED BY OOPS

Criteria	Pitfall Description	Importance level	Cases
Consistency	No detected pitfalls that correspond to consistency	–	0
Completeness	P11 : Missing domain or range in properties	Important	18
	P13 : Inverse relationships not explicitly declared	Minor	11
Conciseness	No detected pitfalls that correspond to conciseness	–	0
Other Pitfalls	P08 : Missing annotations	Minor	45
	P22 : Using different naming conventions in the ontology	Minor	The pitfall applies to the ontology in general
	P41 : No license declared	Important	The pitfall applies to the ontology in general

Figure 10 shows an excerpt of the first important pitfall (P11: Missing domain or range in properties). It shows a missing domain and range for some properties. But this pitfall was reported for the properties which were already mentioned as inverse properties in the IBPMO. Eighteen cases were detected for this pitfall as they represented 18 object properties without domain and range. The OD101 provided the guidelines regarding this property's facet. The effect of range and domain constraints as axioms is the most common problem in OWL [29] [30]. In IBPMO, the domain and range of properties are not assigned to avoid the above problems. Thus, no ontology repair action was carried out for this pitfall.

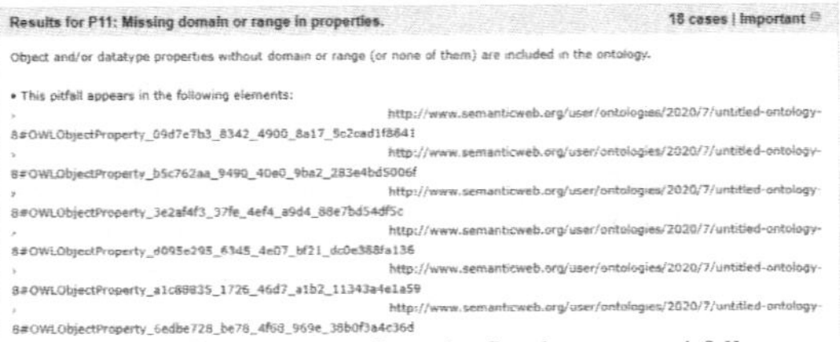

Figure 10. An excerpt from the first important pitfall.

Figure 11 shows the second and the last important pitfall in IBPMO (P41: No license declared). It reports about uses of no license agreement in the IBPMO. The pitfall concerns the ontology metadata aspect, which does not have any guidelines in OD 101. The repair recommendation by OOPS! was to include a statement containing the license information using any of the following properties: dc:rights, dcterms:rights, dcterms:license, cc:license or xhv:license.

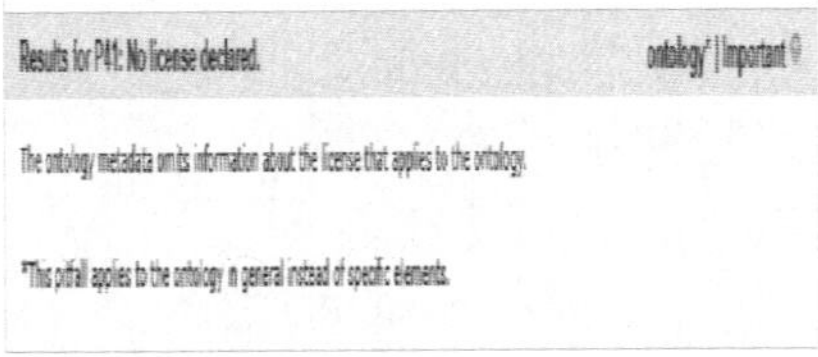

Figure 11. Second important pitfall.

In Protégé, the metadata annotations are under the ontology header view. Figure 12 shows the interface of metadata annotations where the license of the IBPMO is declared. The predicate for the license declaration of the IBPMO was taken from the dcterms:license and assigned to the CC-BY license [31], which is the most popular open Creative Commons Attribution License.

Figure 12. License declaration.

The IBPMO has three minor pitfalls. Figure 13 shows the first minor pitfall (P08: Missing annotations). The description of this pitfall was in creating an ontology element, human readable annotations have failed to be attached to it. The label annotation properties (rdfs:label) and the description annotation properties (rdfs:comment) were considered to define annotations of the IBPMO elements. These are the two most commonly used annotation properties, besides owl:versionInfo [32]. This pitfall will be repaired for further reuse.

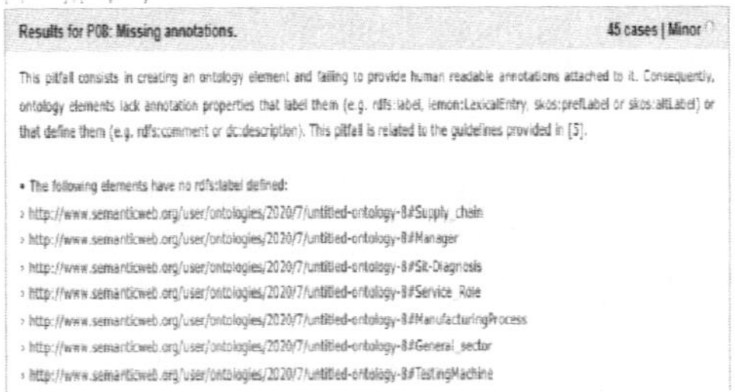

Figure 13. First minor pitfall.

The second minor pitfall is P13 : Inverse relationships not explicitly declared. It suggested some object properties which can be declared as inverse. The description of this pitfall was when any relationship (except for those that were defined as symmetric properties using owl:SymmetricProperty) did not have an inverse relationship (owl:inverseOf) defined within the ontology. OOPS! listed all of the object properties in IBPMO, which did not have the inverse relationship (see Figure 14). OD 101 provided the guidelines regarding inverse relationships. Poveda-Villalón et al. [33] stated that the specification of the inverse properties is needed for completeness.

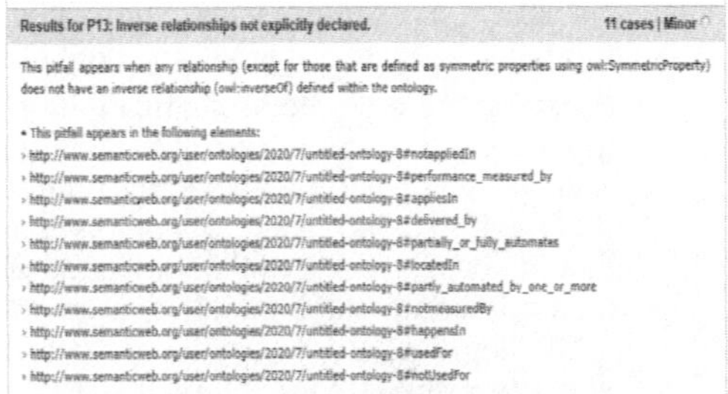

Figure 14. Second minor pitfall.

The final minor pitfall is P22: Using different naming conventions in the ontology (see Figure 15). It detected uses of different naming conventions in the IBPMO. This was reported because for some long class names the symbol "-" (dash) was used, but for short class names, it was not used. A modification was not necessary. OD 101 provided guidelines on naming conventions. It emphasized consistency with the chosen naming conventions. The benefits from the consistency help to avoid modeling mistakes, improve readability, and ease the understanding of the ontology.

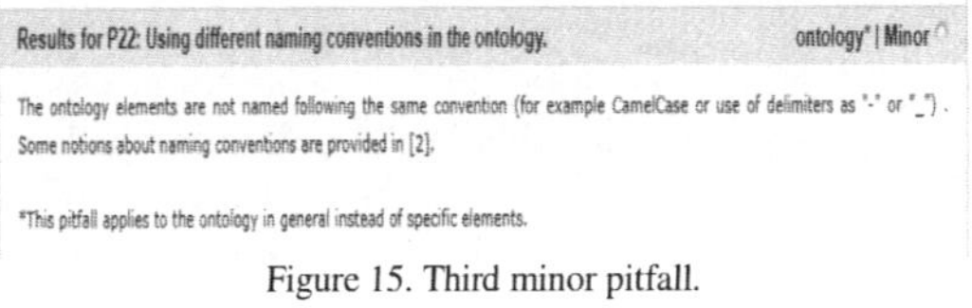

Figure 15. Third minor pitfall.

After correcting the observed errors, the pitfall scanner is run again to ensure all errors are corrected and no new ones are detected. OOPS! plays a significant role in ensuring the ontology is free from the common pitfall by double checking the modeling guidelines provided by the Ontology Development 101. For example, it supports the latest common modeling errors that are not listed in the Ontology Development 101, such as the annotation issue. The main advantage of OOPS! is the repair recommendation made by it. It shows how the ontology element can be repaired to improve the ontology technical quality. In the IBPMO, the evaluation results from OOPS! have improved the inferencing, understanding, clarity and metadata aspects. Nevertheless, OOPS! has a limitation. It still needs to be revised manually in some cases of the pitfall.

C. Application-based evaluation

The last step of the evaluation process consists of using the ontology in a dedicated application. In the present evaluation approach, the IBPMO is evaluated by providing an application-based approach to assess the ability of the IBPMO to serve as a knowledge base for a computer system. The effectiveness of the IBPMO has been assessed by putting it to the real application. It was designed to work for as a knowledge base. The IBPMO is validated by providing the following applications.

- **IBPMO database and interface:** A standalone application, which enables the visualization of knowledge modeled in the IBPMO, was developed. The interfaces provided by the application are designed to configure user needs on selection criteria. In order to provide an easy means to configure each criterion, three User Interface (UI) components can be used, which allow modifying a criteria's configuration. The UI components concern the performance criteria, the BP languages and the application fields. Such interfaces display the selection criteria. Figure 16-18 show interface examples of the application : interface for performance criteria (Figure 16), interface for BP languages (Figure 17) and interface for application fields (Figure 18).

- **BPIGuide tool:** The IBPMO is used in conjunction with the BPIGuide tool decribed in previous works. The BPIGuide enables the decision rules represented in the IBPMO to be automatically infered. Since, using the ontology-based engine, the result of the execution of these rules are the rank of the recommended technologies 4.0 which will be presented to users and could be used to redesign and implement optimized BPs 4.0. Besides, our validated ontology was used in the context of patient care in the healthcare field. We applied the different rules that we extracted from IBPMO in the surgical monitoring business process.

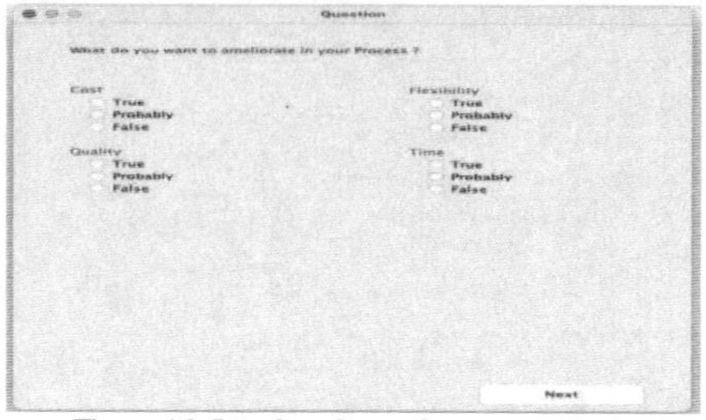

Figure 16. Interface for performance criteria

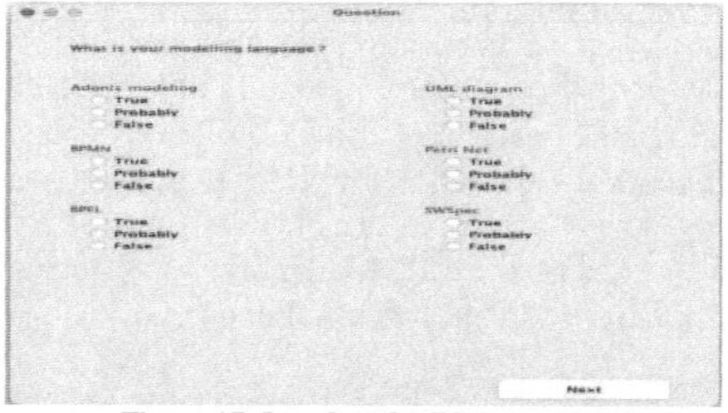

Figure 17. Interface for BP languages

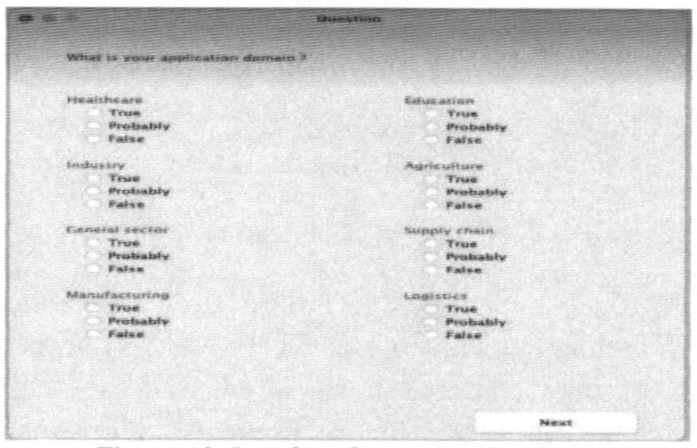

Figure 18. Interface for application fields

VI. DISCUSSION

The evaluation of the IBPMO indicates that the ontology is well-designed and suitable for its application. Only minor changes and adaptations regarding the lexical and structural layer are made. The conducted evaluation revealed that the developed IBPMO is : correct since it meets the completeness, conciseness, and consistency standards, and effectiveness since it can be used concretely in a variety of applications. Nevertheless, evaluating the IBPMO demonstrated that most probable no automatic method will ever be enough to perform a complete ontology evaluation. The evaluator has to decide on the criteria relevant for the evaluation, has to evolve the CQs and has to make decisions based on the evaluation results over each metric. But as good science should exclude subjectivity, it is advisable that more than one person performs the evaluation. Experts should be included for a satisfactory result in the evaluation.

VII. CONCLUSION AND FUTURE WORK

Ontology evaluation is a main task in the process of ontology development that takes a lot of effort and thought-process as each ontology needs an individual approach for evaluation adapted to the intended application of the ontology. The ontology evaluated in this study, IBPMO, has been developed to select the most suitable technologies 4.0 for BPs. We mainly focused on the end-to-end evaluation methodology. First, the IBPMO is evaluated against CQs. This first phase focuses on reformulating CQs as queries, which are expressed in DL and SPARQL language to retrieve data from the ontology and to verify whether the CQs are answered or not. During the second phase, a technology-based evaluation approach is addressed to specify quality criteria in order to ensure that the IBPMO is rid from pitfalls. At last, the ontology is evaluated using an application-based approach to assess the effectiveness of the IBPMO. For future work, the IBPMO will be upgraded with linked open data to enable domain knowledge sharing and reuse.

REFERENCES

[1] S. Mejri and S. Ghannouchi. "Towards a New Approach for Intelligent BPM Based on Technologies 4.0". New Trends in Intelligent Software Methodologies, Tools and Techniques: Proceedings of the 20th International Conference on New Trends in Intelligent Software Methodologies, Tools and Techniques (SoMeT_21). vol. 337, pp. 313-326, September 2021. https://doi.org/10.3233/FAIA210030.

[2] V. R. Sampath Kumar, et al. "Ontologies for Industry 4.0". The Knowledge Engineering Review. vol. 34, pp. e1-e17, November 2019. https://doi.org/10.1017/S0269888919000109.

[3] S. Jaskó, A. Skrop, T. Holczinger, T. Chován, and J. Abonyi. "Development of manufacturing execution systems in accordance with Industry 4.0 requirements: A review of standard-and ontology-based methodologies and tools". Computers in Industry. Vol. 123, pp. 1-18, December 2020.

[4] C. Kaar, J. Frysak, C. Stary, U. Kannengiesser, and H. Müller. "Resilient Ontology Support Facilitating Multi-Perspective Process Integration in Industry 4.0". Proceedings of the 10th International Conference on Subject-Oriented Business Process Management. pp. 1–10, April 2018.

[5] A. Annane, N. Aussenac-Gilles, and M. Kamel. "BBO: BPMN 2.0 Based Ontology for Business Process Representation." 20th European Conference on Knowledge Management (ECKM 2019). pp. 49–59, September 2019.

[6] M. Poveda-Villalón, MC. Suárez-Figueroa, and A. Gómez-Pérez. "Validating ontologies with oops!" Knowledge Engineering and Knowledge Management: 18th International Conference, EKAW 2012. Galway City, Ireland, pp. 267–81, October 2012.

[7] A. A. Alsanad, A. Chikh, and A. Mirza. "A Domain Ontology for Software Requirements Change Management in Global Software Development Environment". IEEE Access. vol. 7, pp. 49352-49361, January 2019. https://ieeexplore.ieee.org/abstract/document/8684236/ (accessed January 30, 2023).

[8] A. Abdelghany, N. Darwish, and H. Hefni. "An Agile Methodology for Ontology Development". IJIES 2019. Vol. 12, pp. 170–181, April 2019. https://doi.org/10.22266/ijies2019.0430.17.

[9] N. Noy and DL. McGuinness. "Ontology development 101". Knowledge Systems Laboratory, Stanford University 2001. vol. 2001, pp. 1-18, January 2001.

[10] W. Chansanam, K. Suttipapa, and A.R. Ahmad. "COVID-19 ontology evaluation". International Journal of Management. vol. 11, pp. 47-57, October 2020.

[11] N. M. Yusof and S. A. M. Noah. "Malaysian food composition ontology evaluation". International Journal of Machine Learning and Computing. vol. 9, pp. 700–705, October 2019.

[12] C. Bezerra, F. Freitas, F. Santana da Silva. "Evaluating Ontologies with Competency Questions". pp. 284-285, November 2013. https://doi.org/10.1109/WI-IAT.2013.199.

[13] M. Poveda-Villalón, A. Gómez-Pérez, and MC. Suárez-Figueroa. "Oops!(ontology pitfall scanner!): An on-line tool for ontology evaluation". International Journal on Semantic Web and Information Systems (IJSWIS). vol. 10, pp. 7–34, April 2014.

[14] S. Jain, V. Meyer. "Evaluation and refinement of emergency situation ontology". Int J Inform Educ Technol. vol. 8, pp. 713–719, July 2018.

[15] M. Richard, X. Aimé, M.C. Jaulent, M.O. Krebs, and J. Charlet. "From Patient Discharge Summaries to an Ontology for Psychiatry". MEDINFO 2017: Precision Healthcare through Informatics, IOS Press. pp. 930–934, June 2017.

[16] D. Kalita, and D. Deka. "Ontology for preserving the knowledge base of traditional dances (OTD)". The Electronic Library. vol. 38, pp. 785–803, October 2020.

[17] T. Pizzuti, G. Mirabelli, Grasso G, and G. Paldino. "MESCO (MEat Supply Chain Ontology): An ontology for supporting traceability in the meat supply chain". Food Control. vol. 72, pp. 123–133, Février 2017.

[18] M. Uschold and M. King. "Towards a methodology for building ontologies". Citeseer. pp. 1-13, July 1995.

[19] M. Gruninger. "Methodology for the design and evaluation of ontologies". Proc. IJCAI'95, Workshop on Basic Ontological Issues in Knowledge Sharing. April 1995.

[20] M. Fernández-López, A. Gómez-Pérez, and N. Juristo. "Methontology: from ontological art towards ontological engineering". pp. 33-40, March 1997.

[21] N. F. Noy, and D. L. McGuinness. "Ontology development 101: A guide to creating your first ontology". Stanford knowledge systems laboratory technical report KSL-01-05. pp. 1-25, March 2001.

[22] H. S. Pinto, S. Staab, and C. Tempich. "DILIGENT: Towards a fine-grained methodology for DIstributed, Loosely-controlled and evolvInG Engineering of oNTologies". ECAI. vol. 16, pp. 1-393, January 2004.

[23] M. C. Suárez-Figueroa, A. Gómez-Pérez, and M. Fernández-López. "The NeOn methodology for ontology engineering. Ontology engineering in a networked world". pp. 9–34, Springer; December 2011.

[24] F. Giustozzi, J. Saunier, C. Zanni-Merk. "Context modeling for industry 4.0: An ontology-based proposal". Procedia Computer Science. vol. 126, pp. 675–684, January 2018.

[25] H. Hlomani and D. Stacey. "Approaches, methods, metrics, measures, and subjectivity in ontology evaluation: A survey". pp. 1-11, August 2014.

[26] Z. C. Khan." Evaluation metrics in ontology modules". pp. 1-13, April 2016.
[27] Kurukshetra, S. Jain S, and V. Meyer. "Evaluation and Refinement of Emergency Situation Ontology". IJIET. vol. 8, pp. 713–719, January 2018. https://doi.org/10.18178/ijiet.2018.8.10.1127.
[28] J. D. Warrender and P. Lord . "How, What and Why to test an ontology". pp. 1-4, Mai 2015.
[29] A. Rector, et al. "OWL pizzas: Practical experience of teaching OWL-DL: Common errors & common patterns". Engineering Knowledge in the Age of the Semantic Web: 14th International Conference, EKAW. Whittlebury Hall, UK, pp. 63–81, October 2004. Proceedings 14, Springer.
[30] D. Allemang and J. Hendler. "Semantic web for the working ontologist: effective modeling in RDFS and OWL". pp. 1-510, May 2011.
[31] M. Poblet, et al. "Assigning Creative Commons Licenses to Research Metadata: Issues and Cases". In: Pagallo U, Palmirani M, Casanovas P, Sartor G, Villata S, editors. AI Approaches to the Complexity of Legal Systems, vol. 10791, pp. 245–256, October 2018. https://doi.org/10.1007/978-3-030-00178-0_16.
[32] M. Horridge, et al. "A practical guide to building owl ontologies using protégé 4 and co-ode tools edition1". vol. 2. pp. 1-107, March 2011.
[33] A. Gangemi, C. Catenacci, M. Ciaramita, and J. Lehmann. "Modelling ontology evaluation and validation". The Semantic Web: Research and Applications: 3rd European Semantic Web Conference, ESWC. Budva, Montene, pp. 140–154, June 2006.

OSS-Fuzzgen: Automated Fuzzing of Open Source Java Projects

Sheung Chi Chan
Ada Logics
London, England, UK
arthur.chan@adalogics.com

Adam Korczynski
Ada Logics
London, England, UK
adam@adalogics.com

David Korczynski
Ada Logics
London, England, UK
david@adalogics.com

Abstract—**OSS-Fuzz is an open source service for managing the fuzzing of open source projects. Open source projects integrate into OSS-Fuzz by adding a set of fuzzing harnesses targeting their project and relevant build logic for the OSS-Fuzz infrastructure. OSS-Fuzz will then build and run these harnesses continuously and report when finding any security or reliability issues. To date, OSS-Fuzz has reported tens of thousands of bugs in software and the list is continuously growing. Unfortunately, the process of integrating projects into OSS-Fuzz is still largely manual and both the creation of fuzzing harnesses and build setup are time-consuming tasks. In this paper, we propose OSS-Fuzzgen, a system that can automatically generate OSS-Fuzz integrations for open source Java projects, including fuzzing harness synthesis and build infrastructure generation. The input to OSS-Fuzzgen is a GitHub URL to a given open source project. The output is a list of ranked OSS-Fuzz integration candidates that can be run by OSS-Fuzz. We empirically evaluate our setup by running the system through more than 200 open source projects, which resulted in more than 100 generated OSS-Fuzz integrations. We manually inspect the results and submit 31 of these to OSS-Fuzz resulting in more than 50 reported bugs across the 31 projects. For 11 of these bugs, we submitted fixes to the relevant open source projects, and 9 fixes were accepted and merged into the upstream open source project. We have open-sourced OSS-Fuzzgen and the code is available on GitHub[1].**

Keywords*—*OSS-Fuzz; Fuzz-Introspector; Java; fuzzing; security testing; libfuzzer.

I. INTRODUCTION

Fuzzing is an effective technique for finding security and reliability issues in software. The high-level idea behind fuzzing is to pass arbitrary inputs to a given application and monitor if unexpected behaviour happens. There are many success stories from fuzzing, both in terms of finding difficult-to-catch issues and also rapidly catching regressions in software. OSS-Fuzz is an open source fuzzing service that currently manages fuzzing infrastructure for more than 1000 widely used open source projects and has reported tens of thousands of security and reliability bugs in these projects[2][3].

To integrate fuzzing in a project, coverage-feedback fuzzing specifically, the general approach is to write fuzzing harnesses that execute the target software package with input seeded by data from the fuzzing engine. In coverage-guided fuzzing, a harness is a small program that aims to explore the target code base by continuously mutating its input and collecting seeds (inputs) that trigger unique code execution in the target. They are often similar to unit tests, but instead of testing a specific input, the harnesses test a generalised domain of inputs, and the domain is often much larger than what is feasible to brute-force, e.g. arbitrarily large buffer, hence the use of genetic mutational algorithms in the fuzzing engine. During execution, the fuzzing engine observes the execution of the target code and uses coverage data to guide the input generation and mutation, resulting in the creation of inputs to the fuzzing harness that incrementally explore the target code base[4].

The harnesses comprise a central role when fuzzing a software package and many projects have several harnesses to trigger different parts of the project's code base. For example, OSS-Fuzz has around 1100 projects integrated into the fuzzing service but runs more than 4500 fuzzing harnesses daily[5]. Another central component when fuzzing is to have a build infrastructure in place that makes it possible to build the target software using an environment that supports fuzzing. Specifically, the target codebase needs to be instrumented appropriately, which happens during the compilation stage and the harnesses need to be appropriately linked to the project.

The process of writing harnesses for a software package as well as constructing the built environment that makes fuzzing possible is cumbersome and time-consuming. It can often take several weeks to integrate fuzzing into medium-sized software packages, and many years to integrate fuzzing into extensive code bases such as modern browsers or operating systems. Furthermore, despite the success of OSS-Fuzz fuzzing more than 1100 software packages continuously, there remain tens of thousands of open source software packages that are not being fuzzed.

There has been efforts into automating fuzzing harness writing[6][7][8][9][10][11] and also related efforts for inferring API specifications[12][13]. In general, a fuzzing harness requires the effort from OSS-Fuzz to observe and mutate the input to extensively cover the underlying code base of the target projects. Otherwise, there is no difference compared to unit testing. These efforts are, however, not targeted open source projects and are only generating fuzzing harnesses but not the full OSS-Fuzz integrations. Some of the efforts require manual studying of the target projects to specify target methods or classes for the fuzzing harnesses generation. This setting makes it difficult to automatically generate the full OSS-Fuzz integration and requires extensive manual efforts before and after the automatic generation process.

In this paper, we introduce OSS-Fuzzgen, a system for automatically generating OSS-Fuzz integrations for open source Java projects. Our system takes as input a list of GitHub repositories and will output a set of fuzzing harnesses and build infrastructure for the projects such that the projects can be fuzzed by way of OSS-Fuzz. Our system relies on static and dynamic program analysis techniques, which are developed as extensions to Fuzz Introspector[14]. To verify our system, we present an empirical evaluation of running our system against 257 open source projects which resulted in more than 100 possible project submissions to OSS-Fuzz. We submit 31 resulting projects with high coverage and fuzzing performance to OSS-Fuzz. For several of the bugs found by the generated harnesses, we reported them to the relevant open source projects, which confirmed that the bugs found were legit and accepted our patches to fix the issues.

Contributions This paper makes the following contributions:

- We present a novel system for automatically synthesising Java fuzzing harnesses.
- We present the first system to automatically construct OSS-Fuzz project integrations.
- We present an extensive empirical evaluation of more than 200 open source projects and verify that our system finds real bugs in widely used Java projects.

The remainder of this paper is structured as follows. In Section II, we introduce the OSS-Fuzz and Fuzz Introspector services. In Section III, we give an overview of the OSS-Fuzzgen tool. In Section IV, we illustrate the detailed design of the OSS-Fuzzgen tool. In Section V, we give details of the empirical evaluation of the OSS-Fuzzgen tool. We then discuss the limitation and future enhancement plan for the OSS-Fuzzgen tool in Section VI and conclude the paper in Section VII.

II. Background

In this section, we introduce OSS-Fuzz and Fuzz Introspector, each comprising a central role in our system. Specifically, our solution is built as an extension to Fuzz Introspector while we rely on OSS-Fuzz as the runtime environment for our generated harnesses.

A. OSS-Fuzz

OSS-Fuzz[2] is a free online service that manages the execution of fuzzing harnesses for open source projects. The process for integrating into the service is that an open source project develops a set of fuzzing harnesses targeting the project and also some necessary glue for OSS-Fuzz to build these harnesses. This glue is composed of a *project.yaml* file with metadata, a *Dockerfile* to construct the container in which the harnesses are built and also a shell script, *build.sh*, that holds the commands for building the target project and harnesses inside the container.

To submit the project for OSS-Fuzz integration, a pull request is made to the OSS-Fuzz repository with the specific glue in the dedicated project directory. Once the pull request is merged OSS-Fuzz will daily build the fuzzing harnesses using the latest upstream code. OSS-Fuzz then runs these harnesses for an extended period and reports to the people listed in the *project.yaml* metadata if any of the harnesses find any bugs. OSS-Fuzz provides the infrastructure to build and run harnesses locally for each project integrated into OSS-Fuzz. In this way, there is a unified interface for building and running more than 4500 fuzzing harnesses spread across more than 1100 projects.

B. Fuzz Introspector

Fuzz Introspector[14] is a tool for providing introspection capabilities into the fuzzing of a given software package. Fuzz Introspector can, for example, analyse the static reachability of fuzzing harnesses, find candidate methods in the target code that are likely good targets for fuzzing and combine runtime code coverage data with static analysis capabilities to identify potential runtime blockers for the fuzzing harnesses [15].

Fuzz Introspector is architecturally split between multiple frontends and a single backend. The frontends are language-specific static analysis tools, often in the form of compiler extensions, which extract data about the software under analysis. The Java frontend of Fuzz Introspector is built on top of SOOT[16] and this is the primary component of Fuzz Introspector that OSS-Fuzzgen uses.

III. OSS-Fuzzgen Overview

OSS-Fuzzgen takes as input one or more URLs to a given set of open source projects on GitHub. OSS-Fuzzgen outputs a set of OSS-Fuzz integrations for each of the provided open source projects, where each integration includes the base OSS-Fuzz files (*Dockerfile, build.sh and project.yaml*) and a fuzzing harness. Each of these integrations can be built and run locally using the OSS-Fuzz setup.

The mechanics behind OSS-Fuzzgen are divided into five sequential stages, and these five stages happen for each open source project input to OSS-Fuzzgen:

- **Stage 1: Build system generation.** This stage creates a build system comprising the OSS-Fuzz Dockerfile and build.sh to build the target codebase. The challenge of this stage is to automatically build a Java project purely based on the GitHub URL.
- **Stage 2: Target project static analysis.** This stage uses static program analysis to extract details, such as method signatures, of the target code which can be used for fuzzing harnesses generation. This stage relies on building the target code and performing static program analysis during the building.
- **Stage 3: Fuzzing harness generation.** This stage takes as input the data generated from Stage 2, and uses it to generate a candidate set of fuzzing harnesses. These harnesses are Java source code files that can be linked to the target's project build artefacts.
- **Stage 4: Fuzzing harness validation.** This stage combines the output from stage 1 and stage 3 into a set of candidate OSS-Fuzz project integrations and then builds and runs the fuzzing harness for each candidate project. The output of this stage is a set of logs showing the result of running the fuzzing harness for each candidate integration.

- **Stage 5: Fuzzing harness integration ranking.** This stage interprets the output from stage 4 and ranks each of the candidate OSS-Fuzz integrations. The output of this stage is a list of viable OSS-Fuzz integrations that are ranked according to which is the best integration.

IV. OSS-FUZZGEN DESIGN

This section describes the stages of OSS-Fuzzgen in detail, including implementation details and higher-level design decisions.

A. Stage 1: Build system generation

The first stage generates the OSS-Fuzz *Dockerfile* and *build.sh*, which are used to build the project in the OSS-Fuzz container image. The general problem to be solved is how to build a given arbitrary Java project and instructions for building fuzz harnesses against the project's build artefacts.

Java projects can be built in many different ways, such as directly compiled by *Javac* or using managed build systems like Maven or Gradle. To this end, OSS-Fuzzgen supports three build systems Maven, Gradle and Ant. OSS-Fuzzgen has heuristics for recognizing which build system is used by the target project by traversing the files of the target repository in the search for build files related to each build system. Specifically, OSS-Fuzzgen looks for *pom.xml* for Maven, *build.gradle* or *build.gradle.kts* for Gradle and *build.xml* for Ant. If multiple build properties exist, it indicates that the project can be built using multiple different build systems, OSS-Fuzzgen will use the first supported build system from the order: Maven, Gradle, Ant.

In addition to the build system, OSS-Fuzzgen needs to support different versions of the Java Development Kit (JDK). The default JDK version adopted by OSS-Fuzz is OpenJDK-15 at the time of writing. However, many projects require a different version of JDK to compile. To support this, OSS-Fuzzgen tries building the project using different versions of JDK until a successful build is found. The order of the JDK used are OpenJDK-15, OpenJDK-17, OpenJDK-11 and OpenJDK-8 and OSS-Fuzzgen will record and use the first successful build.

Finally, in addition to the build system and JDK version, an important step is identifying the class and jar files produced by the project, as these are necessary when linking fuzzing harnesses to the code. To support this, OSS-Fuzzgen traverses the folder of the project post-building to find the class files generated by the build and packs these class files into a single jar file. Additionally, OSS-Fuzzgen locates possible project jars, including dependencies, and moves them to a suitable classpath location so the generated fuzzing harnesses can use them.

B. Stage 2: Target project static analysis

The next task is to extract information about the target code for generating fuzzing harnesses. To do this, OSS-Fuzzgen relies on the Java frontend of Fuzz Introspector to retrieve a list of methods and classes of the target project. The list includes type information for each function, including both return type and argument types.

The Java frontend logic analyses the project's class and jar files, including third-party dependencies. However, OSS-Fuzzgen is not interested in generating harnesses for third-party dependencies, and, therefore, limits the analysis to the code within the source code directory of the target project. This is achieved by introspecting the source code location of the methods and classes within the jar files.

The static analysis component depends on the Soot framework, and a limitation of this is that the Soot framework fails to discover generic types and lambda expressions in the target code. For this reason, OSS-Fuzzgen can only generate general parameters for methods requiring generic type parameters or lambda expressions as input.

Following the static program analysis step, OSS-Fuzzgen creates a base OSS-Fuzz project integration directories and generates the correct set of base files from the template and the build configurations obtained in stage 1. OSS-Fuzzgen also includes an empty base fuzzing harness in the directory. At this point, OSS-Fuzzgen has created a Dockerfile, build.sh and a fuzzing harness, although the fuzzing harness is empty. The setup can now be tested in the OSS-Fuzz container images.

C. Stage 3: Fuzzing harness generation

This stage uses the output of the static analysis stage to create fuzzing harness source codes and combine them with the build artefacts from stage 1 to create working OSS-Fuzz integrations. To do this, OSS-Fuzzgen uses three steps to transform the raw data from Fuzz Introspector to a set of candidate OSS-Fuzz integrations, each with a fuzzing harness targeting the project.

The first step is extracting the specific methods in the target code to add metadata describing how to call these methods. Fuzz Introspector iterates through all the possible methods and classes in the project where each method may require different handling to execute. For example, some methods may be declared static which allows direct invocation, and some methods may require object creation or other code initialization. Furthermore, some methods may be class constructors or throw exceptions that need specific handling. This step extracts this information from the Fuzz Introspector result and groups the target methods accordingly.

The second step is filtering methods to reduce the candidate set of target methods. It is not uncommon for a medium-sized Java project to have more than a thousand methods, where many of them are not good targets to fuzz. OSS-Fuzzgen applies four filters to discard non-relevant methods:

- **Inaccessible methods filter.** This filter discards inaccessible classes and methods. This includes abstract classes, interfaces or protected / private elements which are not accessible by fuzzing harnesses and will likely fail in the fuzzing harnesses validation stage.
- **Helper methods filter.** This filter discards methods that do not have a lot of complexity. This includes general

methods from the Object class, methods with no parameters or helper methods that only get or set variables.
- **Out-of-scope methods filter.** This filter discards methods that do not belong to the target project. Some projects include third-party dependencies in their resulting jar files. OSS-Fuzzgen identifies the source code location for the target project and filters out all methods and classes which are not part of the source files for the target project.
- **Method call-depth filter.** This filter discards methods that may be hit by other possible entry points. Specifically, OSS-Fuzzgen extracts the call tree of each method and discards methods if other possible entry points will reach the given method. This filter consists of two stages. The first stage sorts all target methods by calling tree depth descendingly. Target methods with deeper call trees likely cover more logic which is a desired property when fuzzing. OSS-Fuzzgen then keeps the top 20% of the sorted method target list. The second stage adds any methods that are not called by any other methods, as these are considered public APIs which are determined to be good candidates for fuzzing.

Following the filtering step, OSS-Fuzzgen now has the list of method candidates to target and metadata on how to invoke each of these methods. Next, OSS-Fuzzgen proceeds to apply 10 heuristics for creating fuzzing harnesses against the target methods. These heuristics create a fuzzing harness that calls the target method in a manner where the arguments to the method are seeded with fuzzer-provided data. Some of these heuristics may produce code that won't run for a given target method.

The idea behind this step is to generate a lot of potential fuzz harness candidates and then use runtime evaluation later in the process to assess the quality of each harness. These heuristics are summarised in Table I. We came up with these heuristics by studying the existing OSS-Fuzz projects and abstracting existing fuzzing harnesses into higher-level code patterns.

In addition to creating the logic around the heuristics, OSS-Fuzzgen adds possible exception handling by traversing the call tree of each method, as well as including the import statements necessary for the code. OSS-Fuzzgen augments the code with comments that indicate the target methods and heuristics used.

Heuristics 1-4 are simple heuristics that consider different ways to execute static methods and instance methods directly. Static methods can be invoked directly while instance methods require object initialisation. For these four heuristics, OSS-Fuzzgen handles methods with up to 20 parameters where the parameters have to be primitive types, an array of primitive types and String (or CharSequence in general). Each argument is seeded with data from the fuzzing engine.

Heuristics 6-10 are more complicated than heuristics 1-4. Heuristic 6 considers some method execution that requires prerequisite settings and auto-discover possible settings methods and invokes them before the target method is executed. Heuristic 7 considers testing the consistency of method calling of some supposedly deterministic method. Heuristic 8-10 considers complicated parameters in addition to simple object creation, primitive types, an array of primitive types and string considered in heuristic 1-4. Those complicated parameter types include Class object, Enum object and parameters that require a fixed set of choices. Last but not least, heuristic 11 considers various kinds of parameters for executing public and concrete class constructors.

TABLE I. HEURISTICS FOR GENERATING FUZZING HARNESSES

Heuristic 1	Each possible target contains a fuzzing harness calling to one of the static methods in the target method list directly.
Heuristic 2	Each possible target contains a fuzzing harness calling to one of the instance methods in the target method list after the creation of the required object with the object constructor. It will search for a constructor from the subclass if the target object is an abstract class or interface.
Heuristic 3	Each possible target contains a fuzzing harness calling to one of the instance methods in the target method list after the creation of the required object using a static method like get instance or else.
Heuristic 4	Each possible target contains a fuzzing harness calling to one of the instance methods in the target method list after the creation of the required object with static or instance factory methods. It will also create an instance of the class containing the factory methods if necessary.
Heuristic 6	Similar to Heuristic 2-4, but before the target method is called, some setting methods will be called to simulate the case that some methods have some prerequisite method before the real execution logic.
Heuristic 7	Similar to Heuristic 2-4, but it will execute the target method twice and compare the result to fuzz for a deterministic result.
Heuristic 8	Similar to Heuristic 2-4, but it will handle enum type parameters with random choice of enum value.
Heuristic 9	Similar to Heuristic 2-4, but it will handle parameters that request a static number of choices.
Heuristic 10	Similar to Heuristic 2-4, but it will handle class type parameters of the target method.
Heuristic 11	Each possible target contains a fuzzing harness calling to one of the class constructors from classes in the project, excluding throwable classes or test classes.

The result of this stage is a set of candidate fuzzing harnesses where each of them is stored in an OSS-Fuzz integration directory together with the generated Dockerfile, build.sh and project.yaml. At this point, each of these directories represents a candidate OSS-Fuzz project.

A sample fuzzing harness is shown in Figure 1. The target method in this example is *feign.template.UriUtils::encode* and the heuristic applies is Heuristic 1. The heuristic simply calls into the static method using arguments seeded with data from the fuzz engine.

D. Stage 4: Fuzzing harness validation

Following the fuzzing harness generation, OSS-Fuzzgen has assembled a list of possible fuzzing harness integrations. OSS-Fuzzgen then validates each fuzzing harness by building and running it using the wrapping OSS-Fuzz project integration. The output from the runtime execution is logged and the return value and messages are used to judge if the execution

```
import com.code_intelligence.jazzer.api.FuzzedDataProvider;
import feign.template.UriUtils;

// jvm-autofuzz-heuristics-1
public class Fuzz {
  public static void fuzzerTestOneInput(FuzzedDataProvider data) {
  // Heuristic name: jvm-autofuzz-heuristics-1
  // Target method: [feign.template.UriUtils] public static java.lang.String
  //                  encode(java.lang.String,boolean)
  feign.template.UriUtils.encode(data.consumeString(100),data.consumeBoolean());
  }
}
```

Figure 1. Sample fuzzing harness generated by OSS-Fuzzgen on feign.template.UriUtils::encode method of project feign using heuristic 1

is successful or not. The runtime execution time can be set by the user of OSS-Fuzzgen and is by default set to 20 seconds.

OSS-Fuzzgen determines the status of the run with some additional fuzzing statistics including coverage information. These logs are stored in a separate directory together with a summary.json recording key statistical data for later analysis purposes. Both the building and running of the harness may break, either due to limitations in the artefacts produced, SOOT, Fuzz Introspector or the generated code.

E. Stage 5: Fuzzing harness integration ranking

The OSS-Fuzzgen results are ready to use after the fuzzing harnesses validation phase, however, OSS-Fuzzgen may have generated several hundred successful runs for any given project. To aid the analysis and choosing of the best result to be integrated into OSS-Fuzz, OSS-Fuzzgen also provides some post-processing and summarization of data. OSS-Fuzzgen ranks the possible targets according to the maximum code coverage achieved and the maximum difference in coverage between the start and finish of each fuzzing run.

OSS-Fuzzgen also comes with several utilities for extracting an overview when analysing many open source projects at the same time, to ease the efforts needed to identify the best performing harnesses. The resulting OSS-Fuzz integration directories for each successfully generated target can be integrated directly into OSS-Fuzz.

V. Empirical Study of OSS-Fuzzgen Process and Generated Fuzzing Harnesses

In this section, we present the empirical evaluation of our work. The evaluation process consists of two experiments: a large-scale study running OSS-Fuzzgen autonomously and an extension of this study where we integrate a subset of the successful projects into OSS-Fuzz with minor manual additions.

A. Large scale evaluation

To empirically verify OSS-Fuzzgen, we ran it against 257 open source Java projects not covered by OSS-Fuzz yet. We made an effort to pick popular Java libraries or frameworks, where popularity was based on the number of GitHub Star and GitHub Watch rankings. There were no UI applications in the target projects and in general, we picked libraries that are meant for use by applications rather than stand-alone applications as such. To set up the experiment, we created a text file containing the URLs to each of the 257 projects and provided it as input to OSS-Fuzzgen. For the validation phase of OSS-Fuzzgen, we set the fuzzing harnesses to run for 20 seconds. We divide the results into the following categories:

1) **S1: Successful build and generate fuzzing harness.** A build script and some fuzzing harnesses were generated. Fuzzing harnesses may not be runnable.
2) **S2: Successful build and generate fuzzing harness that runs.** A build script and fuzzing harnesses were generated. Some fuzzing harnesses are built and run successfully.
3) **S3: Successful build and generate fuzzing harness that runs and increases coverage.** A build script and fuzz harnesses were generated. Some fuzzing harnesses build and run successfully and explore more than one code path within 20 seconds of execution.

TABLE II. RESULTS FROM RUNNING OSS-FUZZGEN ON OPEN SOURCE SOFTWARE

#	Total java project targets	257	100%
S1	Successful build and generate fuzzing harness	123	47%
S2	Successful build and generate fuzzing harness that runs	116	45%
S3	Successful build and generate fuzzing harness that runs and increases coverage	94	37%

Table II shows the results of our evaluation. Amongst the 257 total targets, OSS-Fuzzgen succeeded in generating project integrations that match category S2 for 116 (45% of the total) projects. However, 22 of these generated projects failed to increase coverage during the initial 20 seconds of fuzzing harnesses validation, meaning a total of 94 projects (37% of the total) got results matching group S3.

B. Submitting projects to OSS-Fuzz

The goal of OSS-Fuzzgen is to generate OSS-Fuzz integrations that are useful in testing and fuzzing the code of the target projects. To empirically validate this goal, we submitted 31 of the 94 resulting OSS-Fuzz integrations where we picked those projects with the most promising signs of code exploration. We identified this by looking at the code coverage delta of the harnesses achieved from the 20-second initial fuzzing run. The goal was to monitor if the fuzzing harnesses found any issues in the target projects and ensure the projects ran continuously.

Before submitting the generated projects to OSS-Fuzz, we applied some manual efforts on several resulting projects. First, when OSS-Fuzzgen generated multiple targets for a given project, we hand-picked the best targets, in terms of code coverage and target method call depth, and merged them into a single directory. Second, sometimes the auto-generated code may reveal additional entry points in the target code that are good for fuzzing. For example, additional functions that are fuzzable within the same class as an auto-generated fuzzing harness, and we added these. Third, some of the promising generated harnesses would run into issues early in the execution due to missing initialization code and in these cases, we added logic to the fuzzing harnesses that would properly initialise the relevant logic. Finally, we went over the auto-generated code to improve readability by e.g., setting the names of variables appropriately and cleaning up code formatting.

Amongst the 31 projects we submitted to OSS-Fuzz, we received more than 50 bug reports. Commonly, projects with issues have 2 to 3 issues reported whereas a few projects have a significantly higher amount. For example, Joni has 7 bugs reported, however, after root-cause analysis we found that they are caused by triggering 2 core bugs via different entry points, meaning the two bugs are triggered in a handful of ways. The types of bugs found include out-of-memory errors, integer overflow errors, regular expression Denial-of-Services, index out-of-bounds errors for array or string accesses, and string encoding errors.

TABLE III. UPSTREAM BUG FIXING STATUS

Projects	# bug fixes	Status
https://github.com/fusesource/jansi	2	Accepted
https://github.com/jruby/joni	2	Accepted
https://github.com/openfeign/feign	2	Accepted
https://github.com/virtuald/curvesapi	1	Accepted
https://github.com/xdrop/fuzzywuzzy	1	Accepted
https://github.com/graphql-java/graphql-java	1	Accepted
https://github.com/fasseg/exp4j	1	Submitted
https://github.com/locationtech/jts	1	Submitted

To verify that the issues found by the fuzzing harnesses are valid, we performed a root-cause analysis of 11 of these from 8 different projects. Most of the bugs are invalid input checking or memory overflow issues. We then generate bug fixes and make pull requests with fixes on the relevant repositories. 9 bugs from 6 projects have been accepted and merged by the project maintainers with positive comments. Table III summarises the bug reports.

VI. Limitation and Future work

OSS-Fuzzgen has several limitations in the implementation domain. First, extending the system to support more build systems and more versions of JDK would enable more targets to be processed. For almost half the projects tested OSS-Fuzzgen created an OSS-Fuzz integration that builds the project with a fuzzing harness that runs. Extending to further JDK and build systems will likely increase this proportion.

Additionally, we can extend the system to support lambda expressions and generic types for fuzzing harness generation. To do this, we can migrate the existing Fuzz Introspector frontend with SootUp[17].

A limitation in OSS-Fuzzgen is the scope of generating fuzzing harnesses. Currently, it's limited to 10 different heuristics. We can extend this to support additional heuristics to increase the possible set of fuzzing harnesses to generate.

An interesting avenue for improving fuzzing harness generation is extending the system with more general approaches. For example, recent work has explored using Large Language Models to generate fuzzing harness code which shows promising results[18].

To integrate the projects in OSS-Fuzz, we picked the best projects constructed by OSS-Fuzzgen based on how much a given integration achieved in code coverage exploration. A limitation is that we made manual assessments in this case, and further work would explore how we can improve the ability to rank the auto-generated projects. This includes features such as automatically identifying the threat model of a project and matching this with auto-generated fuzzing harnesses; automatically assessing how security-critical an open source project is to enable selection of those where vulnerabilities are most important and also include more data from Fuzz Introspector as to how promising a given harness is.

VII. Conclusion

In this paper, we introduce OSS-Fuzzgen, a first effort in automatic OSS-Fuzz project integration. OSS-Fuzzgen enables automatic fuzzing of open source Java projects by generating fuzzing harnesses, constructing appropriate build scripts and validating the generated harnesses to identify those that perform the best.

OSS-Fuzzgen significantly lowers the barrier of entry for continuous fuzzing and to demonstrate these capabilities, we ran OSS-Fuzzgen against a dataset of 257 open source Java projects. As a result, OSS-Fuzzgen produced 116 valid OSS-Fuzz project integrations with some fuzzing harnesses that build and run. Furthermore, to prove the use of the generated fuzzing harnesses we added 31 of these projects to OSS-Fuzz which resulted in more than 50 issues being found. Finally, we submitted bug fixes for 11 reported issues, 9 of which have been accepted and merged by the open source projects.

In conclusion, OSS-Fuzzgen provides a good entry point for open source project fuzzing. This setting could encourage open source project maintainers to start fuzzing their projects and adopt OSS-Fuzz for continuous security issues and bug discovery.

ACKNOWLEDGMENT

We would like to thank the OSS-Fuzz team for responding to our issues on GitHub and reviewing our contributions. We would also like to thank the maintainers who reviewed our bug fixes.

REFERENCES

[1] "OSS-Fuzzgen." https://github.com/AdaLogics/OSS-Fuzzgen, 2023. Retrieved: October, 2023.
[2] "OSS-Fuzz." http://github.com/google/oss-fuzz, 2023. Retrieved: October, 2023.
[3] Z. Y. Ding and C. L. Goues, "An empirical study of OSS-Fuzz bugs," *2021 IEEE/ACM 18th International Conference on Mining Software Repositories (MSR)*, pp. 131–142, 2021.
[4] V. M. Manes, H. Han, C. Han, S. Cha, M. Egele, E. J. Schwartz, and M. Woo, "The art, science, and engineering of fuzzing: A survey," *IEEE Transactions on Software Engineering*, vol. 47, pp. 2312–2331, nov 2021.
[5] "Fuzzing Introspection of OSS-Fuzz projects." https://introspector.oss-fuzz.com/, 2023. Retrieved: October, 2023.
[6] D. Babic, S. Bucur, Y. Chen, F. Ivancic, T. King, M. Kusano, C. Lemieux, L. Szekeres, and W. Wang, "FUDGE: Fuzz Driver Generation at Scale," in *Proceedings of the 2019 27th ACM Joint Meeting on European Software Engineering Conference and Symposium on the Foundations of Software Engineering*, 2019.
[7] Y. Fu, J. Lee, and T. Kim, "autofz: Automated fuzzer composition at runtime," in *32nd USENIX Security Symposium, USENIX Security 2023, Anaheim, CA, USA, August 9-11, 2023* (J. A. Calandrino and C. Troncoso, eds.), USENIX Association, 2023.
[8] K. K. Ispoglou, D. Austin, V. Mohan, and M. Payer, "Fuzzgen: Automatic fuzzer generation," in *29th USENIX Security Symposium, USENIX Security 2020, August 12-14, 2020* (S. Capkun and F. Roesner, eds.), pp. 2271–2287, USENIX Association, 2020.
[9] B. Jeong, J. Jang, H. Yi, J. Moon, J. Kim, I. Jeon, T. Kim, W. Shim, and Y. H. Hwang, "Utopia: Automatic generation of fuzz driver using unit tests," in *44th IEEE Symposium on Security and Privacy, SP 2023, San Francisco, CA, USA, May 21-25, 2023*, pp. 2676–2692, IEEE, 2023.
[10] P. Godefroid, N. Klarlund, and K. Sen, "Dart: Directed automated random testing," in *Proceedings of the 2005 ACM SIGPLAN Conference on Programming Language Design and Implementation*, PLDI '05, (New York, NY, USA), p. 213–223, Association for Computing Machinery, 2005.
[11] C. Rahalkar, "Automated fuzzing harness generation for library APIs and binary protocol parsers," 06 2023.
[12] M. Pradel and T. R. Gross, "Automatic generation of object usage specifications from large method traces," in *2009 IEEE/ACM International Conference on Automated Software Engineering*, pp. 371–382, 2009.
[13] M. Pradel and T. R. Gross, "Leveraging test generation and specification mining for automated bug detection without false positives," in *2012 34th International Conference on Software Engineering (ICSE)*, pp. 288–298, 2012.
[14] "Fuzz Introspector." http://github.com/ossf/fuzz-introspector, 2023. Retrieved: October, 2023.
[15] W. Gao, V. Pham, D. Liu, O. Chang, T. Murray, and B. I. P. Rubinstein, "Beyond the coverage plateau: A comprehensive study of fuzz blockers (registered report)," in *Proceedings of the 2nd International Fuzzing Workshop, FUZZING 2023, Seattle, WA, USA, 17 July 2023* (M. Böhme, Y. Noller, B. Ray, and L. Szekeres, eds.), pp. 47–55, ACM, 2023.
[16] P. Lam, E. Bodden, O. Lhotak, and L. Hendren, "The soot framework for java program analysis: a retrospective," October 2011. Event Title: Cetus Users and Compiler Infastructure Workshop (CETUS 2011).
[17] "SootUp, howpublished = https://soot-oss.github.io/sootup/, year = 2023, note = Retrieved: October, 2023."
[18] "Fuzz target generation using LLMs." https://google.github.io/oss-fuzz/research/llms/target_generation/, 2023. Retrieved: October, 2023.

INTERACT: a Tool for Unit Test Based Integration of Component-based Software Systems

Nils Wild
Research Group Software Construction
RWTH Aachen University
Aachen, Germany
email: wild@swc.rwth-aachen.de

Horst Lichter
Research Group Software Construction
RWTH Aachen University
Aachen, Germany
email: lichter@swc.rwth-aachen.de

***Abstract*—Testing complex component-based software systems is hard. Unit tests are focused but are not effective in exposing integration faults. However, integration test cases are difficult to develop and maintain. This paper presents a tool that uses unit tests to expose integration faults in component-based software systems. This is done by observing the component's unit test cases to derive the component's expectations of its interactions with other components. These expectations are validated using newly generated component integration test cases. Because the approach requires no new tests to be written, we consider it economical and effective.**

Keywords – component-based software; integration testing.

I. INTRODUCTION

Testing aims to expose faults and to assess that customer requirements are fulfilled. Many approaches have been developed to test software systems [1]. Testing isolated components of a software system - called *unit testing* - is an industry best practice. However, exposing certain types of faults at the unit level is impossible. Thus, tests on the integration level are needed that test the interaction of a component with other components - its environment [2]. However, creating and maintaining these integration tests is tedious. Architectural changes of the system and changes of the components require changes in the unit and integration tests [3]. We aim to automate this process for certain types of integration tests. To overcome some challenges of integration testing, we present a tool-supported approach that relies on existing unit tests. The knowledge encoded therein is used to determine how components expect to interact with their environment and to manipulate the unit tests such that integration aspects are tested. The thereby generated component integration test cases are related to each other such that they are equivalent to traditional integration tests that test those expectations.

The proposed approach and the tool were developed with the following research questions in mind:

- How can interaction expectations of components be extracted from unit test cases?
- How can tests, checking the interaction between a component and its environment, be derived from the unit test cases of the participating components?
- How to determine if a system can be integrated considering those component integration tests to continuously check the integration of a system as it evolves?

This paper is structured as follows: First, challenges of integration testing are presented in Section II. Section III introduces the **U**nit **T**est **B**ased **I**ntegration (UTBI) model which is the conceptual core of the approach. In Section IV we describe how UTBI models are used to derive the expectations components have regarding their environment and how these can be verified. Section V presents the tool INTERACT, implementing the proposed approach. Related work is discussed in Section VI. The planned next steps and future work conclude this paper in Section VII.

II. CHALLENGES OF INTEGRATION TESTING

Whenever a system is changed, tests need to be re-executed, and new tests are needed for new and changed features. In addition to knowing when a component is ready to be integrated, testers need to know how each component expects to interact with other components. Dedicated test specifications or any other form of documentation specify these interactions. However, creating integration tests is difficult, and studies show that documented specifications start to diverge from the implemented system over time [4] [5].

Furthermore, integration tests must be adapted when the underlying components change. Given an arbitrary number of interactions, there are a huge number of possible integration tests. Each interaction between two components can be tested separately by component integration tests as well as each possible subpath of interactions contained in the interaction path of all components that realize a customer feature. Creating and maintaining these tests is generally not feasible. Because of this, often only the most important integration tests are automated [1], [2], [6]. This contradicts the principle of testing as early as possible because these tests require all components to be ready for integration.

An automatable approach to keep the specification, which is used to test the integration, up-to-date with the system's implementation is needed to ensure that each component is integrated with all components as expected.

III. THE UNIT TEST BASED INTEGRATION META-MODEL

In the following, we introduce the UTBI meta-model (see Figure 1) which defines elements and relationships to model structural as well as behavioral information needed to test the integration of components based on existing unit tests. A more detailed definition of the model and its foundations is already published. [7]

Components are core elements of the model. To abstract from various types of communication protocols, any interaction between components is treated as an activation of a component by a *Message* through an *Interface* that is *provided by* the component. A distinction is made between an *Incoming Interface* and an *Outgoing Interface*. Through an incoming interface, a message is *received by* a component, whereas messages are *sent by* an outgoing interface. An incoming interface is *bound to* an arbitrary number of outgoing interfaces and vice versa. Which interfaces are bound to each other depends on the concrete communication protocol. The protocol data is an attribute of the interface, e.g., for the Advanced Message Queueing Protocol (AMQP), the respective bindings are defined depending on the exchange type and queue bindings, while URLs and methods are used for (Representational State Transfer (REST).

For each component, the respective unit test cases are modeled. To this end, *Abstract Test Cases* for each Component Under Test (CUT) are included, which are templates without concrete input and expected values. A *Test Case* is *derived from* an abstract test case by providing concrete *values*.

Once a test case gets executed, a sequence of messages is *triggered by* it. We distinguish three types of messages:

- A *stimulus* is a message received by the CUT from the test case.
- A *component response* is a message sent by the CUT back to the test case or to other components (those components are called the CUT's *environment*).
- An *environment response* is a message sent by a component of the CUT's environment back to the CUT as a reaction to a received component response.

Instances of the UTBI meta-model are called *UTBI component models*. They provide the core information for the automated integration testing process, introduced next.

IV. Integration testing based on UTBI models

In the following section, we describe the activities of the automated integration testing process based on such UTBI component models (see Figure 2).

Create UTBI component models (A1): To create all UTBI component models, the Unit Test Suites (UTS) of all components are executed. During execution, information regarding the unit test cases, the sent and received messages, and the used interfaces are extracted into a UTBI component model.

Derive interaction expectations (A2): To test the integration of all components, it is necessary to know how these components expect to interact with each other. These expectations towards their environment are implicitly defined by the messages triggered during UTS execution. Given a UTBI component model, every environment response that follows after a component response defines an expectation of that component towards the reaction of its environment. Resulting in a list of interaction expectations for each component.

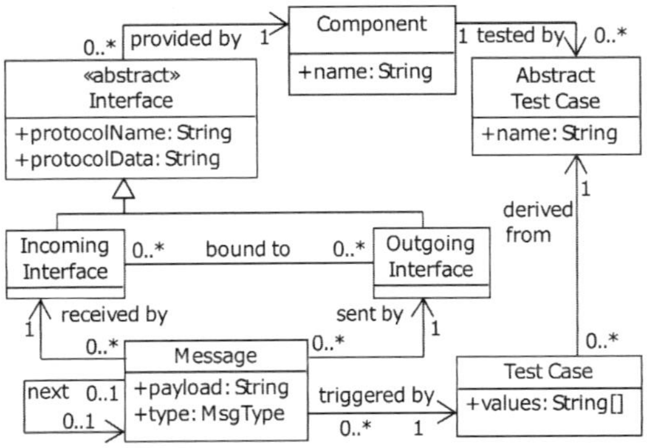

Figure 1. Unit Test Based Integration Meta-Model.

Create the UTBI system model (A3): To validate that all interaction expectations are fulfilled by the integrated system, all UTBI component models need to be merged into one *UTBI system model*. For this purpose, incoming and outgoing interfaces that are bound to each other are determined. This is done using protocol-specific interface matching based on the protocol information attached to the interfaces. The resulting UTBI system model is complete concerning the provided UTSs.

Lookup possible interaction paths (A4): Each interaction expectation can be validated by searching for interaction paths from the interface via which the component response was sent by, to the interface that received the environment response. This might result in multiple paths, each spanning two or more components and interactions. However, which path is activated by the concrete component response depends on its content and the component's behavior.

Create interaction tests (A5): To validate the interaction expectations, the determined paths can be executed by exchanging the original stimulus message in a unit test case with the respective component response. We call these generated component integration test cases *Interaction Test Cases* (ITC) because they test exactly one interaction on an interaction path.

Run interaction tests (A6): When an ITC is successful, a new component response can be observed that replaces the originally mocked environment response in an additional interaction test case that is derived from the original UTC. If all ITCs on an interaction path are successful the interaction expectation is validated.

V. InterACt - an integration testing tool

The presented concept is implemented in the InterACt tool (code: https://github.com/NilsWild/InterACt, video: https://owncloud.swc.rwth-aachen.de/s/NtbMqMSByUoxv0q). InterACt is designed to support different protocols and their implementations. As shown in Figure 3 *Interface Observers* collect the messages that are sent by and sent to the CUT. The collected data is stored in the *UTBI model store* to create the UTBI component models and the UTBI system

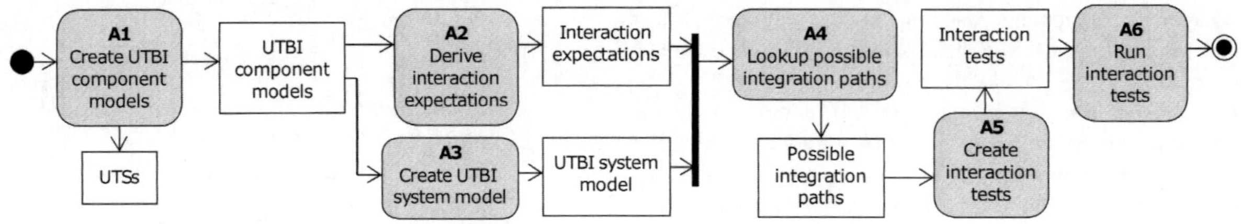

Figure 2. The integration testing process based on UTBI models.

model. INTERACT implements an extension mechanism to specify how the interfaces contained in the UTBI component models are bound via so-called *Interface Binders* to create the UTBI system model. Based on the UTBI system model, the *Interaction Test Harness* retrieves integration data from the *ITC generator* and provides alternative parameters to the abstract test cases according to the derived interaction expectations and the corresponding interaction paths that need to be tested. INTERACT needs to be re-executed until no more interaction paths are untested or all interaction expectations are validated successfully.

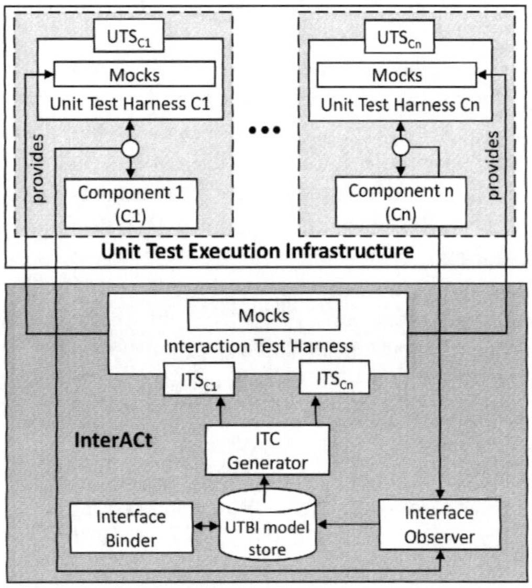

Figure 3. Embedding INTERACT in a unit test execution infrastructure.

A. An example application

To explain INTERACT'S integration testing process we present an example project (available on GitHub https://github.com/NilsWild/InteractionTestExample). This simple banking project consists of three components implemented as microservices using Spring Boot:

- `MoneyTransfer` (MT): Transfers money if the target IBAN is valid and the user's balance is sufficient.
- `IBANValidator` (IV): It checks if a given IBAN is valid.
- `BlacklistChecker` (BLC): It checks if a given IBAN is on the bank's blacklist.

Triggered by a transfer request, these components collaborate as follows (see Figure 5): First, the `MoneyTransfer` component asks the `IBANValidator` to validate the IBAN. To do so, the `IBANValidator` checks the IBANs format and requests the `BlacklistChecker` to check if the receiving IBAN is on the blacklist before it returns the validation result to the `MoneyTransfer` component. For each component, a unit test suite was created as well as mocks needed to test the components as shown in Figure 4.

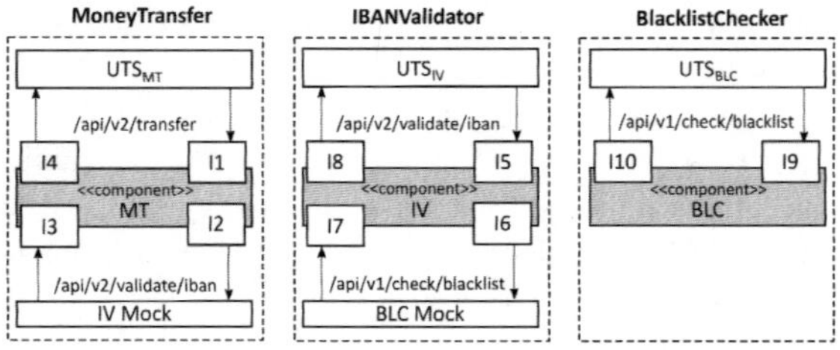

Figure 4. Components, unit test suits, and mocks of the example application.

Using this example, the integration process activities A1 to A6 are explained below.

Create UTBI component models (A1): To create the UTBI component models, INTERACT, its REST interface binder, and the UTBI model store (a neo4j database) are started. Then the unit test suites of all components are executed. The unit test cases are implemented similarly to JUnit parameterized tests. The same argument sources can be used but the tests are annotated with `InterACtTest` instead of `ParameterizedTest`. The parameters of each test case are the stimulus and environment response messages the CUT receives during test execution plus additional expected values for validation. For the `MoneyTransfer` component, three unit tests exist:

- MT-UT1: The `IBANValidator` mock returns that the IBAN is not valid. Thus, the transfer should fail.
- MT-UT2: The `IBANValidator` mock returns that the IBAN is valid but the test sets the state of the `MoneyTransfer` component such that the balance is insufficient. Thus, the transfer should fail.
- MT-UT3: The `IBANValidator` mock returns that the IBAN is valid and the test sets the state of the

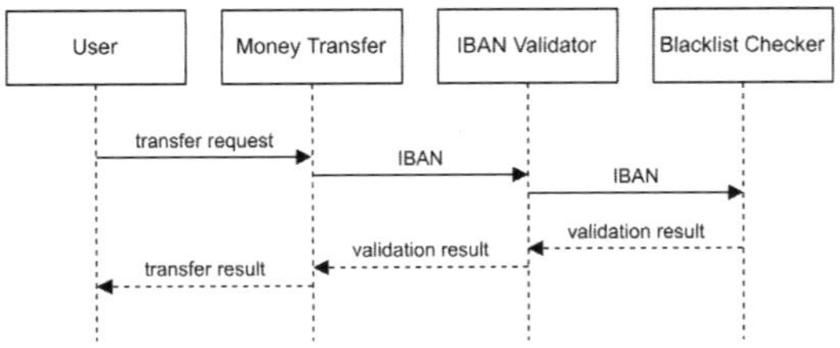

Figure 5. Target sequence of messages triggered by a transfer request.

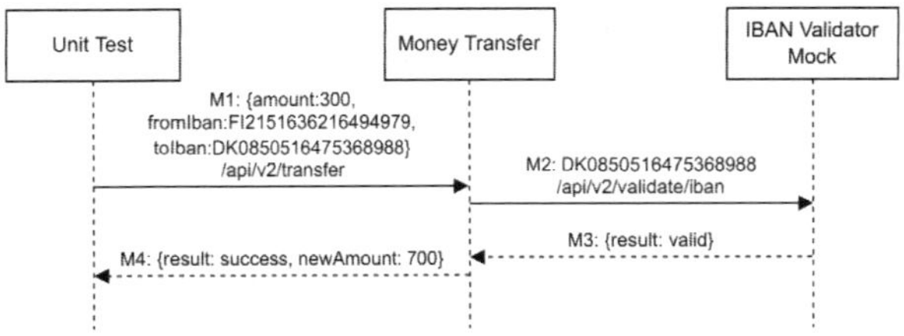

Figure 6. Sequence diagram showing the execution of unit test MT-UT3.

`MoneyTransfer` component such that the balance is sufficient. Thus, the transfer should succeed.

When they are executed, the UTBI component model for the `MoneyTransfer` component is created. It contains the triggered interfaces and the three collected message sequences. This model is stored in the UTBI model store. This is done for each component.

For the `IBANValidator` three unit tests exist:

- IV-UT1: The IBAN is valid but the `BlacklistChecker` mock returns that it is on the blacklist. Thus, the IBAN should be invalid.
- IV-UT2: The IBAN is valid, the `BlacklistChecker` mock returns that it is not on the blacklist. Thus, the IBAN should be valid.
- IV-UT3: An invalid IBAN is provided. Thus, the `BlacklistChecker` is not requested and the IBAN should be invalid.

For the `BlacklistChecker` two unit tests exist:

- BLC-UT1: The test provisions a blacklist that contains the given IBAN. Thus, the `BlacklistChecker` should respond with a match message.
- BLC-UT2: The test provisions a blacklist that does not contain the given IBAN. Thus, the `BlacklistChecker` should respond with a no-match message.

After all UTSs have been executed, all three UTBI component models are in the UTBI model store.

Derive interaction expectations (A2): Whenever new data is added to a UTBI component model INTERACT checks if an interaction expectation is contained in the new data. For the test case MT-UT3 (Figure 6), an interaction expectation from `M2` to `M3` is derived. For the other two behaviors of the `MoneyTransfer` component and the behaviors of the other components, interaction expectations are derived accordingly.

Create the UTBI system model (A3): After the UTBI component models are stored, INTERACT tries to bind the incoming and outgoing interfaces of each component using the provided interface binders. In our example, the REST interface binder handles the captured interfaces shown in Figure 4. They are bound such that the sequence of messages shown in Figure 5 is represented by the resulting UTBI system model. Specifically, the following interface pairs are bound together: (`I2` and `I5`), (`I6`, `I9`), (`I10`, `I7`), (`I8`, `I3`).

Lookup possible interaction paths (A4): Given the interaction expectations and the interface bindings, INTERACT tries to find path candidates to validate the expectations. For the interaction expectation from `M2` to `M3`, it tries to find a path from the outgoing interface `I2` with the URL `/api/v2/validate/iban` of the `MoneyTransfer` component to the incoming interface `I3` where `M3` was received. This is done with a breadth-first path expansion algorithm.

First, messages `M2` and `M3` are mapped to the interfaces `I2` and `I3` the messages were sent to, respectively received from. Next, all outgoing interfaces that are bound to the incoming interface `I3` that `M3` was received from, are collected. In this case `I8`. These are the interfaces that terminate the following path expansion. Starting with `I2` all incoming interfaces that are bound to it – in this case `I5` – and could thus receive `M2` are looked up. For all found interfaces, test cases that triggered messages on them are retrieved (IV-UT1, IV-UT2, IV-UT3). To keep the intention of the test cases, the found test cases are filtered such that only those that triggered `stimulus` messages on that interface are considered. This is true for all three of them. Next, all outgoing interfaces that are triggered as a reaction to a message on the respective incoming interface during these tests are collected. For IV-UT1 and IV-UT2 this is `I6`. For IV-UT3 this is `I8`, as the `IBANValidator` responds directly and the `BlacklistChecker` is not requested via I6. If one of those interfaces is a terminal interface the path is added to the list of possible interaction paths (IP). In the following, the IPs are represented by the unit test sequences that trigger the corresponding interfaces.

IP1 : MT-UT3→IV-UT3→MT-UT3

Then the remaining paths are further expanded starting with the found outgoing interface (`I6`) instead of `I2`. In our example the only interface bound to `I6` is `I9`. The test cases that triggered messages on `I9` are BLC-UT1 and BLC-UT2. `I10` is the outgoing interface that reacts to messages on `I9`. It is the start of the next expansion step as it is no terminal interface. The only interface bound to `I10` is `I7`. IV-UT1 and IV-UT2 triggered messages on `I7`. However, those messages were *environment response* and no *stimulus* messages. But as the tests have already been visited with the *stimulus* message and they are the next incoming message triggered during test execution, the path expansion is continued. This ensures that the integration path remains consistent with the unit test's intention. In both cases (IV-UT1, IV-UT2), a message on `I8` is triggered as a reaction to the message on `I7`. `I8` is a terminal interface. Thus, these paths are added to the list of possible interaction paths:

IP2 : MT-UT3→IV-UT1→BLC-UT1→IV-UT1→MT-UT3
IP3 : MT-UT3→IV-UT1→BLC-UT2→IV-UT1→MT-UT3
IP4 : MT-UT3→IV-UT2→BLC-UT1→IV-UT2→MT-UT3
IP5 : MT-UT3→IV-UT2→BLC-UT2→IV-UT2→MT-UT3

When no further expansion is possible, all interaction paths are found. Each found path is transformed into a *test execution plan*. Such a plan consists of the list of test cases in conjunction with the required information to replace the *stimulus* and *environment response* message with those triggered by the preceding test cases. All five paths and the resulting test execution plans are stored as candidates to validate the interaction expectation.

Create interaction tests (A5): When the test suites are re-executed the INTERACT JUnit extension requests the test execution plans for the CUT from INTERACT. Based on these plans, INTERACT determines parameter sets for the abstract test cases of the CUT based on the messages that were triggered by the components on that path so far. These parameter sets are sent to the JUnit test templates that represent the abstract test cases, resulting in new interaction test cases.

Run interaction tests (A6): When an interaction test gets executed and fails, the corresponding interaction path is not able to validate the interaction expectation. If every interaction test of an interaction path succeeds, the path validates the interaction expectation.

In our example, the process looks like this:

- IP1: Test case IV-UT3 which originally used an invalid IBAN and thus responded with a validation-failed message is parameterized with the IBAN contained in `M2` (DK0850516475368988) that was sent in MT-UT3 by `I2`, resulting in a new interaction test. With the now provided valid IBAN on `I5`, the test fails as the behavior that was tested by IV-UT3 was about receiving an invalid IBAN. The interaction path is not further considered.
- IP2-IP5: Based on IV-UT1 and IV-UT2 respectively, new interaction tests are generated that use the IBAN sent in MT-UT3 as well. As the IBAN format is valid like the one used in the unit test cases, both tests succeed. The paths get evaluated further. For IP3 and IP5, a new interaction test based on BLC-UT2 is generated. Therein the blacklist check received by `I9` contains the IBAN that originated from the unit test case of the `MoneyTransfer` component. As the test gets this message as a parameter, it sets the state such that the IBAN is not on the blacklist. The `BlacklistChecker` responds with a no-match message and the test succeeds. The response is sent via `I10` and is fed back to the `IBANValidator` test cases IV-UT1 and IV-UT2 as expected. In the two resulting interaction tests the `IBANValidator` receives the IBAN (DK0850516475368988), sends the blacklist check to the mock and the mock responds with the no-match response that was just observed in the preceding interaction test. The interaction test based on IV-UT1 fails, as the unit test case covered and asserted the behavior when the `BlacklistChecker` found a match. As the test failed, the path candidate IP3 was skipped for further evaluation. The one based on IV-UT2 succeeds accordingly. IP5 is evaluated further and the response triggered on `I8` is used as the mock response on `I3` in another interaction test based on test case MT-UT3. It succeeds and thus IP5 contains the unit tests that check the components' behaviors that are needed to satisfy the interaction expectation derived in A2. The expectation is validated by IP5. Note, that the response does not need to be equal to the mocked response `M3` in the unit test but leads to a validation of the defined assertions.

B. Detecting integration faults

Leung and White [3] presented a taxonomy for integration faults. Accordingly, integration faults are the result of misinterpretations of the documented specification on the providing or consuming side of a service as components are always developed based on an interpretation of their documented specifications.

INTERACT captures these interpretations by observing the sent and received messages by the executed UTSs and utilizes that information to validate that the consumer component and provider component interact compatibly with respect to their expectations. By analyzing the UTBI system model certain interaction fault types can be detected.

Mismatching interface definitions are detected as the replaced messages in the interaction test cases cannot be deserialized by the receiving component if the interface contract is broken. Furthermore, the assertions implemented in the UTS fail if the replaced environment responses or triggered component responses do not match the specified expectations. *Wrong function faults* are detected similarly.

In addition, *extra function faults* and *missing function faults* are detected, by querying the UTBI system model for unbound incoming and outgoing interfaces. If these are not public APIs they are either an indicator for such faults or an indicator for test gaps.

VI. RELATED WORK

Instead of testing the implementation, specification-based approaches like *protobuff* ensure the structural consistency of APIs by generating the actual implementation from specified documents. – These approaches lack behavioral information [8]. Thus, only interface faults can be prevented.

Approaches like consumer-driven contracts were developed to test early. However, these require additional tests and do not replace integration tests [9]. – In contrast to our approach, consumer-driven contracts cannot be used to check pass-through APIs, which are common in choreography-based architectures [10].

To test message-oriented systems, Santos et al. [11] propose a testing technique, that requires specifying the behavior of a system in advance. It is closely related to other specification-based testing approaches that use Linear Temporal Logic (LTL) to test such systems [12] [13]. – This is only possible if the specification is kept up-to-date with the actual specification of the system under test, which is rarely the case.

Benz [14] presents an approach that requires existing models of components and systems to generate test cases that cover critical interaction scenarios. – Our approach reconstructs the models from the observation of the unit test cases and allows to execute the integration tests on a per-component basis.

Elbaum et al. [15] present an approach, called *differential unit testing,* that contrasts with our approach. Instead of using isolated unit test cases to derive integration test cases, they use system test cases to derive unit test cases to test for differences in implementations of the same component in isolation. – This is only applicable if multiple implementations of the same component are developed.

Gälli et al. [16] present the *EG-meta-model* to create composable test cases. Since tests contain examples of how to use the units, these examples are extracted to composite new more complex tests. – The idea of composing unit test cases that serve as examples for the use of a component is also the basis of the presented approach. However, *InterACt* considers different kinds of communication protocols and extracts expectations towards other components from those examples to generate tests automatically.

Schätz and Pfaller [17] propose an approach to validate a component after it is embedded into a system without instrumenting the component itself, treating it as a black-box test. – While our approach aims to assess the functionality of the system by reusing unit tests, their approach aims to verify the functionality of a component through system tests.

VII. Conclusion & Future Work

InterACt allows testing component-based systems using the implicitly specified interaction expectations encoded in the unit test cases. However, it is currently limited to those expectations encoded within the unit test cases and requires looking into the UTBI model store to verify that all interaction expectations are validated. To overcome these limitations and to widen the applicability of our approach, the following improvements are planned:

- Creating a report generator that provides an overview regarding the fulfillment of all interaction expectations.
- Extend InterACt to validate state expectations and extend the UTBI model by higher order interaction expectations. For example, once an "add IBAN to blacklist" request is sent and a 200 response code was received a transfer with that IBAN fails. This would allow testing that both parties interpret "IBAN was added to the blacklist" in the same way.
- Extending the approach to support asynchronous interfaces, where a request should result in some action but the result is not observed by the component that issued the request. Such expectations are not part of unit test cases and would require a separate specification approach. However, the validation process of InterACt could be reused.

InterACt as it is right now requires to parameterize the UTSs by the messages the CUT receives. However, unlike traditional integration testing which requires a resource-intensive integration environment, the interaction tests require the same resources as the UTSs. Furthermore, InterACt is capable to detect certain types of interface faults, missing function faults, and wrong function faults. Last but not least the interaction test cases adapt to architectural changes, as they are generated based on the provided interfaces and resulting interaction paths. We expect that our approach decreases the burden for integration testers, by reducing the amount of integration tests that need to be written manually. We plan to evaluate our approach and InterACt in a larger industry case study to not only show the concepts effectiveness but also evaluate its effectiveness and efficiency in a larger project.

References

[1] B. Lima and J. P. Faria, "A survey on testing distributed and heterogeneous systems: The state of the practice," in *Software Technologies*, E. Cabello, J. Cardoso, A. Ludwig, L. A. Maciaszek, and M. van Sinderen, Eds. Cham: Springer Int. Publishing, 2017, pp. 88–107.

[2] V. Garousi and T. Varma, "A replicated survey of software testing practices in the canadian province of alberta: What has changed from 2004 to 2009?" *Journal of Systems and Software*, vol. 83, no. 11, pp. 2251–2262, 2010.

[3] H. K. N. Leung and L. J. White, "A study of integration testing and software regression at the integration level," *Proceedings. Conference on Software Maintenance 1990*, pp. 290–301, 1990.

[4] S. Mahmood and A. Khan, "An industrial study on the importance of software component documentation: A system integrators perspective," *Information Processing Letters*, vol. 111, no. 12, pp. 583–590, 2011.

[5] M. Nasution and H. Weistroffer, "Documentation in systems development: A significant criterion for project success," in *2009 42nd Hawaii International Conference on System Sciences*, 2009, pp. 1–9.

[6] A. Mann, A. Brown, M. Stahnke, and N. Kersten, "State of devops report," Puppet, Circle CI, Splunk, Tech. Rep., 2019.

[7] N. Wild and H. Lichter, "Unit test based component integration testing (to be published)," in *30th Asia-Pacific Software Engineering Conference (APSEC 2023)*. IEEE Computer Society, 2023, [retrieved: Oct, 2023]. [Online]. Available: https://swc.rwth-aachen.de/docs/2023_APSEC__Wild_Preprint.pdf

[8] Google, "Protocol buffers," http://code.google.com/apis/protocolbuffers/, [retrieved: Oct, 2023].

[9] C.-F. Wu, S.-P. Ma, A.-C. Shau, and H.-W. Yeh, "Testing for event-driven microservices based on consumer-driven contracts and state models," in *2022 29th Asia-Pacific Software Engineering Conference (APSEC)*, 2022, pp. 467–471.

[10] C. K. Rudrabhatla, "Comparison of event choreography and orchestration techniques in microservice architecture," *Int. Journal of Advanced Computer Science and Applications*, vol. 9, no. 8, pp. 18–22, 2018.

[11] A. Santos., A. Cunha., and N. Macedo., "Schema-guided testing of message-oriented systems," in *Proceedings of the 17th International Conference on Evaluation of Novel Approaches to Software Engineering - ENASE,*, INSTICC. SciTePress, 2022, pp. 26–37.

[12] A. Michlmayr, P. Fenkam, and S. Dustdar, "Specification-based unit testing of publish/subscribe applications," in *26th IEEE Int. Conference on Distributed Computing Systems Workshops (ICDCSW'06)*, 2006, pp. 34–34.

[13] L. Tan, O. Sokolsky, and I. Lee, "Specification-based testing with linear temporal logic," in *2004 IEEE International Conference on Information Reuse and Integration, IRI 2004*, 2004, pp. 493–498.

[14] S. Benz, "Combining test case generation for component and integration testing," in *3rd International Workshop on Advances in Model-Based Testing*, ser. A-MOST '07. New York, USA: ACM, 2007, p. 23–33.

[15] S. Elbaum, H. N. Chin, M. B. Dwyer, and M. Jorde, "Carving and replaying differential unit test cases from system test cases," *IEEE Transactions on Software Engineering*, vol. 35, no. 1, pp. 29–45, 2009.

[16] M. Gälli, R. Wampfler, and O. Nierstrasz, "Composing tests from examples." *Journal of Object Technology*, vol. 6, pp. 71–86, 2007.

[17] B. Schätz and C. Pfaller, "Integrating component tests to system tests," *Electronic Notes in Theoretical Computer Science*, vol. 260, pp. 225–241, 2010, Proceedings of the 5th International Workshop on Formal Aspects of Component Software (FACS 2008).

Bridging the Gap: Introducing a Universal Data Monetization Method from Information and Game Theories

Domingos S. M. P. Monteiro, Felipe Silva Ferraz, Silvio R. L. Meira
Center of Advanced Studies and Systems of Recife
Recife, Brazil
E-mail: {dsmpm, fsf, srlm}@cesar.school

Domingos S. P. Salazar
Distance Education and Technology Unit
Rural Federal University of Pernambuco
Recife, Brazil
domingos.salazar@ufrpe.br

Abstract— **Despite significant research on data monetization in recent years, the academic literature lacks universally applicable methods for this endeavor. This study seeks to introduce a versatile method suitable for various databases and prevalent challenges in both academic and commercial realms. Our methodology draws from information theory and game theory, leveraging the Return On Investment (ROI) metric as a value determinant. The derived method calculates the ROI contributed by distinct databases for binary decision-making, incorporating the Shapley Value concept from cooperative game theory. We tested this method on a practical dilemma—underwriting car insurance policies in Brazil. Our method adeptly pinpointed the financial contribution of each dataset to the assessed decisions. It can be adapted for other binary decision contexts where financial outcomes of decisions are either provided or quantifiable. Given the novelty of this research domain, we anticipate this study to spur further exploration into data valuation in the realm of data science and Big Data.**

Keywords-Big Data; Data Value; Big Data Monetization; Artificial Intelligence; Game Theory; Information Theory; Shapley Value; Digital Assets.

I. INTRODUCTION

Despite the advancements in Big Data applications, in research related to the subject, and in the widespread application of analytical and artificial intelligence solutions in recent decades, a method has not yet been established that can be widely disseminated to determine the intrinsic value of a specific piece of data (or specific database) within a Big Data context. Academic research, in this context, has provided little emphasis on the dimension of Data Value, especially when contrasted with investigations directed at the other three classic dimensions of Big Data, namely: Volume, Velocity, and Variety [1]. In the more specific context of financial or economic value, research is even scarcer, and available studies do not share a common view on methods for its measurement [2].

The aim of this research is to create a flexible method that can be applied to any database that becomes available to solve a specific problem, both in the academic and business environments. At this moment will center our proposal on the binary decision-making problem involving risk as explaned in section III. The exploration of this method aims to shed light on a gap in the domain of data analysis and valuation, providing a methodological structure that can be used effectively and relevantly in different contexts, regardless of the specifics inherent to the data.

Every day, new data is collected from various sources, formats, and domains. A lack of information can lead to inefficient decision-making, thus making the impacts of these decisions less predictable or riskier [3]. Given this scenario, our research questions were:

- Is it possible to develop a method to measure the financial impact (value) of new data available for a binary decicion making problem?
- Can the new information lead to more predictable and efficient decision-making?

The data monetization method proposed in this study is based on the concept of Return On Investment (ROI) [4] provided by different databases that become available for binary decision-making. In the Big Data context, this is a common and realistic scenario since new data is constantly arriving in larger volumes, with greater speed (velocity) and variety [1]. In the research phase, in the searching for suitables methods, we evaluated the application of both information theory [5] and game theory, and the final formulated method was based on the Shapley Value concept borrowed from cooperative game theory [6].

To validate our method, we have executed a series of controlled experiments applied to a real decision-making problem of underwriting car insurance policies in the Brazilian market. For our experiments, we used two databases provided by a partner company of the project, Neurotech SA (Neurotech) [7], and conducted eight (8) different experiments considering the results of each database individually and the combined databases for two (2) distinct real problems with two (2) distincts combination arrangements:

1. Claims: represents the occurrence of a covered risk during the insurance plan's validity period, and;
2. Theft: represents the occurrence of subtraction of the insured asset during the insurance plan's validity period.

The application of the proposed method was able to precisely isolate the financial value added by each of the databases used for the different decisions evaluated, and these results shed significant light on the research problem in focus.

The proposed method offers the possibility of replication in a multitude of scenarios characterized by problems of a similar nature [8]. Essentially, it is pertinent to those that constitute binary decisions, in which the assessment of the financial gain or loss of each decision, in itself, is provided by concrete information or can be duly inferred or measured. The reach of this method goes beyond its initial application, extending to various contexts that share similar characteristics.

We hope that this study can stimulate the development of other methodological approaches, whether derivations of the method proposed in this study or as new proposals themselves. We also hope that this stimulation can contribute to a more comprehensive and insightful understanding of data value in the universe of data science, when inserted into the complex environments that characterize Big Data.

This article is structured as follows: in Section 2, we explore the context that we have adopted in our study related to the topic of Big Data Monetization and detail our main objective; in Section 3, we present the data our experiments relied on; in Section 4, we discuss how to apply information and games theorie to the problem; in Section 5, we proposed the method; in Section 6, we provide details on the related experiments; in Section 7, we present the method results to the available data; in Section 8, we present the conclusion and suggest further future studies.

II. Data: a Valuable Digital Asset

In a 2016 review comprising over a thousand and five hundred studies that mentioned the term "Big Data", De Mauro et al. [9] proposed the following definition that would be able to bundle most of the assessed texts: "Big Data is the information asset characterized by such a High Volume, Velocity and Variety to require specific Technology and Analytical Methods for its transformation into Value". This definition is the one taken into consideration in our study and what makes the proposed method even more relevant, once it highlights that the explicit objective of a Big Data environment is to turn digital assets into Value.

The debate on how "value" itself was formed has been going on for millennia, since pre-Christian era, when Aristotle argued that value is based on the need for exchange (Aristotle, 350 BC) [11]. This concept is in the core of economic adjustment and is the basis to define what will be produced, how it will be produced and who will produce it.

Another key discussion in economic theory includes questioning the reasons for a product or service to be priced the way it is, that is, how the value of a product or service is determined and how to calculate it correctly [12].

The theory was formulated and applied in a world where products and services were in their entirety represented by physical assets with well-defined characteristics: raw material, finished products and services provided by physical living beings (humans and animals) [13].

The advent of computers brought the world a new category of assets, digital ones, represented in a discrete numerical way and used in digital devices with computational processing. These digital assets are capable of delivering a new category of products and services: better decisions, increased performance, competitive advantages and they can even be sold directly as a product [10]. It is in this context of "data" as a digital asset and as a product itself that we will propose a way for its monetization in this study.

Our objective in this project was to apply a strategy that can accurately estimate the value of data in a real-world situation, using concepts from information theory and game theory in conjunction with machine learning. We will center our proposal on finding value of data to the binary decision-making problem involving risk. This decision was driven by two primary reasons:

1. The operational focus of our partner company, Neurotech, which has developed and implemented thousands of solutions for binary decision problems, impacting millions of decisions made daily by its clients related to credit risk analysis, underwriting insurance policies, among other areas (retail, finance, health plans, etc.);
2. Being a class of problems well-known and researched by the academic community [14];

Although our proposal concentrates on the binary decision-making problem, most used for classification purposes, these types of solutions can be grouped into decision trees that are applicable for both multiple classifications and regression [15]. Hence, the generalization of this method can encompass both classes of problems.

A. Value Search

The price of data can depend on various premises, such as its acquisition cost, its storage and update cost, its scarcity, etc. However, as Warren Buffett remarked regarding financial assets, "Price is what you pay, value is what you get" [16]. In other words, the value of an asset is an intrinsic characteristic that differs from its price. In the case of investments, Buffet evaluates a company, for instance, based on its ability to generate future profits.

An analogy with data assets would be that their value, and not their price, depends on their ability to inform better decision-making [17], which is often directly linked to a company's operational profit. In this way, the value of data can be mapped to the quantification of this data's capacity to enhance decision-making.:

$$Value\ of\ data = V(data, decision) \tag{1}$$

It's interesting to note that the decision is part of the equation. In other words, even if the acquisition cost remains unchanged, data can have different values for different decision-making processes. Thus, it is expected that a rational agent would only purchase specific data if it were traded at a price equal to or less than its added value; for our method, this would be represented by a positive ROI upon the addition of the new data. However, quantifying this value can be a complex issue.

We evaluated information theory and game theory as potential paths for our method. We will delve deeper into these possibilities in the following sections using a subset of our experimental data, which we detail from this point forward.

III. AVALIABLE DATA SET

The data used in this study were provided by the partnering organization of this research. The company, Neurotech SA, is a leading data and analytics provider for the Brazilian market that serves over 200 major corporations, including large retailers, banks, financial institutions, and insurance companies in Brazil. We considered the initial database (*DB1*) as that containing Neurotech's proprietary and public collected data consisting of roughly 3.3 million vehicles, and their respective owners.

In our experiments, we have joined the former database (*DB1*) with a new database provided by a third-party company specialized in collecting data on automatic payments via radio-frequency identification (RFID) [18], often used in toll payments, commonly known as TAG. This database was considered to represent the new data available for the problem (*DB2*).

We investigated how the value of this new data *(DB2)* could be determined for monetization purposes, using the method detailed here. We selected an auto insurance company to test our method.

Currently, Neurotech has millions of car insurance quotes transacted monthly on its platforms that consider the initial database (*DB1*) in their analyses. In this project, we will supplement these quotes with the data from the new database to understand if this new data can assist in the risk decision-making of policy underwriting compared to decisions based solely on the original base.

For our project, a sample of 120 million transactions from *DB2* was provided. A transaction in this context means an event related to a TAG, such as passing through a particular toll. While toll usage is the most common application for a TAG, the market now allows TAG use in transactions at affiliated networks that involve not just tolls, but also use in parking lots, refueling at gas stations, and even purchases at some fast-food drive-thrus and restaurants. These 120 million transactions involve 2.2 million TAGs, roughly 2.2 million vehicles, and their respective owners.

The next step was to combine the consolidated new data (*DB2*) with the original database (*DB1*). Of the 2.2 million TAGs provided, we found similar keys (vehicle/owner) in the original base for 540,000 of these TAGs. The result leads us to an initial conclusion that approximately 25% of the TAG holders present in *DB2* sample also went through *DB1* of the partner company seeking insurance for their car.

As a result, we were able to enrich 540,000 policies from the original database *(DB1)* with the data from the new database *(DB2)*. This represented 16.5% of the partner company's original database, meaning 16.5% of the policies transacted in the original database involved individuals who had transaction data from their TAGs available for enrichment from the new database. We summarize these conclusions in the Venn diagram below.

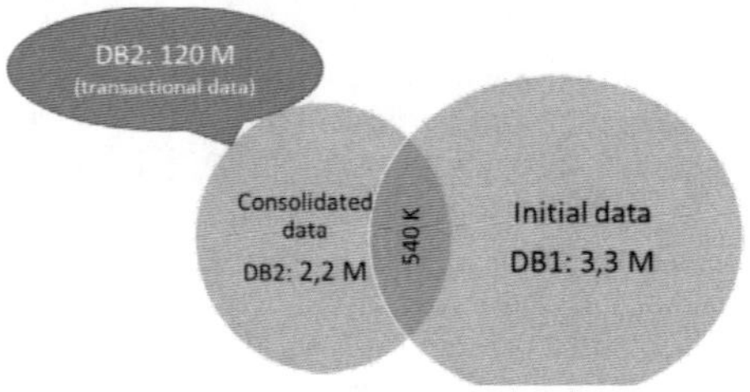

Figure 1. Data: Transformations and Enrichment.

IV. VALIDATING THE THEORIES

Our goal in this project was to apply a strategy that can accurately estimate the value of data in a real-world situation, by applying concepts from information theory and game theory in conjunction with machine learning.

A. Testing theories with a data samples

For the purpose of comparing theories and defining our strategy, we initially considered only one of the focal problems: identification of Theft or Robbery. In this example, we used a random sample from the available database consisting of 328,565 annual car insurance policies. Among them, 756 had an occurrence of a certain type of theft or robbery claim (0.23% of the cases), and 327,809 did not record the occurrence of this type of claim. The database consists of various explanatory variables that were available (or known) at the beginning of the underwriting process. The goal is to quantify the value that this information has with the aim of predicting the occurrence of the claim. For this, we will use the approach of information theory based on mutual information [5] and game theory considering the Shapley Value [6].

Consider the following variables and their respective descriptions.

TABLE I. VARIABLE DESCRIPTION

Variable	Descriptions
MEDIA_DISTANCIA_PARCEIROS	Average distance between the residential address and the nearest point of interest.
STD_VALOR_TRANSACAO	Standard deviation of the historical transactional values (in BRL) of the vehicle with partners..
QTD_NOITE	Number of vehicle transactions during the nighttime.
QTD_MADRUGADA	Number of vehicle transactions during the early morning hours.
MAIOR_DISTANCIA_PARCEIROS	Minimum distance between the residential address and the nearest point of interest.
QTD_TAGS	Number of tags registered for the vehicle in question.
QTD_TARDE	Number of vehicle transactions during the afternoon.
MIN_VALOR_TRANSACAO	Minimum among the historical transactional values (in BRL) of the vehicle with partners..
MEAN_VALOR_TRANSACAO	Average of the historical transactional values (in BRL) of the vehicle with partners.
QTD_PARCEIROS	Number of points of interest registered for the vehicle in question.

The selected variables are numerical, and depending on their value, one may observe a greater or lesser quantity of the target class (occurrence of Theft or Robbery). The dependency between each variable and the target class (Y=1) was represented in a bivariate analysis, and we will present below, for illustrative purposes, the result for the variable QTD_TAGS. The bivariate analyses for the other variables are available at the following Kaggle reference [19]. Those analysis supported the Entropy calculation when applying Information Theory.

TABLE II. FREQUENCY OF THEFT AND BURGLARY OCCURRENCES FOR THE VARIABLE QTD_TAGS

QTD_TAGS	Y=1	Y=0	Total
1.0 - 1.0	0,1%	22,9%	23%
2.0 - 3.0	0,1%	27,1%	27%
4.0 - 4.0	0,0%	12,3%	12%
5.0 - 7.0	0,0%	21,8%	22%
8.0 - 345.0	0,0%	15,6%	16%
TOTAL	0,2%	99,8%	100%
QTD_TAGS	Y=1	Y=0	Total

B. *Apply Information Theory*

Shannon's information theory is not directly applied to determine the specific value of a piece of data itself, but rather to quantify the information contained in a dataset or to understand how information is transmitted and processed. However, information theory can be used to address prediction and probability problems, and thus we will test an approach considering Shannon's information theory. Consider the Shannon entropy of a given information X [5],

$$H(X) = -\sum_i \quad p(x_i)\, log_2\, p(x_i) \qquad (2)$$

Where:

- $H(X)$ is the entropy of the information source X
- $p(x_i)$ is the probability of occurrence of the symbol xi na fonte de informação.
- The logarithm is in base 2, which measures information in bits.

Note that this magnitude depends solely on the given data X in question, but it does not depend on the decision for which the data X will be used. For this reason, it does not meet our value criteria in (1) and therefore would not be applicable to our method. One possible way to incorporate information theory into our method, to quantify the impact that a data point X has on a decision Y, would be to measure the mutual information:

$$I(X;Y) = -\sum_i \quad p(x_i,y_i)\, log_2\, [p(x_i,y_i)/p(x_i)q(y_i)], \qquad (3)$$

Where:

- $I(X;Y)$ is the mutual information between sources X and Y.
- $p(x_i,y_i)$ is the joint probability of xi and yj occurring in sources X and Y, respectively.
- p(xi) and q(yi) are the marginal probabilities of X and Y, respectively.
- Y is the target, we would like to predict.

In a binary decision problem, Y would be 0 or 1, suggesting two possible events (or decisions). Meanwhile, p(x,y) represents the probability of observing the data X=x and the target Y=y simultaneously, while p(x) and q(y) are the probabilities of observing X=x and Y=y, respectively. Intuitively, mutual information is the gain in information we have regarding the decision Y, given that X is known. In terms of entropy, it can be written as:

$$I(X;Y) = H(Y) - H(Y|X), \qquad (4)$$

Where H(Y|X) is the conditional entropy.

$$H(Y|X) = -\sum_i \quad p(x_i,y_i)\, log_2\, [p(x_i)/p(x_i,y_i)], \qquad (5)$$

Where:

- $H(Y|X)$ is the conditional entropy of Y given X
- $p(x_i,y_i)$ is the joint probability of xi and yi occurring in sources X and Y, respectively.

Note that, if X and Y are independent, we have $p(x_i,y_i) = p(x_i)q(y_i)$, which would result in *H*(*Y*|*X*)=*H*(*Y*) and (*X*;*Y*)=0. That is, the information gain is null when knowing data X, since the decision Y does not depend on this data. In this specific case, it's expected that the data holds no value for this decision-making process. Alternatively, if X truly provides some information gain regarding the decision Y, we should have *I*(*X*;*Y*)>0, and the value of the information X can be given by:

$$Valor(X) = V(I(X;Y)). \qquad (6)$$

In summary, the value of data X depends on the decision Y through the information gain (or mutual information). For the value to be consistent, the function V(.) must be increasing and V(0)=0. In the following example, we will quantify the value of data X for the binary event Y that indicates the occurrence (Y=1) or non-occurrence (Y=0) of a claim on a car insurance policy over a one-year validity period, as per the bivariate analysis shown in Table II and others available on Kaggle [19] for the variables presented in Table III.

TABLE III. APPLYING ENTROPY DEFINITION, CONDITIONAL ENTROPY AND MUTUAL INFORMATION

Variable	H(X)	H(Y)	H(Y|X)	I(X;Y)
MEDIA_DISTANCIA_PARCEIROS	2,3212402	0,0234799	0,0234632	1,68E-05
STD_VALOR_TRANSACAO	2,3329737	0,0234799	0,0234459	3,40E-05
QTD_NOITE	2,3204087	0,0234799	0,0234735	6,50E-06
QTD_MADRUGADA	2,2215431	0,0234799	0,0234482	3,17E-05
MAIOR_DISTANCIA_PARCEIROS	2,3212402	0,0234799	0,0234564	2,36E-05
QTD_TAGS	2,2686251	0,0234799	0,0234591	2,08E-05
QTD_TARDE	2,3215146	0,0234799	0,0234591	2,08E-05
MIN_VALOR_TRANSACAO	1,6651711	0,0234799	0,0234486	3,14E-05
MEAN_VALOR_TRANSACAO	2,3329732	0,0234799	0,0234725	7,40E-06
QTD_PARCEIROS	2,3135011	0,0234799	0,023463	1,70E-05

One way to assess the value of the data from the Table III is as follows. Since a value function V(.) is increasing, it is expected, for instance, that the variable X1=MIN_VALOR_TRANSACAO holds more value for the business in question (which involves the decision Y) than the variable X2=QTD_NOITE, as I(X1;Y)=3.14E-05 > I(X2;Y)=6.50E-06. However, note that X1 has a lower entropy than X2, with H(X1)=1.665 and H(X2)=2.32. This result demonstrates that having higher entropy, and therefore more information, is not always synonymous with a better decision, as what matters in reality for our method is the mutual information I(X;Y) that data X1 and X2 have concerning decision Y. Thus, information theory does not determine specific data values but helps quantify the uncertainty or information contained in probabilistic events. To determine the specific value of data, we need to consider other methods, depending on the context and the data involved.

C. Game Theory in Action

The same variables from the previous section were assessed based on their SHAP values [20]. SHAP (SHapley Additive exPlanations) values are a model interpretability technique that quantifies the relative impact of individual features on the output of a machine learning model [21]. Within the realm of binary classification tasks, SHAP values are employed to discern the proportional contribution of each feature to a model's prediction.

This method becomes particularly valuable when dealing with highly complex models, such as Random Forests or Deep Neural Networks [22], where the functional relationship between the input features and the model's output can be highly non-linear and intertwined. SHAP values, grounded in cooperative game theory, provide a solution to the problem of fairly distributing "rewards" (in this context, the contribution to the model's prediction) to each "player" (feature).

Such distribution considers both the marginal contribution of each feature as well as all potential synergistic interactions among them. For this analysis, the variables were used to train an XGBoost binary classification model aiming to predict the target class (Y=1). Subsequently, the average absolute SHAP value of each feature was calculated and represented in Table IV.

TABLE IV. SHARP VALUE FOR EACH VARIABLE USED IN THE MODEL

Variável	mean(SHAP value)
MEDIA_DISTANCIA_PARCEIROS	0.09022027
STD_VALOR_TRANSACAO	0.07902433
QTD_NOITE	0.05610221
QTD_MADRUGADA	0.05555103
MAIOR_DISTANCIA_PARCEIROS	0.04823394
QTD_TAGS	0.04670959
QTD_TARDE	0.04214765
MIN_VALOR_TRANSACAO	0.02885941
MEAN_VALOR_TRANSACAO	0.0260881
QTD_PARCEIROS	0.0217269

In Table IV, the variable STD_VALOR_TRANSACAO had an absolute average SHAP value of 0.079 and ranks second among the variables, despite the same variable having shown the highest mutual information with the target class in the table from the previous section (Information Theory). Such behavior is expected since different methods were used, and although they quantify the variable's impact on the decision in some way, they won't necessarily agree on the importance of the variables and, consequently, the value of the data. Even considering the different methods, it's interesting that there's an agreement between them that STD_VALOR_TRANSACAO is a significant variable. Fig. 2 shows the relevance of each variable in the final constructed model.

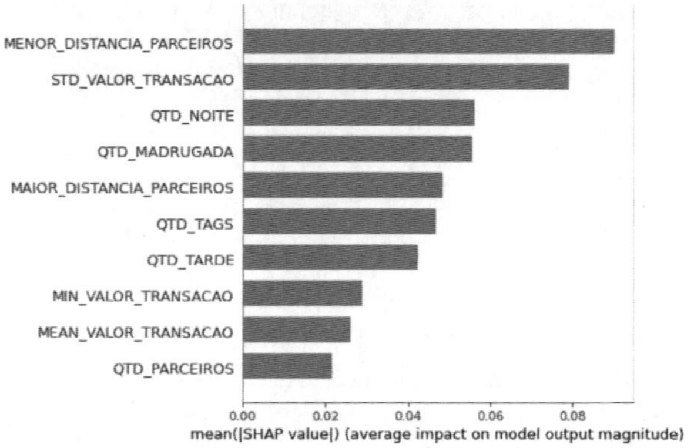

Figure 2. Variable importance according to Shapley Value.

D. Theory Selection

While we validated the potential use of both theories in the last two sessions, it became evident that we would face a much greater generalization challenge with Information Theory compared to Game Theory when applied to real-world problems.

In the case of the analysis presented based on the entropy formula and the mutual information of Information Theory, we simplified our problem to a bivariate analysis for each of the available attributes in a selected small sample. We would face a significant challenge in generalizing our method using this theory as the number of attributes or, equivalently, the number of databases to be combined and jointly evaluated increased.

When analyzing the Shapley Value (SHAP) calculation method from game theory, we discerned an objective very similar to what our method aims for. Analogously to SHAP, our method seeks to provide a solution to the problem of fairly distributing Monetary Value based on the contribution of each of the databases used for decision-making. To reach this conclusion, the financial gains obtained from decisions considering all possible combinations between the databases, both in isolation and combined, must be evaluated, precisely as proposed by the method based on game theory. By doing so, we will determine how the gains should be distributed. In our case, each "player" (resource) would be one of these available databases.

Such distribution considers both the marginal contribution of each resource and all possible synergistic interactions between them, and it's precisely for this reason that from this point forward, we'll be developing our method using Game Theory as the foundation.

V. THE METHOS BASED ON ROI

The data monetization method resulting from this study employs the concept of ROI added by a new database that becomes available for a binary decision-making when applied to a decision through a decision score (decision model) [23].

This is an anticipated scenario in the Big Data context as new data are continuously emerging.

ROI is a widely used financial indicator to assess the effectiveness and profitability of an investment. It compares the net gain achieved against the initial investment cost. Calculated as the difference between the net gain and the investment cost, divided by the investment cost, it's expressed as a percentage. ROI offers insights into an investment's efficiency, allowing organizations to evaluate the value produced relative to the invested resources [4].

We will illustrate the method using our experiment related to the decision-making process of analising insurance policies, in the underwriting process of a given quote. Specifically, car insurance underwriting may use data and/or an individual predictive score to determine whether an individual will be granted insurance (underwriting) or will be denied access following the quote process. An individual might be rejected, for instance, if there's any indication of potential fraud or risky behavior the insurer does not want to price.

In this case, the policy price is not shown, and the individual is said to have been declined during underwriting. Typically, this process does not reject a significant portion of the quotes. Underwriting rules tend to decline between 1% to 10% of the quotes, and this can vary among regions and profiles.

This process is beneficial for estimating data value since the operational outcome with an underwriting rule can be gauged on a historical policy base (backtest). This outcome is calculated based on the issued premium (in currency), which corresponds to the amount the insured pays to the insurer to access the insurance, and the observed indemnity during the policy period, which is the amount the insured received in the event of a claim. The insurer's operational gain equates to the difference between the premiums received from the insured (net of brokerage commission) and the compensations paid out resulting from occurred claims (indemnities).

$$Result_0 = \sum_{i=1}^{N} Premium(i)\big(1 - \%Commission(i)\big) - Indemnity(i), \quad (7)$$

Where:

- $Result_0$ is the insurer operational Gain.
- $Premium(i)$ is the amount payed by insured i.
- $\%Commission(i)$ is the percentage commission payed by the insurer to the brokerage of the insured i.
- $Indemnity(i)$ is compensations paid out by the insurer resulting from occurred claims of insured i policy

A good underwriting rule can reject some of these policies that, in general, would have resulted in a loss. In this way, a new operational gain can be calculated without them, considering only the policies that have a risk score above a given cutoff point. This rule can be written as follows:

$$Result_1 = \sum_{i=1}^{N} \theta(Score(i) - cutoff\_point) [Premium(i)(1 - \%Commission(i)) - Indemnity(i)], \quad (8)$$

Where:

- θ(x) is the Heaviside step function [24].
- $Score(i)$ is is insurer i risk score.
- $cutoff\_point$ is minimum score for acceptance.
- The remaining itens are the same in (7).

Finally, the gain with an underwriting rule can be written as the difference between the results above (with and without the rule).

From this point on, we will build the artificial intelligence solutions (models) that will transform the raw data into the scores that will be used in the decision-making for the different scenarios of our experiment.

The models will transform the data into different scores according to the databases used (DB1, DB2, or both) and with the problem being addressed (target objective of the modeling). Table V summarizes all the models that were built in this research. At the end of each of the experiments, we apply (8), and the results are presented in section VIII.

VI. EXPERIMENTS

We conducted controlled experiments applied to real databases in a laboratory setting. The initial application assesses the ability to highlight the gain in understanding the risk of a new insurance quote when considering all the different scenarios including both available databases (DB1 and DB2) and how this gain can be measured in terms of ROI. We have used all the available data in our experiments, i.e., all the 540 thousands records (Fig. 1) where used for the modeling phase.

The experiments were repeated for different strategic decision-making, within the same domain (risk decision), allowing us to learn from the process and develop a generalizable method by the end of the study.

A. Model Construction (Risk Scores)

After the data was collected and processed, we moved on to the modeling phase, also known as knowledge discovery [25]. At this juncture, the data mining process begins. Algorithms will automatically sift through the data, trying to create the best possible representation of this data through scores. We split the dataset into two samples: one used for model training, with 75% of the available data, and the other for testing the model, where we assessed the performance of the built solutions, with the remaining 25%. For training, older insurance policies were used, while the newer ones were set aside for model testing.

With the datasets prepared, we could conduct experiments combining all possible scenarios. We had two databases (DB1 and DB2), two possible targets/objectives (claims and theft/robbery), and we also selected two different approaches to combine the resulting models: Stacking and linear combination.

All these possibilities resulted in eight different experiments as presented in Table V below.

TABLE V. 8 (EITGH) EXPERIMENTS

#Experiment	Description
1	DB2 x theft/robbery
2	DB2 x claims
3	DB1 x theft/robbery
4	DB1 x claims
5	Stacking x theft/robbery
6	Stacking x claims
7	Combinação Linear x theft/robbery
8	Combinação Linear x claims

B. The Choosen Technics

We chose two Machine Learning (ML) techniques to be applied in the model building for our project: Multilayer Perceptron (MLP) and eXtreme Gradient Boosting (XGBoost). The former was selected as it's a more traditional and widely used technique with a known performance track record for various problems. XGBoost has gained prominence in recent years for outperforming various ML algorithms [26]. For each of these techniques, different hyperparameter combinations were tested (For MLP: number of layers, number of neurons in each layer, etc. For XGBoost: depth, learning rate, lambda, etc.).

Each constructed model resulted in a risk scoring system (risk score) with the score indicating the risk level of that policy (claims or theft/robbery). A lower score indicates higher risk, while a higher score signifies lesser risk. After each model was built, to standardize our analyses, we divided the scored population into a uniform distribution with 10 bands (10 deciles), with the first decile (decile 1) representing the top 10% at highest risk, and the last decile (decile 10) representing the 10% at lowest risk.

We consider the model construction as a preliminary and necessary stage for our method and therefore will not delve deep into the details of each of the eight experiments. We will only detail the results of the third experiment here since it has the highest KS [27] among all (see summarized results in Table II).

C. Models Results

In the chart shown in Fig. 3 below, the average percentage of Theft/Robbery is depicted by the dashed line (0.45%). The chart displays the results of the model application to the test set of the third experiment conducted. The results for the other experiments can be found at the following Kaggle link [19]. The frequency of theft or robbery is represented by the red curve. We observed that the percentage of theft or robbery in the first score band (decile 1) is 283% (1.69% in the band) higher than the overall theft or robbery frequency of the base. In the last band (decile 10), this percentage is 91% lower (0.04% in the band).

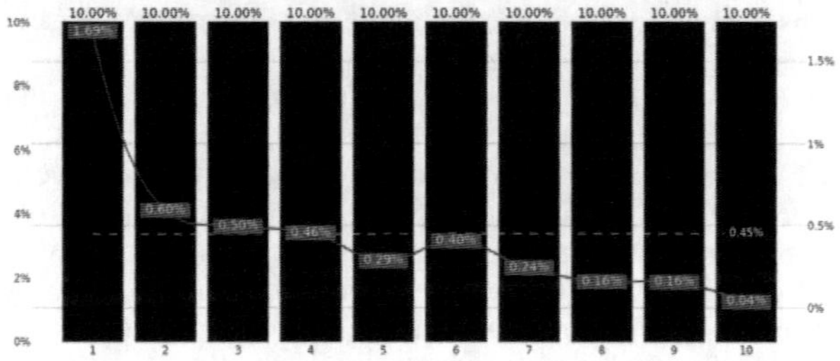

Figure 3. Histogram and risk curve by decile for the experiment 3.

The KS for this model was 33.4%, meaning we cannot assume the null hypothesis [28], and the model can distinguish the policies that will result in theft or robery from those that will not. We present in Table VI the results for the 8 (eight) experiments conducted:

TABLE VI. SUMMARY OF TECHNICAL RESULTS OF SOLUTIONS CONSIDERING THE ISOLATED AND COMBINED DATABATES

Model Database	Theft / Robery	Claims
DB2	28	4.2
DB1	33.4	5
Stacking Comb	33	5.6
Linear Comb	33	6.5

D. Experiment Conclusion

When evaluated individually, the solutions developed using the original database have a technically superior performance compared to those developed with the new database provided for both defined objectives. This was expected since the original database was developed and adjusted for this application by the partner company. The results from combining the databases were vastly different for the different objectives.

For the goal of predicting theft or robbery, none of the combinations achieved a technical result superior to the solution developed exclusively with the original database. We will investigate further to determine whether it's still possible to compute an added economic value to the addition of these new data using the proposed ROI method.

For the goal of predicting claims, both combinations achieved technically superior results to solutions developed with each of the databases exclusively. We will further investigate if this superior technical result can also be estimated in terms of ROI.

VII. RESULTS

To reach a conclusion about our method, we applied (8) to the 8 (eight) solutions developed during the experimental phase, considering a real database from a major Brazilian insurance company.

We are using a sample with R$ 100 million (one hundred million reais) in issued premium in the original portfolio (before the underwriting rule) and a 60.3% claims rate. We also considered an 18.2% commission. All these parameters were extracted from Table VII, which presents the comparison disclosed by SUSEP (Superintendency of Private Insurance) concerning the operational performance among all car insurance companies for the year 2023.

We used the parameters related to the month of April from this table in (8). Although the report provides data for each insurance company individually, we refrained from using the parameters of the insurance company under study due to confidentiality reasons.

TABLE VII. PUBLISHED DATA ABOUT OPERACIONAL RESULTS OF INSURANCE COMPANIES

Ranking do Seguro de Automóvel - Dados SUSEP SES Ramos (20, 25, 26, 31, 42, 44, 53)											
Rank	Grupo seguradoras	Janeiro a Abril									
		Prêmio Emitido		Evol	Share	Sinistralidade (S/P)			Comissão		
		2022	2023	23/22	2023	2022	2023	Dif pp	2022	2023	Dif pp
1	**Grupo Porto Seguro**	3.862.088	4.727.351	22,4%	27,2%	65,6%	58,7%	-6,8	22,3%	20,3%	-2,1
	+ Porto Seguro	2.550.669	3.209.031	25,8%	18,5%	61,2%	57,7%	-3,5	22,7%	20,7%	-1,9
	+ Azul Seguros	1.311.419	1.518.320	15,8%	8,7%	74,0%	61,0%	13,0	21,7%	19,3%	2,4
2	**Grupo HDI**	2.671.751	3.426.472	28,2%	19,7%	77,9%	57,0%	-20,9	20,4%	18,8%	-1,6
	+ HDI	967.262	1.218.194	25,9%	7,0%	83,2%	61,8%	-21,4	19,5%	17,3%	-2,2
	+ Santander Auto	36.894	66.519	80,3%	0,4%	29,4%	27,4%	-2,0	22,0%	22,0%	0,0
	+ Sompo	414.790	325.996	-21,4%	1,9%	82,2%	67,8%	14,4	21,0%	19,0%	-2,0
	+ Liberty	1.239.424	1.800.548	45,3%	10,4%	73,9%	52,9%	-21,0	20,7%	19,5%	-1,1
	+ Indiana	13.380	15.215	13,7%	0,1%	55,0%	51,7%	-3,3	33,9%	34,2%	0,2
3	**Tokio Marine**	1.794.876	2.375.724	32,4%	13,7%	72,4%	54,5%	17,9	21,2%	19,0%	-2,1
4	**Bradesco**	1.693.879	2.116.061	24,9%	12,2%	70,8%	58,8%	-12,0	16,3%	14,8%	-1,5
5	**Grupo Allianz**	1.855.147	2.019.188	8,8%	11,6%	85,6%	69,8%	-15,8	19,5%	17,2%	-2,3
6	**Mapfre**	1.139.785	1.179.671	3,5%	6,8%	78,9%	63,5%	-15,4	19,7%	20,5%	0,8
7	**Suhai**	261.670	393.607	50,4%	2,3%	67,4%	68,7%	1,3	24,1%	21,0%	-3,1
8	**Zurich**	327.234	352.462	7,7%	2,0%	81,6%	66,3%	-15,3	19,0%	19,3%	0,4
9	**Alfa**	184.185	130.194	-29,3%	0,7%	79,1%	75,7%	-3,4	18,1%	16,6%	-1,5
10	**Sura**	92.056	112.013	21,7%	0,6%	91,5%	67,6%	-23,9	18,6%	16,4%	-2,1
11	**Grupo Caixa**	140.151	106.012	-24,4%	0,6%	77,6%	61,3%	-16,2	11,8%	12,4%	0,6
12	**Gente**	65.681	82.827	26,1%	0,5%	86,3%	71,8%	-14,5	13,3%	11,7%	-1,6
13	**Mitsui**	93.470	69.065	-26,1%	0,4%	86,3%	61,7%	-24,6	22,9%	18,9%	-4,0
	Total Mercado	14.288.934	17.374.879	21,6%	98,4%	74,1%	60,3%	14,1	20,3%	18,6%	1,7

Fonte: Susep

-	**Sancor**	22.715	22.979	1,2%	0,1%	94,4%	66,2%	-28,2	17,1%	18,2%	1,0

The two available databases (DB1 and DB2) on individuals were used to create separate underwriting rules. Subsequently, two new rules were created from the combination of the two databases using the different combination methods as explained in the section on Experiments. The operational gains from the four situations, extracted through backtesting, are listed in tables VIII and IX below. For this, an optimization of the cut-off point was considered, which would result in a refusal of 10% of the policies applying (8).

A. Calculating ROI for Each Scenario

To arrive at these results, we applied (8) for calculating the financial return for all the scenarios simulated in our experiment according to Lifts (applying an approval cut-off point at the 10th percentile) and their respective gains (ROI) presented in Tables VIII and IX.

TABLE VIII. RESULTS FOR THE THEFT AND ROBERY TARGET.

Modelo	Lift	Gain
DB2 isolated	170%	R$ 5.137.858,00
DB1 isolated	283%	R$ 10.711.628,20
Stacking Comb.	293%	R$ 11.204.882,20
Linear Comb.	296%	R$ 11.352.858,40

TABLE IX. RESULTS FOR THE CLAIM TARGET.

Model	Lift	Gain
DB2 isolated	19%	-R$ 2.310.277,40
DB1 isolated	40%	-R$ 1.274.444,00
Stacking Comb	33%	-R$ 1.619.721,80
Linear Comb	50%	-R$ 781.190,00

From the calculation of the result for all possible combinations, we can apply the Shapley Value to isolate the contributions of each of the databases to the final combined result.

B. Calculating the Data Value

Finally, by applying the values shown in Tables VIII and IX and using the SHAP formula, we can come to an exact conclusion about the value of each data for each of the selected problems and for each of the combinations made.

Just to recap, the formula for the data value we want to solve is presented below (as detailed in section II.A:

$$Value\ of\ data = V(data, decision)$$

As defined in our method, we will use the SHAP value to determine how much each of the Databases used contributes to the final value of the coalition (combination of the two databases). Recalling the Shapley Value formula that will be used in this calculation is presented below:

$$vi = \sum_{(S \subseteq N \setminus \{i\})} \frac{|S|!\,(|N| - |s| - 1)!}{|N|!} * (v(S \cup \{i\}) - v(S)),$$

Where:

- N is a players set.
- is a coalition that does not include player i.
- v(S) is the coalition value S.
- v(S∪{i}) is the coalition that includes player i.

From now on we present the computation of the value of the both datbases calculated according to our method for each of the databases in each of the combinations carried out in our experiments.

1) Value of DB1 and DB2 for Theft and Robery Using Stacking

Table X shows all possible coalitions and their respective ROIs for the Theft and Robery problem using Stacking as a technique to combine DB1 and DB2 in their coalition.

TABLE X. RESULTS FOR THE THEFT TARGET WITH STACKING.

Coalisões	ROI
C({Ø})	R$ 0,00
C({DB1})	R$ 10.711.628,20
C({DB2})	R$ 5.137.858,00
C({DB1,DB2})	R$ 11.204.882,20

We can interpret the Result as follows: The coalition (combination) of the two databases yields a Result greater than any other coalition that has only one of the two databases.

By applying the SHAP formula, we arrive at the following division of Gains between DB1 and DB2:

TABLE XI. DATA VALUE OF DB1 AND DB2 FOR THEFT USING STACKING.

Player	Result (SHAP)
DB1	R$ 8.389.326,20
DB2	R$ 2.815.556,00

As we can see from Table XI, although the coalition with the two databases yields a higher result for the decision being made, the result for each of the databases is less than the ROI of each one individually. This outcome is expected because the new data added for decision-making is unlikely to be entirely independent of the data previously available. These characteristics and discussions regarding the results are also applicable to the other experiments, so we will present the results in a summarized form for the remaining experiments.

2) Value of DB1 and DB2 for Theft and Robery Using Linear Combination

TABLE XII. RESULTS FOR THE THEFT TARGET WITH LINEAR COMBINATION

Coalision	ROI
C({Ø})	R$ 0,00
C({DB1})	R$ 10.711.628,20
C({DB2})	R$ 5.137.858,00
C({DB1,DB2})	R$ 11.352.858,40

Applying SHAP formula, it possible to get to these gains between DB1 and DB2:

TABLE XIII. DATA VALUE FROM DB1 AND DB2, USING LINEAR COMBINATION

Player	Result (SHAP)
DB1	R$ 8.463.314,30
DB2	R$ 2.889.544,10

3) Value of DB1 and DB2 for Claims Using Stacking.

TABLE XIV. RESULTS FOR THE CLAIM WITH STACKING

Coalision	ROI
C({Ø})	R$ 0,00
C({DB1})	-R$ 1.274.444,00
C({DB2})	-R$ 2.310.277,40
C({DB1,DB2})	-R$ 1.619.721,80

Applying SHAP formula it is possible to get the following division between DB1 e DB2:

TABLE XV. VALUE OF DATA DB1 AND DB2 FOR CLAIMS USING STACKING.

Player	Result(SHAP)
DB1	-R$ 291.944,20
DB2	-R$ 1.327.777,60

4) Value of DB1 and DB2 for Claims Using Linear Combination.

TABLE XVI. RESULTS FOR CLAIMS USING LINEAR COMBINATION.

Coalision	ROI
C({Ø})	R$ 0,00
C({DB1})	-R$ 1.274.444,00
C({DB2})	-R$ 2.310.277,40
C({DB1,DB2})	-R$ 781.190,00

Applying the sharp method it was possible to calculate the following gaing between bases DB1 and DB2:

TABLE XVII. DATA VALUE OF DB1 AND DB2 FOR CLAIMS USING LINEAR COMBINATION.

Player	Result (SHAP)
DB1	R$ 127.321,70
DB2	-R$ 908.511,70

From the calculated data values from DB1 and DB2 for all the different combined experiments (Tables XI, XIII, XV and XVII) it became clear that a database value would depend cleary on the problem and the decision we are puirsuiting. We found situations where both data brought value do the decision (Tables XI, XIII), cases where none of the databases where able to add value do the decision (Tables XV) and situation where only one of then brought additional value (Table XVII).

VIII. CONCLUSIONS AND FUTURE WORK

In conclusion, this study addresses a significant gap in the field of data monetization, proposing a method that provides a systematic and adaptable approach to assess the value of data across various databases and problem domains. While data monetization has garnered substantial attention, the absence of widely applicable methods in academic literature has hampered the realization of its full potential [2]. By integrating information theory, game theory, and the ROI metric, this research introduces a new method rooted in the Shapley Value concept from cooperative game theory.

The successful application of the method to the real-world decision-making problem of underwriting car insurance policies in the Brazilian market exemplifies its efficacy in precisely quantifying the financial contribution of individual datasets to binary decision outcomes. By isolating the added ROI generated by each data set, this approach offers a comprehensive perspective on data's value in decision-making processes. Notably, the versatility of the proposed method extends to analogous scenarios featuring binary decisions with measurable financial implications.

Venturing into this emerging research domain, we anticipate this study will serve as a catalyst for the development of future methodologies. These methodologies might build on the foundations laid out in this work or introduce innovative frameworks further illuminating the multifaceted value of data in the dynamic landscape of data science in Big Data environments. As organizations continue to recognize data's strategic importance, the proposed method presents a promising avenue for maximizing the benefits derived from data monetization efforts.

Despite its contributions, the proposed method is not without limitations. Firstly, its application is confined to binary decision problems where financial gains and losses can be explicitly quantified. This constraint may hinder its direct applicability to scenarios with more complex decision structures or non-monetary objectives. Additionally, the method relies on the availability of accurate and reliable data to compute ROI, making it susceptible to inaccuracies stemming from data quality issues.

Moreover, while the Shapley Value provides a fair value attribution in cooperative games, its implementation may demand computational resources that could become burdensome for exceptionally large datasets or high-dimensional decision spaces [29].

Regarding future research directions, several paths merit exploration. A fundamental area is extending the proposed method to accommodate more complex decision structures, potentially involving multiple parties or sequential decisions. This could entail adapting concepts from cooperative game theory to capture such scenarios' dynamics.

Furthermore, as the data monetization field continues to evolve, exploring alternative value metrics beyond ROI could offer a more comprehensive understanding of data's value. This could involve incorporating qualitative factors, long-term strategic impact, or even societal implications.

Additional investigations into methods for dealing with noisy or incomplete data might enhance the proposed approach's robustness. Exploring machine learning techniques, data preprocessing, and statistical analysis could help mitigate data quality issues' impact.

Lastly, a broader application of the method across various sectors and contexts would provide empirical evidence of its versatility and limitations. Comparative studies involving different decision problems and data sets could shed light on the proposed approach's generalization and efficacy in diverse settings.

In conclusion, while the current method offers a valuable contribution to evaluating data's value in binary decision scenarios, it's imperative that future research overcome its limitations and broaden its scope to address the complexities of real-world decision-making environments. By embracing these challenges and pursuing innovative directions, researchers can propel the advancement of data monetization methodologies and pave the way for more informed, data-driven decisions in an increasingly data-rich world.

REFERENCES

[1] ORACLE, "What Is Big Data? Big Data Definition -," Jul. 11, 2020. https://www.oracle.com/br/big-data/what-is-big-data.html (accessed Jul. 11, 2020).

[2] D. Monteiro, L. Monteiro, F. Ferraz, and S. Meira, "Big Data Monetization: Discoveries from a Systematic Literature Review," Oct. 2020.

[3] A. McAfee and E. Brynjolfsson, "Big Data: The Management Revolution," *Harv. Bus. Rev.*, 2012.

[4] R. S. Kaplan and D. P. Norton, "The Balanced Scorecard—Measures that Drive Performance," *Harvard Business Review*, Jan. 01, 1992. Accessed: Aug. 31, 2023. [Online]. Available: https://hbr.org/1992/01/the-balanced-scorecard-measures-that-drive-performance-2

[5] C. E. Shannon, "A Mathematical Theory of Communication," p. 55, Jan. 1948.

[6] L. S. Shapley, "A value for n-person games," in *Contributions to the Theory of Games*, Princeton University Press, 1953, pp. 307–317.

[7] Neurotech SA, "Neurotech SA." [Online]. Available: https://www.neurotech.com.br/

[8] D. S. Johnson, "The NP-completeness column: An ongoing guide," *J. Algorithms*, vol. 11, no. 4, pp. 434–451, 1990.

[9] A. De Mauro, M. Greco, and M. Grimaldi, "A formal definition of Big Data based on its essential features," *Libr. Rev.*, vol. 65, no. 3, pp. 122–135, 2016, doi: 10.1108/LR-06-2015-0061.

[10] K. Ruan, "Digital Assets as Economic Goods," in *Digital Asset Valuation and Cyber Risk Management*, K. Ruan, Ed., Academic Press, 2019, pp. 1–28. doi: 10.1016/b978-0-12-812158-0.00001-6.

[11] Aristotle, *Nicomachean Ethics*. Publisher Not Specified, 350AD.

[12] A. Smith, *An Inquiry into the Nature and Causes of the Wealth of Nations*. Publisher Not Specified, 1776.

[13] K. Marx, *Das Kapital*. Publisher Not Specified, 1867.

[14] M. R. Garey and D. S. Johnson, *Computers and Intractability: A Guide to the Theory of NP-Completeness*. W. H. Freeman, 1979.

[15] L. Breiman, J. H. Friedman, R. A. Olshen, and C. J. Stone, *Classification and Regression Trees*. CRC Press, 1984.

[16] W. E. Buffett and L. A. Cunningham, *The Essays of Warren Buffett: Lessons for Corporate America*. Cunningham Group, 2013.

[17] F. Provost and T. Fawcett, *Data Science for Business: What you need to know about data mining and data-analytic thinking*. O'Reilly Media, 2013.

[18] R. Journal, "What is RFID?" 2023. [Online]. Available: https://www.rfidjournal.com/what-is-rfid

[19] "Data Monetization - Auto Isurance data." https://www.kaggle.com/datasets/domingosmonteiro/auto-insure-data (accessed Sep. 05, 2023).

[20] S. Lundberg and S.-I. Lee, "A Unified Approach to Interpreting Model Predictions," in *Proceedings of the 31st International Conference on Neural Information Processing Systems*, 2017.

[21] J. Li, B. Shao, J. Xu, H. Li, and Q. Wang, "A big data based product ranking solution," in *2016 IEEE International Conference on Service Operations and Logistics, and Informatics (SOLI)*, Jul. 2016, pp. 190–194. doi: 10.1109/SOLI.2016.7551685.

[22] K. He, X. Zhang, S. Ren, and J. Sun, "Deep Residual Learning for Image Recognition," in *Proceedings of the IEEE Conference on Computer Vision and Pattern Recognition (CVPR)*, 2016.

[23] S. Lohiya, *Decision Trees for Decision Making*. Springer, 2018.

[24] E. Kreyszig, "Advanced Engineering Mathematics, 10th Edition | Wiley," *Wiley.com*, 2010. https://www.wiley.com/en-us/Advanced+Engineering+Mathematics%2C+10th+Edition-p-9781119455929 (accessed Aug. 31, 2023).

[25] G. Piatetsky-Shapiro, *Knowledge Discovery in Databases*. AAAI/MIT Press, 1991.

[26] Q. Tang, G. Xia, X. Zhang, and F. Long, "A Customer Churn Prediction Model Based on XGBoost and MLP," in *2020 International Conference on Computer Engineering and Application (ICCEA)*, Guangzhou, China: IEEE, Mar. 2020, pp. 608–612. doi: 10.1109/ICCEA50009.2020.00133.

[27] J. Berkson, "A Note on the Kolmogorov-Smirnov Test," *J. Am. Stat. Assoc.*, vol. 40, no. 230, pp. 269–272, 1945.

[28] D. S. Moore, G. P. McCabe, and B. A. Craig, *Introduction to the Practice of Statistics*. W. H. Freeman, 2017.
[29] W. S. Jewell and C. H. Owen, *Cooperative Game Theory and Applications*. Oxford University Press, 1999.

Combining Retrieval and Classification: Balancing Efficiency and Accuracy in Duplicate Bug Report Detection

1st Qianru Meng
LIACS
Leiden University
Leiden, Netherlands
mengqr@vuw.leidenuniv.nl

2nd Xiao Zhang
CLCG
University of Groningen
Groningen, Netherlands
xiao.zhang@rug.nl

3rd Guus Ramackers
LIACS
Leiden University
Leiden, Netherlands
g.j.ramackers@liacs.leidenuniv.nl

4th Visser Joost
LIACS
Leiden University
Leiden, Netherlands
j.m.w.visser@liacs.leidenuniv.nl

***Abstract*—In the realm of Duplicate Bug Report Detection (DBRD), conventional methods primarily focus on statically analyzing bug databases, often disregarding the running time of the model. In this context, complex models, despite their high accuracy potential, can be time-consuming, while more efficient models may compromise on accuracy. To address this issue, we propose a transformer-based system designed to strike a balance between time efficiency and accuracy performance. The existing methods primarily address it as either a retrieval or classification task. However, our hybrid approach leverages the strengths of both models. By utilizing the retrieval model, we can perform initial sorting to reduce the candidate set, while the classification model allows for more precise and accurate classification. In our assessment of commonly used models for retrieval and classification tasks, sentence BERT and RoBERTa outperform other baseline models in retrieval and classification, respectively. To provide a comprehensive evaluation of performance and efficiency, we conduct rigorous experimentation on five public datasets. The results reveal that our system maintains accuracy comparable to a classification model, significantly outperforming it in time efficiency and only slightly behind a retrieval model in time, thereby achieving an effective trade-off between accuracy and efficiency.**

Keywords-Duplicate Bug Detection; Deep Learning; Natural Language Processing; Transformer; Running Time; Accuracy.

I. INTRODUCTION

Bug reports are crucial in the software development and maintenance phase, providing valuable information to software developers [1][2]. It commonly comprises structured text (e.g., timestamp, version, component, and bug status) and unstructured text, such as title and description [3]. Typically, bugs are recorded in the Bug Database (also known as Bug Tracking System) by developers, testers and users [3][4][5]. Unfortunately, the inconsistent understanding of bug descriptions by different writers leads to the continuous generation of numerous duplicate bug reports [6], which increases maintenance costs. Consequently, significant research efforts have been devoted to detecting duplicate bugs, aiming to reduce redundant work involving the testing of bugs that have already been resolved [5][7][8], thereby enhancing the efficiency of the bug fixing process [9].

DBRD task can be defined as: the automatic process of identifying and comparing the semantic content in bug reports to discover new reports that are duplicate or highly similar to existing reports. As shown in Table I, there are two instances

TABLE I: COMPARISON OF DUPLICATE BUG REPORTS FROM ECLIPSE

Bug_id	178
Title	Maintain sync view expansion state when switching modes
Description	It would be nice if when things got filtered out, their expansion would be remembered, so that when the item is revealed again it has the correct expansion. For example, if you have one outgoing change; switch to the catchup pane and then come back, the tree is completely collapsed.
Bug_id	226
Title	Switching between sync UI modes should preserve expansion state
Description	When you switch between Catch Up and Release modes, it loses the expansion state of the tree. It should remember this and probably the selection and top item (scroll bar position) as well.

of duplicate bug reports where similar features have been highlighted. These features are not limited to exact word matching, but also extend to semantic similarity and context. Therefore, this places high demands on the capacity of automatic text processing techniques.

Traditionally, the automatic approach to DBRD has been divided into two distinct tasks: Information Retrieval (IR) and classification[1]. Early methods for IR primarily relied on word-based approaches (e.g., Vector Space Model), as well as topic-based models like Latent Dirichlet Allocation (LDA) and Latent Semantic Analysis (LSA), which transformed bug reports into feature vectors. More recently, embedding models, such as Word2Vec [10][11], GloVe [12], and sentence BERT [13] have gained traction. These models generate embeddings that are then utilized to calculate similarities between bugs, typically using distance measurements, such as Cosine similarity. These retrieval methods have demonstrated promising performance, particularly in terms of recall rate [1]. Simultaneously, classification models, particularly deep-learning-based approaches, have emerged as prominent research focus in DBRD [1][5][9]. Initially, the classifier employed the Convolutional Neural Network (CNN) [6][11][14][15], followed by the Recurrent Neural Network (RNN) [15] and eventually transitioning to the Long Short-Term Memory (LSTM) model [15]. However, due to the challenges associated with processing lengthy text, the performance of these three models has been surpassed in recent years by transformer-based classifiers, most notably BERT [3][5], sentence BERT [3][13] and RoBERTa [3]. These large language models are pre-trained on large corpus and fine-tuned on domain-specific data, which enables them to capture contextual semantic information and generate word and sentence representations efficiently. Not surprisingly, transformer-based models became the state-of-the-art for this task [3].

However, in previous studies, we found that commonly used dataset splitting methods have data leakage issues, which may lead to biased results. Specifically, it is possible for a single data within a pair in the train set to be combined with another data and consequently appear in the development or test set. This unintentional leakage has not been explicitly addressed by most existing methods, with only one work taking this matter into account without explicitly acknowledging it [3]. Therefore, one of the main contributions of our work is the design of a Cluster-based dataset partition mechanism to address this problem.

Most importantly, while there has been a considerable emphasis on performance metrics, such as recall and precision in existing studies, the evaluation of these approaches' efficiency in terms of speed has often been overlooked. As highlighted by Haruna et al. [13] in their research, with the advent of large language models, such as BERT, the performance of retrieval and classification tasks has shown remarkable advancements. Nevertheless, the deployment and execution of these models can present difficulties due to their relatively slower inference times. Especially when it comes to practical applications, the speed plays a critical role. As a result, it's essential to evaluate a model not just based on its accuracy, but also on its efficiency.

In our research, we propose a novel system based on the transformer architecture that combines the advantages of retrieval model and classification model. Our approach integrates retrieval techniques to retrieve an initial set of potential duplicate instances, which is then fed into a classification model for further triage. This innovative methodology enables us to achieve faster performance without compromising accuracy. By effectively merging these two components, we attain a balance between efficiency and accuracy in DBRD task.

The contributions of our work are as follows:

- Cluster-based dataset partition mechanism: To address the problem of train set leakage, we introduce a cluster-based dataset partition mechanism. This mechanism ensures that duplicate instances are evenly distributed across the train and test sets, effectively mitigating any potential data leakage issues.
- Comparison with previous models: We conduct a comprehensive comparison between the performance of the transformer-based models and that of previous methods in retrieval and classification. Through rigorous experiments and evaluations, we demonstrate that our transformer-based models outperform on both tasks, surpassing the performance of previous models.
- Integration of retrieval model and classification: Our proposed system leverages the strengths of both retrieval models and classification models. As demonstrated in the experiments, our system can achieve a balanced between speed and accuracy in two real-world scenarios.

We introduce the related work in Section II, detail our approach in Section III and validate the experiments in large open source projects to demonstrate the effectiveness in Section IV and Section V.

II. Related Work

As previously mentioned, solutions to DBRD can be viewed as IR task and classification task. Approaches to IR tasks focus on identifying duplicates by computing similarities between textual representations, while classification tasks typically utilize deep learning techniques to train models in distinguishing between "duplicated" and "non-duplicated" instances based on learned patterns. In the following subsections, we present related work on these methods.

1) Information Retrieval Methods: Hiew [16] introduces a retrieval method for unstructured text including titles and descriptions. Textual fields are converted to TF-IDF vectors, which are then organized into clusters based on their similar characteristics to identify duplicates. Runeson et al. [7] utilized a Vector Space Model to present text-based information and determined the text similarity by using three similarity calculation methods. Wang et al. [17] integrated execution data into their strategy to detect similar bug reports. Sun et al. [18] proposed a REP model that incorporates similarity of lexical features and categorical features from bug reports. Nguyen et al. [9] introduced the DBTM model that processes topic features extracted by LDA model and unstructured textual features. It combines topic model and retrieval model to show both similarity and dissimilarity between bug reports. Some follow-up studies [19][20][21] adopt a similar approach to previous studies, also implementing topic models for retrieval, but differentiate their studies by analyzing distinct corpora and utilizing varied feature inputs in bug reports.

Therefore, traditional IR methods primarily focus on the calculation of word frequency feature to detect duplicates, which show advantages in processing structured text and keyword-based queries. However, IR methods exhibit limitations in processing contextual information and complex semantic features, areas where deep learning (DL) methods demonstrate proficiency.

2) Deep Learning Methods: Deshmukh et al. [14] were the first to introduce deep learning into duplicate bug report detection, proposing a model that uses Siamese Convolutional Neural Networks and Long Short Term Memory to process hybrid input from bug reports for retrieval and classification. Budhiraja et al. [22][23] proposed Deep Word Embedding Networks (DWEN), a framework designed to retrieve similar reports by processing unstructured input, including bug report titles and descriptions. Xie et al. [10] introduced a deep learning framework named DBR-CNN, which enhances traditional CNN by integrating domain-specific features extracted from bug reports. The hybrid features are fed into the CNN model to obtain concatenated vectors, which are utilized for classification task. Poddar et al. [24] proposed a neural architecture for multi-task learning, with joint tasks of classifying duplicates and clustering latent topics, operating on unstructured descriptions as input. Building upon the CNN framework, He et al. [11] subsequently developed a Dual-Channel CNN (DC-CNN) method to classify duplicate bug reports using hybid-structured text as input. Kukkar et al. [6] presented a deep learning based classification model applied on hybrid features, also leveraging CNN to extract relevant features that are subsequently used to compute similarities for classification purposes.

Following these advancements, transformer-based language models have gained considerable attention and popularity within the present landscape of duplicate bug report detection, due to their rich context-based learning capabilities. Isotani et al. [13] introduced transformer-based deep learning embedding model of SBERT to vectorize the unstructured textual features (title and description) and then computes the similarity of the embedding representations, enabling retrieval of similarly ranked bug reports. Rocha et al. [5] proposed a SiameseQAT approach, using BERT and MLP to concatenate structured and unstructured features and features extracted based on corpus topics for retrieval and classification tasks respectively. Messaoud et al. [3] proposed a BERT-MLP model for classifying duplicate bug reports, which considers only unstructured data. The model utilizes BERT to generate contextualized word representations and applies an MLP for classification. Jiang Y et al. [25] suggested a CombineIRDL method, which utilizes different deep learning models to extract lexical, categorical, and semantic features from hybrid input and then employs a retrieval model to obtain ranked duplicates.

Building on these deep learning methods discussed in the literature, we find that most of them accomplish duplicate detection by implementing retrieval and classification tasks separately [5][6][14] or focus on a single task [3][10][11][13][22][23][24][25]. Furthermore, deep learning methods have demonstrated significant effectiveness in both tasks. In IR tasks, deep learning enhances similarity assessments by employing advanced word embedding models, such as transformer models. In classification tasks, it trains models (such as CNN, LSTM or transformer models) to predict whether two bug reports are duplicates by leveraging their learning capabilities to discern complex textual patterns. By employing these advanced deep learning models, classification tasks can achieve higher accuracy than IR tasks through the extraction of comprehensive textual features, but at the cost of thousands of computations to achieve such precision. Conversely, IR tasks can achieve more significant efficiency in reducing the search space than classification tasks. However, previous work has not considered the trade-off between accuracy and efficiency. Therefore, our approach combines those two tasks in order to fully exploit their strengths in terms of efficiency and accuracy, thereby achieving a balance. In doing so, we apply transformer-based models in our approach, which are widely recognized as the state-of-the-art for Natural Language Processing (NLP) tasks by exploiting their ability to learn semantic and contextual information. These models are utilized to generate embedding representations in the retrieval task and to identify duplicate pairs in the classification task. The following section contains more details of our methodology.

III. Methodology

In this section, we outline our methodology for the DBRD task, including the overall architecture, pre-processing, data split, and model fine-tuning.

A. Overall Architecture

The overall architecture of our proposed approach is shown in Figure 1, which consists of three important phases: data split, retrieval and classification.

- **Data split** is to split the test and train set for preparing for the training of retrieval and classification models and we introduce it detailed in Section III-C.
- In the **Retrieval** phase, the retrieval model is responsible for generating the embedding representation of bug report input. Using cosine similarity [26], it calculates the embedding similarity and selects the Top K similar bug reports. This "ranking" is primarily used to identify the top-K candidates, which serve as the target input for the subsequent classification model.
- In the **Classification** phase, the model takes the top-K candidates from the retrieval phase and aims to output the final results by labeling them as duplicates or non-duplicates.

B. Pre-processing

In DBRD task, the input of bug reports can typically be unstructured input containing only unstructured textual fields, or hybrid input including both unstructured textual features and structured categorical features. Our emphasis lies on unstructured input, specifically title and description. These text constitute the most critical component of bug reports and they are also noisy and complex, covering a large number of domain-specific technical fields. To eliminate the redundant and invalid data in the content of bug report datasets, the following operations are used to clean the datasets:

- Remove all non-English words from the text (note: adjust this based on the primary language of the dataset)
- Remove some special characters but keep periods and commas
- Remove stop words
- Unify all letters to lowercase

C. Data Split

As outlined in Section I, most prior studies have neglected the leakage from the train set to the development and test set. To address this issue, we introduce a cluster-based dataset generation method, as illustrated in the Data Split Phase of

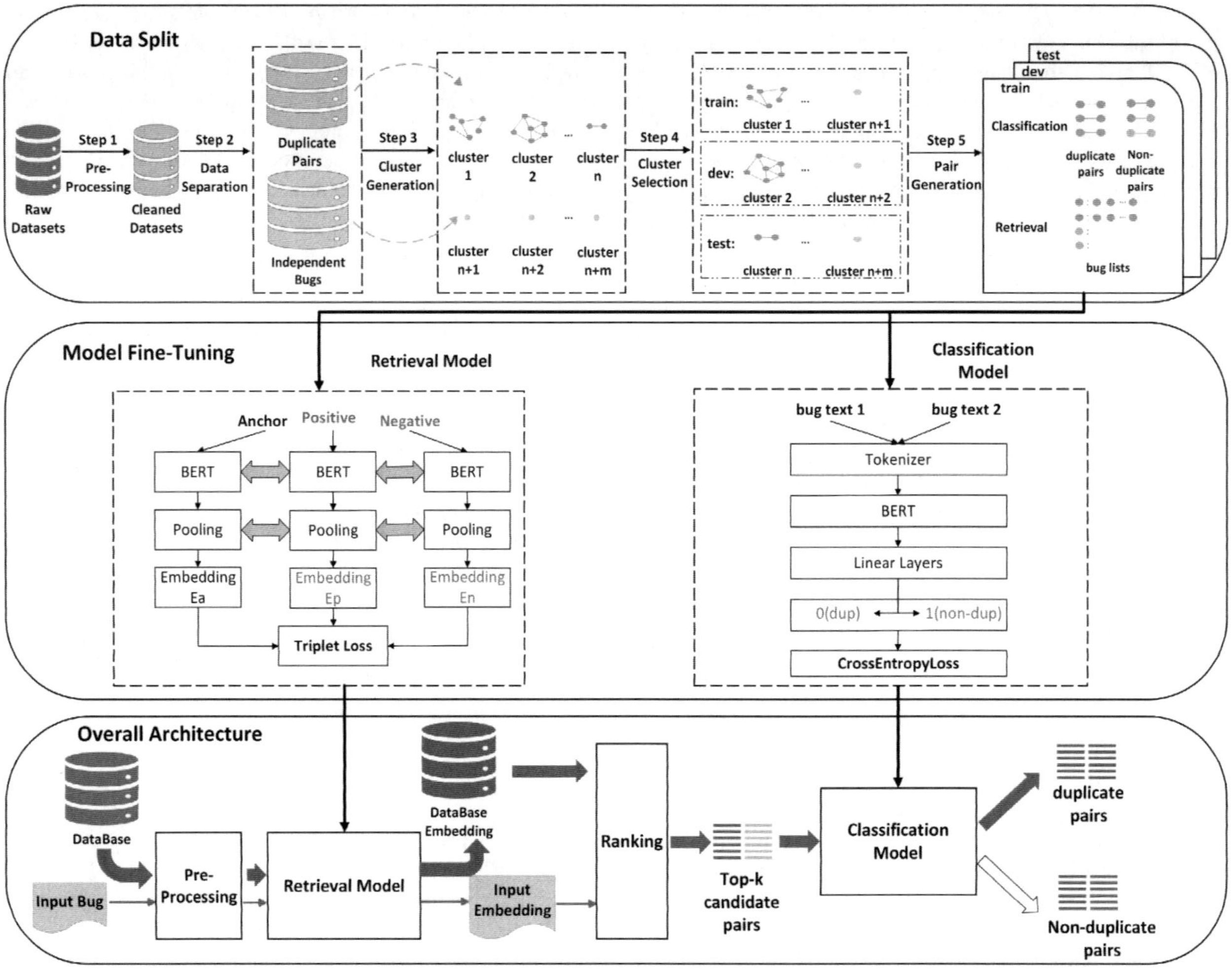

Fig. 1: Transformer-Based Framework split into Two Phases: 1). Data Generation Phase and 2). Model Fine-Tuning Phase

Figure 1. This approach ensures a stringent separation between the train set, development set, and test set.

Data Separation. After pre-processing, the bug reports are categorized into two groups: independent bug reports and duplicate bug reports. Independent bug reports refer to those that do not have any duplicates among the dataset.

Cluster Generation. In this particular step, we adopt the assumption of transitivity in the relationship between duplicate bug reports. This means that if Bug A is a duplicate of Bug B, and Bug B is a duplicate of Bug C, then Bug A and Bug C are also considered duplicates. Consequently, based on our example, Bugs A, B, and C would be grouped together in a single distinct cluster. Leveraging this assumption, we employ a cluster-based method to group pairs of duplicated bug reports into distinct clusters. Within each cluster, every two bugs are marked as duplicates.

Cluster Selection. Unlike prior studies that randomly select duplicate pairs for train/test sets, we choose clusters to form train, development, and test sets. This ensures each bug appears only once in any set, and the clusters across these sets are distinct. This method reduces potential biases and data leakage from directly selecting duplicate pairs.

Pair Generation. In this step, we generate two train/test datasets with different data structures for retrieval and classification models respectively. The retrieval dataset follows the format of [Bug ID: Bug IDs], where bugs sharing the same cluster are considered duplicates of each other. On the other hand, the classification dataset comprises both duplicated pairs and non-duplicated pairs in a one-to-one format of [Bug ID: Bug ID], which are generated based on the clusters. For a cluster with n bugs, $\frac{n*(n-1)}{2}$ duplicated pairs can be derived. Furthermore, for two clusters (with sizes n and m, respectively), we can generate $n * m$ non-duplicated pairs.

Notably, the train set is carefully balanced in terms of positive (duplicate) and negative (non-duplicate) data, while the development and test sets are intentionally left unbalanced. This setting aims to reflect the real-world scenario, where the number of non-duplicate bug pairs far exceeds the number of duplicate bugs.

D. Model Fine-tuning

As shown in Figure 1, Model Fine-tuning phase encompasses the process of training two models: the retrieval model and the classification model.

To adapt SBERT for the retrieval task, we modify the dataset structure into triplets [Anchor, Positive, Negative], where we aim to fine-tune the model's ability to distinguish between relevant (positive) and irrelevant (negative) instances. The loss function employed is the Triplet Loss [27], represented by 1. In this equation, $||\cdot||$ denotes a distance metric used to assess the similarity between embeddings. It is important to note that this loss function imposes a condition that the distance between the anchor text and the positive text should be at least θ greater than the distance between the anchor text and the negative text.

$$Triplet\ Loss = Max(||E_a - E_p|| - ||E_a - E_n|| + \epsilon, 0) \quad (1)$$

In the context of classification, BERT operates by taking in two texts simultaneously, and using [SEP] token to differentiate them. The embedding of the [CLS] token, obtained from the final layer of BERT, is processed through a linear layer. The softmax function is then applied to generate the final prediction. The loss function employed in this case is the CrossEntropy (CE) Loss, as represented by 2.

$$CE(y,p) = -\sum_{i=1}^{N} y_i \log p_i \quad (2)$$

where the y_i is the true label and p_i is the predicted label.

IV. Experimental Settings

In this section, we detail the experiments, discussing setup, datasets, hyperparameters, evaluation, baselines, and model selection.

A. Setup

To ensure a fair and consistent comparison between the models, we maintain uniformity by implementing and building the models using Python within the PyTorch framework. We will provide the structured code in subsequent documentation. All experimental procedures were conducted on a Linux server featuring an AMD EPYC-Rome processor and an NVIDIA A40 GPU card. This setting allows for efficient execution and reliable performance evaluation of the models.

B. Datasets

We use five open source bug report repositories [1] to verify the effectiveness of our system, namely Eclipse, Firefox, Mozilla, JDT, and ThunderBird (TBird), as the experimental datasets in our study. These repositories have been extensively utilized in previous research [1]. We focus on the following statistical attributes to characterize the datasets as Table II shown.

We have detailed the process of Data Split in Section III-C, where we employ an 8:1:1 ratio to split train, development, and test sets respectively. As previously discussed, we introduce skew to the development and test data, while maintaining balance in the train set. Consequently, we adhere to the 'Dup Bug Ratio' as indicated in Table II, to establish the ratio of duplicate pairs in both the development and test sets. Since a substantial number of duplicate and non-duplicate pairs can be generated, we limit the size of the train/test/dev set as shown in Table III.

C. Hyperparameters

We leverage pre-trained transformer-based models along with their respective tokenizers. Fine-tuning of these models is performed using the AdamW optimizer [28] with a learning rate of 10^{-5}.

In the classification scenario with SBERT, we introduce a linear layer comprising two hidden layers of 768 hidden size each. For the Bi-LSTM model, we utilize the SGD optimizer, implementing a learning rate of 0.5 and a decay rate of 0.25. For the CNN model, we adhere to the configurations outlined in DC-CNN [11].

To mitigate overfitting, we apply a 0.5 dropout across all models. We process training data in 32-size batches. To bolster the robustness and reliability of the results, each experiment is conducted five times.

D. Evaluation

1) Individual Evaluation: The performance of retrieval and classification models is individually assessed in our study. For the retrieval model, we evaluate the performance by measuring the recall and precision under different Top-k settings. For the classification model, we employ precision, recall, and the corresponding F1 score to indicate the performance.

Metrics: Utilizing a confusion matrix, which tabulates the counts of True Positives (TP), False Positives (FP), False Negatives (FN), and True Negatives (TN), we characterize the recall, precision, and F1 score as delineated in 3, 4, and 5 respectively. Above fomulas are the performance indicators for classification. However, in the context of retrieval, the computation of recall@k and precision@k deviates slightly, as demonstrated in 6 and 7.

$$Recall = TP/(TP + FN) \quad (3)$$

$$Precision = TP/(TP + FP) \quad (4)$$

$$F1 = \frac{2 * (Precision * Recall)}{(Precision + Recall)} \quad (5)$$

$$Recall@k = \frac{(relevant\ items\ in\ top - k)}{(relevant\ items)} \quad (6)$$

$$Precision@k = \frac{(relevant\ items\ in\ topk)}{k} \quad (7)$$

[1]Datasets available at: [Online]. Available: https://github.com/logpai/bugrepo

TABLE II: STATISTICS OF FIVE OPEN SOURCE DATASETS

Dataset	Bugs	Dup Pairs	Separate Bugs	Dup Bug Ratio	Cluster Numbers	Cluster size
Eclipse	84020(85156)	13231	70752	0.1564	7519	2.760
Firefox	96258(115814)	15742	80000	0.1689	6654	3.366
Mozilla	195248(205069)	34507	160378	0.1786	17263	2.998
JDT	44154(45296)	6513	37608	0.1483	3828	2.701
TBird	24767(32551)	4404	20050	0.1905	2133	3.065

TABLE III: DISTRIBUTION OF BUG PAIRS IN TRAIN/DEV/TEST SET

Dataset	Train		Dev		Test		Total
	Dup	Nondup	Dup	Nondup	Dup	Nondup	
Eclipse	6615	6615	258	1394	258	1394	16534
Firefox	7871	7871	332	1635	332	1635	19676
Mozilla	17253	17253	770	3542	770	3542	43130
JDT	3256	3256	120	693	120	693	8138
TBird	2202	2202	104	445	104	445	5502

2) *Architecture Evaluation:* We conduct a comprehensive evaluation of our proposed system, comparing its performance and efficiency against individual retrieval and classification methods in two common real-world scenarios.

One VS All: In this scenario, when a user enters a bug, the system compares the user's input bug with existing bug reports in the entire database. To evaluate this scenario, we divided the test set into two parts: 20% for user input and 80% for the database.

All VS All: This scenario often arises on the database side, where developers need to locate and eliminate all duplicate errors in the database. It resembles the One VS All scenario, except that we utilize the entire test set as the database.

The applications of our proposed system as well as retrieval and classification methods in the above scenarios are as follows:

One VS All scenario: when a user submits a bug report,

- **retrieval** scans the entire database to find the report most similar to the submitted report;
- **classification** predicts which reports in the database are relevant to the submitted report based on certain characteristics;
- **proposed system** firstly retrieves the top K most similar reports from the database based on user submissions, and then the classifier further predicts these K reports to ultimately determine the duplicate results.

All VS All scenario: each method repeats the One VS All process, aiming to identify and eliminate all duplicates in the database.

In our approach, the classification process primarily serves to enhance the quality of retrieval results, so using the retrieved metrics allows for a more comprehensive comparison of overall performance, while also displaying the improvements attained by the classification part. Therefore, this evaluation consists of the following metrics: recall@k, precision, accuracy (as depicted by 8) and inference time.

$$Accuracy = TP + TN/TP + TN + FP + FN \quad (8)$$

It should be noted that the maximum k set in our experiments is 100 which builds also in the real word scenario. In practical information retrieval settings, users rarely browse beyond the top 100 results due to the huge amount of data and the limitation of their own attention. Therefore, capping k at 100 strikes a balance between presenting enough relevant results and preventing users from being overwhelmed by too many results.

E. Baselines

Based on individual evaluation in retrieval and classification respectively, we employ GloVe [12] and FastText [29] as retrieval baseline methods. Since both methods generate word-level embeddings, we compute sentence embeddings by averaging the word embeddings. In the evaluation of classification models, we incorporate the Bi-LSTM and DC-CNN as the baselines. Both the Bi-LSTM model and the CNN model have been previously applied as classification models in DBRD research [11][14].

In the overall evaluation, we select outperforming retrieval and classification models as baselines and compare them with our combined approach.

F. Model Selection

In our proposed approach, we select transformer-based models for retrieval and classification. For the retrieval model, we leverage sentence BERT (SBERT) to generate text embeddings and evaluate its efficacy on the retrieval task. In the classification task, we choose three transformer-based models as classification models, BERT, ALBERT and RoBERTa, and compare their performance. We selected these transformer-based models because they have demonstrated effectiveness in previous state-of-the-art studies [3][5][13] for DBRD.

V. Experiment Results

We analyze our experimental results by answering following two research questions.

RQ1: Compared to baseline models, how do the transformer-based models perform on retrieval and classification?

In our first evaluation, we conduct experiments on retrieval models and classification models, presenting the results in Table IV and Table V, respectively.

Consistent with previous research, our evaluation of the retrieval model primarily focuses on the recall value. Notably, as the k value increased, we observed a substantial improvement in the recall of the model. This result is expected as increasing the value of k allows for more candidates to be considered,

TABLE IV: RECALL@K OF MODELS IN DUPLICATE BUG RETRIEVAL FOR ALL DATASETS

	Eclipse			Firefox			Mozilla			JDT			TBird			
	r@20	r@60	r@100	r@20	r@60	r@100	r@20	r@60	r@100	r@20	r@60	r@100	r@20	r@60	r@100	Avg r@100
Fasttext	0.489	0.678	0.783	0.596	0.716	0.809	0.414	0.526	0.588	0.608	0.785	0.972	0.627	0.874	**1.000**	0.8304
Glove	0.602	0.727	0.824	0.705	0.789	0.843	0.478	0.608	0.662	0.579	0.798	0.975	0.689	0.888	**1.000**	0.8608
SBERT	**0.848**	**0.935**	**0.960**	**0.892**	**0.956**	**0.973**	**0.771**	**0.892**	**0.919**	**0.872**	**0.990**	**0.997**	**0.880**	**0.983**	**1.000**	**0.9698**

TABLE V: PRECISION, RECALL & F1 SCORES OF MODELS IN DUPLICATE BUG CLASSIFICATION TASK FOR ALL DATASETS

	Eclipse			Firefox			Mozilla			JDT			TBird			
	Precision	Recall	F1	Precision	Recall	F1	Precision	Recall	F1	Precision	Recall	F1	Precision	Recall	F1	Avg F1
Bi-LSTM	0.511	0.506	0.473	0.510	0.515	0.469	0.507	0.506	0.506	0.490	0.490	0.490	0.621	0.510	0.474	0.4824
DC-CNN	0.752	0.813	0.785	0.744	0.765	0.753	0.792	0.765	0.736	0.763	0.781	0.773	0.833	0.752	0.781	0.7660
BERT	**0.825**	0.888	0.848	0.881	0.921	0.899	0.824	**0.892**	0.849	0.772	0.857	0.797	0.870	0.898	0.883	0.8552
ALBERT	0.806	**0.896**	0.834	0.874	0.920	0.893	0.819	0.889	0.845	**0.825**	**0.872**	**0.843**	**0.885**	**0.902**	**0.893**	0.8616
RoBERTa	0.846	0.892	0.866	**0.886**	**0.925**	**0.903**	**0.835**	0.891	**0.857**	0.824	0.868	0.841	0.846	0.898	0.866	**0.8666**

thereby raising the probability of identifying duplicate bugs. Upon setting k to 100, we discovered that nearly all duplicates are successfully detected, resulting in an approximate recall value of 1.

Furthermore, by comparing the retrieval performance of the three models, as shown in Table IV, we find that SBERT achieves the highest recall value, under different k values. It outperforms Glove and FastText in all five datasets by an average lead of 12.42%. This significantly demonstrates the superiority of the transformer model in information retrieval capabilities.

In the classification task, we compared the performance of traditional models, such as Bi-LSTM, DC-CNN, with transformer-based models on the three indicators of precision, recall and f1. Our results in Table V show that f1 is significantly improved by 20% to 38% when using transformer-based models compared to traditional methods. When comparing transformer models, their performance does not exhibit significant variations. However, RoBERTa has emerged as the frontrunner, surpassing the others with a slightly higher F1 score of 0.8666.

Therefore, the above experimental results indicate that transformer-based models outperform traditional models in both classification and retrieval performance.

RQ2: Compared to single retrieval and classification model, how does the proposed system perform in case of recall precision, accuracy and time?

Figure 2 presents a comparative performance overview showing the difference in recall, precision, accuracy and running time for single retrieval model, classification model and proposal system in the One VS All scenario, and Figure 3 presents the overall performance in the All VS All scenario. The results obtained in the One vs All and All VS All scenarios of the five datasets are relatively similar, so we choose one of datasets, firefox, to show the results.

It is important to emphasize that, as shown in Figure 2, the performance of the classification model is not affected by changes in k, thus presenting a horizontal line in the figure.

In Figure 2a, we observed that at lower k, both the retrieval model and our system exhibit lower recall scores compared to the classification model. The reason is that the limited k prevents the retrieval of a large number of duplicate pairs. However, as k gradually increases, after reaching around 20, the recall of the retrieval model exceeds that of the classification model. At the same time, since the classification step of the system may introduce positive and false samples, the recall rate of the system is lower than that of the retrieval model, resulting in a decrease in the overall recall rate. Given that our system incorporates retrieval, such recall aligns with the rising trend demonstrated by retrieval models as k increases, albeit at a slightly slower pace. For example, it is not until "k" equals 40 that the recall of our method starts to be comparable to that of classification. This suggests that as the value of k rises to higher values (e.g., over 100), our recall will continue to rise, thereby establishing an increasingly discernible gap from the recall of classification.

In the Figure 2b, we note that the precision of the retrieval model and our proposed system decrease as k increases, a consequence of increasing the number of retrieved candidates. Nevertheless, it is worth mentioning that compared with the retrieval precision, the decrease of system precision is not obvious. Even when k is equal to 100, the precision of the system is still higher than the classification precision, which demonstrates the effectiveness of our system in terms of precision. Similar to precision in Figure 2c, accuracy also exhibits a sonsistent trend. As the k increases, both the accuracy of the system and retrieval decrease. The decline in system accuracy is also slower compared to retrieval accuracy. This highlights the advantage of our system for introducing a classification step after retrieval, as it can efficiently preserve the performance in precision and accuracy, especially better than classification.

Comparatively, as displayed in Figure 2d, the classification

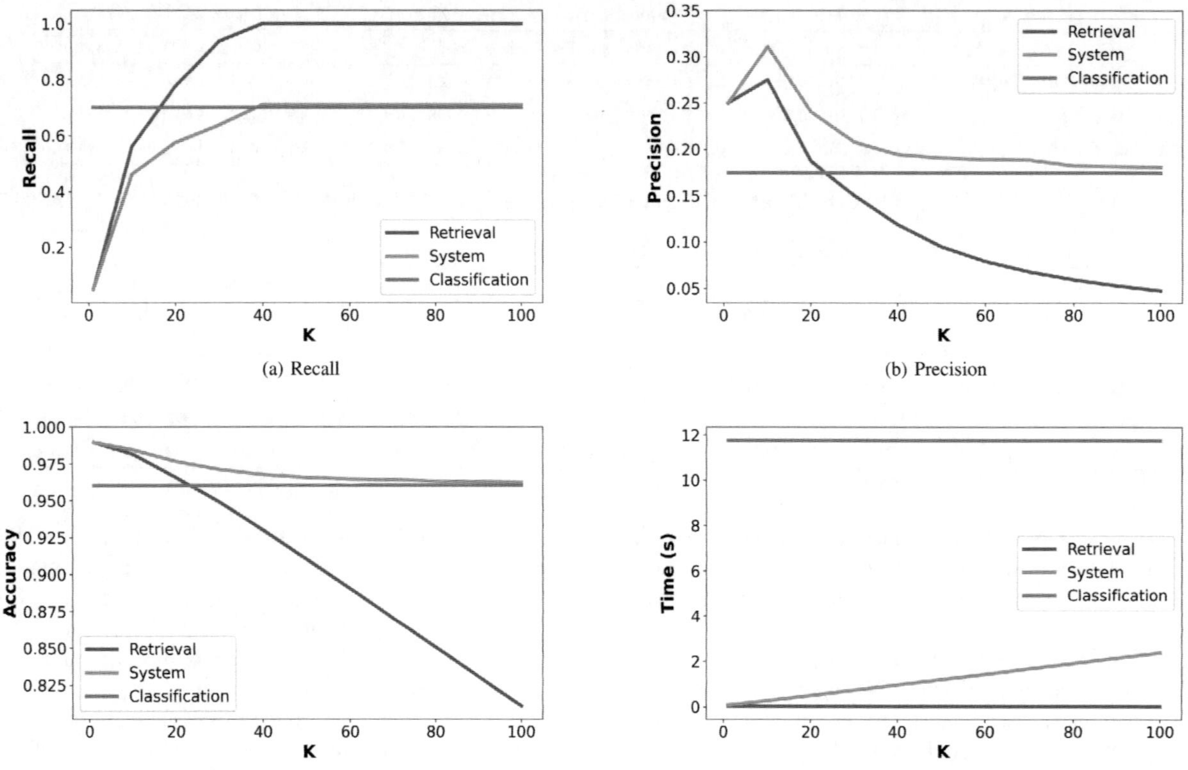

(a) Recall

(b) Precision

(c) Accuracy

(d) Running Time

Fig. 2: Time-Performance Evaluation on Firefox Dataset in One VS All scenario

process is more time-consuming than both retrieval and our system. This observation can be explained through a simple calculation. Assuming we have n user input bugs and m database bugs, and assuming that both the classification model and the retrieval model require the same time for a single inference, the following holds: The classification model requires $n{*}m$ inferences. The retrieval model requires $n{+}m$ inferences, along with $n * m$ calculations of embeddings similarity and subsequent sorting. As the similarity calculation and sorting are considerably faster than model inference, the retrieval process roughly takes n + m seconds per inference. Our system incorporates the results of retrieval. Therefore, it includes the retrieval model inference time $n + m$, similarity calculation, and sorting time, followed by $n * topk$ classifications. Consequently, the system's required time amounts to $n{+}m{+}n{*}topk$ inferences. The preceding calculations are equally applicable to the All VS All scenario as well. It is clear that our method exhibits almost the same remarkable efficiency as retrieval and classification in terms of time. This is proven by the fact that the time consumed by the classification is approximately 60 times greater than our approach.

Figure 3 shows that the All VS All scenario exhibits similar performance trends as the One VS All scenario. The running time in Figure 3d represents the average time taken to match each bug with its similar ones, comparable to Figure 2d.

Overall, our system makes a trade-off by sacrificing some running time in order to maintain robust performance in terms of recall, precision, and accuracy. As k increases from 0 to 100, the recall of our system increases, demonstrating the ability of our model to successfully retrieve all relevant duplicates. At the same time, the accuracy and precision are only slightly reduced, effectively alleviating the sharp decline in retrieval, but never fall below those achieved by classification. The steady improvement in recall between retrieval and classification, coupled with the maintained superior precision, shows that we minimize the time cost while maintaining accuracy performance. This convincingly demonstrates our ability to obtain a trade-off between accuracy performance and time efficiency.

Therefore, selecting the appropriate value for k requires careful consideration. While a smaller k value may improve the time efficiency, it may also lead to a degradation in model performance. On the other hand, choosing a larger k value may result in increased time consumption. Thus, striking a balance between speed and model performance depends on selecting the optimal k value.

VI. Conclusion and Future Work

In our work, we proposed a novel system based on the transformer models, that leverages the strengths of both re-

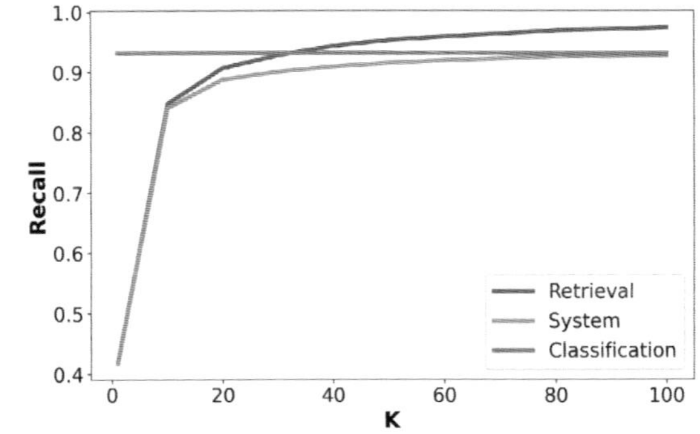

(a) Recall

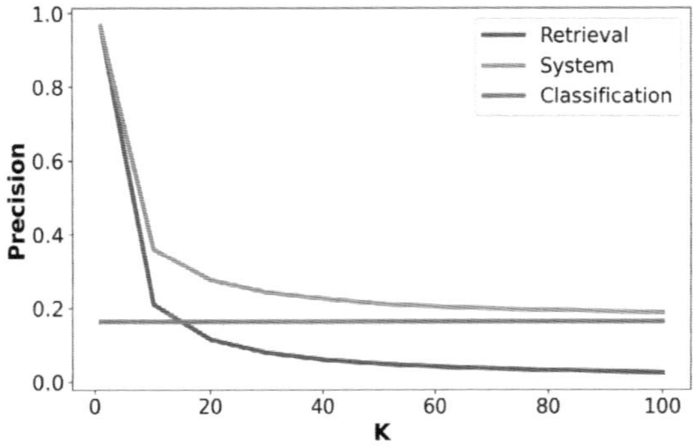

(b) Precision

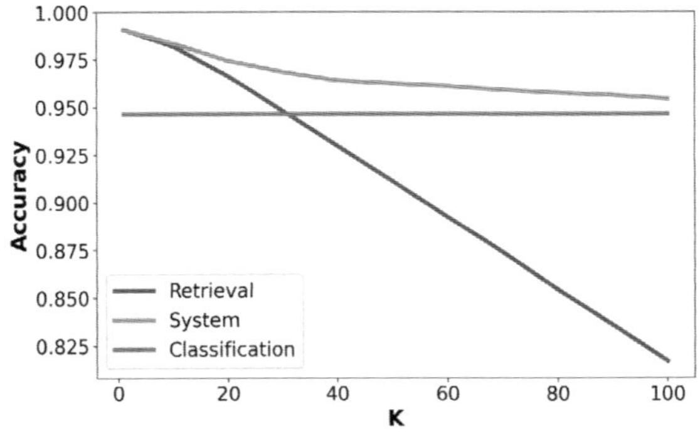

(c) Accuracy

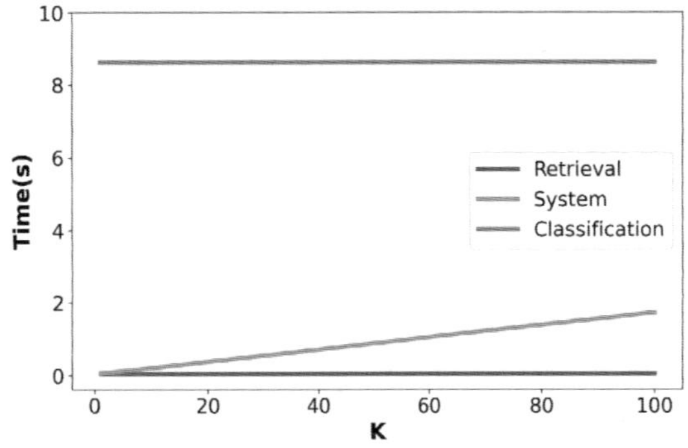

(d) Running Time

Fig. 3: Time-Performance Evaluation on Firefox Dataset in All VS All scenario

trieval and classification approaches for duplicate bug report detection task. We have evaluated the transformer-based models employed by our method on five datasets, demonstrating their effectiveness compared to traditional models for both classification and retrieval. More importantly, our method shows a competitive edge by achieving a balance between time efficiency and accuracy, compared to solutions employing only one of them. This advantage holds significant importance in real-time bug report detection where requires high-quality results in a short time. In other words, under resource constraints, combining retrieval and classification as a novel solution enables dynamic adjustments to efficiently address issues related to changes in data volume and quality, while flexibly adapting to time-sensitivity and shifts in user demands. This approach enhances resource efficiency and ensures the maintenance of response speed and accuracy in a constantly changing environment. Furthermore, our combined strategy can be expanded to tackle similar issues in other tasks, such as recommendation tasks.

While our system addresses the running time concern that previous methods overlooked, and achieves a trade-off between time and accuracy, there are several factors need to be considered for practical application, such as the size of the model. Our system relies on both the retrieval and classification models, resulting in a larger memory space requirement compared to a single model. As a result, future efforts could explore the possibility of employing multi-task learning to integrate these two models, allowing for the completion of both tasks with a single model simultaneously. Additionally, there are some limitations in our study that can be addressed in the future, such as expanding to new datasets. This not only includes datasets that are more current, but also those that are more diverse in terms of types, which would enhance the generalizability of our methods.

ACKNOWLEDGMENT

This work was funded by the China Scholarship Council (CSC) and supported by the Leiden Institute of Advanced Computer Science (LIACS).

REFERENCES

[1] S. Gupta and S. K. Gupta, "A systematic study of duplicate bug report detection," *International Journal of Advanced Computer Science and Applications*, vol. 12, no. 1, pp. 578–589, 2021.

[2] B. S. Neysiani and S. Morteza Babamir, "Automatic duplicate bug report detection using information retrieval-based versus machine learning-based approaches," pp. 288–293, 2020.

[3] M. B. Messaoud, A. Miladi, I. Jenhani, M. W. Mkaouer, and L. Ghadhab, "Duplicate bug report detection using an attention-based neural language model," *IEEE Transactions on Reliability*, pp. 1–13, 2022.

[4] T. Zhang, H. Jiang, X. Luo, and A. T. Chan, "A literature review of research in bug resolution: Tasks, challenges and future directions," *The Computer Journal*, vol. 59, no. 5, pp. 741–773, 2016.

[5] T. M. Rocha and A. L. D. C. Carvalho, "Siameseqat: A semantic context-based duplicate bug report detection using replicated cluster information," *IEEE Access*, vol. 9, pp. 44 610–44 630, 2021.

[6] A. e. a. Kukkar, "Duplicate bug report detection and classification system based on deep learning technique," *IEEE Access*, vol. 8, pp. 200 749–200 763, 2020.

[7] P. Runeson, M. Alexandersson, and O. Nyholm, "Detection of duplicate defect reports using natural language processing," in *29th International Conference on Software Engineering (ICSE'07)*. IEEE, 2007, pp. 499–510.

[8] J. Uddin, R. Ghazali, M. Mat Deris, R. Naseem, and H. Shah, "A survey on bug prioritization," *Artificial Intelligence Review*, vol. 47, pp. 145–180, 2017.

[9] A. T. Nguyen, T. T. Nguyen, T. N. Nguyen, D. Lo, and C. Sun, "Duplicate bug report detection with a combination of information retrieval and topic modeling," in *2012 Proceedings of the 27th IEEE/ACM international conference on automated software engineering*. IEEE, 2012, pp. 70–79.

[10] Q. Xie, Z. Wen, J. Zhu, C. Gao, and Z. Zheng, "Detecting duplicate bug reports with convolutional neural networks," in *2018 25th Asia-Pacific Software Engineering Conference (APSEC)*. IEEE, 2018, pp. 416–425.

[11] J. He, L. Xu, M. Yan, X. Xia, and Y. Lei, "Duplicate bug report detection using dual-channel convolutional neural networks," in *Proceedings of the 28th International Conference on Program Comprehension*, 2020, pp. 117–127.

[12] V. Pankajakshan and M. Sridevi, "Detecting duplicate question pairs using glove embeddings and similarity measures," in *Advances in Automation, Signal Processing, Instrumentation, and Control*. Springer, 2021, pp. 695–702.

[13] H. e. a. Isotani, "Duplicate bug report detection by using sentence embedding and fine-tuning," in *2021 IEEE International Conference on Software Maintenance and Evolution (ICSME)*. IEEE, 2021, pp. 535–544.

[14] J. Deshmukh, K. Annervaz, S. Podder, S. Sengupta, and N. Dubash, "Towards accurate duplicate bug retrieval using deep learning techniques," in *2017 IEEE International conference on software maintenance and evolution (ICSME)*. IEEE, 2017, pp. 115–124.

[15] G. Xiao, X. Du, Y. Sui, and T. Yue, "Hindbr: Heterogeneous information network based duplicate bug report prediction," in *2020 IEEE 31st International Symposium on Software Reliability Engineering (ISSRE)*. IEEE, 2020, pp. 195–206.

[16] L. Hiew, "Assisted detection of duplicate bug reports," Ph.D. dissertation, University of British Columbia, 2006.

[17] X. Wang, L. Zhang, T. Xie, J. Anvik, and J. Sun, "An approach to detecting duplicate bug reports using natural language and execution information," in *Proceedings of the 30th international conference on Software engineering*, 2008, pp. 461–470.

[18] C. Sun, D. Lo, S.-C. Khoo, and J. Jiang, "Towards more accurate retrieval of duplicate bug reports," in *2011 26th IEEE/ACM International Conference on Automated Software Engineering (ASE 2011)*. IEEE, 2011, pp. 253–262.

[19] A. Alipour, A. Hindle, and E. Stroulia, "A contextual approach towards more accurate duplicate bug report detection," in *2013 10th Working Conference on Mining Software Repositories (MSR)*. IEEE, 2013, pp. 183–192.

[20] A. Lazar, S. Ritchey, and B. Sharif, "Improving the accuracy of duplicate bug report detection using textual similarity measures," in *Proceedings of the 11th Working Conference on Mining Software Repositories*, 2014, pp. 308–311.

[21] K. e. a. Aggarwal, "Detecting duplicate bug reports with software engineering domain knowledge," *Journal of Software: Evolution and Process*, vol. 29, no. 3, p. e1821, 2017.

[22] A. Budhiraja, K. Dutta, R. Reddy, and M. Shrivastava, "Dwen: deep word embedding network for duplicate bug report detection in software repositories," in *Proceedings of the 40th International Conference on software engineering: companion proceeedings*, 2018, pp. 193–194.

[23] A. Budhiraja, K. Dutta, M. Shrivastava, and R. Reddy, "Towards word embeddings for improved duplicate bug report retrieval in software repositories," in *Proceedings of the 2018 ACM SIGIR International Conference on theory of information retrieval*, 2018, pp. 167–170.

[24] L. e. a. Poddar, "Train one get one free: Partially supervised neural network for bug report duplicate detection and clustering," *arXiv preprint arXiv:1903.12431*, 2019.

[25] Y. Jiang, X. Su, C. Treude, C. Shang, and T. Wang, "Does deep learning improve the performance of duplicate bug report detection? an empirical study," *Journal of Systems and Software*, p. 111607, 2023.

[26] F. Rahutomo, T. Kitasuka, and M. Aritsugi, "Semantic cosine similarity," in *The 7th international student conference on advanced science and technology ICAST*, vol. 4, no. 1, 2012, pp. 1–2.

[27] N. Reimers and I. Gurevych, "Sentence-bert: Sentence embeddings using siamese bert-networks," *CoRR*, vol. abs/1908.10084, 2019. [Online]. Available: http://arxiv.org/abs/1908.10084

[28] I. Loshchilov and F. Hutter, "Fixing weight decay regularization in adam," *CoRR*, vol. abs/1711.05101, 2017. [Online]. Available: http://arxiv.org/abs/1711.05101

[29] P. Bojanowski, E. Grave, A. Joulin, and T. Mikolov, "Enriching word vectors with subword information," *CoRR*, vol. abs/1607.04606, 2016. [Online]. Available: http://arxiv.org/abs/1607.04606

"Elderly, with location data, while shopping?" Spotting Privacy Threats Beyond Software: A Quasi-Experimental Study

Tuisku Sarrala
Faculty of Information Technology
University of Jyväskylä, Jyväskylä, Finland
email: tuisku.rad.sarrala@jyu.fi

Tommi Mikkonen
Faculty of Information Technology
University of Jyväskylä, Jyväskylä, Finland
email: tommi.j.mikkonen@jyu.fi

Abstract—**In software development, privacy has become an increasingly critical aspect due to privacy legislation, the growing complexity of software, and the private nature of many computing systems. However, studies reveal that developers often have security-focused understanding of privacy and expect user privacy needs to align with their own. This can risk regulatory compliance and potentially lead to harm to individuals. In this paper, we present a quasi-experimental study that explores how a card-based privacy threat modeling method using systems thinking elements could help to think about privacy threats on a broader scope and from another person's perspective. Sixty-five software engineering course participants used the same card deck. The experimental group created several scenarios, whereas the control group described their software with the cards. Both reflected against privacy principles. The experimental group's threats had broader and more often social scope, showed consideration for individuals, and were more often context-based. The control group's threats were more security focused and had software artifact focused scope. These findings help to understand how developers' understanding of privacy could be broadened. On a practical level, they have the potential to improve current privacy-by-design tools and methods, ultimately leading to more robust privacy protection in software development.**

Keywords—Privacy; privacy impact; software development; card-based modeling; systems thinking; personas; scenarios; process improvement.

I. INTRODUCTION

Today's companies processing personal data cannot avoid addressing privacy, which involves protecting personal information and assessing potential impacts on individuals. Privacy-related legislation enforces the requirement for understanding and mitigating harmful impact, such as the EU General Data Protection Regulation (GPDR) [1] and the forthcoming EU AI Act [2]. A lack of understanding of privacy threats, the source of privacy impact, can eventually expose customers to the risk of subjective and objective harms, and the company to significant financial losses. Consequently, privacy has become an important non-functional property to consider when building and deploying software systems.

Previous studies show that software developers have a narrow security-focused understanding of privacy [3]. During development, software is typically considered as a technical artifact. However, when the software is in use, it becomes a socio-technical system operating in the rich real world with real privacy-vulnerable individuals as its users. Threats arising from this complex context can go unnoticed by developers if their focus is merely on the security of the technical artefact. Therefore, to be successful in mitigating privacy threats in software development, studies suggest developers' understanding of privacy ought to be broadened [3]–[5]. Moreover, improving privacy tooling could help the situation, since developers prefer practical solutions and rely on privacy tools [3]. Furthermore, tools based on traditional reductionist approaches are a poor fit for broadening one's understanding of complex socio-technical issues [6].

Our research seeks to improve the situation, based on the following:

- **Engineering activity**: We target *privacy threat modeling* since it is a practical privacy thinking exercise which developers take part in.
- **Approach**: We apply *systems thinking*, which is an approach that
  - helps to understand *complex* issues, such as today's socio-technical software and privacy;
  - helps to develop one's thinking; and
  - involves techniques suited for broadening developers' understanding of privacy, through offering multiple perspectives, narrative and human focus.
- **Implementation**: We utilise on practical familiar techniques that fit systems thinking approach, namely *personas* and *scenarios* techniques, and *ideation cards*.

In this paper, we present a quasi-experimental study with 65 software engineering course participants during a short course where they developed a piece of software in small teams. We experimented with a card-based privacy threat modeling approach and examined its outcome, hoping to see threats that focus on privacy, consider harm to individuals, and have a broader scope beyond the technical artifact. In particular, we were interested in how a method with systems thinking features compares to a method with traditional features in privacy threat discovery in terms of identified threats.

"Systems thinking" analyzes complex situations by examining interactions and dependencies among system components [7]. The study revealed that with the systems thinking based method the identified privacy threats were wider in scope, less security-focused, more contextual and human-focused. Our results suggest that moving attention from the technical artifact to the wider context and directing it to the users' potential privacy vulnerabilities and interaction with the artifact appear to be key factors in improving privacy threat modeling outcome, leading to an enhanced understanding of privacy as a whole.

The rest of this paper is structured as follows. In Section 2, we present the background for the work. In Section 3, we describe our research approach and method. In Section 4, we provide the results of the study. In Section 5, we present a discussion regarding the key findings. In Section 6, we draw some final conclusions.

II. Background

A. Privacy and Privacy Threats

Privacy is a multifaceted concept that has many definitions, such as the right to be let alone [8] or one's control over their data [9]. A particular characteristic of privacy is that it touches people through the lack of it, resulting in harm which we call the *privacy impact*. Hence, it has been argued that rather than asking what privacy is, we should focus on the negative impacts and harms to address privacy [10]. Along similar lines, Daniel J. Solove, an influential privacy researcher, offers a taxonomy of privacy violations [11]. Privacy legislation too recognises the harms and impacts viewpoint. For example, the GDPR [1] mandates the anticipation of negative impacts arising from personal data processing to ensure the protection of individuals. In this article, we take the harms and impacts focused approach to privacy, and define *privacy impact* as any negative impact to individuals arising from the processing of personal data, in line with the GDPR. Similarly, we define *privacy threat* as something that has the capability of causing privacy impact to an individual.

Engineering is dominated by an approach that considers privacy as pre-definable through the application of compliance requirements and privacy principles [12]. Privacy-related legislation dictates the generic approach to privacy threat identification. Privacy impact and data protection impact assessment methods and templates from authorities [13] are commonly followed. Specifically for technical audience, there are privacy engineering methods for privacy threat and impact identification [14][15]. Typically, extensive modelling or description of the target is required and then compliance requirements, privacy principles or privacy goals are iterated against it. However, many threats can arise from the rich real world context where the system operates, and the traditional narrow focus on pre-defined privacy issues and the artifact model can leave these threats unnoticed.

B. Developers' Understanding of Privacy

Understanding privacy is imperative for software developers, for several reasons. The developers are required to (1) make privacy-safe and ethical design decisions, (2) spot and escalate privacy issues that they observe from their deeply technical viewpoint, and (3) collaborate effectively with business owners and company legal experts. These objectives consolidate the developers' contribution to the company achieving its main goal, legal compliance.

Recent research [4][5] points out that supporting developers' privacy understanding and practical privacy work is an under-researched area that requires attention. Security dominates when it comes to privacy in software development, but privacy is much more than security. Security is prominent in privacy research related to developers, developers understanding, and privacy tools for developers [3]–[5]. Previous research [3][16] shows that developers use security vocabulary to discuss privacy, which limits their perception of privacy to external threats, such as a hacker gaining access to personal data.

There are further aspects narrowing down developers' views. Developers have a practical rather than theoretical understanding of privacy, which does not match the policy makers' view [3][16]. Developers' understanding is built through practical work and online communities, as well as by observing the (at times questionable) privacy practices of big tech companies [4][17][18]. User privacy appears to be considered through the developer's own privacy persona [17][19], whose privacy needs may vastly differ from the needs of the individuals that become the users [19][20].

Due to the lack of skills in implementing privacy in practice, developers rely heavily on privacy tools and methods to carry out the necessary tasks [4]. Simultaneously, effective use of these tools is hampered due to developers still lacking a mental model of privacy. Training alone appears to be insufficient in bridging this gap, due to the lack of its practical relevance [4].

C. Systems thinking

"Systems thinking" is a conceptual approach used to understand and analyze complex situations, problems, or phenomena by focusing on the interactions and interdependencies among various components or elements within a larger system [7][21]. "System" could be comprised of physical entities, processes, people, organizations, or even abstract concepts. Arnold and Wade [7] propose the following definition for the purpose of systems thinking: "*Systems thinking is a set of synergistic analytic skills used to improve the capability of identifying and understanding systems, predicting their behaviors, and devising modifications to them in order to produce desired effects. These skills work together as a system.*". In practice, systems thinking commonly involves taking a holistic view, examining the dynamic interconnections of the different elements and observing the behaviour of the system that arises from the interconnections and the system's structure (i.e., behaviour that cannot be seen by examining the parts in isolation) [21]. Specific techniques include probing from different angles, multiple perspectives and narrative techniques [21].

The need for systems thinking skills for dealing with complex socio-technical systems and problem situations is recognised in literature [6][22]. Many of today's software systems can be seen as social systems [23]. They are embedded in their environment and constantly evolving [24]. This makes them complex and their boundaries blurred. Privacy is a complex social-technical issue, and more complex and ever-evolving software has more potential to create dangerous combinations for privacy. Both generic and engineering approaches for identifying privacy threats commonly rely on a detailed description and analysis of all the parts of the target. This traditional reductionist engineering approach can be heavy and poorly matched to today's complex software systems and privacy threats [6]. Where traditional approaches may struggle, systems thinking is suited for understanding complex human of problem situations [6].

D. Understanding Users and Their Privacy Vulnerabilities

Personas is a technique to model actual users as fictitious personas so that the software design can better fit their needs and expectations. Personas are commonly generated based on focus groups, interviews and workshops [25]. In the case of privacy personas, the unveiled privacy preferences of the users are used for privacy persona creation [26][27]. Understanding gained through personas can be enriched and strengthened by the use of scenarios [28]. *Scenarios* are a general non-standardised way of creating narratives around user activities. Personas based on users' preferences may not, however, help to identify privacy threats towards them, since their source may not be known to the user. The users may not be aware of their privacy vulnerabilities nor understand how threats may arise through their interaction with the software. Modeling personas with a variety of privacy vulnerabilities, rather than privacy preferences, could address this. This approach would be similar to the suggestion to model personas with various disabilities [29].

E. Card-based Implementation

Card-based design tools are virtual or physical cards commonly used for various design, planning, brainstorming, and collaborative activities. The cards typically represent individual pieces of information, concepts, tasks, or elements, and can be arranged, grouped, and manipulated by the users. A review of card-based design tools [30] shows that the most worthwhile outcomes appear to be produced by cards that stimulate creativity, facilitate early user participation, and summarise design or good practice guidelines. The review called for independent scientific trials since the cards had been evaluated mostly by their developers. Recent studies with privacy-related cards list accessibility and potential for communicating complex ideas as their benefits, and well as how cards intertwine with practice rather than separate privacy to be considered in separate forms [18]. Cards can enhance understanding at an introductory level, bring practical value and engage participants with the topic [17][31]. Weaknesses include overloading user with information, topic oversimplification, and being difficult to use, apply and update [30].

Next, studies with setups similar to ours are discussed. In contrast to our study, the identified privacy threats were neither studied nor reported in detail. Rather, the studies focused on the process of using the cards, so their findings will be more relevant for our future studies. We were interested in card-based methods that have a threat discovery element and scoped out methods that see privacy as pre-definable [12], such as compliance and privacy principle checklists.

1) Security and Privacy Threat Discovery Cards: The method [32] has some elements that are present in systems thinking approach, namely multiple perspectives and combining cards to create new viewpoints. The focus is on security threats by an attacker, but impact on humans is considered. The deck has four suits: human impact, adversary's motivations, adversary's resources and adversary's methods. Cards can be added. The eight human impact cards cover impacts on a wide scope: emotional, financial, physical and societal wellbeing, relationships, security of personal data, the biosphere and 'unusual impacts'. Different activities with the cards are suggested, such as combining, sorting, considering the unusual, and risk assessment.

2) An Ideation Card Study "Playing the legal card": The study was carried out by Luger et al. [31]. The systems thinking element of multiple user perspectives is present but the card usage was very linear. The target scenario was created specifically for the study. The card deck contained cards covering four GDPR requirements (data breach notification, use of consent, right to be forgotten and privacy by design), cards providing context (a description of a system), cards providing user groups (e.g., older people, ex-offenders, women of all cultures and faiths), and cards with system constraint descriptions. System architects and programmers took part along with HCI and research oriented players. The players drew one card of each category for discussion at five minute intervals and then discussed all of them for 15 minutes. The user cards reportedly had a significant effect on the system design. The groups saw the users through a stereotype, but these stereotypes highlighted several privacy issues.

3) An Ideation Card Study: The study by Tang et al. [17] elaborated the "Playing the legal card" study and involved teams of undergraduate students completing an industry-sponsored software development project. All the projects were different. The deck was similar to the "Playing the legal card" deck. From systems thinking perspective, the elements were the same. The cards included personas with qualities such as age, mental health, language, country, gender spectrum and physical health. The teams drew user, constraint and regulation cards from the deck, discarding cards which they felt were not applicable to their software. Teams could draw more cards, time permitting. The teams discussed each card for five minutes, and then all the drawn cards together. A week later, the teams provided a list of changes to be made in their projects based on the session. The teams struggled to understand the privacy concepts on the cards and rarely were able to generalise the concept to the team's context. Nevertheless, the authors suggest that privacy ideation cards are a promising pedagogical tool and should be used in student projects to help students learn about privacy.

III. RESEARCH APPROACH

A. Research Question and Experiment Design

To investigate how the problem situation could be improved, we set up a quasi-experiment. We selected privacy threat modeling as the practical engineering activity and implemented it as an experimental card-based tool with added systems thinking features. To control the experiment, we implemented a similar tool but with traditional features instead. The research question we sought to answer was:

RQ: How does a method with systems thinking features compare to a method with traditional features in privacy threat discovery in terms of identified threats?

In the experimental version, the systems thinking elements were the following:

- Multiple perspectives: looking at the situation through the persona cards' perspectives
- Narrative technique: creation of scenarios with the personas and explaining these to others
- Exploring interconnections and system behaviour arising from them: creation of scenarios from different elements and observing what privacy threats they may generate
- System's blurred boundary, context, environment: The modeling was not bounded by the software artifact boundaries or centred to that. The artifact was not modeled but was to be kept in mind.

Our reasoning for including personas was that they would:

- add a social dimension and thus broaden the scope where threats can appear (not bounded to the technical artifact);
- reveal impacts – privacy is easier to understand through its impacts, than through the abstract privacy concepts;
- illuminate in depth why privacy matters, since they amplify privacy threat effects for the particular persona due to their special vulnerabilities [31]; and
- offer an alternative for the participants reflecting against their own personas.

In the control version, the traditional features were the following:

- The modeling steps: the target is first described and then a check through privacy principles is carried out
- Focus: the technical artifact in the centre
- Pre-defined and checklist-based approach to privacy: the target is compared to privacy principles.

Although not a traditional feature but a compromise, we opted to ask the control group to describe their target with the given cards rather than words or diagrams, so that the cards available to both teams would be the same.

For the visual design and user instructions, we took into account the recommendations from the other card based studies. The cards were designed to be aesthetically pleasing and the threat modeling was organised as fun game, with short descriptions and no jargon, as recommended [17]. Along the recommendations, we provided an information session about privacy before the exercise and provided the teams all the cards as a reference, rather than restricting participants to drawn cards. In the experimental game, the user scenario was designed to be considered before the privacy principles. This is in line with "Playing the Legal Card" [31] where the participants saw the user and technology cards forming one inseparable whole, and ranked them higher in importance than the privacy regulation cards. Furthermore, the experimental game was designed to move focus from the technical artifact to threat scenarios, which is supported by a machine learning ethics cards study [33] stating that,"focus should be less on technology and more on consequences and implications". In another ethics focused card based study [18], it was observed that participants 'clustering' cards together enabled more nuanced discussions and communicating about complex threats. The experimental teams 'cluster' cards together into scenarios.

To narrow down the exercise, the discovered threats were not required to be a risk assessed. Free threat brainstorming was encouraged on the basis that a larger number of threats, less criticism on the ideas, allowing unusual ideas, and building on the ideas of others would produce more quality threats [34] and therefore be more valuable for the risk assessment process that would normally follow. The experiment focus was on initiating broader privacy thinking, rather than a final plausible threat listing. The participants were explained that in an industry setting, the threats would be the raw material for a risk assessment process, where their quality, likelihood and impact would be weighed, but that would not be part of this exercise.

B. Participant Selection and Experiment Setting

The experiment was conducted during a five-week remotely taught (online) software engineering course. The course was open both to persons already in the industry as well as to current students at master's level. Sixty-five participants gave research consent. The participants responded to a pre-course survey that asked how confident they were in any programming language and how many years of work experience in software engineering or development they had. The participants' work experience varied from none to over 10 years. Twenty participants had no relevant work experience; 19 had less than 1 year; 20 had 1-5 years; and 6 had over 6 years.

The main course assignment was to develop a piece of working software in teams of 3-5 participants. Participants were arranged in 16 teams, which were split to experimental and control group, as shown in Table I. The majority's experience in each team is in bold. It was not disclosed to the participants whether they belonged to the experimental or control group. The split was based on the confidence scores and then the experience scores, making the groups equal and avoiding variance within teams, as far as practicable.

The developed software was to be an online auction system, where users could sell and buy goods by bidding. The required features included email registration, user authentication, seller and buyer interfaces, system operator functions, and currency conversion. The course had an industry sponsor, and the team who delivered the best solution was promised a low-value prize.

In week two, all the participants were given a 30-minute basic lecture about privacy. In week four, the participants were given a 15-minute lecture focusing on privacy threats, and introducing the privacy threat modeling game that was created for the experiment. At the end of the lecture, the participants were instructed to play the privacy threat game within their

TABLE I
CONFIDENCE LEVEL AND YEARS OF WORK EXPERIENCE IN PROGRAMMING.

Experimental Team	Confidence 0-10	Work experience in yrs 0-10+
Team E1	1.8-3	**0**, 1-5
Team E2	3.6-4	**<1**
Team E3	4.1-5	0, **<1**, 1-5
Team E4	6	0, **<1**, 1-5
Team E5	6.9-7	**<1**, 1-5
Team E6	7-8	0, **1-5**, 6-10
Team E7	7-8.5	0, **<1**, 1-5
Team E8	9	1-5, **6-10**, 10+
Control Team	**Confidence 0-10**	**Work experience**
Team C1	0-1	**0**, <1, 6-10
Team C2	4	0, 1-5
Team C3	5-5.5	**0**, <1, **1-5**
Team C4	5.5-6	0, <1
Team C5	6-6.9	**0**, 1-5
Team C6	7.5-8	**0**, <1, 10+
Team C7	4.5-8.5	<1, **1-5**
Team C8	9-10	<1, **1-5**

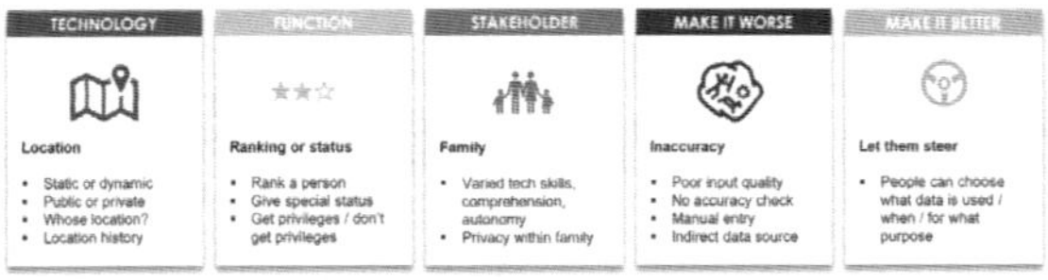

Figure 1. Examples of each card.

teams at their chosen time, with the aim of identifying privacy threats relating to the software they were designing. It was not disclosed to the participants that there were two different versions of the game.

C. Experimental and Control Game Implementation

The experimental card deck design was similar to the deck in the "Playing the legal card" [31] study. The cards depicted personas, technological context and privacy principles. Both games included the same cards, examples shown in Figure 1. There was a difference in usage of the software aspect cards and the game board, as shown in Figure 2.

The five categories of the cards were:

- Software aspect cards, describing the following:
  - Technology: 10 technologies that may be utilised in software (chat bot, office software, AI/machine learning, sensor, wearable, mobile phone, website, wireless, photos and video, location)
  - Function: 9 software functions (marketing, profile, ranking or status, security, shopping, social, access and identification, customer service, incidents and accidents)
  - Stakeholder: 10 personas that the stakeholders could be (elderly, family, influencer, knowledge worker, person with a past, child/teen, contractor, temporary staff, very important person, visitor)
- 12 "Make it worse" cards describing things that may weaken privacy in software, like anti-privacy principles

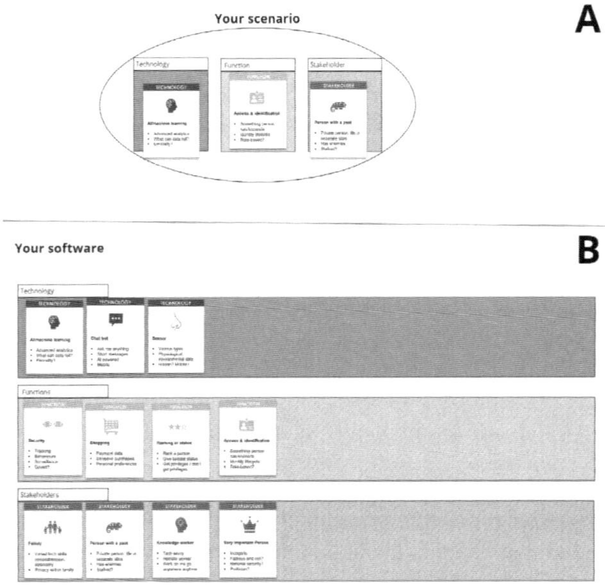

Figure 2. Experimental teams' board A and control teams' board B.

(1) Familiarise yourself with the game board. You can add your own cards by using the blank ones, if the ones provided are not enough.
Experimental teams: "Your scenario" area is used to represent different scenarios relating to the team software with one blue, one green and one purple card.
Control teams: "Your software" area is used to represent different aspects of the team software. From the blue, green and purple cards, choose all the technologies, functions and stakeholders that could represent your software now or in the future. Place them in the purple, green and blue boxes below ("Your software").

(2) Play the game. The cards are meant to give you ideas, rather than restrict you. So don't be bound by the exact things written on them.
Experimental teams: First make a scenario that could relate to your software, now or in the future. Pick one purple, green and blue card and place them in the middle under "Your scenario".
Both teams: Split into two roles: Baddies vs Goodies. Play takes place in turns. The Baddies' aim is to come up with privacy problems with the (**E**: software scenario)/(**C**: software). Baddies have the "Make it worse" cards to help them with bad ideas. The Goodies' aim is to mitigate baddies' ideas. Goodies have the "Make it better" cards to help them to mitigate the bad ideas. The Baddies go first. Baddies choose one card to worsen the software scenario and describe verbally a privacy problem that would happen, relating it to the software in a believable way. Then it is Goodies' turn to mitigate it, with the help of one or more "Make it better" cards. The aim is that the Goodies can mitigate all the privacy problems that the Baddies come up with, and keep the software safe for people to use. After each round, write down the privacy problem and its mitigation in the "Privacy problems catalogue" below the game board.
For the next round, swap roles and re-use all cards as you like! (**E**: You can change the scenario. Mix and match to make new scenarios) Come up with as many problems as you can. Play for 30-45 mins.

Figure 3. Instructions as given to the teams.

(more is more, inaccuracy, kept forever, vague purposes, identity and access, revealed, not available, no secrets, don't tell them, take advantage, sensitive data, combination)
- 12 "Make it better" cards describing things that may strengthen privacy in software, like privacy principles (use and reuse controlled, fair and ethical, minimise, expiry date, identity and access, let them steer, tell them about it, fresh and accurate, basic data, data segregation, availability, it's confidential)

Each card listed privacy vulnerabilities or related considerations about the topic or persona, to help the participant to think of the topic from the privacy angle. The cards were not specifically tailored for the target, but generic in their nature. All the card categories included also one "invent your own" card.

Written instructions to the teams are shown in Figure 3. The experimental teams were instructed to consider three software aspect cards of their choice at a time (1 technology, 1 function, 1 stakeholder) to come up with threats. The control teams had an additional step in the beginning, to choose all the software aspect cards that related to their software and lay them out on the game board. After that, they could start freely identifying threats.

The game was delivered through a Miro board[1]. A separate password-protected board was created for each team. The boards included a gaming area, cards movable with a mouse, a table where to record the identified threats and mitigations, and written instructions on how and why to play the game. Participants were instructed to record their online gaming session (showing a shared screen, with no participant video required). Everyone participated remotely. There was no facilitator. Using a game format instead of workshop format allowed participants to play without a facilitator, thus minimising external influences. A previous study [17] had listed strict time limits as a limiting factor for higher level cognitive processes. In our study, the teams could ultimately decide themselves how long they would play, but 30-45 minutes was instructed.

IV. Results

Once the teams had carried out the privacy threat exercise, the resulting privacy threat catalogues were collected from each team for analysis. The threats that the teams identified were categorised from different viewpoints to reveal differences in the number of threats discovered by the experimental and control groups based on threat type, scope, contextuality and the description for the harmed party, as well as the overall number of threats. In addition, the time taken to do the exercise was noted.

The threat analysis was done by coding the threat descriptions by the main author. For the initial coding the group codes were hidden and the threats were mixed, after which a sample of approx. 20% was reviewed by a researcher outside of this project. The final codings were adjusted based on the reviewer

[1]miro.com

TABLE II
Type of threats discovered.

Type	Experimental teams	Control teams
Privacy	31	21
Security	4	16
Other	8	6
Total	43	43

TABLE III
Scope of the threats.

Scope	Experimental teams	Control teams
Software	15	**26**
Malicious	5	**14**
Social	**21**	3
Society	**2**	0

comments. Codings which had no room for interpretation were not validated, such as merely highlighting the word used to describe the harmed party.

A. Number of Threats and Time Taken

It was found that teams in both experimental and control groups reported similar number of threats, between 4 and 7, approximately 5 each. Coincidentally, both groups' total was 43 threats. Among both experimental and control groups, the more experienced teams found fewer threats than the less experienced (around 4.4 against 6). No instructions on how many threats should be identified had been given to the teams, but the privacy threat catalogue template included three numbered rows and a help text how to add more.

The teams were instructed to play for 30-45 minutes, and they actually played for 28-65 minutes based on the lengths of the video recordings. On average per team, those in the experimental group played for 42:23 in mm:ss (5:39:07 in total, hh:mm:ss), whereas those in the control group played for 38:56 (5:11:27 in total). On average per team, those in the experimental group played approximately 3.5 minutes longer than those in the control group.

B. Types of Threats

The threats were categorised under three different types of threats:

- Privacy threats: Threat relates to how the person's personal data is used or exposed, or how their private life is exposed. Example: "The system collects data without telling the user and uses the data for other purposes." (Team C3)

TABLE IV
Descriptions of the harmed party.

-	Experimental teams	Control teams
None	12	**18**
Neutral	12	**25**
Persona	**19**	0

- Security threats: Threat is a security issue without a distinct privacy element. Example: "Database credentials reveals from public GitLab repository and gives full access to database." (Team E8)
- Other threats: Threat is about harm to a person, but does not relate to privacy or personal data use or exposure. Example: "Shopping website can have secretly extra fees hidden from customers." (Team E3)

Table II shows that experimental group uncovered a higher number of privacy threats than the control group.

C. Contextuality of Threats

The contextuality of the threats was analysed as either:

- Pre-definable: Threat could have existed on a generic checklist and the context does not matter much. Example: "Sensitive and unnecessary data is collected from users." (Team C8)
- Context-based: The threat is such as it would not have existed on a generic checklist, but it arises from the context. Example: "Financial status of the user can be identified though his purchase history." (Team C3)

Control group found 24 pre-definable threats and 19 context-based threats. Experimental group found 14 pre-definable threats and 29 context-based threats.

D. Scope of Threats

The scope of each threat was categorised, from narrow to wide scope:

- Software: Threat description is limited to the scope of software, where something is wrong with the software and it can be fixed there. Example: "Transactional data is never removed, regardless of success or date of the auction" (Team C6)
- Malicious party: Threat materialises through a malicious party, a greedy company or an attacker, internal or external. Example: "If forms are not controlled enough, user can input malicious data on input fields such as SQL injection and destroy or steal user data from database." (Team C4)
- Social: Threat materialises through how people interact with the software and touches people's social sphere. Example: "An elderly user inputs wrong payment data (account number, telephone number, address)." (Team E8)
- Society: Threat touches the society. "The app could collect excess amounts of GPS data from user's phone, the user could be e.g., a member of the parliament. Threat to national security." (Team E3)

Table III shows that most of the experimental group's threats were on the social scope. The control group uncovered threats on a narrower scope, with most of their threats being on the software and malicious scope. Only three social threats and no society threats were identified by the control group.

E. Descriptions of the Harmed Party

The words used by the experimental and control groups to describe the harmed party were as follows:

- Experimental teams: Child, family, elderly, famous person, influencer, knowledge worker, member of parliament, teenager, VIP, seller, customer, person, 'they', user, (or: no description)
- Control teams: Buyer, customer, person/people, someone, user, (or: no description)

The description of the harmed party for each threat was categorised as follows:

- No description: The threat description did not describe the harmed party in any way. Example: "Some page contains forgotten debug lines that reveal too much data." (Team C3)
- Neutral description: The harmed party was described as user, seller, buyer, customer, person/people, someone/they/who. Example: "Without authentication and with shared credentials user would see other user's info." (Team C4)
- Persona description: The harmed party has a persona. Example: "Customer service worker is obsessed with a famous individual, which happens to contact our customer service. Now he/she learns lots about his/her target of obsession!" (Team E4)

Table IV shows that that the control group's descriptions were limited to neutral descriptions of buyer, customer, person or people, someone and user. Experimental group used persona descriptions from the cards as well as descriptions that appear to be inspired by the cards (famous person, member of parliament) in addition to neutral descriptions. Both groups had threats where they had not described the harmed party at all. The neutral descriptions were invented by the individual teams. Within the experimental group, team E1 did not use any personas, and in contrast, team E4 only used personas. The rest of the experimental teams used a mix of personas, neutral descriptions and no descriptions.

The control group were instructed to choose the relevant cards in the beginning. Thus, their game boards were analysed to ascertain to what extent that had narrowed their selection of stakeholder cards. One control team had picked 9 out of the 10 stakeholder cards, five teams had picked 4-6 stakeholder cards, and two teams had picked 1-2 cards and supplemented their selections with 5-6 invented neutral stakeholders (such as seller, buyer and product owner). The experimental group chose relevant cards as the game went on. Based on the average number of threats found, the teams in the experimental group had picked 1-5 different stakeholder cards during the game.

V. Discussion

In this study, we set out to find ways to broaden developers' understanding of privacy beyond security and bring more focus to the harm to individuals via improving the threat modeling process. The research question to be addressed was:

RQ: How does a method with systems thinking features compare to a method with traditional features in privacy threat discovery in terms of identified threats?

The findings to the question were that the experimental group's threats had broader and more often social scope, were more often context-based and described the harmed party more often in a personal way. The control group's threats were mostly security-focused, their scope was the software artifact and the harmed party was described in a non-personal way.

The control group's results were in line with existing research regarding developers' understanding of privacy. The experimental group's results showed a positive result, pointing to that systems thinking features may improve the situation and is a promising direction of research. The findings could be used to inform the design of privacy threat modeling and privacy impact assessment methods for developers as well as privacy education.

A. Why Did the Same Card Deck Yield Different Results?

1) More Material to Consider: The experimental group used the software aspect cards to create several scenarios and the control group used them in a static way, for describing the software. The experimental group's changing scenarios introduced new additional viewpoints for every round, which means that they had more new material to consider than the control group. Having more material did not result in higher number of threats identified, but it may have contributed to the wider scope and contextuality of the threats. The experimental teams played approximately 3.5 minutes longer each. Therefore the experimental group was slightly slower, but not considerably, taking into account the extra scenario creating.

2) Scenarios Before Privacy Principles: The control group relied on the privacy principle cards for identifying threats, which may have led them to describe their threats more often in a pre-definable way, stating what is written on the card. The learning value of cards for understanding privacy *concepts* (privacy principle cards) is not well supported [17]. The experimental group had to be already thinking of threats when constructing the scenarios before applying the privacy principle cards. The threat scenario creation stage likely led to the threats being not pre-defined, but unique.

3) Mixing and Matching: Connected to scenario creation, mixing and matching cards may have contributed to the experimental group threats having a wider scope and more contextual, since mixing and matching is a different sense-making activity to concept generalisation. Whilst this study did not analyse the interaction with the cards, the instructions were that the experimental teams should mix and match cards, whereas control teams were instructed to pick a card (privacy principle / anti-priciple). The other card-based studies reported on the varying usage of the cards, such as sorting, grouping and so on, but not on the effects of this. It is likely that the card sorting was done in an attempt to increase understanding of the cards and possibly for getting more ideas.

4) Personas for Social Threats: Each scenario had a stakeholder card depicting a persona. This meant that the experimental group was first focused on the persona's privacy story, rather than the privacy concepts. This likely led the experimental group to use the personas in their threat descriptions. In "Playing the legal card" [31], the persona cards had a major effect, causing the players to see threats through their individual circumstances. Similarly in our study the experimental teams described nearly half of their threats through the personas and centred their threats to them. The control group did not describe any personas, probably since their focus was foremost on the static, described software artifact. This in turn may explain the very low number of social threats for the control group. In contrast, the experimental group's scenarios were inherently social since they always involved a persona, and the scenarios were natural interactions rather than happening inside the software artifact.

B. What May Have Affected the Results?

1) Time and Available Threats To Be Found: The combined effect of time, potential threats to be found, and the participants' effort, motivation and privacy-related experience, is difficult to establish. Neither the time for the task nor the threats to be identified were controlled. It is not known how many potential threats there were to be found in each software, which were all slightly different. This made the task more realistic but less controlled. Furthermore, this study was interested in non-pre-defined contextual threats in particular.

2) Controls for Persona Use: Whilst personas appear to have improved the experimental group's threats in our study, persona use comes with challenges [25] that may have affected this experiment. The experiment did not include detailed instructions about how to consider the persona cards, so it is possible that the participants did not know how to apply them against their software. For example, it was not explicitly stated that the personas depicted in the stakeholder cards had privacy vulnerabilities, although the bullet points under each hinted that way. It is possible that the experimental group relied on the personas too much, since all but one team used them in their threat descriptions. Due to the storytelling nature of scenarios and the personas not being directly representative of the software's users from the viewpoint of its functionality (buyers, sellers, etc.), it is possible that threat scenarios became a stories of their own, rather than tightly relating to their software. The control group did not use any of the personas given on the stakeholder cards in their threat descriptions although six out of the eight teams had selected them to represent their software. Again this could be due to the personas appearing unrepresentative. In addition, the control group was not challenged on their stakeholder card selections after they had selected them in the beginning.

3) Controls for Participants: The participants' programming confidence and software engineering related work experience was varied. Having variety is natural in the industry and being in a group somewhat helped to balance the variety. Participants were arranged in groups based on experience and confidence, so that the difference between the results of high and low confidence and experience could be also compared. No information about participants' understanding of privacy was collected beforehand. The effects of this was mitigated by delivering all participants the same lectures about privacy. No training on the delivery platform, Miro, was given, but it was excepted that due to its simplicity, the possible learning curve would not be too steep. Participants were instructed to familiarise themselves with the platform functionality before beginning the exercise. Since the exercise was completed only once, the teams could not enjoy the benefits of learning the platform and the tool. The participants' physical environment was not controlled but all individuals were remote.

C. Threats to External Validity

1) Presence of Complexity and Systems Thinking: One of the drivers for the research was using systems thinking for understanding complex systems. Although privacy and socio-technical systems are complex phenomena and the results may be generalizable to those, the teams' modeling targets were not complex from a technical viewpoint. Hence, the results' applicability to technically complex systems remains open. Traditional approaches may work well with simple systems [6], but so far as our control method can be considered "traditional", it was outperformed by the experimental method from our research perspective. Systems thinking approach uses various techniques, some of which can be found in other settings too but here they were applied from the systems thinking perspective. For example, the personas technique is commonly used to model the actual users, whereas here it was used to bring in multiple perspectives and probe the issues. However, it would be worth exploring whether the general approach or the specific techniques made the difference, or perhaps their interplay.

2) Realistic Control Method: Instead of using an existing traditional method for the control groups, the control method was specifically designed for the experiment, making it somewhat artificial and simplified. This was a compromise to increase control of the experiment, but it can lower the generalizability of the results. The control group version was designed based on the traditional way of identifying privacy threats, where the teams built a representation of the software (their selection of relevant cards) and then examined it against the privacy principles and anti-principles. The control group's 'traditional' results indicate that the control version design was successful and provided appropriate control for the experiment.

3) Plausibility of the Threats: Due to the threat scenario building encouraging story-telling, there is a chance that the experimental group threats came out as far fetched stories about the personas and were not so closely related to the software. This is not a major concern since in this study we were interested in what can evoke broader and human centred privacy thinking, rather than focusing on the threats' quality from the impact and likelihood assessment viewpoint. It is also possible that any implausible threat scenarios can be modified to plausible ones in the risk assessment stage.

4) Generalizability to Developers and Industry Setting: The experiment was not carried out with software developers in an industry setting. Two thirds of the participants had no or very little relevant work experience, while the remaining third been in the industry for at least one year. When looking at the teams, all but two teams had participants with at least one year of industry experience, which helps to increase the generalizability of the results. Other aspects that made the set-up more realistic were that the course had an industry sponsor acting as the client, who evaluated and commented on the final pieces of software at the end of the course, and the experiment was embedded as a natural element in the software development process.

D. Directions for Future Work

To address the threats to validity and limitations discussed above, we plan to validate the findings in an industrial environment with a more complex target and extend the analysis to the plausibility of the threats. Secondly, we plan to analyse the session recordings so that comparisons to the other card-based studies can be made, which concentrated on the participants' interaction with the cards. To investigate the participants' understanding of privacy, the session recordings could be analysed for cognitive processes, as done in study by Tang et al. [17].

In terms of the experimental method, in addition to reviewing and refining all of the cards, the persona cards and related guidance should be developed further. Each persona's privacy vulnerabilities should be stated more clearly and users should be instructed clearer on their usage for reflection.

VI. Conclusion

In this paper, we were motivated by the potentially harmful combination of the impact that developers can have on user privacy and their limited security-focused understanding of this subject. In response, we designed a quasi-experiment that targeted the privacy threat modeling activity and investigated how an experimental method with systems thinking features compared to a traditional-style method in terms of identified threats.

The threats identified within the experimental group prominently considered wider contextual factors and human interactions, which equals to a positive result showing a broader view of privacy. The control group, employing the traditional-style method, generated more security-focused threats, aligning with the prevailing norms. We attribute the experimental group's result to the shift of focus from the software artifact and privacy principles to the human interaction with the software beyond its technical boundaries. The shift was achieved with the use of personas and scenarios with a systems thinking approach. These techniques can be inserted in privacy tools and methods to improve current practice and ultimately help to produce more privacy safe software. Following these results, we plan to gain additional insights by analysing the session recordings, refine the cards and the user guidance accordingly, and finally validate the results in the industry.

REFERENCES

[1] Regulation (EU) 2016/679, "General Data Protection Regulation (GDPR). Regulation (EU) 2016/679 of the European Parliament and of the Council of 27 April 2016, on the protection of natural persons with regard to the processing of personal data and on the free movement of such data, and repealing Directive 95/46/EC," 2016. [Online]. Available: https://eur-lex.europa.eu/eli/reg/2016/679/oj [Retrieved: October, 2023]

[2] Proposal for Regulation (EU) COM/2021/206 final, "Proposal for a regulation of the European Parliament and of the Council laying down harmonised rules on artificial intelligence (Artificial Intelligence Act) and amending certain Union legislative acts." 2021.

[3] I. Hadar et al., "Privacy by designers: software developers' privacy mindset," *Empirical Software Engineering*, vol. 23, no. 1, pp. 259–289, 2 2018.

[4] M. Tahaei, "The Developer Factor in Software Privacy," Ph.D. dissertation, The University of Edinburgh, 2021.

[5] M. Peixoto et al., "The perspective of Brazilian software developers on data privacy," *Journal of Systems and Software*, vol. 195, p. 111523, 1 2023.

[6] P. F. Katina, C. B. Keating, and R. M. Jaradat, "System requirements engineering in complex situations," *Requirements Engineering*, vol. 19, no. 1, pp. 45–62, 2014.

[7] R. D. Arnold and J. P. Wade, "A definition of systems thinking: A systems approach," in *Procedia Computer Science*, vol. 44, no. C. Elsevier, 2015, pp. 669–678.

[8] S. D. Warren and L. D. Brandeis, "The Right to Privacy," *Harvard law review*, vol. 4, no. 5, pp. 193–220, 1890.

[9] A. F. Westin, *Privacy and freedom*. New York: Atheneum, 1970.

[10] W. Hartzog, "What is Privacy? That's the Wrong Question," *U. Chi. L. Rev.*, vol. 88, p. 1677, 2021.

[11] D. J. Solove, "A Taxonomy of Privacy," *University of Pennsylvania Law Review*, vol. 154, no. 3, pp. 477–564, 2006.

[12] R. Y. Wong and D. K. Mulligan, "Bringing Design to the Privacy Table," in *Proceedings of the 2019 CHI Conference on Human Factors in Computing Systems*. New York, NY, USA: ACM, 5 2019, pp. 1–17.

[13] Information Commissioner's Office, "Sample DPIA template," 2018. [Online]. Available: https://ico.org.uk/for-organisations/guide-to-data-protection/guide-to-the-general-data-protection-regulation-gdpr/accountability-and-governance/data-protection-impact-assessments/ [Retrieved: October, 2023]

[14] M. C. Oetzel and S. Spiekermann, "A systematic methodology for privacy impact assessments: a design science approach," *European Journal of Information Systems*, vol. 23, no. 2, pp. 126–150, 3 2014.

[15] K. Wuyts, L. Sion, and W. Joosen, "LINDDUN GO: A Lightweight Approach to Privacy Threat Modeling," in *2020 IEEE European Symposium on Security and Privacy Workshops (EuroS&PW)*. IEEE, 9 2020, pp. 302–309.

[16] M. Peixoto et al., "On Understanding How Developers Perceive and Interpret Privacy Requirements Research Preview," in *Requirements Engineering: Foundation for Software Quality*, ser. Lecture Notes in Computer Science, N. Madhavji, L. Pasquale, A. Ferrari, and S. Gnesi, Eds., vol. 12045. Cham: Springer International Publishing, 2020, pp. 116–123.

[17] Y. Tang, M. L. Brockman, and S. Patil, "Promoting Privacy Considerations in Real-World Projects in Capstone Courses with Ideation Cards," *ACM Transactions on Computing Education*, vol. 21, no. 4, p. 34, 12 2021.

[18] L. D. Urquhart and P. J. Craigon, "The Moral-IT Deck: a tool for ethics by design," *Journal of Responsible Innovation*, vol. 8, no. 1, pp. 94–126, 2021.

[19] A. R. Senarath and N. A. G. Arachchilage, "Understanding user privacy expectations: A software developer's perspective," *Telematics and Informatics*, vol. 35, no. 7, pp. 1845–1862, 10 2018.

[20] S. Sheth, G. Kaiser, and W. Maalej, "Us and Them: A Study of Privacy Requirements across North America, Asia, and Europe," in *Proceedings of the 36th International Conference on Software Engineering*, ser. ICSE 2014. New York, NY, USA: Association for Computing Machinery, 2014, pp. 859–870.

[21] J. P. Monat and T. F. Gannon, "What is Systems Thinking? A Review of Selected Literature Plus Recommendations," *American Journal of Systems Science*, vol. 2015, no. 1, pp. 11–26, 2015.

[22] K. E. Dugan, E. A. Mosyjowski, S. R. Daly, and L. R. Lattuca, "Systems thinking assessments in engineering: A systematic literature review," *Systems Research and Behavioral Science*, vol. 39, no. 4, pp. 840–866, 7 2022.

[23] R. L. Ackoff, "Systems thinking and thinking systems," *System Dynamics Review*, vol. 10, no. 2-3, pp. 175–188, 1994.

[24] M. M. Lehman, "Program evolution," *Information Processing & Management*, vol. 20, no. 1-2, pp. 19–36, 1 1984.

[25] D. Karolita, J. McIntosh, T. Kanij, J. Grundy, and H. O. Obie, "Use of personas in Requirements Engineering: A systematic mapping study," *Information and Software Technology*, vol. 162, p. 107264, 10 2023.

[26] E. Kim, J. K. Yoon, J. Kwon, T. Liaw, and A. M. Agogino, "From innocent irene to parental patrick: Framing user characteristics and personas to design for cybersecurity," in *Proceedings of the International Conference on Engineering Design, ICED*, vol. 2019-August. Cambridge University Press, 2019, pp. 1773–1782.

[27] M. Rudolph, S. Polst, and J. Doerr, "Enabling users to specify correct privacy requirements," in *Requirements Engineering: Foundation for Software Quality: 25th International Working Conference, REFSQ 2019, Essen, Germany, March 18–21, 2019, Proceedings 25*, 2019, pp. 39–54.

[28] J. Salminen, K. Wenyun Guan, S. G. Jung, and B. Jansen, "Use Cases for Design Personas: A Systematic Review and New Frontiers," in *Conference on Human Factors in Computing Systems - Proceedings*. Association for Computing Machinery, 4 2022, pp. 1–21.

[29] J. T. Nganji and S. H. Nggada, "Disability-Aware Software Engineering for Improved System Accessibility and Usability," *International Journal of Software Engineering and Its Applications*, vol. 5, no. 3, pp. 47–62, 7 2011.

[30] R. Roy and J. P. Warren, "Card-based design tools: A review and analysis of 155 card decks for designers and designing," *Design Studies*, vol. 63, pp. 125–154, 7 2019.

[31] E. Luger, L. Urquhart, T. Rodden, and M. Golembewski, "Playing the legal card: Using ideation cards to raise data protection issues within the design process," in *Conference on Human Factors in Computing Systems - Proceedings*, vol. 2015-April. Association for Computing Machinery, 4 2015, pp. 457–466.

[32] T. Denning, B. Friedman, and T. Kohno, "The Security Cards," 2013. [Online]. Available: http://securitycards.cs.washington.edu/index.html [Retrieved: October, 2023]

[33] K. E. K. Bilstrup, M. H. Kaspersen, and M. G. Petersen, "Staging reflections on ethical dilemmas in machine learning: A card-based design workshop for high school students," in *DIS 2020 - Proceedings of the 2020 ACM Designing Interactive Systems Conference*. Association for Computing Machinery, Inc, 7 2020, pp. 1211–1222.

[34] J. E. Danes, J. Lindsey-Mullikin, and K. Lertwachara, "The sequential order and quality of ideas in electronic brainstorming," *International Journal of Information Management*, vol. 53, p. 102126, 8 2020.

An Empirical Investigation of Usability Measurement in Canvas Educational Applications

A Case Study at the University of North Texas

1st Shabbab Algamdi
Computer Science Department
University of North Texas
Denton, Texas
shabbab.algamdi@unt.edu

2nd Stephanie Ludi
Computer Science Department
University of North Texas
Denton, Texas
stephanie.ludi@unt.edu

***Abstract*—A Learning Management System (LMS) is a computer software that enables teachers and students to become more actively involved in their studies and learn more effectively. The Canvas LMS is one of the best examples in this field as it is a widely adopted LMS. It is extensively utilized throughout a range of educational institutions, involving K-12 schools as well as universities. The platform has received recognition for its intuitive user interface and comprehensive selection of impacts educational resources.This study is conducted on computer science students at the University of North Texas because this sample of students is more familiar with the terminologies used in the study regarding gauging usability in Canvas applications. This is done in accordance with the Jacob Nielsen usability factors study. The goal of this study is to identify the most significant problems with the usability of the Canvas application. This study simultaneously examines and classifies them according to several aspects, and then determines how to address and improve the responses for each of these factors. This methodologies adopted in this study serve as a tool for the main investigation, and the 104 students successfully completed it. The overall scale in the study had a Cronbach's alpha rating of 0.969, which shows that the reliability and consistency of the questionnaire in this study are quite high.The survey's framework was built upon the principles outlined by Jacob Nielsen for mobile usability. During the pilot testing phase of the survey, the results revealed a substantial percentage of reliability and validity. Despite minor fluctuations, the findings consistently demonstrated a commendable level of reliability. These results open the door for further investigations.**

Keywords*—*Usability; Human-Computer Interaction; Learning Management Systems; User Reviews; Mobile Application Platform.

I. Introduction

During the COVID-19 pandemic, the evolution and enhancement of Learning Management Systems (LMS) have been notably pronounced, with Canvas emerging as a prominent example. Canvas LMS boosts a comprehensive set of features that benefit both students and instructors, contributing to the positive development of online education during this challenging period [1]. The Canvas app is one of the most significant LMS applications [2]. These platforms offer a variety of functions and resources to help in managing courses, distributing content, and grading students. The ease of use and steep learning curves of these platforms greatly influence their efficiency. A LMS is highly useful when it is simple for users to use, efficient, and requires minimal effort on their part to fulfill tasks. The value of the Canvas app has been examined in a few of studies [1][3] when compared to other educational apps, the usefulness of the Canvas application is proven to be high. It is discovered that students using Canvas scored higher on its navigation easiness and friendly layout.

Mobile learning has a lot of educational potential. The most recent iteration of mobile technology makes it simple to provide digital material using portable wireless mobile devices. Because of the inherent limitations of mobile devices, such as their small screens, lack of input capabilities, and low computing capacity, creating mobile learning applications is not an easy task [4].

In a separate investigation, Hossain [5] conducted a survey involving college students, revealing a paradox in their perceptions of Canvas. While they granted Canvas high marks for its usability, their assessment of the platform's search features and mobile usability was notably unfavorable. In addition to these studies, a collection of articles and blog posts also underscores the apparent simplicity of using Canvas. Similarly, within the domain of educational technology, a blog post emphasized Canvas's adaptability and functionality compared to Blackboard (another widely used LMS), further affirming the significance of customization and usability within different LMS platforms [6].

One notable tool that contributes to enhancing the user experience of educational apps, such as Canvas, is the utilization of app reviews. As the usage of smartphones and tablets by students surges, mobile usability becomes an increasingly crucial aspect determining the performance of mobile apps. The usability of an app on mobile devices pertains to its ease of use and its efficient functionality. A mobile application is considered user-friendly when it is intuitive, performs seamlessly, and minimizes user effort. In 2023, the task of identifying high-quality educational apps appears to be a challenging endeavor, particularly considering the staggering number of over 567,000 educational apps available [7]. Thus, instead of relying solely on app reviews, this study opted for a more empirical approach by conducting a usability survey for the Canvas app. The rest of this paper is organized as follows. Section II highlights the recent research endeavors related to the scope of this study. Section III presents the main core of the methodology adopted. Section IV presents the results and discussions achieved. Section V discusses the correlation between the variables, and finally Section VI concludes this paper and presents recommendations for future work.

II. Related Work

Related work is investigated on two levels. One is addressing the mobile application usability in general, while the other is focusing on education apps usability specifically.

A. *Mobile Application Usability*

Building upon Shackel's model, Nielsen [4] in 1993 presented his own conceptualization of usability. Initially encompassing four attributes (Learnability, Effectiveness, Efficiency, and Satisfaction). Nielsen subsequently revised this by eliminating 'Effectiveness' and introducing 'Memorability' and 'Errors', culminating in a five-attribute framework. This conceptualization garnered substantial recognition within the Human-Computer Interaction (HCI) community, particularly due to its emphasis on users' perceptions of the system and aspects of recall, as highlighted by the inclusion of 'Satisfaction' and 'Memorability'[8] [9].
Usability in mobile applications is delineated based on the International Standards Organization's (ISO) definition, characterizing it as the degree to which a designated user can employ such an application to realize predetermined objectives with accuracy, proficiency, and contentment within a given usage context [10] [11]. Usability studies focus on how system features and user interactions interact when placed within particular activities and expected results. Due to the fact that many software products have been found to be less than ideal in meeting user needs, a variety of thorough study projects that go under the general heading of "usability" have been started. These efforts aim to promote more profound understanding and relevant measurement, with the goal of capturing all relevant phenomena in a single framework or model [12].

B. *Education Apps usability*

Several academic studies have been conducted to evaluate the effectiveness of educational applications. A recent investigation employed deep learning models to discern usability issues within mobile applications in the education applications [13]. This research has focused alot on how application functionality and design affect student learning results [14]. Mobile learning offers a paradigm wherein educational acquisition is untethered from traditional spatial and temporal constraints. Instead of being confined to established settings like classrooms or predefined schedules, it facilitates pedagogical engagement across diverse locales and at any chosen moment[15].

This literature review delves into pertinent insights extracted from recent research concerning the usability of educational applications. Earlier investigations have primarily focused on appraising the efficacy of employing educational apps for instructing young children [16] [17]. Their analysis culminated in the observation that the efficacy of educational apps predominantly hinged on factors such as the quality of the user interface, the ease of navigation, and the capacity to engage with content. In a similar vein, Perera and Yacef's investigation underscored that student motivation and engagement were profoundly impacted by the visual and experiential aspects inherent in educational app design [18]. Tailoring learning experiences to individual students stands as another pivotal attribute of educational apps, contributing to their user-friendliness. In this context, Lee et al. examined the influence of personalized learning approaches on the ease of utilizing educational apps[19]. Their findings underscored students' inclination toward personalized learning features, particularly adaptive content and feedback mechanisms. These attributes emerged as effective tools for sustaining student interest and motivation [20]. The usability of educational apps presents a multifaceted and intricate challenge, encompassing numerous elements that influence student engagement, motivation, and learning achievements. Through the adoption of a comprehensive perspective encompassing app design and functionality, coupled with the integration of attributes that foster personalization and usability, developers can elevate the overall usability of educational apps and thereby elevate the quality of student learning experience [21].

Based on the Jakob Nielsen factors, the scope of this study can be formulated as follows: For the Canvas LMS application, and as outlined by Nielsen's study, to what extent are the interrelationships between the different usability factors observable, and what are their effects?

III. Methodology

To comprehensively understand the usability factors of the Canvas LMS application in light of Nielsen's criteria, we adopted a structured approach. This section delineates the methods we used, starting with a foundation in the information background, followed by an exploration of the general challenges users encounter.

A. *Information Background and General Challenge*

In Table 1 valuable insights into the Information Background and General Challenges encountered by users of Canvas within the study. The breakdown of users by educational level indicates a majority of Graduate students (72.1%), followed by Undergraduate (23.1%) and Doctoral (4.8%) students. This diversity of academic levels engaging with the LMS is noteworthy.
The duration of usage of the Canvas mobile app displays an even distribution, with a significant portion of respondents (30.8%) using it for 6 months to 1 year and 19.2% for 1 year to 2 years. This result suggests a moderate level of familiarity with the platform. Interestingly, fewer users have used the app

for longer durations, implying that turnover among users could impact the interpretation their experiences and challenges.
Within the Computer Science Engineering (CSE) department, a considerable number of respondents (92.3%) are enrolled in various programs, with Computer Science (62.5%) emerging as the predominant academic department. This concentration highlights the potential for tailoring Canvas features to address this department's specific needs and requirements. Notable representation is also seen from other departments, such as Computer Engineering (13.5%), AI (16.3%), and Cybersecurity (4.8%), underscoring the platform's adaptability across diverse fields of study. These findings emphasize the importance of comprehending the CSE department's educational backgrounds, usage patterns, and program enrollments. Such understanding can guide the enhancement of Canvas to better serve the distinct needs and challenges faced by users at different academic stages and within various fields of study. These demographics are visually represented in Figure 1.

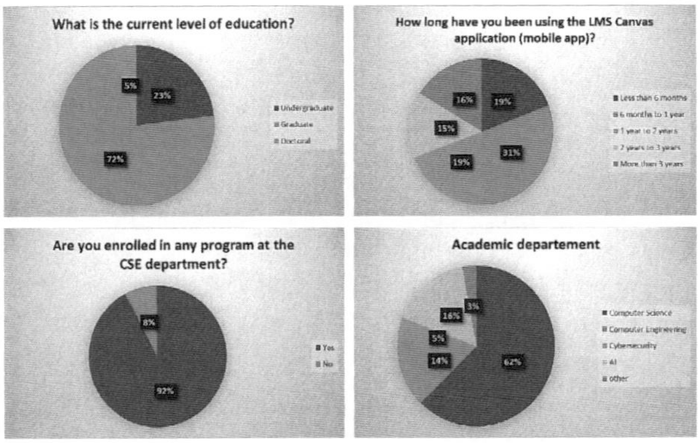

Fig. 1. Information Background for Canvas Users in the Study

TABLE I
INFORMATION BACKGROUND FOR CANVAS USERS IN THE STUDY

Items	N	%
What is the current level of education?		
Undergraduate	24	23.1%
Graduate	75	72.1%
Doctoral	5	7.8%
How long have you been using the LMS Canvas app on mobile?		
Less than 6 months	20	19.2%
6 months to 1 year	32	30.8%
1 year to 2 years	20	19.2%
2 years to 3 years	15	14.4%
More than 3 years	17	16.3%
Are you enrolled in any program at the CSE department?		
Yes	96	92.3%
No	8	7.7%
Academic departement		
Computer Science	65	62.5%
Computer Engineering	14	13.5%
Cybersecurity	5	4.8%
AI	17	16.3%
other	3	2.9%

B. *Reliability analysis*

In Table 2 the Cronbach alpha levels of the study variables concerning the Canvas users is presented. The conducted reliability analysis on the Canvas user study variables offers a comprehensive evaluation of the key factors influencing user satisfaction and experience. The Cronbach's alpha values assigned to each variable serve as internal consistency and measurement reliability indicators, thus shedding light on the robustness of the study's conclusions. Remarkably, the notably high Cronbach's alpha values for several variables such as Visibility of System Status (0.920), Aesthetic and Minimalistic Design (0.900), and User Control and Intuitiveness (0.911) underline the robust reliability and interconnectedness of these aspects. While certain variables exhibit somewhat lower Cronbach's alpha values, such as Recognition Over Recall (0.737) and Realistic Error Management (0.667), they still indicate a reasonable level of reliability.
Furthermore, Consistency and Standards, Efficiency of Use and Performance, and Alignment Between System and Real-World Context display satisfactory Cronbach's alpha values of 0.772, 0.798 and 0.777, respectively. Finally, Cronbach's alpha level for the total scale in the study was 0.958, indicating that this questionnaire has excellent reliability and consistency.

TABLE II
THE RELIABILITY ANALYSIS OF THE FACTORS IN THE STUDY

Variable	No. of items	Cronbach alpha
Visibility of System Status	2	0.920
Match Between System and Real World	2	0.777
Aesthetic and Minimalistic Design	2	0.900
Recognition Rather than Recall	2	0.737
Effective Design to Lesson User's Workload	2	0.870
Flexibility and Efficiency of use	2	0.680
User control and obviousness	2	0.911
Realistic error management	2	0.667
Consistency and standards	3	0.772
Efficiency of use and performance	2	0.798
Total scale	21	0.958

C. *Validity Analysis*

Table 2 exhibits the outcomes of the validity analysis conducted on the factors within the Canvas user division. The validity of the factors was determined via a Pearson correlation analysis. To establish their construct validity, each item of the scale was correlated with the entire scale. All items showcased an immensely significant positive correlation with the entirety of the scale they are associated with. Thus, the essential items sufficiently established the concept of the factors and effectively expressed their significance in assessing the impressions of Canvas users.

IV. DESCRIPTIVE STATISTICS ANALYSIS

Table 3 and Figure 2 show the descriptive statistics, including mean, standard deviation, and the agreement levels of the Canvas users factors in the study. The "Visibility of System Status" factor reflects a positive user sentiment. The users

TABLE III
USABILITY MEASUREMENT SCORES

Factor	Mean	Std. Dev.	Level
Visibility of System Status			
The status of icons is clearly indicated in the application.	4.36	1.153	Agree
Graphical user interface menus make obvious whether deselection is possible.	4.11	1.187	Agree
Visibility of System Status mean score	4.23	1.126	Agree
Match Between System and Real World			
The selected colors correspond to common expectations about the color codes.	4.22	0.996	Agree
Function keys labeled clearly and distinctively, even if this means breaking consistency rules.	4.06	1.153	Agree
Match Between System and Real World mean score	4.14	0.974	Agree
Aesthetic and Minimalistic Design			
Field labels are brief, familiar, and descriptive.	4.32	1.138	Agree
The large objects, bold lines, and simple areas have been used to distinguish icons.	4.32	1.193	Agree
Aesthetic and Minimalistic Design mean score	4.32	1.112	Agree
Recognition Rather than Recall			
The system provides mapping: do the relationships between controls and actions appear to the user?	4.19	1.176	Agree
There is a good color and brightness contrast between image and background colors.	4.32	1.099	Agree
Recognition Rather than Recall mean score	4.26	1.013	Agree
Effective Design to Lesson User's Workload			
A simple design canvas is easy to navigate and understand and it can significantly reduce the amount of cognitive load required to complete a task.	4.40	1.030	Agree
Feedback and error messages can help users quickly identify and correct mistakes, reducing the time and effort needed to complete a task.	4.27	1.193	Agree
Effective Design to Lesson User's Workload mean score	4.34	1.048	Agree
Flexibility and Efficiency of use			
The canvas supports both beginner and expert users, are multiple levels of error message detail available.	4.34	1.151	Agree
Canvas offer "find next" and "find previous" shortcuts for database searches.	3.99	1.364	Agree
Flexibility and Efficiency of use mean score	4.16	1.098	Agree
User control and obviousness			
Canvas has design and services which make it customizable and easy to use	4.28	1.177	Agree
Canvas is customizable and simple to use because to its design and service features.	4.21	1.163	Agree
Realistic error management			
Canvas is providing clear and concise error messages that communicate what went wrong and how the user can fix it.	3.72	1.282	Agree
Realistic error management mean score	3.93	1.059	Agree
Consistency and standards			
Canvas symbols, icons, and symbolism should be consistent.	4.38	0.818	Agree
When users interact with content on Canvas categories, they should expect a clear and familiar experience	4.54	0.743	Agree
Consistency and standards mean score	4.45	0.706	Agree
Efficiency of use and performance			
The Canvas application offers specific features and tools that can help users to quickly locate the information they need, potentially making it more efficient than other learning management systems.	4.22	1.109	Agree
Efficiency of use and performance mean score	4.18	1.026	Agree
Other Considerations			
Users may be accessing the device in a variety of settings, such as while walking, standing in a crowded area, or sitting in a quiet space.	4.40	1.091	Agree

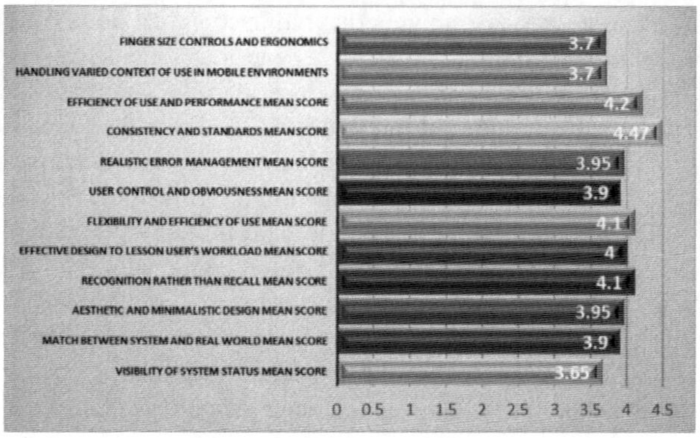

Fig. 2. All Canvas Users' Factors Mean in The Study

agree that icons are clearly indicated (M= 4.36, SD = 1.153), and the graphical user interface menus clarify deselection (M= 4.11, SD = 1.187). The whole mean score factor was 4.23, indicating a high agreement of the Canvas users toward its Visibility of System Status. Similarly, the factor "Match Between System and Real World" garners agreement, with users finding that selected colors align with common expectations (M= 4.22, SD= 0.996) and function keys are distinctly labeled (M= 4.06, SD= 1.153). Also, the overall mean score of this factor was 4.14, reflecting the higher matching between the Canvas system and the real world.

In terms of "Aesthetic and Minimalistic Design," users appreciate the use of brief, familiar, and descriptive field labels (M= 4.32, sd= 1.138) and the incorporation of large objects and bold lines to distinguish icons (M= 4.32, SD= 1.193). Likewise, the overall mean score of this factor was also 4.32. Furthermore, the "Recognition Rather than Recall" factor emphasizes user-friendly design, with users recognizing the presence of mapping between controls and actions (M= 4.19, SD= 1.176) and appreciating good color and brightness contrast (M= 4.32, SD= 1.099). The overall mean score of this factor was 4.26, indicating the increased agreement from the Canvas users toward this factor.

In addition, the "Effective Design to Lessen User's Workload" factor suggests that a simple design reduces cognitive load (M= 4.40, SD= 1.030), and users find feedback and error messages helpful (m= 4.27, SD= 1.193) in streamlining tasks. The overall mean score showed a high agreement degree with a mean score of 4.34. similarly, the "Flexibility and Efficiency of Use" factor demonstrates Canvas's support for both beginner and expert users (M= 4.34, SD= 1.151), although the "find next" and "find previous" shortcuts receive slightly lower agreement (M= 3.99, SD= 1.364). However, the overall mean score of this factor was high (4.16), indicating the flexibility and efficiency of the Canvas use by the participants in the study.

Moreover, the "User control and obviousness" factor underscores Canvas's customizability and ease of use (M= 4.28, SD= 1.177), aligning with users' positive perceptions of its design and services (M= 4.21, SD= 1.163). In this context, the User control and obviousness mean score was 4.24. In terms of "Realistic error management," users agree that Canvas provides clear error messages (M= 3.72, SD= 1.282) and emphasizes plain language over technical jargon (M= 4.14, SD= 1.160). Although this factor has the lowest overall mean score (3.93) among other factors, it still has an agreement level of response.

On the other hand, The "Consistency and standards" factor reflects users' positive reactions to consistent symbols and icons (M= 4.38, SD= 0.818), familiar interaction experiences (M= 4.54, SD= 0.743), and a navigational design standard on the homepage (M= 4.41, SD= 4.41). The overall mean score was consistent with these variable scores, with 4.45. Lastly, the "Efficiency of use and performance" factor highlights Canvas's potential efficiency in locating information (M= 4.22, SD= 1.109) and the potential workflow improvements brought by shortcuts (M= 4.14, SD= 1.142). The overall mean score of this factor was 4.18, suggesting a highly effective use and good performance of the Canvas application.

Overall, these results indicate a generally positive perception of Canvas, with users agreeing on its effectiveness in delivering a user-friendly, efficient, and consistent experience. The findings offer actionable insights for further enhancing the platform's usability and addressing specific areas for improvement.

V. Correlations Between Variables

Figure 3 show the correlation analysis among the variables within the Canvas user scale. It yields valuable insights into the connections between different facets of user experience and system functionality. The matrix of correlation coefficients presents a glimpse into the interrelationships of these variables, illuminating potential patterns and interdependences.

All the variables in the scale show a positive significant correlation with each other, indicating a high interconnection between these factors. Where, X1= Visibility of System Status mean score, X2= Match Between System and Real World, X3= Aesthetic and Minimalistic Design, X4= Recognition Rather than Recall, X5= Effective Design to Lessen User's Workload, X6= Flexibility and Efficiency of use, X7= Handling varied contexts of use in mobile environments, X8= User control and obviousness, X9= Realistic error management, X10= Consistency and standards, X11= Efficiency of use and performance. Also, P-value calculated by a Pearson correlation test.

VI. Conclusion and Recommendations for Future Work

As for the research question addressed in this study, and following the discussion of the significance of The validity analysis of the factors pertaining to Canvas user division is presented herein. A questionnaire was implemented on 104 CSE students to evaluate the different usability factors. To ascertain the validity of each factor, a Pearson correlation analysis was employed. Construct validity was gauged by correlating each item on the scale with the totality of the scale. Notably, all items exhibited a robust and statistically significant positive

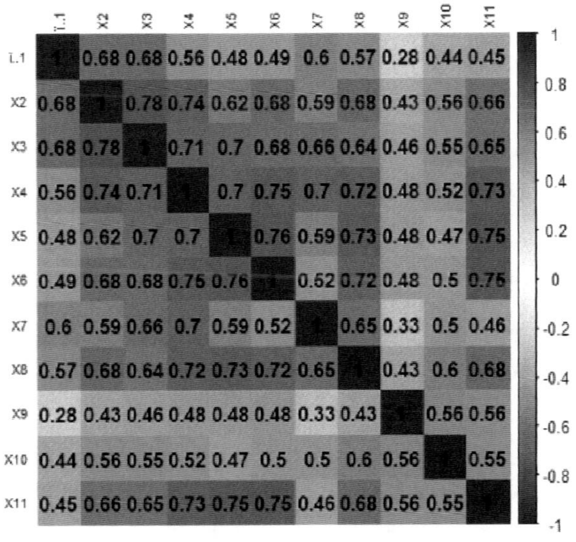

Fig. 3. The Heat Correlation Map of the Variables within the Canvas User Scale

correlation with their respective scales. Consequently, these items are deemed competent in representing the conceptual underpinnings of the factors and are pivotal in assessing the perceptions of Canvas users. An explanation of the interactions between the elements is made possible by Figure 3, which clearly shows the correlations among them.

The achieved results open the door for further comparative examination between the components in the investigated Canvas LMS and other apps such as the Blackboard application.

References

[1] M. J. J. Gumasing, A. B. Vasquez, A. L. S. Doctora, and W. D. D. Perez, "Usability evaluation of online learning management system: Comparison between blackboard and canvas," in *2022 the 9th international conference on industrial engineering and applications (europe)*, 2022, pp. 25–31.

[2] K. Haan, *Best Learning Management Systems (LMS) Of 2023*, https://www.forbes.com/advisor/business/best-learning-management-systems/, Jul. 2021.

[3] M. N. Yakubu and S. I. Dasuki, "Factors affecting the adoption of e-learning technologies among higher education students in nigeria: A structural equation modelling approach," *Information Development*, vol. 35, no. 3, pp. 492–502, 2019.

[4] A. A. Arain, Z. Hussain, W. H. Rizvi, and M. S. Vighio, "Evaluating usability of m-learning application in the context of higher education institute," in *Learning and Collaboration Technologies: Third International Conference, LCT 2016, Held as Part of HCI International 2016, Toronto, ON, Canada, July 17-22, 2016, Proceedings 3*, Springer, 2016, pp. 259–268.

[5] A. A. M. S. Hossain, "Evaluating and testing user interfaces for e-learning system: Blackboard usability testing," *J. Inf. Eng. Appl*, vol. 5, no. 1, p. 23, 2015.

[6] J. Kaliski, J. Kalinowski, P. Schumann, T. Scott, D. Shin, *et al.*, "Competition in the elearning industry: A case study," *Journal of Business Case Studies (JBCS)*, vol. 4, no. 2, pp. 106–122, 2008.

[7] G. A. Store, *Educational Applications on Store*, https://www.educationalappstore.com/app-lists/apps-for-education/, [Online; accessed 02-October-2023], 2023.

[8] J. Nielsen, *Usability engineering*. Morgan Kaufmann, 1994.

[9] W. Ali, O. Riaz, S. Mumtaz, A. R. Khan, T. Saba, and S. A. Bahaj, "Mobile application usability evaluation: A study based on demography," *IEEE Access*, vol. 10, pp. 41 512–41 524, 2022.

[10] N. A. N. Ahmad and M. Hussaini, "A usability testing of a higher education mobile application among postgraduate and undergraduate students.," *International Journal of Interactive Mobile Technologies*, vol. 15, no. 9, 2021.

[11] H. Hoehle and V. Venkatesh, "Mobile application usability," *MIS quarterly*, vol. 39, no. 2, pp. 435–472, 2015.

[12] P. Weichbroth, "Usability of mobile applications: A systematic literature study," *Ieee Access*, vol. 8, pp. 55 563–55 577, 2020.

[13] S. Alagmdi, A. Albanyan, and S. Ludi, "Investigating the usability issues in mobile applications reviews using a deep learning model," in *2023 IEEE 13th Annual Computing and Communication Workshop and Conference (CCWC)*, IEEE, 2023, pp. 0108–0113.

[14] A. H. Safar, A. A. Al-Jafar, and Z. H. Al-Yousefi, "The effectiveness of using augmented reality apps in teaching the english alphabet to kindergarten children: A case study in the state of kuwait," *EURASIA Journal of Mathematics, Science and Technology Education*, vol. 13, no. 2, pp. 417–440, 2016.

[15] B. A. Kumar and P. Mohite, "Usability of mobile learning applications: A systematic literature review," *Journal of Computers in Education*, vol. 5, pp. 1–17, 2018.

[16] D. O'Brien, K. A. Lawless, and P. Schrader, "A taxonomy of educational games," in *Gaming for classroom-based learning: Digital role playing as a motivator of study*, IGI Global, 2010, pp. 1–23.

[17] P. G. Schrader and K. A. Lawless, "The knowledge, attitudes, & behaviors approach how to evaluate performance and learning in complex environments," *Performance Improvement*, vol. 43, no. 9, pp. 8–15, 2004.

[18] T. Hidayati and S. Diana, "Students' motivation to learn english using mobile applications: The case of duolingo and hello english," *JEELS (Journal of English Education and Linguistics Studies)*, vol. 6, no. 2, pp. 189–213, 2019.

[19] Y.-C. Hsu and Y.-H. Ching, "Mobile app design for teaching and learning: Educators' experiences in an online graduate course," *International Review of Research in Open and Distributed Learning*, vol. 14, no. 4, pp. 117–139, 2013.

[20] D. Zhang, "Delivery of personalized and adaptive content to mobile devices: A framework and enabling technology," *Communications of the Association for Information Systems*, vol. 12, no. 1, p. 13, 2003.

[21] N. S. A. Rashid, X. W. Chen, M. F. Mohamad Marzuki, *et al.*, "Development and usability assessment of a mobile app (demensia kita) to support dementia caregivers in malaysia: A study protocol," *International Journal of Environmental Research and Public Health*, vol. 19, no. 19, p. 11 880, 2022.

Ecosystems in Business

A systematic literature review of ecosystems and its dimensions

Luiz Henrique N. G. Moreira, Silvio R. L. Meira[1], Andre Neves, Felipe Silva Ferraz
Center of Advanced Studies and Systems of Recife
Recife, Brazil
E-mail: {lhgm}@cesar.school, [1]lhgondim@gmail.com

Abstract—**Business leaders and scholars struggle to separate Business Ecosystem (BE), Digital Ecosystem (DE), Digital Platform Ecosystem (DPE), and Innovation Ecosystem (IE). Uncertain ecosystem definitions affect business performance, innovation, and decisions. The objective of this paper is to conduct a systematic literature review of ecosystem and its dimensions in order to achieve clarity and precision about the definition of the concept. Snowball technique was used to identify relevant articles and mining techniques to examine how ecosystems have been defined. The results of the review revealed different meanings of digital ecosystems, but key similarities were identified.**

Keywords-ecosystems; digital ecosystems; business ecosystems; innovation platforms; business innovation; systematic literature review.

I. INTRODUCTION

The term ecosystem is a set of actors that includes a focal firm and other participants who share the same vision of value creation and are willing to work together through multi-lateral co-specializations under mutually agreed governance mechanisms [9]. The use of the term 'ecosystem' has increased in frequency as it entered the lexicon of technological and commercial companies; the concept of which can include different forms of associations of organizations like platforms, clusters, networks, and incubators [4]. Within the specific context of innovation, ecosystems refer to a complex and interconnected network that collaborate and interact with each other to drive innovation through the creation of new products, services, or solutions.

The terms Business Ecosystem (BE), Digital Ecosystem (DE), Digital Platform Ecosystem (DPE), and Innovation Ecosystem (IE) are often used interchangeably. These terms generally refer to the system that is in place for innovation in a business company to be created or developed [21]. However, these terms pertain to different aspects of ecosystem.

Unclear ecosystem definitions can affect the performance, innovation, and decisions of businesses. Having multiple definitions of a concept within a business company can lead to confusion and misalignment among employees, hindering effective communication and decision-making. It can also result in inconsistent implementation of strategies or objectives, impacting the company's overall efficiency and performance.

To address this problem, this research will attempt to examine how the concept ecosystem and its dimensions have been defined using previous research studies. Specific focus will be given to the business setting, where the concept of digital ecosystem is necessary for competitive advantage and sustainability [14].

The research questions of the study are the following: 1. How has ecosystem been defined in business? and 2. What are the core similarities of the different terms that have been used to define ecosystem in business? These two research questions served as the basis that grounds this study.

The purpose of this research is to conduct a Systematic Literature Review (SLR) of ecosystem and its dimensions in order to achieve clarity and precision about the definition of the concept. Through this SLR, core similarities about the different definitions of ecosystem in the business setting can be identified.

This research is limited by the approach of SLR. The quality of SLR is dependent on the quality of the studies included. If the studies included have flaws and biases in their methodology, these issues may carry over to the SLR itself. Moreover, because of the heterogeneity of studies included in SLR, the methods, populations, and outcomes can vary, making the process of synthesizing and drawing clear conclusions challenging.

The structure of the paper will include several sections that will cover the entire study. Section II will cover the methodology of the SLR. Section III will present the different definitions and dimensions of ecosystem based on the SLR. Section IV will present the conclusions and future work recommendations.

II. METHODOLOGY

The methodology of the study will be informed by SLR. Systematic literature reviews aim to provide a comprehensive summary of existing research on a specific topic [20]. This comprehensive summary can be instrumental in helping other researchers and decision-makers acquire a deeper understanding of the current state of knowledge in a particular area of topic. The selection of SLR as a methodology was appropriate because the current study aims to examine how ecosystem and its related terms have been defined by previous researchers. Through this information, the researcher will be able to have a more precise definition of the core characteristics of this term.

The objective of this SLR is to examine the different definitions that have been made to define ecosystem and its other related terms. This SLR can be instrumental in the determination of themes or patterns from previous research that can lead to a deeper and more precise understanding of the concept of ecosystem. This review can identify primary studies that focus on different definitions of the ecosystem, how it can be clarified and how it can be applied inside organizations. The review will also focus on key differentiations that can help in the understanding of the multi-dimensional nature of the concept of ecosystems.

A. Search Strategies

The databases considered in the study are listed below:

- ACM Digital Library (see Table 1)
- IEEE Xplore (see Table 1)
- ScienceDirect – Elsevier (see Table 1)

Many different terms were created to guarantee that important information would not be excluded when querying different search engines and databases. As a result, four search strings were created:

1. "Innovation"
2. "Decentralized Innovation" or "Regional Innovation"
3. "Regional Innovation Systems" and "Regional Innovations"
4. "Digital Business Strategy"

Within the search, the criteria below were applied in each database:

- Articles published after 2015 for qualitative analysis
- Studies that are published in the English language
- Studies that are available online
- Studies not based on research that express only the official opinions of governments and field experts
- Duplicated articles (see Table 1)

TABLE I: AMOUNT OF STUDIES FOUND ON EACH DATABASE

Database	Number of studies
ACM Digital Library	271
IEEE Xplore	2603
ScienceDirect – Elsevier	1656
Studies Duplicated – Removed	803
Manual Process Added	

B. Studies Selection Process

In the process of selecting information from the databases, the search strings were used separately on each database, all grouped later using Zotero software to adjust duplication and mine references, using a snowball approach. The searches were performed for articles not older than 2015. Table 1 shows the number of studies found on each database.

A total of 83 primary studies were selected, supplemented by adopting backward snowballing [19]. In snowballing, additional papers are identified either from the paper's reference list (backward snowballing), or from the citations to that paper (forward snowballing). As a result, an additional two primary studies were identified from backward snowballing, increasing the final tally to 85.

TABLE II: AMOUNT OF STUDIES FILTERED IN EACH STEP OF SELECTION PROCESS

Phase of Selection Process	Number of studies
1. Databases Search	3726
1.1 Database cleansing (before 2015)	303 removed | 3423
2. Title Analysis (contain Ecosystem, Systems, Innovation, Hub)	1571 removed | 1852
3. Abstract Analysis (contain Business, Ecosystem)	1769 removed | 83
4. Last articles for Quality Analysis	83

C. Quality Assessment

For quality and quantitative assessment, six questions were used to help in the quality assessment of the SLR. The questions are:

1. Does the study provide a definition of ecosystem or its related terms?
2. Is the study peer-reviewed?
3. Is the study based on research – not merely on specialists' opinions?
4. Is the context of the study adequately described?
5. Were research results adequately explained and described?
6. Does the study contribute to research related to innovation, where business ecosystems are described?

III. DEFINITIONS & DIMENSIONS OF ECOSYSTEMS

In the context of ecosystem research, our systematic literature review has not only provided valuable insights into the various definitions and dimensions of ecosystems in the business setting but has also laid the foundation for future investigations, which may explore barriers to ecosystem adoption, the potential for establishing a culture of innovation collaboration, and a deeper understanding of the components essential for the functionality of ecosystems in diverse organizational contexts.

A. Definitions

Ecosystems, derived from the field of biology, pertain to collections of mutually reliant entities. Complementarities are a necessary condition for their functioning, as they must be present in both the consuming and production domains. Ecosystems inside organizations undergo changes as partners engage, disengage, allocate investments, or redirect their efforts. The promotion of a diversified environment has the potential to provide useful knowledge and facilitate accelerated learning [18].

Business ecosystems refer to "a distinctive organizational form consisting of members co-evolving their capabilities and aligning themselves with a common interest" [13]. In another research, business ecosystem has been defined as a group of actors who are economically connected to each other in order to produce valuable goods and services to customers [22].

The term digital ecosystem has been defined in terms of being a virtual environment that consists of various digital entities such as software applications, hardware, and related processes [12]. Another definition of digital ecosystem focuses on the interconnectedness of different businesses with shared interest in order to utilize digital technology in order to generate products or services [3].

Digital platform ecosystem refers to the context that facilitates the configuration of a new model based on the ability to combine different processes, technology, actors, and interests in order to create new services or products [6]. Another study operationalizes the concept in terms of its five key characteristics, which include "generativity, convergence, share-ability, modularity, multiplicity and sustainable business model innovation" [11].

Innovation ecosystem pertains to the processes that allow the adaptation needed for sustainable transition and transformation of a particular context [5]. The term has also been defined as the loose connection among different business entities that evolve each other's capabilities based on shared technology, knowledge, or skills [8].

B. Dimensions

The scope of ecosystem research is contingent upon the chosen unit of analysis. There are three broad categories that can be identified: the "business ecosystem," which emphasizes the relationship between enterprises and their surrounding environment; the "innovation ecosystem," which revolves on the concept of innovation and the actors that support it; and the "platform ecosystem," which investigates how players organize themselves in relation to a platform. Our primary focus will be on the examination of innovation ecosystems.

The concept of an ecosystem may be described as a framework that comprises several stakeholders who are crucial for the realization of a value proposition [1]. The aforementioned interconnections exhibit a state of multilateral interdependence, which distinguishes them from conventional economic frameworks.

Ecosystems can be characterized as assemblies of agents that possess multilateral, non-generic complementarities, rather than being governed in a hierarchical manner [10]. The primary area of interest lies in the temporal and causal factors contributing to the emergence of ecosystems.

The concept of business ecosystems centers on the interplay between a company and various external entities, such as other businesses, institutions, and individuals. These interactions have a significant influence on the enterprise itself, as well as its consumers and suppliers [15].

The concept of innovation ecosystems centers around the examination of innovations and its various components and complements. It places particular emphasis on the collaborative efforts of interdependent actors in the creation of customer-facing solutions [2].

Platform ecosystems consist of both organizational and market intermediary platforms. These platforms are characterized by a core platform that is surrounded by peripheral companies. These companies are connected through shared technologies, which facilitate the process of value co-creation [16].

Platform ecosystems exhibit distinct features in the form of intricate inter-organizational connections, resembling commercial networks. These connections facilitate entrepreneurial endeavors and facilitate transactions across diverse user groups [7]. In essence, ecosystems encompass intricate interdependencies and diverse complementarities, presenting different viewpoints on their functioning, be it in the realms of business, innovation, or platforms.

IV. CONCLUSION AND FUTURE WORK

The purpose of this research is to conduct a Systematic Literature Review (SLR) of ecosystem and its dimensions in order to achieve clarity and precision about the definition of the concept. Through this SLR, core similarities about the different definitions of ecosystem in the business setting can be identified. The results of the SLR suggest that the different terms highlight themes of interconnectedness of different entities and the creation of a new product or services. The results also reaffirmed the existence of different dimensions of ecosystems.

Based on the results that were presented, future research could further examine the barriers in the adoption or success of ecosystems in business setting. Future researchers could also explore the question of whether companies can establish a culture of innovation collaboration that is independent of their core. More detailed information of the components of a well-functioning ecosystem can also be pursued by future researchers.

REFERENCES

[1] R. Adner, "Ecosystem as structure," J. Manag., vol. 43, pp. 39–58, 2017.

[2] R. Adner, "Match your innovation strategy to your innovation ecosystem," Harv. Bus. Rev., vol. 84, pp. 98–107, 2006.

[3] T. H. Bui and V. P. Nguyen, "The impact of artificial intelligence and digital economy on Vietnam's legal system," International Journal for the Semiotics of Law, vol. 36, pp. 969-989, 2023.

[4] S. Y. Barykin, I. V. Kapustina, T. V. Kirillova, V. L. Yadykin, and Y. A. Konnikov, "Economics of digital ecosystems," Journal of Open Innovation: Technology, Market, and Complexity, vol. 6, pp. 1-16, 2020.

[5] J. Boyer, J., Ozor and P. Rondé, "Local innovation ecosystem: structure and impact on adaptive capacity of firms," Industry and Innovation, vol. 28, pp. 620-650, 2021.

[6] M. Calabrese, A. La Sala, R. P. Fuller and A. Laudando, "Digital platform ecosystems for sustainable innovation: Toward a new meta-organizational model?," Administrative Sciences, vol. 11, pp. 1-14, 2021.

[7] C. Cennamo and J. Santalo, "Platform competition: strategic trade-offs in platform markets," Strateg. Manag. J., vol. 34, pp. 1331–1350, 2013.

[8] O. Granstrand and M. Holgersson, "Innovation ecosystems: A conceptual review and a new definition," Technovation, vol. 90, pp. X-X, 2020.

[9] H. Hou and Y. Shi, "Ecosystem-as-structure and ecosystem-as-coevolution: A constructive examination", Technovation, vol. 100, p. x-x, 2021.

[10] M. G. Jacobides, C. Cennamo and A. Gawer, "Towards a theory of ecosystems," Strat. Manag. J., vol. 39, pp. 2255–2276, 2018

[11] X. Li, L. Zhang and J. Cao, "Research on the mechanism of sustainable business model innovation driven by the digital platform ecosystem," Journal of Engineering and Technology Management, vol 68, pp. 1-48, 2023.

[12] P. K. Senyo, L. Liu, and J. Effah, "Digital business ecosystem: Literature review and a framework for future research,"

International Journal of Information Management, vol. 47, pp. 52-64, 2019.

[13] M. M. Shin, S. Jung, and J. S. Rha, "Study on business ecosystem research trend using network text analysis. Sustainability, vol. 13, pp. 1-17, 2021.

[14] M. Subramaniam, "Digital ecosystems and their implications for competitive strategy," Journal of Organization Design, vol. 9, pp. 1-10, 2020.

[15] D. J. Teece and G. Linden, "Business models, value capture, and the digital enterprise," Journal of Organization Design, vol. 6, pp. 1-14, 2017.

[16] L. D. Thomas, E. Autio and D. M. Gann, "Architectural leverage: Putting platforms in context. Academy of Management Perspectives, vol. 28, pp. 198-219, 2014

[17] J. Wareham, P. B. Fox, and J. L. Cano Giner, "Technology ecosystem governance," Organ. Sci., vol. 25, pp. 1195–1215, 2014.

[18] P. J. Williamson and A. De Meyer, "Ecosystem advantage: How to successfully harness the power of partners," Calif. Manag. Rev., vol. 55, pp. 24–46, 2012.

[19] C. Wohlin, M. Kalinowski, K. R. Felizardo and E. Mendes, "Successful combination of database search and snowballing for identification of primary studies in systematic literature studies," Information and Software Technology, vol. 147, pp. X-X. 2022

[20] Y. Xiao and M. Watson, "Guidance on conducting a systematic literature review," Journal of Planning Education and Research, vol. 39, 93-112, 2019.

[21] S. Yablonsky, S., "A multidimensional platform ecosystem framework," Kybernetes, vol. 49, pp. 2003-2035, 2020.

[22] S. T. D. Yuan, S. Y. Chou, W. C. Yang, C. A. Wu, and C. T. Huang, "Customer engagement within multiple new media and broader business ecosystem–a holistic perspective," Kybernetes, vol. 46, pp. 1000-1020. 2017.

Prerequisites for Simulation-Based Software Design and Deployment

Radek Kočí and Vladimír Janoušek

Brno University of Technology, Faculty of Information Technology
Bozetechova 2, 612 66 Brno, Czech Republic
emails: koci@fit.vut.cz, janousek@fit.vut.cz

Abstract—**The fundamental problem associated with software development is correctly identifying, specifying, and realizing the software system requirements. Many methodologies are not formally defined and rely on intuitive use. In contrast, the formal description techniques clearly describe the user requirements and their specific solutions. We are involved in modeling the requirements and behavior of software systems using formal models used in a specific manner. The approach combines intuitive modeling with the precise expression of specified requirements and a detailed implementation description. Models serve for analysis, system design, validation, and simulation. Models can also be directly deployed in real environments of developed systems. This paper summarizes the current state of the approach to system development, which is being developed by our team.**

Keywords—Modeling; simulation-based design; model-driven engineering; model-continuity.

I. INTRODUCTION

Software Engineering deals with the issues of efficient development of correct and reliable systems. Correctness means that the system fits perfectly with the intentions and goals of deploying this system. Reliability means the system does not contain errors or provide for damage caused by unexpected and wrong behavior. The primary development cycle of each software product is divided into several phases that are continuously linked to each other. The first phases are mainly analysis and specification of requirements, system design, implementation and testing, and finally, system deployment. Many software development methodologies work with phases in different ways. It is possible to follow the phases one by one accurately, to overlap or iterate them. In any case, they are part of every development process. One of the fundamental problems is the correct specification and validation of the requirements for the system [1]. A use case diagram from the Unified Modeling Language (UML) is often used to specify the requirements, which is then developed with other UML diagrams [2]. The disadvantage of this approach is the difficulty in validating the specification models. In response, methods for working with modified UML models having executable form have been developed, such as the Model Driven Architecture (MDA) methodology [3], the Executable UML language (xUML) [4] or the Foundational Subset for xUML [5]. However, these approaches still need to solve the problem of model transformations as it is difficult to transfer back to the model all the changes that result from the validation process. Another approach, for example, uses a modified subset of the UML, called fUML, with the formal language Alf [6][7]. This approach is supported by modeling and analysis tools [8].

The fundamental prerequisite for achieving the correct and reliable system is continuous verification or validation of specification documents, design documents, and implementation [9]. Another area for improvement is the transition between different development process phases, from one document type to another. An example may be the transition from an informal specification to the model or from a design model to the implementation. In these cases, mistakes often occur due to misinterpretation of the outgoing model or by simply overlooking any model element. Two main reasons for these mistakes are the complexity and informal semantics. Many elements of the used modeling means need a clearly defined syntax and semantics, and their use is relatively intuitive. In this paper, we summarize the concepts of software product development and deployment using a combination of formal and informal models, programming languages, and simulation.

The paper is structured as follows. We discuss related work in Section II. In Section III, we specify basic requirements for reliable software development and deployment. Section IV introduces models that may appear during the development life cycle. Section V addresses techniques needed for exploiting the potential of visual and formal languages in the simulation-based design.

II. RELATED WORD

The approach that combines formal models, simulations, and their deployment or transformation is mainly applied in control software. Many of these approaches [10]–[12] propose to generate models in a particular language (e.g., System Modeling Language—SysML) from UML models, usually from a class diagram. Other work, such as [13], transforms different levels of diagrams. Some approaches attempt to transform conceptual models, described, i.e., in SysML, into simulation models [14]. The approach most closely resembles ours is based on the network-within-networks (NwN) formalism, with which the Renew tool is associated [15]. In the design of more general software systems, an example is already mentioned xUML or fUML. The resulting system can often be generated from the designed models [16][17]. However, freely available tools only allow partial output (often, only a skeleton in the chosen language is generated). However, these approaches also do not allow formal models to implement the system but only for simulation runs. Our proposed approach retains the generated models throughout the software development and deployment. We aim to create more efficient representations of models and their simulators for deployment purposes on commonly used platforms and languages (Java, C++).

III. Prerequisites for a Simulation-Based Approach

This section briefly summarizes the basic requirements for reliable software design and defines the prerequisites for meeting these requirements.

A. Basic requirements

First, we define points that have to be met to create the correct and reliable software system.

1) understand the goals of the software project and precisely specify the specific requirements whose implementation meets the declared objectives,
2) verify that the requirements specification is in line with the objectives,
3) based on a verified specification, create a system design that reflects the conditions of a particular implementation environment,
4) verify that the system design complies with the requirements,
5) implement the verified design,
6) verify that implementation is consistent with the design,
7) verify accuracy and reliability of implementation under real conditions

In the following sections, we explain the basic principles of our approach and how they fulfill the above points.

B. Model Continuity

The primary means for specifying requirements is plain text in the native language. In this form, the specification is also part of the contract between the developer and the customer. Validation of the text description of requirements specification is, however, difficult and very often impossible. This validation can not be performed in an automated manner but by a person. Nevertheless, someone is limited by his/her memory and cannot analyze multi-page text in all its dependencies.

Visual models with a clear formal foundation make it possible to capture a particular aspect of requirements unequivocally, helping to understand the developed system better and detect errors. For these reasons, the ideal state is to use one type of model that captures everything. However, such a model would be too extensive to get into the same problem as the text description.

A more appropriate approach is to combine models capturing the system at different levels of abstraction so that it is possible to view and analyze system models as a whole and their details. This approach is complemented by other models or text descriptions that include those features or requirements that can not be captured in the existing models; eventually, their capture would be very complicated. *It satisfies the point 1 from the list in Section III-A.*

An important feature that extends the capability of validating specification models is the ability to simulate these models. It allows live testing of models in simulated conditions instead of simply passing through a document. Another aspect that affects validation capabilities is the environment or context in which the simulation is performed. If models are integrated into a realistic environment, the credibility of simulation results increases. *It satisfies the point 2 from the list in Section III-A.*

After the validation of specification models, the question of a correct transition to the design models and the subsequent implementation in the chosen environment remains. We aim to work with the same models in all development phases, especially the specification, design, and implementation, with no transformation and minimization of errors. The models are only complemented with further details while preserving the possibility of previewing models at different levels of abstraction from the specification to the implementation view. *It satisfies points 3 and 4 from the list in Section III-A.*

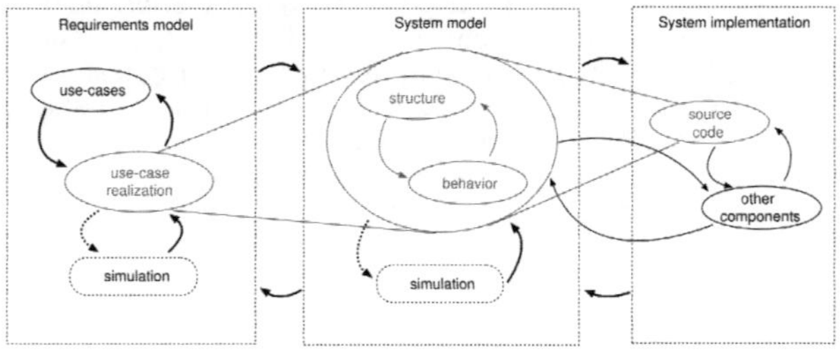

Figure 1. Model Continuity: Basic principle.

At the end of the development process, we have functional models that fully reflect the system requirements. In certain situations, especially concerning performance, these models can serve as implementation models, i.e., become part of the target system. If this is inappropriate or impossible for the above reasons, we must implement or exploit the ability to generate code from such models. Consistency with the design does not need to be checked, as the same set of models is still being developed. Verification accuracy and reliability under real conditions are proved in the same or partially modified manner. *It satisfies points 5, 6, and 7 from the list in Section III-A.*

The prior text presents the basic principle of the continuity model, which is depicted in Figure 1. Design models complement and extend each other in the development process, and there is no need to transform or create new models based on existing ones. If the nature of the resulting application permits, it is possible to maintain the models in the target system.

IV. Models in the Simulation-Based Development Life-Cycle

In this section, we will introduce the types of models that may appear during the life cycle of simulation development of software systems. One of the basic principles of simulation development is the continuity of models over the entire development process until deployment in the application environment. We define categories of models and typical representatives and evaluate their applicability in simulation development.

The process of modeling software systems consists of several phases that follow and interleave [18]. Various modeling tools may be used in each phase, but there must be a way of interconnecting them. We distinguish between *Domain Model*, *Behavioral Model*, and *Design Model* that are supplemented by *Architecture Model*.

In the following text, we will explain and analyze the importance of each model in more detail. We will proceed from a simple example of a robotic system, which we now briefly specify. The example, which is based on the case study presented in [19], presents a robot control system whose motion is controlled by a pre-specified algorithm.

A. Domain Model

Domain Model captures concepts of the domain system as identified and understood during the requirements analysis process. The class diagram modeling conceptual classes and their links is usually used. The domain model is the initial model for modeling functional requirements and creation of design models and is one of the first models to use when designing the software.

B. Behavioral Model

Behavior Model captures an external view of the system's functionality, specific behavior, and system interaction with its surroundings. The behavior model can be divided into two complementary types:

- *User Requirements Model* captures an external view of the system functionality. Use case models are used.
- *Scenario Model (Model of Functional Requirements)* captures specific behavior and interaction of individual use cases. Different descriptions are used, e.g., structured text, activity diagrams, or state charts. Generally speaking, it is possible to use such models that describe the workflow of the use case supplemented by communication mechanisms.

Use case diagrams are used to model user requirements. The goal of modeling is to identify system users, user requirements, and how the user works with these requirements. The essential elements are *users* of the system, their *role*, and *activities*. Roles are modeled through *actors* and activity through individual *use cases* in the use case diagram. Interconnected scenarios (activity nets or role nets) then specify the behavior of the individual elements (see Figure 2) and can be described by different formalisms.

Activity diagrams, state diagrams, or interaction diagrams can model case scenarios (activities). However, formal models or formal languages, such as *Petri nets*, can also be used with advantage. An important feature is an interconnection between use case diagrams and scenarios modeled by specific diagrams since both models represent a different view of the system under development.

Figure 3 shows an example of the scenario model for the elements Robot (role) and Execute Scenario (activity). The

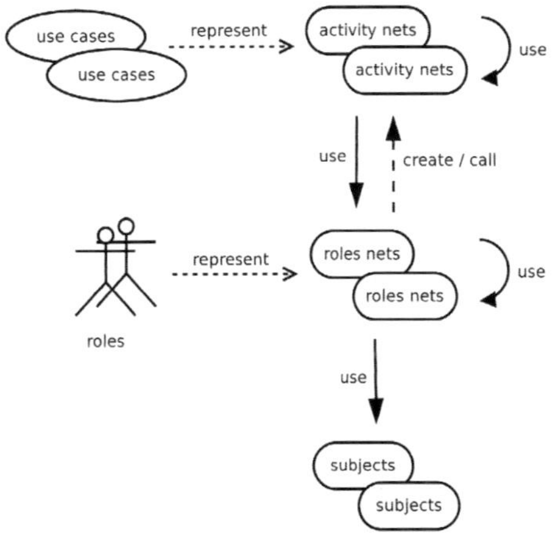

Figure 2. Interrelation of elements and their descriptions.

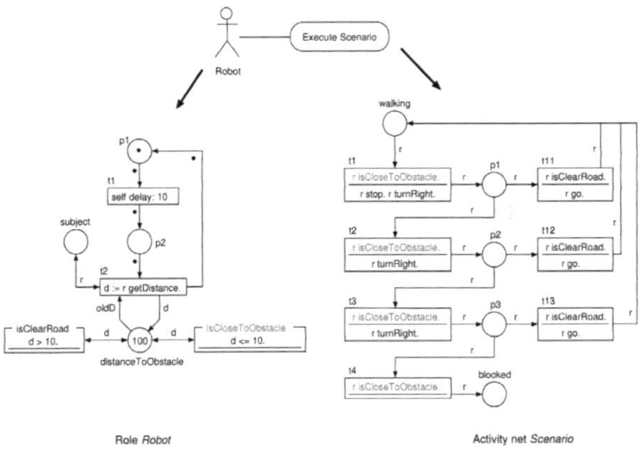

Figure 3. Sample scenario model for role and use case.

formalism of Petri nets, its variant Object-Oriented Petri nets, models the scenarios and uses its inherent synchronous port mechanism (e.g., isCloseToObstacle) to synchronize with each other [20].

C. Design and Architecture Model

Design Model is based on the domain and behavioral models. Generally speaking, these are elaborate models of the domain, requirements, and behavior that can be directly implemented. Class diagrams, activity diagrams, or state diagrams are used. The *Architecture Model* captures the organization of the design classes. Class diagrams and grouping diagrams or deployment diagrams are used. Usually, the architecture model merges with the design models.

D. Interrelation of Models

As indicated in Figure 4, the scenario models at the level of behavioral and design models merge into a single concept. Therefore, the class diagram is also included in this concept. The scenarios associated with the diagram of use cases correspond to classes from the design model. A specific class type models each element. Thus, we can identify groups of classes modeling *actors*, *use cases*, and other classes based on the domain model. As behavioral models evolve, they become design models that also serve the purpose of requirements specification. The basic view of requirements is conveyed by use case diagrams, class diagrams provide the architectural view, and individual scenarios are represented as workflows specified by Petri nets. Additional objects from the domain environment can be used in the workflow to simulate the system or run it under realistic conditions without displaying these implementation details at the scenario level. Thus, the same model can be used both for requirements documentation and for the developed system's executable version (prototype, implementation).

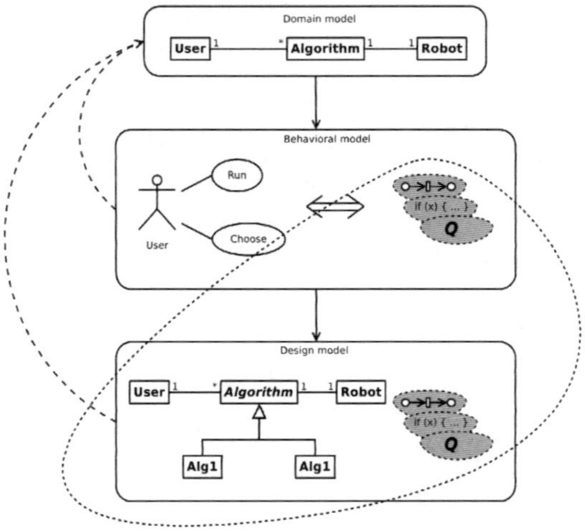

Figure 4. The role of models in the development process.

V. Supporting Techniques

The mentioned prerequisites need to be complemented by supporting techniques that exploit the potential of visual and formal languages in the simulation-based design. Many of these techniques have already been developed and introduced in previous papers.

A. Components

The possibility of exchanging parts of the software to debug and verify the correctness or behavior of the system under different conditions. The exchange should be enabled on the fly (simulation). For this purpose, a component concept based on the Discrete Event System Specification formalism (DEVS) [21][22] was chosen. It makes possible to associate the formal models described by High-level nets with an executable code that is incorporated into DEVS formalism structures. DEVS formalism is abstract concept that can be easily adapted to a particular environment.

B. Debugging and Constraints

An important aspect is, of course, the possibility of debugging and stepping. Simulation stepping is an obvious functionality of the simulation tool. We have also explored tracking and reverting the model run using Petri nets [23]. However, the presented concept still needs to consider all possible applications.

We also introduced the basic concept of requirements validation and its implementation through scenarios described by sequence diagrams [24]. Scenarios can be created manually or generated from running (simulation) models. It allows us to obtain assumed scenarios of the behavior of the use case under study and real scenarios reflecting the design that can be compared.

We introduced the concept of constraints and exceptions over the Petri net formalism, which can be used to verify the consistency of component interfaces or the correctness of the behavior of the modeled system [21].

C. Models Supported by Programming Languages

Models can be combined with programming (or other formal) languages that can be interpreted together with the model. Thus, they can also use concepts (e.g., objects) from another environment or programming languages. Current simulator can work with only Smalltalk objects.

D. Transformations

Transform the model into the chosen programming language for more efficient running. In the case of a transformed model, using some of the above resources is limited. Currently, we have the experimental implementation of transformations to Java and C++ languages done by our master students.

VI. Conclusion

This paper summarized the concept of simulation-based software development in conjunction with model-continuity principles and the current state of the art that our research team has achieved. The simulator has experimentally implemented many of the techniques presented but is only partially suitable for wider use (experimental implementation in a Smalltalk environment). We are, therefore, currently working on a new implementation of the simulator and a comprehensive model editor in Java. The goal is to create a comprehensive tool for modeling, designing, and verifying software systems with the possibility of direct deployment (with a lightweight version of the virtual machine for running models) or direct transformation into a programming language for more efficient running.

Acknowledgment

This work has been supported by the internal BUT project FIT-S-23-8151 – Reliable, Secure, and Intelligent Computer Systems.

References

[1] K. Wiegers and J. Beatty, Software Requirements. Microsoft Press, 2014.

[2] N. Daoust, Requirements Modeling for Bussiness Analysts. Technics Publications, LLC, 2012.

[3] R. France and B. Rumpe, "Model-driven development of complex software: A research roadmap," in International Conference on Software Engineering, FOSE, 2007, pp. 37–54.

[4] C. Raistrick, P. Francis, J. Wright, C. Carter, and I. Wilkie, Model Driven Architecture with Executable UML. Cambridge University Press, 2004.

[5] S. Mijatov, P. Langer, T. Mayerhofer, and G. Kappel, "A framework for testing uml activities based on fuml," in Proc. of 10th Int. Workshop on Model Driven Engineering, Verification, and Validation, vol. 1069, 2013, pp. 11–20.

[6] T. Buchmann and A. Rimer, "Unifying modeling and programming with alf," in SOFTENG 2016: The Second International Conference on Advances and Trends in Software Engineering, 2016, pp. 10–15.

[7] E. Seidewitz, "UML with meaning: executable modeling in foundational UML and the Alf action language," in HILT '14 Proceedings of the 2014 ACM SIGAda annual conference on High integrity language technology, 2014, pp. 61–68.

[8] Z. Micskei and et al., "On open source tools for behavioral modeling and analysis with fuml and alf," in 1st Workshop on Open Source Software for Model Driven Engineering, MODELS 2014, pp. 31–41, [online; retrieved: September, 2022]. [Online]. Available: http://ceur-ws.org/Vol-1290/paper3.pdf

[9] D. Cetinkaya, A. V. Dai, and M. D. Seck, "Model continuity in discrete event simulation: A framework for model-driven development of simulation models," ACM Transactions on Modeling and Computer Simulation, vol. 25, no. 3, 2015, pp. 17:1–17:24.

[10] T. Hussain and G. Frey, "UML-based Development Process for IEC 61499 with Automatic Test-case Generation," in IEEE Conference on Emerging Technologies and Factory Automation. IEEE, 2010.

[11] C. A. Garcia, E. X. Castellanos, C. Rosero, and Carlos, "Designing Automation Distributed Systems Based on IEC-61499 and UML," in 5th International Conference in Software Engineering Research and Innovation (CONISOFT). IEEE, 2017.

[12] I. A. Batchkova, Y. A. Belev, and D. L. Tzakova, "IEC 61499 Based Control of Cyber-Physical Systems," Industry 4.0, vol. 5, no. 1, November 2020, pp. 10–13.

[13] S. Panjaitan and G. Frey, "Functional Design for IEC 61499 Distributed Control Systems using UML Activity Diagrams," in Proceedings of the 2005 International Conference on Instrumentation, Communications and Information Technology ICICI 2005, 2005, pp. 64–70.

[14] G. D. Kapos, V. Dalakas, A. Tsadimas, M. Nikolaidou, and D. Anagnostopoulos, "Model-based system engineering using SysML: Deriving executable simulation models with QVT," in IEEE International Systems Conference Proceedings, 2014.

[15] L. Cabac, M. Haustermann, and D. Mosteller, "Renew 2.5 - towards a comprehensive integrated development environment for petri net-based applications," in Application and Theory of Petri Nets and Concurrency - 37th International Conference, PETRI NETS 2016, Toruń, Poland, June 19-24, 2016. Proceedings, 2016, pp. 101–112. [Online]. Available: http://dx.doi.org/10.1007/978-3-319-39086-4_7

[16] F. Ciccozzi, "On the automated translational execution of the action language for foundational uml," Software and Systems Modeling, vol. 17, no. 4, 2018, doi: 10.1007/s10270-016-0556-7.

[17] E. Seidewitz and J. Tatibouet, "Tool paper: Combining alf and uml in modeling tools an example with papyrus," in 15th Internation Workshop on OCL and Textual Modeling, MODELS 2015, pp. 105–119, [online; retrieved: September, 2022]. [Online]. Available: http://ceur-ws.org/Vol-1512/paper09.pdf

[18] C. Larman, Applying UML and Patterns: An Introduction to Object-Oriented Analysis and Design and Iterative Development. Prentice Hall, 2004.

[19] R. Kočí and V. Janoušek, "Formal Models in Software Development and Deployment: A Case Study," International Journal on Advances in Software, vol. 7, no. 1, 2014, pp. 266–276.

[20] R. Kočí and V. Janoušek, "Specification of Requirements Using Unified Modeling Language and Petri Nets," International Journal on Advances in Software, vol. 10, no. 12, 2017, pp. 121–131.

[21] R. Kočí and V. Janoušek, "The Object Oriented Petri Net Component Model," in The Tenth International Conference on Software Engineering Advances. Xpert Publishing Services, 2015, pp. 309–315.

[22] R. Kočí and V. Janoušek, "Incorporating Petri Nets into DEVS Formalism for Precise System Modeling," in ICSEA 2019, The Fourteenth International Conference on Software Engineering Advances. Xpert Publishing Services, 2019, pp. 184–189.

[23] R. Koci and V. Janousek, "Possibilities of the reverse run of software systems modeled by petri nets," International Journal on Advances in Software, vol. 12, no. 3, 2019, pp. 191–200.

[24] R. Kočí, "Requirements validation through scenario generation and comparison," in The Fifteenth International Conference on Software Engineering Advances, ICSEA 2020. Xpert Publishing Services, 2020, pp. 129–134.

Engineering IoT-based Software Systems for Forestry: A Case Study

Marko Jäntti
School of Computing
University of Eastern Finland
P.O.B. 1627, 70211, Kuopio, Finland
Email: marko.jantti@uef.fi

Markus Aho
UEF Business School
University of Eastern Finland
Yliopistokatu 2, 80100 Joensuu, Finland
Email: markus.aho@uef.fi

Markus Aho
Funlus Oy
Sepontie 15, 73300 Nilsiä, Finland
Email: markus.aho@funlus.fi

***Abstract*—The Internet of Things (IoT) is a rapidly growing technology that offers huge possibilities for optimizing processes and increasing productivity in various domains. The IoT technology connects software services, devices, various types of sensors, and machines to the internet and enables real-time data collection, analysis and sharing. However, ensuring the quality of the IoT is a complex challenge for software engineers and requires new development skills, as well as coordination of third party service providers. In this case study, we use embedded single case design with two Internet of Things experiments to study the quality factors in IoT system implementation. The research problem of this study is: How quality aspects should be taken into account while designing and implementing IoT-based software systems for forestry inventory management? The main contribution of this paper is to present lessons learnt from two experiments with different monitoring targets: liquid level monitoring and continuous mass monitoring of oil canister pallets. Both IoT experiments were performed in facilities of the second largest forest harvesting company in Finland.**

Keywords*—*Internet of Things; software system; software engineer; sensor; ICT quality.

I. Introduction

The Internet of Things (IoT) is a fast-growing network of interconnected devices that exchange data and enable a wide range of applications. From smart homes and cities to industrial automation and intelligent machinery, the IoT has the potential to transform our lives, workplaces, communication and processes. However, implementing IoT systems is not a straightforward task even for experienced software engineers. Building IoT-based software systems of high quality requires careful planning and integration of various technologies, devices, services and sensors together.

Especially for forestry domain where actors still operate with traditional non-digital practices, IoT technology provides numerous opportunities for improvement and ways to improve productivity and increase level of automation. While forest machines involve high tech components, such as machine vision, robotics and intelligent sensors, the support and maintenance of forest machines including orders for liquids and other supplies, includes a large number of manual work activities.

Previous studies on using Internet of Things in forestry domain have mainly focused on monitoring forest assets [1], creating IoT-based systems for forest environment monitoring systems [2], improving the safety of forestry workers [3], establishing IoT-enabled plantation monitoring systems [4] and studying IoT implementation challenges in experiments conducted in rural areas [5]. However, surprisingly few of these studies focus on discussing how to ensure quality in IoT systems implementation. Identification of these quality aspects would help IoT engineers and developers to make better informed decisions on selecting IoT sensor components, services and platforms. Information on IoT quality aspects would also help IoT customers, consultants and coordinators of IoT projects to produce better quality and more accurate invitations for tender and make acquisition of IoT systems smoother.

There are several quality factors that software engineers in IoT projects should take into account. One of the most important quality aspects of the IoT is reliability. Reliability means that various IoT devices, sensors, software services and platforms must work together seamlessly to deliver accurate and timely data. In Finland, poor network coverage is a real challenge [6], especially in eastern and northern parts of Finland. Network failures can lead to significant consequences, such as loss of data, severe information security breaches, and unavailability of systems. Thus, it is critical to ensure that all IoT components are reliable and no weak links shall exist in the infrastructure. Additionally, when an IoT service is running in the operation phase, the service provider should provide frequent reports on the service quality which is part of a broader service-oriented philosophy [7].

Information security is another important quality aspect related to the IoT technology. While increasing amount of data is exchanged over the internet, security breaches have become a significant concern in Internet of Things projects. Cyberattacks may be performed even through very standard IT components, such as web cameras [8].

Fortunately, large cloud service providers have addressed security concerns of IoT, established security controls by using IT governance frameworks, such as COBIT [9], created security roadmaps and cybersecurity reference architectures [10] and presented mechanisms for ensuring secure access control, authentication of various types of devices and detecting potential security vulnerabilities and providing secure connections from sensors to IoT cloud services. Cybersecurity plays a very important role for IoT systems that can control critical systems or services, such as heating, ventilation, lighting and access control in smart buildings [11].

The results of this article are aimed at IoT system developers, companies in IoT customer role, Internet of Things consultancy companies and persons responsible for coordinating IoT projects to increase their awareness of quality aspects related to IoT implementations in Finland, especially in forestry sector.

In Section 2, research methodology of the study is presented. In Section 3, case study results are presented. Section 4 is the analysis and finally, the conclusions are given in Section 5.

II. Research Problem & Methodology

This study aimed at answering the following research problem: How quality aspects should be taken into account while designing and implementing IoT-based software systems for forestry? The forestry domain was selected because it has a large financial impact in Finland. We admit that oil and gas industries may be forerunners in IoT but they play a very minor role in Finland compared to forest industry. In this study, we utilized a case study research method to answer the research problem with a single case organization (Motoajo Oy, a forest machine operator from Finland) with an embedded structure involving two IoT experiments. The research problem was divided into following three research questions:

- What types of IoT monitoring needs does a forest machine operator company have?
- How quality attributes are visible in building IoT solutions?
- How IoT monitoring shall support forest operations?

The case study can be defined as "an empirical inquiry that investigates a contemporary phenomenon within its real-life context" [12]. The real life context refers to daily operations management of a forest machine operator company. Figure 1 shows the context of this study.

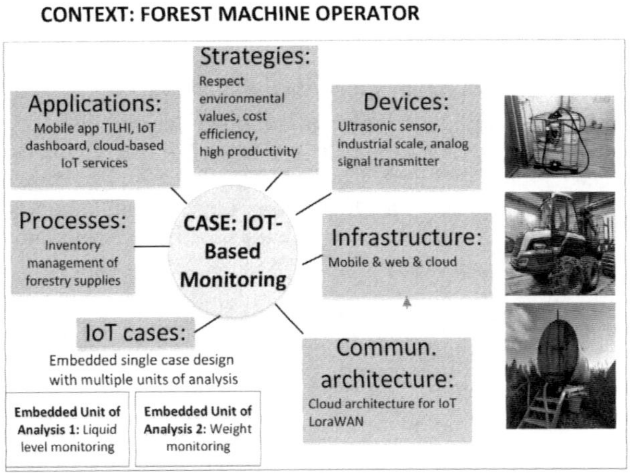

Fig. 1. The context of the case study.

A. Case Organization

Our target organization Motoajo Oy (SME) is a forestry contractor company located in Nurmes, Eastern Finland. The company is Finland's second largest harvesting company. Motoajo operates as a family-owned company with 51 forest machines and 81 employees. Additionally, the company has in possession 3 Volvo transport trucks, 2 Volvo excavators, 1 wheel loader, 5 MB Sprinter light trucks and 64 Pick-up trucks. Regarding the staff, there are 35 harvester operators, 28 forwarder operators, 2 transport truck drivers, 3 excavator operators, 5 mechanics and 8 management staff. Reliable inventory management and order management of liquids and other supplies for forest machines are critical business functions for Motoajo. Forest machines cannot operate without these liquids and supplies and even short operational outages may cause remarkable costs for the company.

During the case study, the research team including the authors of this paper collaborated with various Motoajo employees but especially foreman, CEO, financial administrator and development manager. The collaboration occurred in joint digital experiment workshops, work meetings on preparing the experiment handbook, experiment status reporting meetings (Motoajo, AIKA DIH, DIH-World coordinator), joint webinars and seminars (2 DIH community days, 2 other regional dissemination events on digital transformation).

Digital Innovation Hubs (DIH) [13] are one-stop shops that help companies, especially SMEs and start-ups become more competitive with regard to their business/production processes, products or services using digital technologies. The funding for the first IoT case was received from the 1st call of experiments of DIH-World project (funded by Horizon 2020). The idea for the second IoT case was identified in the continual improvement workshop that was organized at the end of the first IoT case.

B. Data Collection Methods

Qualitative data for this case study were collected by using multiple sources of evidence between August 2021 - May 2023. Most of the data were captured while visiting Motoajo's facilities (main storage in Nurmes, Finland as well as remote storage areas). The following sources of evidence were used:

- Documentation: IoT device specification for Tekelek tank alert sensor (ultrasonic), Enless Wireless Transmitter product specification, supporting documentation sent by IoT providers during the bidding process of weight monitoring system, safety instruction documentation of diesel exhaust fluid and log marking colour.
- Archival records: Data records (JSON) from the IoT provider, online forms for truck drivers and forest machine operators (triggered by QR codes in containers), LoraWAN data conversion Excel sheet by Enless Wireless.
- Interviews/discussions: Online meeting discussions with 9 Internet of Things providers, live discussions in Solver X reverse pitching event in April 19th, 2023, interviews with CEO of Motoajo, project discussions during work meetings with foreman of Motoajo, phone discussions with CEO.
- Participative observation: digital experiment work meetings, several field visits to case organization's facilities, such as the main storage area, the remote

storage area, a logging site in Nurmes, Finland; participative observation in DIH webinars and dissemination meetings related to Green and Digital Forest Service Management experiment.

- Physical artifacts: Artifacts related to case 1 included Tekelek ultrasonic sensor module, various types of liquid containers, such as a portable fuel container, a fungicide container, plastic Intermediate Bulk Containers (IBC) containing log marking colour and diesel exhaust fluid. Artifacts related to case 2 included oil canister pallet, industrial scale PCE RS 2000 by PCE Instruments and Enless Wireless Analog Transmitter.
- Direct observations: Monitoring forest machine operational work in logging site (January 11th, 2022)

C. *Data Analysis*

Data analysis of this study was performed by case comparison technique with two units of analysis. The case comparison analysis technique [14] is a common way to compare and analyze data from multiple cases. Our units of analysis were two different types of Internet of Things experiments. The first experiment focused on liquid level monitoring and the second experiment on weight monitoring.

During the article writing period, the second experiment was still ongoing. The analysis was performed by two researchers that are also authors of this paper. The case comparison was based on predefined categories (=patterns) describing the nature and settings of experiments and reflecting the quality aspects of IoT.

III. Results of the Study: Engineering IoT-based Software System for Forestry

The results of this exploratory case study are presented in this section as case narratives with Situation, Task, Action, Results (STAR) approach. The STAR approach includes four steps: 1) Situation describing the context within the IoT development was performed, 2) Tasks describing responsibilities or tasks to be done in that particular situation, 3) Action describing how the task was completed or how the challenge was resolved, and 4) Results describing the outcomes or results generated by the action.

A. *Situation*

Case A: According to the data we received from our site visits and conversations with the case organization, we noticed that the process for refilling and retrieving liquids from containers is mostly done manually. Additionally, we observed that the online form is not consistently used by truck drivers and forest machine drivers. The primary issue is that the company lacks an accurate view of their forestry liquid inventories, which can lead to a scenario where drivers of forest machines do not receive the necessary liquids they require. Motoajo and Digital Innovation Hub AIKA Ecosystem applied and received funding for the digital transformation initiative from DIH-WORLD project around 90 Keur.

Case B: The idea for Case B, continuous mass measurement using sensor technology, was received in the end of Case A when the research team asked case organization what would be next potential improvement targets for IoT based monitoring. A joint research consortium was established to find solutions for the problem. The first research organization provided expertise on metrology (purchasing and calibration of the scale) and the second research organization took care of designing cloud services. No external regional or international funding was related to this experiment.

B. *Task*

Case A: The EU funding for the experiment enabled the research consortium to design, implement, test and validate the monitoring solution. When the experiments started, no sensors were used for liquid level monitoring and the company did not have sensor platform in use. Monitoring consumption was based on manual checks and required traveling to remote sites frequently (1-2 monthly visits). The expected benefits involved, first, increased productivity and quality of operations for a forest machine operator due to decreased number of interruptions in production. Significant costs are caused if a forest machine cannot operate due to lack of liquids; in worst case scenario, salaries need to be paid to forest machine drivers also when a machine does not operate and fixed costs, such as insurance fees are still running. Second, IoT based monitoring reduces costs associated to travelling to remote storage areas due to checking whether there is sufficient amount of liquids available.

Third, monitoring of containers provides more accurate and timely information on inventory in containers through real-time consumption monitoring. Fourth, the company can order refilling of containers proactively and organize pick up for waste from storage areas. Fifth, our goal was also to increase operational safety related to dealing with liquids (fungicide, AdBlue, fuel) that may also lead to decreased workload for forest machine drivers. Finally, more automated process will decrease the number of contact requests from employees to work managers due to unclear or missing liquids-related work instructions.

Case B: The main task in case B was to design a continuous mass measurement system using smart sensors and state of the art cloud services. Our goal was to place an industrial class "scale" under the standard IBC container to continuously measure the mass of the liquid container. The public LoraWAN was selected as the data network solution because the research team had positive experiences from the first pilot.

The planned work tasks included research work to design the solution and select the components, make a build or buy decision, test and experiment the selected solution, and identify constraints in Motoajo's warehouse environment.

C. *Action*

Case A: The main purpose of the action was to plan, design, implement, test and validate the IoT based monitoring system for forestry liquids including tank level sensors and install sensor modules into plastic IBC containers containing log marking colour and Diesel Exhaust Fluid. The following list contains action items from the beginning to the end of the experiment:

- Kick off for the experiment (objectives and deliverables of the experiment presented and discussed, SME and DIH plan the work to the Trial Handbook)
- Capturing user stories for the system
- Technical specification (technical features of the mobile application, technical details of IoT sensors and dashboard)
- Development (development of mobile, IoT dashboard, configuring and coding)
- User Interface design (User interface design of the mobile app, IoT dashboard design)
- User feedback (collect information from forest machine drivers and work managers, implementation of corrections and changes)
- Testing (sensor testing, data network and integration testing, testing related to alerts, agile test report)
- Deployment (deploy solution for diesel exhaust fluid and marking colour container)
- User training (train related user groups)
- Experiment closure meeting (conduct closure meeting, reflect to the experiment objectives, capture lessons learnt, plan further dissemination and exploitation opportunities)

Case B: The main purpose of the action was to implement a continuous mass measurement system. However, the monitoring target was changed to the oil canister pallet that is delivered to the warehouse or a remote storage and the goal was to find out when there are only few canisters (200 kg/1000 kg) left. The following list contains action items for the case B:

- Study the required components for the system (scale, IoT services, signal transmitter, etc.)
- Purchase and integrate selected hardware components (PCE RS 2000, Enless Wireless Signal Transmitter)
- Conduct meetings with AWS specialists to identify potential ways to implement the system
- Sign up an Open Cloud Research Environment Contract to make purchase of services smoother (however, we decided not to wait this contract to be signed)
- Establish and test the connection between the signal transmitter and Digita IoT network (this part went successfully)
- Participate in Solver X reverse pitching event in Helsinki, Finland to identify potential IoT providers for the cloud system
- Negotiate with IoT providers and initiate a public bidding process on implement the system in our own AWS subscription (we have reached this step)
- Start implementation (our next step)

D. Results: Case A

Case A: The experiment was considered successful in the case organization. As the results of Case A, the company has now an IoT-based monitoring system for liquid containers (Diesel Exhaust Fluid, log marking colour) that enables monitoring liquids in remote storage areas. The monitoring system includes a mobile application that machine drivers use when they pick up supplies and liquids from storage areas. Through the mobile application work managers are able to monitor containers and see the level of liquids. The system also enables sending alerts when most of the content in liquid containers has been consumed. Three sensor modules were installed during the experiment and according to our knowledge, the company has ordered more similar sensor modules from the IoT sensor provider in 2023.

Case B: As main results of Case B, we defined a system architecture for the continuous mass measurement system. Figure 2 shows the architecture with key system components. Based on discussions with customer, data transmission frequency can be approximately one hour and the test site would be in Nurmes, Eastern Finland in Motoajo's main storage area. Our aim was to establish a system where sensor data is directed to a cost-effective cloud-based IoT environment where data is stored and a simple graph (for example, generated by open source visualization tools) is constructed. By implementing the system to our own AWS premises, we try to avoid potential vendor lock-in. The scale shall be placed on the warehouse floor and the system allows lifting goods onto the scale with a forklift. The prototype of the system is almost ready (at the time of submitting this paper) and we are preparing to deliver the system to the customer's storage facilities.

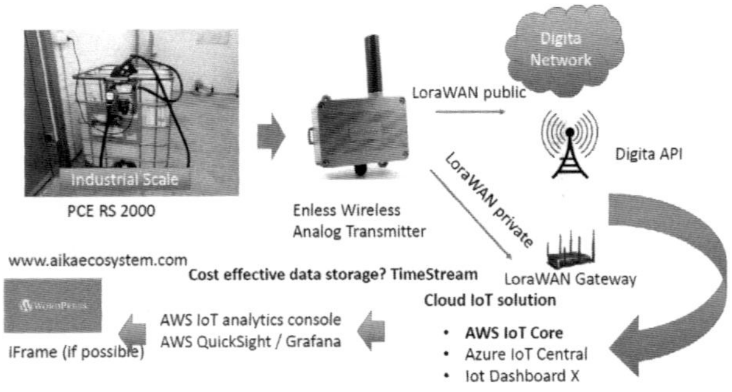

Fig. 2. The IoT sensor architecture.

IV. ANALYSIS

The data analysis for the study was performed by case comparison technique. The results of this exploratory case study are presented in this section according to three research questions: 1) What types of IoT monitoring needs does a forest machine operator company have?, 2) how quality attributes are visible in building IoT solutions for forestry domain? and 3) how IoT-related challenges and barriers can be solved?. In Table 1, analysis of case study results reflecting the three research questions of the study is presented.

The following lessons learnt can be identified based on our cases:

TABLE I. ANALYSIS OF THE CASE STUDY WITH TWO IOT EXPERIMENTS AS UNITS OF ANALYSIS

Category	Case A
Monitoring needs	Monitoring liquid containers Proactive orders for liquids Sending alerts on low levels Ordering refilling containers in time
Quality	Accurate view on liquid level Data conversion on distance to percent Data frequency 6 hours Install sensor to cap of container Calibration of sensors
Benefits	Check liquid levels remotely Setting alerts on critical liquid levels Proactive way to ensure availab. of liquids Provides data on liquid consumption trends May reveal container leaks
Category	**Case B**
Monitoring needs	Contin. mass monitoring Proactive orders for supplies: oil canisters Sending alerts on low levels Oil orders in time
Quality	Number of canisters 4-20 mA to kg Data frequency 1 hours Scale under pallet Calibration of scale
Benefits	Number of oil canisters Setting alerts on only few oil canisters left Enables monitoring any tangible items Consumption of oil canisters May detect that items are stolen

Lesson 1: Security is a top priority quality aspect: As IoT devices are connected to the internet, they are prone to cyber attacks. It is important to ensure that security is top priority when designing and implementing IoT solutions. In our cases, data does not control anything and IoT platform was protected by usernames and passwords. Data was sent from sensors to IoT platform and further to mobile app. The mobile app showing virtual version of the container forces users to use strong passwords.

Lesson 2: Scalability is crucial: IoT solutions may need to handle large amounts of data and devices. It is important to design solutions that can scale to accommodate growth. Regarding case A, our mobile app Alfa was running in AWS cloud to ensure scalability. In case B, we also aim at using scalable cloud services instead of third party IoT platforms to ensure scalability of the system.

Lesson 3: Interoperability is key: IoT devices and platforms need to be able to communicate with each other seamlessly. It is important to ensure that devices and platforms are interoperable and can work together. Data in our case A was delivered by using JSON, standard communication protocol. It is very likely that case B shall be using the JSON or the MQTT protocol. We observed in case A that data transmission from sensors was conducted every 6th hour (the goal was to transmit data on hourly basis). In case B, we put data transmission frequency clearly to Invitation for tender document.

Lesson 4: Maintenance is important: IoT devices need to be maintained and updated regularly to ensure they are functioning properly and securely. Battery life is impacted by cold weather. Offers from IoT providers could have clearlier statements on battery life and maintenance of IoT devices. Most of the providers are offering their own platform instead of implementing IoT in customer's premises.

Lesson 5: Data management is critical: IoT devices generate large amounts of data. It is important to have proper data management and analytics tools in place to make sense of this data. Third party IoT platform was responsible for receiving data from Digita LoraWAN network. Data was further stored in AWS MySQL database. The application server of Alfa application has access only to database server that increases security of data management.

Lesson 6: User experience is important: IoT solutions should be designed with the end user in mind. The user interface should be intuitive and easy to use. In the mobile application Alfa, visualization of container worked well. We aimed at listening users carefully to address their needs. The online form related to QR codes might need further improvement and clarification.

According to our observations, there are other factors that might also have effects on IoT system implementations in Finland: First, if sensors are placed outdoors, there is significant temperature variation (in extreme cases +35 C - -40 C) between summer and winter seasons in Finland. Second, a large part of forestry operations are performed in remote forest destinations, often without official street addresses. This might cause challenges in producing reliable location data.

Third, there is only one public LoraWAN network provider Digita in Finland. This should be taken into account while software engineers build LoraWAN-based systems in Finland. Creating contracts may take time and thus should not be ignored while planning IoT project schedules. Fourth, Finland is a sparsely populated country. Long distances mean a lot of traveling and eliminating unnecessary traveling creates a good business case for IoT implementation projects. Finding a profitable and viable business case for IoT is often a challenging task.

Fifth, IoT technology also has societal impacts on people living in rural areas of Finland. Through IoT based monitoring [15], one can monitor elderly people, detect potential accidents and incidents both outdoors and indoors or locate injured forestry workers or trigger alerts.

Finally, despite the high level of digitalization, the lack of skilled workforce is a challenge for many cities. This means unavailability of software engineering talents that are able to design cloud-based IoT systems and take care of advanced privacy and security requirements.

V. CONCLUSION

This study aimed at answering the research problem: How quality aspects should be taken into account while designing and implementing IoT-based software systems for forestry inventory management? The main contribution of this paper is to present lessons learnt from two experiments with different monitoring targets: liquid level monitoring and continuous mass monitoring of oil canister pallets. Both IoT experiments were performed in facilities of the second largest forest harvesting company in Finland.

There were three research questions in the study. Regarding the first research question, we observed various IoT monitoring needs in the forest machine operator, such as various types and sizes of containers (fuel containers, water containers, oil containers, fungicide containers, diesel exhaust fluid containers, marking colour containers). However, in addition to liquids there are several tangible supplies that company orders on frequent basis, such as grease tubes, oil filters, oil canister pallets, chain blades and chains. These tangible supplies need another type of monitoring system that we aimed at to design in the second IoT case.

Concerning the second research question, how quality attributes are visible in building IoT solutions, we highlighted activities that were specific to IoT-based digital transformation, such as selecting right sensor and data network solution, performing data conversion, defining data storage mechanism for IoT data, as well as installing the sensor modules. All of these require work efforts.

Finally, related to the third research question, we studied how IoT monitoring shall support forest operations. First of all, IoT-based monitoring allows proactive approach on ordering both liquids and supplies. The monitoring system enables sending alerts on low inventory levels, as well as showing visualization as graphs or tables based on the ingested IoT data. In the future, this data can be used and analyzed to optimize the ordering process based on consumption patterns.

The following limitations are related to this study: There are certain limitations related to the case study research method. First, case study does not allow the generalization of results to other organisations but we can use our results to extend the theory related to planning, designing and building realtime IoT-based systems. Second, Case B is still ongoing and we have no detailed information how the selected IoT provided has done the actual implementation in AWS cloud. However, the prototype is close to delivery to the customer site. Third, more staff from user side could have been interviewed to receive more feedback on improved liquids ordering process. Further research could focus on ICT quality aspects in cloud-based Internet of Things projects, for example, in Amazon Web Services projects or Azure IoT implementations.

ACKNOWLEDGMENT

We would like to thank the case organization for valuable collaboration during the study and DigiCenterNS DIH and AIKA Ecosystem DIH for research data collection. DigiCenterNS was supported by Digiteknologian TKI-ympäristö project A74338 (ERDF, Regional Council of Pohjois-Savo). AIKA Arctic Data Intelligence and Supercomputing Ecosystem in Kainuu project (A78688) is funded by European Regional Development Fund and Regional Council of Kainuu. The IoT-based liquid level monitoring case was created in DIH World experiment co-funded by the Horizon 2020 Framework Programme of the European Union under grant agreement no 952176.

REFERENCES

[1] J. Gabrys, "Smart forests and data practices: From the internet of trees to planetary governance," *Big Data & Society*, vol. 7, no. 1-10, pp. 362–377, 2020.

[2] S. K. Mohammed, S. M. Kamruzzaman, A. Ahmed, A. Hoque, and F. Shabnam, "Design and implementation of an iot based forest environment monitoring system," in *2019 IEEE 5th International Conference on Computer and Communications (ICCC)*, 2019, pp. 2152–2156.

[3] A. Hinze, J. Bowen, and J. König, "Wearable technology for hazardous remote environments: Smart shirt and rugged iot network for forestry worker health," *Smart Health*, vol. 23, p. 100225, 12 2021.

[4] Y. Wang, J. Song, X. Liu, S. Jiang, and Y. Liu, "Plantation monitoring system based on internet of things," in *2013 IEEE International Conference on Green Computing and Communications and IEEE Internet of Things and IEEE Cyber, Physical and Social Computing*, 2013, pp. 366–369.

[5] A. Ferrari, M. Bacco, K. Gaber, A. Jedlitschka, S. Hess, J. Kaipainen, P. Koltsida, E. Toli, and G. Brunori, "Drivers, barriers and impacts of digitalisation in rural areas from the viewpoint of experts," *Information and Software Technology*, vol. 145, p. 106816, May 2022.

[6] M. Jäntti and M. Aho, "Improving the quality of ict and forestry service processes with digital service management approach: A case study on forestry liquids," in *Quality of Information and Communications Technology*, A. Vallecillo, J. Visser, and R. Pérez-Castillo, Eds. Cham: Springer International Publishing, 2022, pp. 175–189.

[7] A. Cater-Steel, "It service departments struggle to adopt a service-oriented philosophy," *International Journal of Information Systems in the Service Sector*, vol. 1, no. 2, pp. 69–77, 2009.

[8] Y. Seralathan, T. T. Oh, S. Jadhav, J. Jonathan Myers, P. J. Jeong, Y. H. Kim, and J. N. Kim, "Iot security vulnerability: A case study of a web camera," in *2018 20th International Conference on Advanced Communication Technology (ICACT)*, 2018, pp. 172–177.

[9] COBIT5, *Control Objectives for Information and related Technology: COBIT 5: Enabling Processes.* ISACA, 2012.

[10] A. Kudrati, C. Peiris, and B. Pillai, *Microsoft Cybersecurity Reference Architecture and Capability Map*, 2022, pp. 183–240.

[11] J. Mace, C. Morisset, K. Pierce, C. Gamble, C. Maple, and J. Fitzgerald, "A multi-modelling based approach to assessing the security of smart buildings," in *Living in the Internet of Things: Cybersecurity of the IoT - 2018*, 2018, pp. 1–10.

[12] R. Yin, *Case Study Research: Design and Methods, Fourth edition.* Beverly Hills, CA: Sage Publishing, 2009.

[13] A. Kalpaka, J. Sorvik, and A. Tasigiorgou, "Digital innovation hubs as policy instruments to boost digitalisation of smes," Publications Office of the European Union, Tech. Rep., 2020.

[14] K. Eisenhardt, "Building theories from case study research," *Academy of Management Review*, vol. 14, pp. 532–550, 1989.

[15] M. Bacco, G. Brunori, A. Ferrari, P. Koltsida, and E. Toli, "Iot as a digital game changer in rural areas: the desira conceptual approach," in *2020 Global Internet of Things Summit (GIoTS)*, 2020, pp. 1–6.

Towards Improving Accurate Breast Cancer Diagnosis: Leveraging Pre-trained Convolutional Neural Network for Mammogram Analysis

Marwa Ben Ammar
Research Laboratory of Biophysics and Medical Technologies
Higher Institute of Medical Technologies of Tunis (ISTMT), University of Tunis el Manar
Tunis, Tunisia
marwa.ammar@istmt.utm.tn

Dorra Zaibi
Research laboratory Innov'COM « Innovation of COMmunicant and COoperative Mobiles Laboratory »
Higher School of Communication of Tunis (SUPCOM), University of Carthage
Tunis, Tunisia
e-mail: dorra.zaibi@supcom.tn

Faten Labbene Ayachi
Research laboratory Innov'COM « Innovation of COMmunicant and COoperative Mobiles Laboratory »
Higher School of Communication of Tunis (SUPCOM), University of Carthage
Tunis, Tunisia
e-mail: faten.labbene@supcom.tn

Riadh Ksantini
Department of Computer Science
College of IT, University of Bahrain
Bahrain, Bahrain
e-mail: ksontiniriadh@yahoo.fr

Halima Mahjoubi
Research Laboratory of Biophysics and Medical Technologies
Higher Institute of Medical Technologies of Tunis (ISTMT), University of Tunis el Manar
Tunis, Tunisia
e-mail: halima.mahjoubi@istmt.utm.tn

Abstract— **Breast cancer poses a significant global health challenge, emphasizing the need for improved diagnostic approaches for early diagnosis and intervention. Mammography, a widely used screening method, provides valuable insights into breast tissue anomalies. Nevertheless, its effectiveness is marred by error-prone interpretations and time-consuming analyses. To address this, our study introduces an innovative strategy to enhance breast cancer diagnosis by employing a Three-Stage One-Class You Only Look Once (YOLO) classification framework, harnessing the power of Deep Learning (DL). By incorporating the YOLO-v8 network, cutting-edge convolutional neural network (CNN) architecture, our proposed methodology aims to mitigate the shortcomings of conventional mammography interpretation. To assess the model's effectiveness, we utilize the Mammography Image Analysis Society (MIAS) dataset, which encompasses inherent data imbalances and intricacies. The framework we present is divided into three stages, each contributing to the refinement of the diagnostic process. Through the application of a one-class classification technique, our model effectively distinguishes between normal and abnormal mammograms. Furthermore, it offers a higher level of granularity by categorizing abnormalities into masses or calcifications. Additionally, the model can differentiate between benign and malignant cases, thereby facilitating precise clinical decision-making.**

Keywords- Breast cancer; mammography; deep learning; YOLO; early diagnosis; one-class classification; three stages methodology; data imbalance

I. INTRODUCTION

In this section, we will provide an overview of the research problem, outline the research questions, and delineate the research objectives. This introductory segment aims to set the stage for a comprehensive understanding of the context and purpose of our research.

A. *Research Problem*

Breast cancer has taken the lead as the most commonly diagnosed cancer and the fifth cause of cancer deaths among women worldwide. Therefore, only an early and accurate breast cancer diagnosis can significantly improves patient survival rates and paves the way for effective treatment. Mammography remains the most widely utilized by radiologists for accurate breast cancer diagnosis.

Nonetheless, the ever-increasing volume of daily mammograms presents a real challenge for radiologists and physicians, potentially resulting in diagnostic errors and unnecessary biopsies. Two significant types of errors can occur: False-Positive (FP) and False-Negative (FN). False positives carry negative consequences as they misidentify benign areas as cancerous. More critically, false negatives jeopardize patient lives as they occur when radiologists fail to detect abnormalities. Moreover, studies have shown that to reduce FN diagnoses, biopsies are recommended for lesions with a greater than 2% likelihood of malignancy. Consequently, only 15–30% of patients referred for biopsy are ultimately found to have malignancies [1]. To tackle these challenges, our research proposes a computer-aided diagnosis system using the You Only Look Once version 8 (YOLOv8) Convolutional Neural Network (CNN). It operates in three stages, leveraging a One-Class Classification (OCC) approach to effectively detect normal and abnormal mammograms, categorize abnormalities as masses or calcifications, and identify benign and malignant cases for precise clinical decision-making. In the following section, we highlight key Research Questions (RQs) from existing literature that inform our proposed breast cancer diagnosis model.

B. *Research Questions*

Taking into account the latest advancements in breast cancer diagnosis using deep learning techniques, our research focused on the following key questions: Which imaging method is most effective in detecting breast cancer? Which algorithm can efficiently and accurately detect and classify breast cancer within a unified framework? How can diagnostic accuracy be improved while minimizing the need for biopsies and reducing errors in identifying malignant cancers? Which model has the highest accuracy rate across all databases? Currently, there is no tool capable of diagnosing breast cancer with both a high degree of accuracy and minimal errors, while also minimizing the number of required biopsies.

C. *Outline of Objectives*

Our primary research objective is to develop a novel and highly effective YOLOv8-based model for breast cancer diagnosis using mammograms. Our specific focus includes achieving : (1) Reliability: Our model aims for high accuracy, sensitivity, specificity, precision, False-Negative (FN), False-Positive (FP), F1-score, Receiver Operating Characteristic (ROC) curve, Area Under The Curve (AUC), Intersection Over Union (IOU) score, and mean Average Precision (mAP), as these metrics are crucial in medical images analysis [2]; and (2) Transferability: We want our model to be adaptable across different datasets, even when transitioning from analyzing mammograms to other domains like lung X-ray images These objectives are in direct alignment with the research queries outlined in the preceding subsection focusing on research questions.

The subsequent sections of this study are structured as follows: Section 2 delivers a concise review of the current State-Of-The-Art in breast cancer diagnosis using deep learning algorithms on mammography, accompanied by an overview of their results. Section 3 provides an in-depth exposition of our research methodology. Finally, in Section 4, we wrap up the paper by briefly summarizing the expected research outcomes, detailing the present stage of our research, and offering insights for potential future investigations.

II. LITERATURE REVIEW

In this section, we attempt to cover most recent research works that have been done related to diagnosis of breast cancers with applying various techniques of deep learning along with their results. Muduli et al. [3] proposed a deep CNN model for breast cancer classification in mammogram and ultrasound images. This CNN model achieved 96.55%, 90.68%, and 91.28% accuracy on MIAS, DDSM, and INbreast datasets, respectively. Additionally, it reached 100% and 89.73% accuracy on BUS-1 and BUS-2 datasets. Zhao et al. [4] developed three YOLOv3-based models for breast cancer detection and classification using mammograms: a general model, mass model, and microcalcifications model. Their study achieved detection accuracy rates of 93.667%, 97.767%, and 96.870%, and classification accuracy rates of 93.927%, 98.121%, and 97.045%, respectively, using the CBIS-DDSM dataset. Baccouche et al. [5] used an end-to-end YOLO-based fusion model to detect and classify breast lesions (mass, calcification, architectural distortion) in digital mammograms with the UCHC DigiMammo dataset. The approach incorporated prior mammograms for early detection and retrospective prediction. The evaluation achieved detection rates of 93% for mass lesions, 88% for calcification lesions, and 95% for architectural distortion lesions in current mammography. Zebari et al. [6] constructed a breast cancer detection model from mammograms using a pre-trained CNN-based approach. Testing on the mini-MIAS dataset resulted in an impressive accuracy of 95.71%. Alam et al. [7] applied the Unet3+ architecture for semantic segmentation to enhance breast cancer diagnosis in ultrasound images of 309 patients. The Unet3+ model outperformed other models (FCN, Unet, SegNet, DeeplabV3+, and pspNet) with an average accuracy of 82.53%, an intersection over union of 52.57%, a weighted accuracy of 89.14%, and a global accuracy of 90.99%. Boudouh et al. [8] investigated seven pre-trained CNNs for accurate breast tumor detection: Xception, InceptionV3, ResNet101V2, ResNet50V2, ALexNet, VGG16, and VGG19. They gathered data from three distinct databases: MiniMIAS, DDSM, and CMMD. The results were impressive, particularly for ResNet50V2 and InceptionV3, which achieved the highest accuracy rates of 99.9% and 99.54%, respectively. Despite the accomplishments of these computer-aided diagnostic methods, challenges like high memory complexity, practical implementation, and extended runtime persist. Furthermore, these approaches have the following flaws. First, the accuracy of recognizing probable small lesions is quite poor. Second, except for [4] and [5], techniques only identify breast mass lesions, disregarding other types like microcalcifications in mammography. As a result of these issues, the method's limitations have been discovered. To address the constraints noted above, we focus on the detection and classification of mammograms while also addressing the issues of different types of lesions and small-sized lesions, and we propose a YOLOv8-based computer-aided diagnostic system for mammograms.

Section III summarizes our thorough contributions to the field of breast cancer diagnosis using deep learning techniques and mammography image analysis.

III. METHODOLOGY

Our research aims to develop an accurate breast tumor detection and classification model while reducing FP and FN outcomes. We utilize the publicly available Mammographic Image Analysis Society Digital Mammogram (MIAS) dataset, which can be conveniently accessed through a user-friendly online interface [10]. Our methodology comprises four steps, as illustrated in Fig. 1: data acquisition and splitting, image preprocessing, YOLOv8 deep learning model deployment with OCC approach, and comprehensive performance evaluation. In the subsequent subsections, we will provide detailed insights into each step.

A. *Dataset Description*

The MIAS dataset, established by a UK research consortium, comprises 322 single-slice digital mammograms from 161 patients. The dataset covers various breast abnormalities, as detailed in Table 1. However, The MIAS dataset has limitations: it's small, potentially causing overfitting in deep learning models; it's imbalanced, with 207 normal and 115 abnormal cases, impacting classification algorithms; and it requires preprocessing to remove extraneous data outside the mammary area.

TABLE I. COMPREHENSIVE DATA DISTRIBUTION OVERVIEW

Total number of Patients	161
Total number of Mammograms	322
Total number of Mammograms with Pathology	115
Total number of Mammograms without Lesions (Normal)	207
Number Of Mammograms With Mass Lesions	57
Number of Mammograms with Calcification Lesions	25
Number of Mammograms with Architectural Distortion Lesions	18
Number of Mammograms with Asymmetry Lesions	14

In this section, we've introduced the mammography dataset that forms the basis of our study. The subsequent sections will provide detailed insights into the techniques utilized for image data preprocessing, a clear explanation of our classification methodology, a discussion on model selection, and an overview of our performance evaluation process.

B. *Image Data Preprocessing*

To enhance our dataset's quality and applicability. Our approach includes various techniques like noise removal, contrast enhancement, data augmentation, resizing, and normalization for each mammogram breast image within the MIAS dataset. This dataset contains different noises and imaging artifacts, such as tape artifacts and high-intensity rectangular labels, as illustrated in Fig. 2, which need to be removed. Additionally, MIAS mammograms have limited contrast, prompting us to consider contrast enhancement techniques like Contrast Limited Adaptive Histogram Equalization (CLAHE). Besides, we perform image resizing, data augmentation, and normalization to align input images with CNN requirements and address the small dataset size challenge. Data augmentation involves random transformations like rotation and flipping to diversify and expand the training data.

C. *Image Data Classification*

Our study focuses on developing a YOLOv8-based pipeline for breast mammogram detection and classification. It includes three key stages: detecting abnormalities as normal or abnormal, distinguishing masses from microcalcifications, and classifying benign or malignant cases.

Our selection of the YOLOv8 model for our breast cancer diagnosis study using mammograms is based on several key considerations that collectively make it exceptionally well-suited for this task. Firstly, YOLOv8 is renowned for its efficiency and speed in object detection and classification tasks, aligning perfectly with our goal of providing an efficient model for breast cancer diagnosis. Its real-time capabilities are essential for swift and accurate diagnosis. Additionally, YOLOv8 has demonstrated outstanding accuracy in object detection, a crucial aspect for identifying abnormalities in mammograms, which is fundamental in the context of breast cancer diagnosis.

Moreover, YOLOv8's architectural versatility is a significant advantage. The model is capable of handling various object detection tasks, a valuable trait considering the diverse abnormalities and conditions that can be present in mammograms. In the realm of breast cancer diagnosis, this flexibility is highly advantageous.

Furthermore, our study emphasizes the importance of achieving high transferability across different datasets. YOLOv8's adaptability to varying data distributions and its ability to generalize well across diverse datasets ensure that our model can maintain consistent performance, regardless of the specific dataset it is applied to.

Last but not least, the YOLOv8 model is part of a well-established family of models with a substantial user base and ongoing research efforts. This provides us with access to valuable resources, pre-trained models, and a vibrant community of researchers continually working on model improvements and adaptations. In conclusion, our choice of the YOLOv8 model is well-founded in its remarkable efficiency, accuracy, versatility, and transferability, making it an ideal candidate for enhancing breast cancer diagnosis through deep learning techniques. Its real-time capabilities, combined with its adaptability to different datasets, position it as a robust choice for our mission of advancing breast cancer diagnosis.

The imbalance within the MIAS dataset, consisting of 207 normal cases and 115 abnormal cases, significantly impacts the classification process. Imbalanced datasets often pose challenges for traditional binary or multi-class classification methods, as they tend to favor the larger class, making it difficult to accurately detect the minority class. One effective approach to address these issues is the utilization of OCC. This approach is particularly valuable in domains such as medical image diagnosis, where acquiring data from both healthy and unhealthy patients can be impractical due to high costs or rarity.

In the context of OCC approach, the primary objective is to classify data when information is available for only one group of observations. OCC methods operate with a single dataset, referred to as the "target class," typically representing the class with fewer instances. The aim is to distinguish data belonging to the target class from other potential classes. OCC can be viewed as a specialized form of the two-class classification problem, where only data from one class is considered during the training and validation phases. However, during inference, the classifier encounters data from both the target class and classes outside the target.

In our study, we adopt the terminology of "target" and "outside the target" to differentiate between abnormalities and normal cases, masses and calcifications, and malignant and benign cases. This approach allows us to effectively address the classification challenges presented by the MIAS dataset's class imbalance.

Our choice to primarily employ the MIAS dataset for evaluation was motivated by several key factors. First and foremost, the MIAS dataset stands as one of the most renowned and widely utilized datasets in the realm of mammography image analysis. With a substantial number of mammogram images accompanied by annotations, it serves as a valuable benchmark for our model's performance.

In this study, our principal goal was to construct and benchmark our YOLOv8-based breast cancer diagnosis model within the context of a well-recognized dataset, the MIAS dataset. This approach allows us to assess the model's performance within a known benchmark and aligns with the core objectives of our research.

Moreover, by concentrating our initial evaluation on the MIAS dataset, we intended to establish a solid baseline for our model's performance. Once this robust baseline is achieved, we are fully prepared to extend our evaluation to encompass the other datasets referenced in our literature review.

It is important to acknowledge that evaluating a model on multiple datasets can be resource-intensive and time-consuming. Therefore, it is a customary practice in research to commence with a specific dataset to validate the model's viability before proceeding to a broader spectrum of datasets.

While our preliminary evaluation centers on the MIAS dataset, we are fully cognizant of the significance of future research endeavors that will encompass a wider array of datasets outlined in the literature review. This expansion is vital for a comprehensive assessment of the model's robustness and adaptability across diverse data sources, as envisaged in our research question. We are dedicated to advancing our research to address this aspect thoroughly, ensuring our model's performance is rigorously validated across a broader range of datasets, in line with the goals of our research.

D. *Performance Evaluation*

Our research will primarily center on evaluating the YOLOv8-based model's capacity to accurately identify the position of breast lesions in mammograms. We will employ two key metrics for this assessment: the IOU score and the mAP.

Following that, we will shift our focus to gauge the performance of the YOLOv8 model. In practical terms, the effectiveness of deep learning-based image classification is determined through a range of metrics, including accuracy, sensitivity, specificity, precision, FP and FN rates, the ROC curve, the AUC, and F1-score.

Consequently, as depicted in Fig. 1, our research work will incorporate a total of ten essential metrics for a comprehensive evaluation. The true positive (TP) represents the number of positive classes that have been correctly classified as positive. The true negative (TN) is the number of negative classes that that have been correctly classified as negative. The false positive (FP) represents the number of negative classes that have been misclassified as the positive class. The false negative (FN) represents the number of positive classes that have been misclassified as negative.

Below, we briefly outline the calculation formulas for the evaluation metrics used.

- mean Average Precision (mAP)

$$mAP = \frac{1}{N}\sum_{i=1}^{N} APi. \tag{1}$$

- Intersection Over Union score (IOU)

$$\text{IOU score} = \frac{\text{Area of Intersection}}{\text{Area of Union}} \tag{2}$$

- Accuracy (Acc)

$$Acc = \frac{TP + TN}{TP + TN + FP + FN} \tag{3}$$

- Precision (Pr)

$$Pr = \frac{TP}{TP + FP} \tag{4}$$

- Sensitivity (Sn)

$$Sn = \frac{TP}{(TP + FN)} \tag{5}$$

- Specificity (Sp)

$$Sp = \frac{TN}{(TN + FP)} \quad (6)$$

- F1-Score

$$F1 - Score = 2 \times \frac{Recall \times Precision}{(Recall + Precision)} \quad (7)$$

- ROC-AUC

$$FPR = \frac{FP}{FP + TN} \quad (8)$$

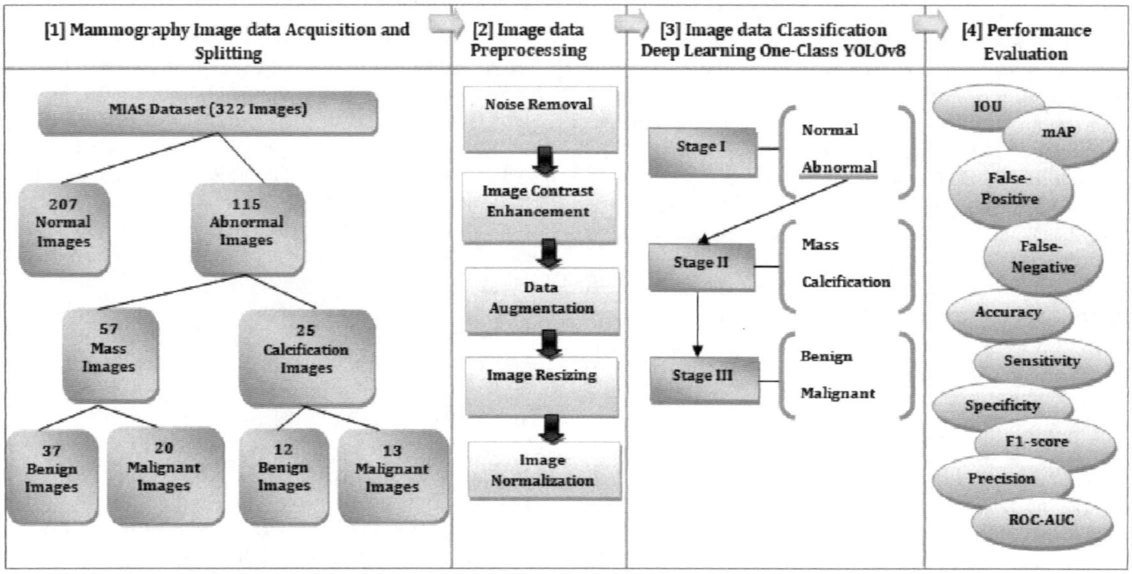

Figure 1. Framework for breast lesions detection and classification using deep learning one-class YOLOv8.

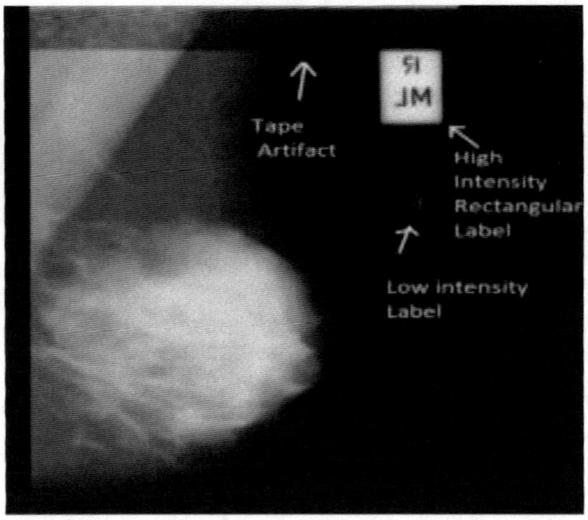

Figure 2. Examples of Noise Artifacts in MIAS Dataset.

IV. CONCLUSION AND FUTURE WORK

In the course of our research endeavor, our primary objective is to develop a state-of-the-art end-to-end learning model designed to diagnose breast cancer by analyzing mammogram images. Our vision for this innovative model centers on two critical aspects: (1) ensuring high reliability and (2) facilitating seamless transferability.

To this end, we have successfully reached several key milestones in our research journey. These milestones encompassed:

- Selection of the most appropriate image modality and dataset.
- Identification of widely adopted image preprocessing techniques.
- Determination of the deep learning model for breast cancer diagnosis and the classification approach.
- Selection of evaluation metrics meticulously designed to assess the proposed model's effectiveness.

Moreover, we have made significant progress by developing an initial YOLOv8-based algorithm. This algorithm, constructed using Python within the Google Colab Notebook, is adept at detecting breast lesions by distinguishing between normal and abnormal cases. The preliminary results of this algorithm, as demonstrated in Fig. 3, illustrate the proficiency of the YOLOv8 model in identifying abnormal breast lesions.

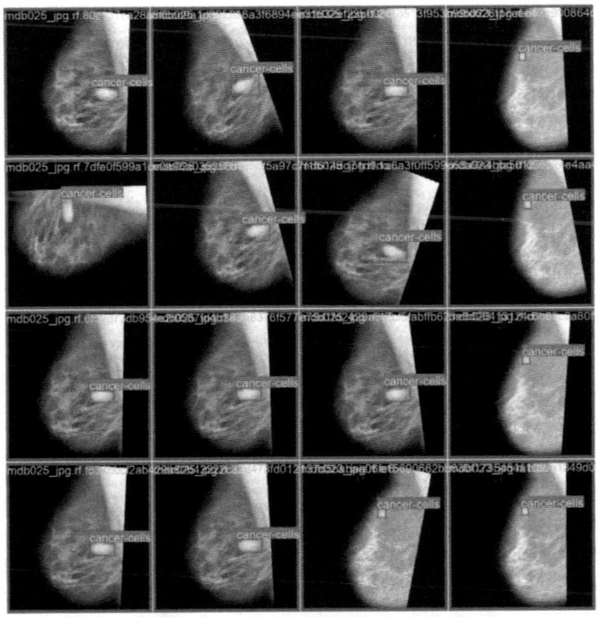

Figure 3. Example of Preliminary Outcomes of the YOLOv8 Model in Detecting Unusual Breast Lesions.

As we draw our research efforts to a close in this exploration of an advanced framework for mammogram image analysis in breast cancer diagnosis, it's important to note that our experiments are currently underway. The preliminary findings are highly promising, and we are on the brink of realizing the full potential of this groundbreaking technology. We eagerly anticipate sharing the final results, which have the potential to reshape the landscape of breast cancer diagnosis.

Looking forward, we propose a novel avenue for future work: a multimodal fusion architecture that leverages both breast images and tabular non-image data. This architecture incorporates a probability fusion approach, often referred to as "late fusion." It operates on the basis of considering the output probabilities from an image-only model and a non-image-only model, with the aim of yielding a final prediction. The underlying idea is that by incorporating non-image data alongside image data, we can significantly enhance predictive performance compared to a unimodal (single-source) approach.

Broadly, our proposal entails a decision-making pipeline that enables a hierarchical classification of breast cancer. To achieve this, we propose to aggregate the predictions from two models: the Deep Support Vector Data Description (DSVDD) and the One-Class Convolutional Neural Network (OCCNN) through a meta-model, consisting of a simple two-layer Multilayer Perceptron (MLP). This approach is geared towards improving the accuracy of breast cancer diagnosis.

For the training of these models, we consider specific combinations of feature subsets and model architectures. In our pursuit of exploring whether the fusion of image and non-image features can enhance breast cancer prediction, we propose to begin by establishing unimodal baseline models that exclusively employ image data and tabular non-image data. Subsequently, we propose to embark on the development of a multimodal fusion model that jointly learns from both image and non-image data.

REFERENCES

[1] E. A. Sickles, "Periodic mammographic follow-up of probably benign lesions: results in 3184 consecutive cases," Radiology., vol. 179, pp. 463–468, 1991.

[2] E. Mahoro, M. A. Akhloufi, "Applying Deep Learning for Breast Cancer Detection in Radiology," Curr. Oncol., vol. 29, pp. 8767-8793, 2022.

[3] D. Muduli, R. Dash, and B. Majhi, "Automated diagnosis of breast cancer using multi-modal datasets: A deep convolution neural network based approach," Biomed. Signal Process. Control., Vol. 71, ISSN. 1746-8094, 2022.

[4] J. Zhao, T. Chen, and B. Cai, "A computer-aided diagnostic system for mammograms based on YOLOv3," Multimed. Tools Appl., vol. 81, pp. 19257–19281, 2022.

[5] A. Baccouche, B. Garcia-Zapirain, Y. Zheng, and A. S. Elmaghraby, "Early detection and classification of abnormality in prior mammograms using image-to-image translation and YOLO techniques," Comput. Methods Programs Biomed., Vol. 221, 2022.

[6] D. A. Zebari, H. Haron, D. M. Sulaiman, Y. Yusoff, and M. N. Mohd Othman, "CNN-based Deep Transfer Learning Approach for Detecting Breast Cancer in Mammogram Images," IEEE 10th Conference on Systems, Process & Control (ICSPC)., pp. 256-261, 2022.

[7] T. Alam, W. C. Shia, F. R. Hsu, and T. Hassan, "Improving Breast Cancer Detection and Diagnosis through Semantic Segmentation Using the Unet3+ Deep Learning Framework," Biomedicines., vol. 11, pp. 1536, 2023.

[8] S. S. Boudouh, M. Bouakkaz, "Breast cancer: toward an accurate breast tumor detection model in mammography using transfer learning techniques," Multimed Tools Appl., vol. 82, pp. 34913–34936, 2023.

[9] G. H. Aly, M. Marey, S. A. El-Sayed, M. F. Tolba, "YOLO Based Breast Masses Detection and Classification in Full-Field Digital Mammograms," Comput. Methods Programs Biomed., Vol. 200, ISSN. 0169-2607, 2021.

[10] https://www.kaggle.com/datasets/kmader/mias-mammography.

Design Pattern Detection in Code: A Hybrid Approach Utilizing a Bayesian Network, Machine Learning with Graph Embeddings, and Micropattern Rules

Roy Oberhauser[0000-0002-7606-8226] and Sandro Moser
Computer Science Dept.
Aalen University
Aalen, Germany
e-mail: roy.oberhauser@hs-aalen.de, sandro.moser@studmail.hs-aalen.de

Abstract—**Software design patterns and the abstractions they offer can support developers and maintainers with program code comprehension. Yet manually-created pattern documentation within code or code-related assets, such as documents or models, can be unreliable, incomplete, and labor-intensive. While various Design Pattern Detection (DPD) techniques have been proposed, industrial adoption of automated DPD remains limited. This paper contributes a hybrid DPD solution approach that leverages a Bayesian network integrating developer expertise via rule-based micropatterns with our machine learning subsystem that utilizes graph embeddings. The prototype shows its feasibility, and the evaluation using three design patterns shows its potential for detecting both design patterns and variations.**

Keywords – software design pattern detection; machine learning; artificial neural networks; graph embeddings; rule-based expert system; Bayesian networks; software engineering.

I. Introduction

While the amount of program source code worldwide continues to rapidly expand, code comprehension remains a limiting productivity factor. Program comprehension may consume up to 70% of the software engineering effort [1]. Activities involving program comprehension include investigating functionality, internal structures, dependencies, run-time interactions, execution patterns, and program utilization; adding or modifying functionality; assessing the design quality; and domain understanding of the system [2]. And code that is not correctly understood by programmers impacts quality and efficiency.

Software Design Patterns (DPs) have been documented and popularized, including the Gang of Four (GoF) [3] and POSA [4]. The application of abstracted and documented solutions to recurring software design problems has been a boon to improving software design quality, efficiency, and aiding comprehension. These well-known macrostructures or associated pattern terminology in code can serve as beacons to abstracted macrostructures, and as such may help identify aspects such as the author's intention or the purpose of a code segment, which, in turn, supports program comprehension.

Possible automated DPD development or maintenance benefits include: quicker comprehension of DP-related structural aspects of some software; supplementing design documentation; automatically documenting DPs; reducing dependence on unreliable or incomplete manual DP documentation; detection of inadequately implemented DPs, e.g., as unknown DPs or DP variants. Yet automated DPD faces challenges, including: 1) tool support for heterogeneous programming languages, as DPs are independent of programming language; 2) internationalization and labeling, since developers may name and comment in their natural language or any way they like; 3) varying pattern abstraction levels, such as design vs. architectural patterns; 4) similarities and intent differentiation, since some similar pattern structures are primarily differentiated by their intention; 6) DP localization, indicating where in code a DP was detected; and 7) detecting variants, since each implementation is unique. While various DPD approaches have been explored [5] [6], no approach has so far achieved significant traction in practice and industry tools, and thus additional investigation into further viable approaches and improvements is warranted.

In previous work, we described DPDML, our ML-based DPD approach [7], and our hybrid DPD approach HyDPD [8], which combines two main components: HyDPD-ML that applies a supervised ML model based on semantic and static analysis metrics, and HyDPD-GA that applies a graph analysis technique.

This paper contributes our new DPD solution approach HyDPD-B (Hybrid DPD using a Bayesian network), which applies a Bayesian network probabilistic reasoning to flexibly integrate various DPD subsystems, including an updated version of HyDPD-ML utilizing graph embeddings, as well as our new knowledge-based expert rule system and language utilizing micropattern detection. The DP rule language supports including developer expertise in refining our DPD. Our prototype shows its feasibility and the evaluation demonstrates its potential for detecting both DPs and DP variations.

This paper is structured as follows: the next section discusses related work. Section 3 describes our solution. In Section 4, our realization is presented, which is followed by our evaluation in Section 5. Finally, a conclusion is provided.

II. Related Work

Surveys including categorizations of DPD approaches include [5] and [6]. Graph-based approaches include: Yu et al. [9] transform code to UML class diagrams, analyze the XMI for sub-patterns in class-relationship directed graphs; Mayvan and Rasoolzadegan [10] use a UML semantic graph; Bernardi et al. [11] apply a DSL-driven graph matching approach; DesPaD [12] extract an abstract syntax tree from code, create a single large graph model of a project, and then apply an isomorphic sub-graph search method. Further isomorphic subgraph approaches include Pande et al. [13] and Pradhan et al. [14], both of which require UML class diagrams.

Learning-based approaches map the DPD problem to a learning problem, and can involve classification, decision trees, feature maps or vectors, Artificial Neural Networks (ANNs), etc. Examples include Alhusain et al. [15], Zanoni et al. [16], Galli et al. [17], Ferenc et al. [18], Uchiyama et al. [19], and Dwivedi et al. [20]. Thaller et al. [21] describe a micro-structure-based structural analysis approach based on feature maps. Chihada et al. [22] convert code to class diagrams, which are then transformed to graphs, and have experts create feature vectors for each role based on object-oriented metrics and then apply ML.

Additional approaches include: reasoning-based approaches such as Wang et al. [23] based on matrices; rule-based approaches like Sempatrec [24] and the ontology-based FiG [25]; metric-based approaches such as MAPeD [26], Uchiyama et al. [19], and Dwivedi et al. [27]; Fontana et al. [28] analyze microstructures based on an abstract syntax tree; semantic-analysis style includes Issaoui et al. [29]; while DP-Miner [30] uses a matrix-based approach based on UML for structural, behavioral, and semantic analysis.

Our graph embedding procedure is conceptionally similar to Gl2vec [31] and Gredel [32], which was applied to drug discovery from biomedical literature.

Our HyDPD-B composite system uses a hybrid approach involving graph analysis as does Singh et al. [33]. However, Singh et al. combine static rules with graph analysis rather than ML. In our opinion, combining knowledge engineering with rules learned from data can address biases in expert knowledge as well as data scarcity. Our HyDPD-ML component utilizes random microstructures. GEML [34] initializes a population of random structures and then applies genetic algorithms to mutate and generate new patterns from the initial population. In contrast, we do not mutate the random patterns initially generated. Instead, ML is applied to determine the weight of each pattern and combine patterns in a linear way, thus enhancing interpretability. Furthermore, HyDPD-B utilizes micro-patterns, a recurring concept in pattern recognition, as does Kouli and Rasoolzadegan [35]. However, instead of binary logic, our work utilizes probabilistic logic, which in combination with micro-patterns can improve system flexibility. HyDPD-B offers a hybrid solution concept integrating multiple DPD subsystems. Utilizing a Bayesian network with probabilistic reasoning, it combines an expert knowledge rule system leveraging graph analysis micropatterns with a ML system utilizing graph embeddings. Additionally, our DPD solution supports multiple programming languages without requiring UML modeling.

III. SOLUTION CONCEPT

DPD approaches can arguably be categorized into three primary approaches: 1) learning-based, where DPs are (semi-)automatically learned (e.g., via supervised learning) from provided data and requiring minimal expert intervention; 2) knowledge-based, whereby an expert defines DPs by describing elements and their associations; and 3) similarity-based, whereby DPs are grouped based on similar metrics or characteristics.

In previous work our hybrid DPD approach (HyDPD) was described that seeks to combine various DPD approaches. To do so, it converts heterogeneous source code into a common format srcML [36], which is then further processed by a hybrid set of subsystems as shown in Figure 1. Our HyDPD-ML machine learning (ML) model in this paper uses knowledge graph embeddings as input to a supervised learning model. Our HyDPD-GA converts the srcML to BSON (Binary JSON) stored in MongoDB, maps it to a graph model stored in Neo4j that supports the Cypher Query Language (CQL) [37] for graph-based DPD analysis.

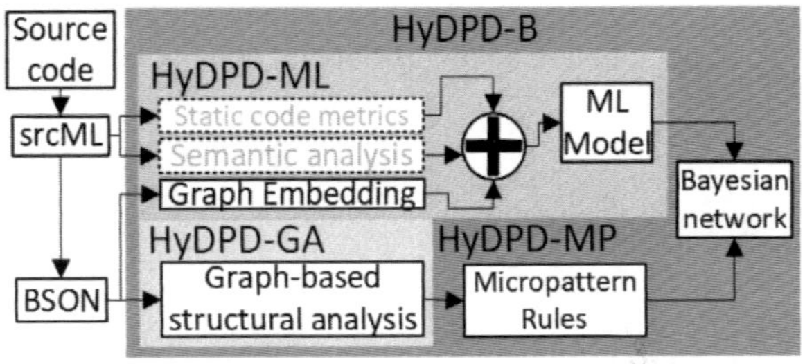

Figure 1. The HyDPD-B solution concept.

This paper describes our new hybrid solution concept HyDPD-B, which integrates results from our various DPD subsystems (HyDPD-ML, HyDPD-GA, HyDPD-MP) with a Bayesian network. It improves HyDPD by: 1) providing a mechanism to engage developers as experts in defining DP rules via a simple DP Rule Language (DPRL), 2) enabling approximate DP matching via micropattern support (HyDPD-MP), 3) utilizing HyDPD-ML results, and 4) enabling known and unknown variant detection. The Bayesian network provides a flexible framework for probabilistic reasoning that is comprehensible and interpretable for humans, and thus offering a hybrid solution for utilizing all three DPD approaches (learning-, knowledge-, and similarity-based).

A. *Design Pattern Rule Language (DPRL)*

Various languages have been proposed to express DPs in a programming language-agnostic but human-readable way. Mainly these consist of logic-, ontology-, or graphical-based languages [38]. As they vary based on purpose, they can be classified as intended for description, analysis, or verification. Most languages described in literature did not fit our purpose, necessitated a steep learning curve for developers, or were generalized and challenging to map to a practical and usable implementation. Since HyDPD-GA already provides a graph-based representation, we chose to start by simplifying Neo4j's CQL to create our own Domain-Specific Language (DSL) called Design Pattern Rule Language (DPRL). DPRL serves as a graph-oriented rule language for developers (i.e., the knowledge experts) that should be relatively easy to learn and comprehend. While CQL is powerful and offers a human-readable interface for formulating graph queries, a developer would nonetheless need to learn the Cypher syntax to formulate these only for the purpose of DPD. Instead, since developers are already well acquainted with the relatively simple JSON format, we chose to store it in JSON and then parse and map values to generate Cypher queries. Consequently, DPRL should be relatively easy to understand for developers and depend primarily on DP knowledge to formulate meaningful queries. The primary language concepts are *participants*, *subpatterns*, and *relations* as shown in the Adapter DP example in Figure 2.

```
1  {
2      "participants": [
3          {
4              "constraints": [
5                  {
6                      "field": "Type",
7                      "operator": "is",
8                      "value": true
9                  }
10             ],
11             "name": "adaptee"
12         },
13         {
14             "constraints": [
15                 {
16                     "field": "Type",
17                     "operator": "is",
18                     "value": true
19                 }
20             ],
21             "name": "adapter"
22         }
23     ],
24     "subpatterns": [
25         {
26             "relations": [
27                 {
28                     "constraints": [
29                         {
30                             "field": "collection",
31                             "operator": "is",
32                             "value": "true"
33                         }
34                     ],
35                     "directed": true,
36                     "operand1": "adaptee",
37                     "operand2": "adapter"
38                 }
39             ],
40             "truthvalue": false
41         },
42         {
43             "relations": [
44                 {
45                     "constraints": [
46                         {
47                             "field": "collection",
48                             "operator": "is",
49                             "value": "false"
50                         }
51                     ],
52                     "directed": true,
53                     "operand1": "adaptee",
54                     "operand2": "adapter"
55                 }
56             ],
57             "truthvalue": true
58         }
59     ]
60 }
```

Figure 2. DPRL example Adapter pattern specification in JSON.

1) Participants: Participants represents a collection of participant objects in a DP. In its simplest form a *participant* consists of the field *name* (line 21) – for instance, if the nature of the participant is irrelevant but the role it plays is of importance. The optional *constraints* field (line 4 and 14) allows a collection of arbitrary unary *constraints* (constraints that only involve the participant variable) to be specified. In Cypher, these constraints may correspond to labels while others may correspond to attributes. The distinction is made by our DSL parser using an internal symbol table. A *constraint* consists of three values: *field* (line 6 and 16) corresponding to the target of the constraint; *operator* (line 7 and 16) corresponding to the truth operator; and *value* (line 8 and 18) corresponding to the desired field value.

2) Subpatterns: Subpatterns (line 24) represents a collection of *subpattern* objects, each of which consists of a collection of binary *relations* (line 26 and 43) and the field *truthvalue* (line 40 and 57), indicating if the *subpattern* should be matched positively or negatively (precluded). While a pattern can contain only a single positive *subpattern*, it can contain an arbitrary number of negative *subpatterns*.

3) Relations: Relations (line 26 and 43) is a collection of *relations* between participants, which are specified by the fields *operand1*, *operand2*, *constraints,* and *directed* (lines 28-37). *Operand1* and *operand2* each contain either a name reference to a participant or a full description of a participant object (as described above). The collection *constraints* contains constraints analogous to those defined on a *participant.*

4) Example Equivalent Cypher Query. Our JSON DSL is parsed to an equivalent Cypher query. For the example in Figure 2, this is shown in Figure 3. For a developer with no knowledge of Cypher, the equivalent Cypher query is more complex to formulate or comprehend.

```
MATCH (adaptee) -[e]-> (adapter)
WHERE adaptee:Type AND adapter:Type AND e.collection = false
AND NOT EXISTS {MATCH (adaptee) -[f]-> (adapter) WHERE adaptee:Type
AND adapter:Type AND f.collection = true AND adaptee <> adapter}
AND adaptee <> adapter RETURN *
```

Figure 3. Example Equivalent HyDPD-GA Cypher Query.

B. *Micro Pattern Catalog (MPC)*

Certain structural aspects of design patterns can ideally be expressed as a set of smaller elementary units or characteristics we refer to as Micro Patterns (MPs) [39], e.g., Instantiation, Inheritance, Delegate, Extend, and Conglomeration. This also supports the reuse of viable MP detection components. Decomposing our existing graph-based queries in the Cypher Query Language (CQL) from our previous work on HyDPD-GA provided derived MPs with appropriate queries.

C. *Randomized Graph Embeddings*

In our previous work, HyDPD-ML was trained on tabular features extracted from source code. These features include the existence of specific keywords, as well as object-oriented metrics, such as the number of classes in a project. This approach is vulnerable to a change in naming convention or code obfuscation. To mitigate this issue, we introduce a new approach, using knowledge-graph-embeddings. Input for those embeddings is provided by the graphs used by HyDPD-GA. We apply a simple embedding approach: we first sample a predetermined number of random substructures in the graph. Those substructures are always extracted from the training set to exclude possible information leakage. Substructures include information about relationship type. From those substructures, we derive a pattern query.

A graph embedding is created by matching all generated pattern queries against a graph. This results in binary vectors, 0 if a pattern matched, else 1. While the number of generated patterns can be treated as a hyper parameter, we decided to work with 500 patterns. Another hyper parameter is the complexity of extracted patterns. We define pattern complexity as the number of edge traversals in the knowledge graph as shown in Figure 4. In a grid search experiment, it was determined, that constraining complexity between 3 and 4 traversals yields optimal results.

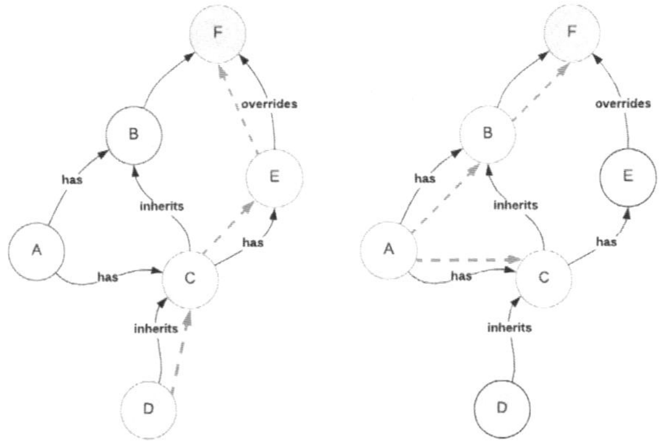

Figure 4. Sampling substructures with complexity 3

The graph embeddings are consumed by a simple logistic regression model with L2 regularization. This enables learning from sparse data. This composition of random feature extraction combined with a regularized linear model is inspired by the ROCKET-algorithm, which is used for time series classification [40]. By using a linear model, the interpretability of any results can be better supported.

D. *Pattern Variant Detection*

DPs often do not conform exactly to some specification, making detection of DP variants challenging. The problem of DP variant detection can be partitioned into 1) the detection of *known* variants, and 2) the detection of *unknown* variants as shown in Figure 5. Assuming DP variants share a substantial degree of MPs, our solution concept should be able to detect *known* pattern variations efficiently. Moreover, by using hidden variables in the Bayesian network, the algorithm can also provide precise information regarding the variant.

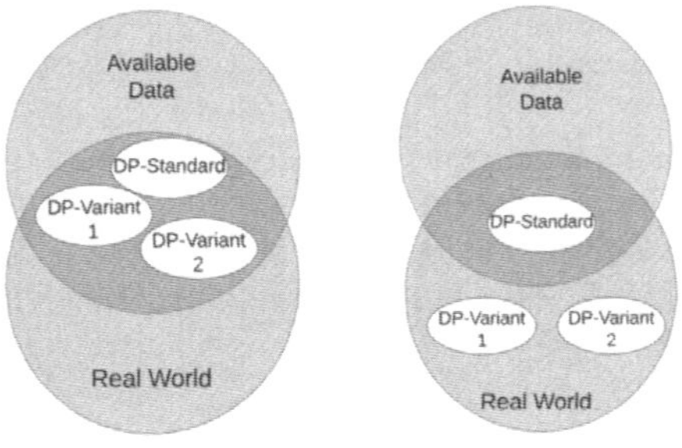

Figure 5. Detecting known (left) and unknown (right) DP variants.

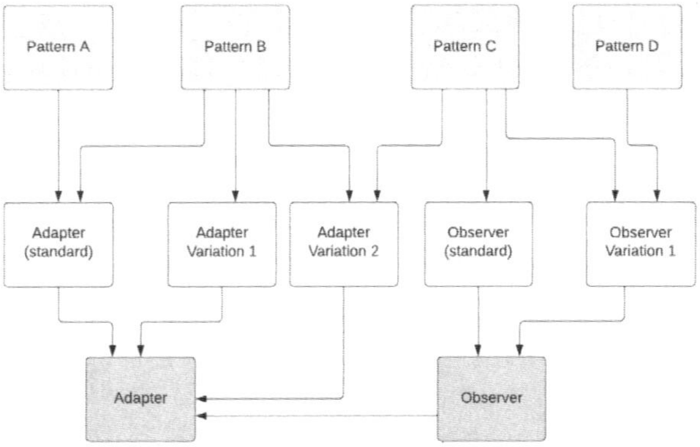

Figure 6. Expressing DP variants in the Bayesian network.

An example for this is depicted in Figure 6. Here, yellow variables correspond to DP variants. To learn probabilities of those variant variables from data, it is necessary to annotate the data accordingly. If uninterested in variants, the intermediate variables could be omitted and all MPs involved wired directly to the DP variables. Probabilities are computed using Bayes theorem, where a hidden variable per variant can be calculated using knowledge of all observed variables [41].

Unfortunately, it is questionable if new variant detection can be done efficiently via a knowledge-based system. This is due to the fact that system is biased by the expert towards DP implementations known to him. However, as the proposed system is more flexible than a classical rule-based approach due to the usage of MPs and probabilistic reasoning, it should be able to better detect new variants that share MPs with known variants.

E. *Metamodel Bayesian Network*

The output of both the ML and MP DPD subsystems is integrated into the Bayesian network HyDPD-B as shown in Figure 7.

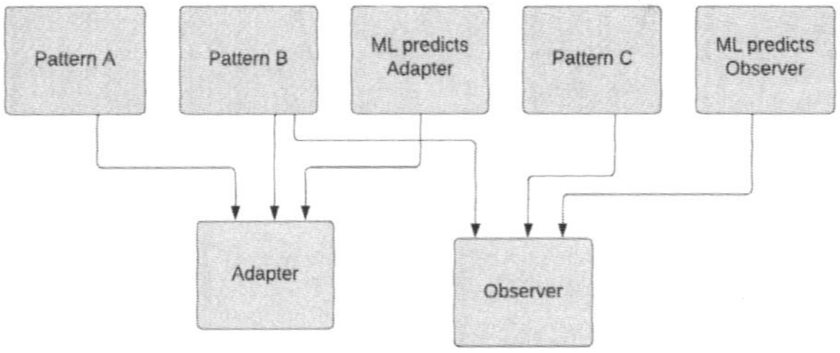

Figure 7. Example HyDPD-B Bayesian metamodel integrating ML and MP inputs.

To enable this, the result of the ML subsystem has to be interpreted as an observed variable in a network. Unfortunately, the system only allows binary variables, while the output cardinality of the ML system is dependent on the number of considered DPs. To avoid this, one can formulate variables in the following way: a binary ML variable is associated with a model, as well as a specific DP. If the prediction of the model equals the specified DP, the variable evaluates to true.

IV. REALIZATION

Software used to realize the solution included: sklearn, numpy, pandas, matplotlib, seaborn, NetworkX, Pomegranate for the Bayesian network, Flask, Jupyter notebooks, Docker, Docker Compose, Neo4j, MongDB, ReactJS, and JointJS.

The core of the backend was realized in Python as a library, which contains all modules necessary to create the Bayesian networks and ML models for DPD.

A. Web-based User Interface (UI)

The UI is implemented using a web-based Single Page Application (SPA). While Jupyter Notebooks can suffice as a frontend for research purposes, they could be inconvenient for software developers, who would have to code in Python and know the API of the library. In contrast, our frontend provides functionalities to create Bayesian networks in a graphical way and train them via graphical UI elements as seen in Figure 8. Here the network can be created (Step 1) and the decision-making process of the model visualized. After training the model (Step 2), data can be loaded (Step 3) and a prediction run (Step 3).

Furthermore, a UI is provided to create, edit, and delete DPRL rules and show the JSON and CQL as seen in Figure 9.

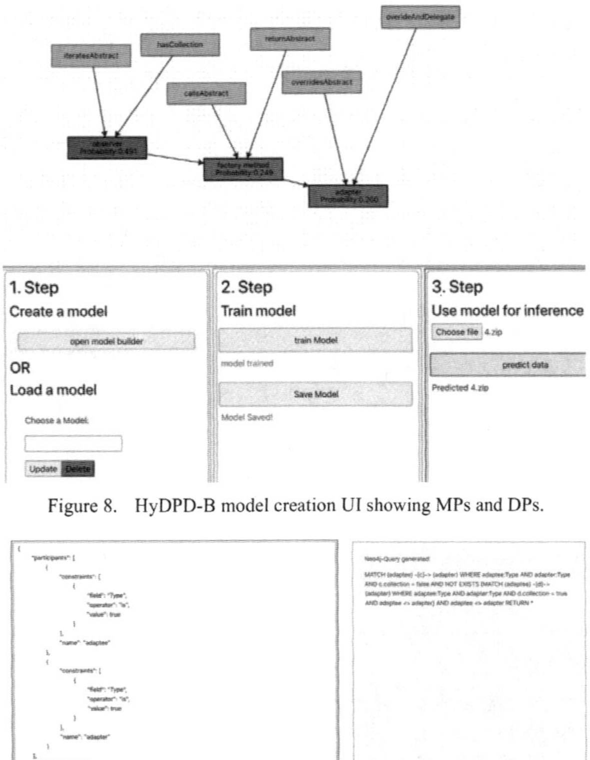

Figure 8. HyDPD-B model creation UI showing MPs and DPs.

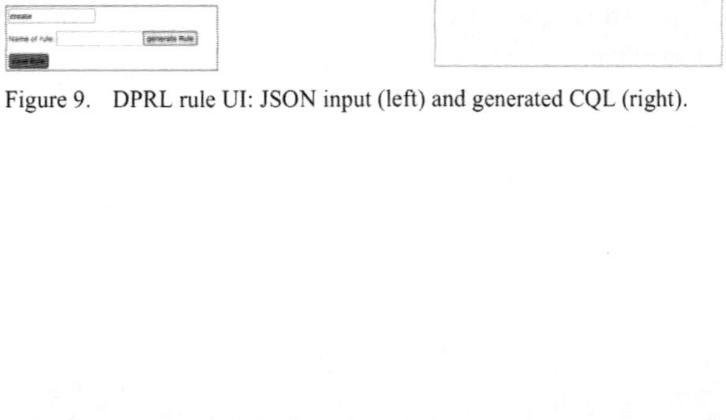

Figure 9. DPRL rule UI: JSON input (left) and generated CQL (right).

B. Micro Pattern (MP) Catalog (MPC) Realization

1) Override Abstract: Derived from the Adapter Cypher query, it is a general MP describing a method that overrides an abstract method.

```
MATCH (adapter:Type)-[:INHERITS*1]->(target:Abstract:Type),
(adapter)-[:HAS]->(adapter_op:Operation),
(target)-[:HAS]->(target_op:Operation),
(adapter_op)-[:OVERRIDES]->(target_op) RETURN *
```

2) Iterate: This MP simply queries if a participant iterates over another participant, and commonly occurs in the Observer DP.

```
MATCH (a)-[:ITERATES]-(b) RETURN *
```

3) Abstract Function Call: This MP describes a call of an abstract function. Such calls occur in the Observer DP, more precisely when a notify function calls an update function.

```
MATCH (c_notify)-[:CALLS]->(update:Operation:Abstract) RETURN *
```

4) Has Collection: This MP queries if there is a participant that owns a collection of abstract types. This MP is frequent in the Observer DP.

```
MATCH
(c_subject:Type)-[:HAS {collection: true}]->(observer:Type:Abstract)
RETURN *
```

5) Override & Delegate: This MP describes a function overriding a function and calling another function, and was extracted from the Adapter DP.

```
MATCH (adapter_op)-[:OVERRIDES]->(target_op),
(adaptee)-[:HAS]->(adaptee_op:Operation),
(adapter_op)-[:CALLS]->(adaptee_op)
WHERE adaptee_op <> target_op RETURN *
```

6) Double Inheritance: This MP describes double inheritance, used in Adapter DP instances. If the Adapter pattern is implemented in the static, class-based way, the Adapter participant should in some way inherit from the adaptee as well as from the target.

```
MATCH (c)<-[:INHERITS]-(a)-[:INHERITS]->(b) RETURN *
```

7) Overriding Method Creates: This MP describes a method that overrides another method and creates an object. It was extracted from the Factory Method DP.

```
MATCH (creator_method)<-[:OVERRIDES]-(method)-[:CREATES]->(object) RETURN *
```

8) Returns Abstract: This MP matches methods that return an abstract class, and was extracted from the Factory Method DP.

```
MATCH
(concrete_create_op)-[:RETURNS]->(abstractproduct)<-[:INHERITS]-(concreteproduct)
RETURN *
```

C. MP Bayesian Network Realization

Each DP is connected to relevant MPs. In HyDPD-GA, DPs were distinguished in a query by excluding certain features that would implicate another DP, as certain patterns exhibit a high degree of overlap in structure and behavior. Unfortunately, such exclusions make DPD more complex. To resolve this, output variables of frequently confused DPs are interconnected with each other. The resulting network can be seen in Figure 10.

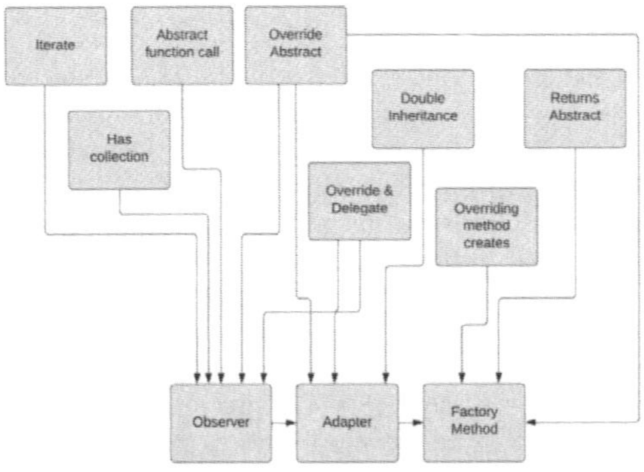

Figure 10. Bayesian network architecture for 3 DPs utilizing 8 MPs.

D. Metamodel Bayesian Network Realization

1) Leaf variables: A leaf variable corresponds to the result of a MP match against the graph. Thus, the value of a leaf variable can be calculated deterministically at inference time. The variable requires a binary output (False or True). While it is feasible to use continuous variables, it would make the system less comprehensible and interpretable.

2) Hidden variables: Hidden variables cannot be directly detected like measurable variables. The output of a hidden variable depends solely on the input of parent variables. To allow a model to learn values of hidden variables from data, the data must be annotated accordingly. A hidden variable can be expressed as a conditional table, which maps each combination of parent variables to a probability value (e.g., T/T->0.8, T/F->0.5, F/F->0.2). In practice, such annotations might indicate the specific pattern variants or participants involved in the pattern. For DPD, hidden variables may correspond to following entities: *DP probability* that code is instance of a specific DP; *DP variant probability* that code is instance of a specific pattern variant; *DP participant probability* that code contains a DP participant; and *MP pattern probability* that code contains a specific MP.

3) Query variables: We are not necessarily interested in all available hidden variables. For DPD, we are specifically interested in the probabilities given to DPs. Consequently, in most use cases, query variables correspond to DPs.

V. EVALUATION

For the evaluation of HyDPD-B, we used the same dataset as used for HyDPD [8] Due to resource constraints, we focused on three common patterns from each of the major pattern categories: from the creational patterns, Factory Method; from the structural category, Adapter; and from the behavioral patterns, Observer. For this, 25 unique single-pattern code projects per pattern small single-pattern code projects from public repositories, 49 in Java and 26 in C# (mostly from github and the rest from pattern book sites, MSDN, etc.). They were manually verified and labeled as examples of a specific pattern. srcML supports these two popular programming languages and the mix of languages demonstrates programming language independence. For HyDPD-ML training data, we applied hold-out validation, selecting 60 of 75 projects (20 per pattern category). with between 60-75% of the code projects being in Java and the remainder in C#. To create the ML test dataset, the remaining 15 projects (5 per pattern, 3 in Java and 2 in C#) were duplicated and their signal words removed or renamed, resulting in 30 test projects (10 per pattern).

A. HyDPD-MP (Bayesian Network without ML)

1) Performance: Repeated cross-validation was used to test the performance of the rule-based system. Simple cross-validation showed high variance leading to inaccurate results. Thus, 5-fold cross-validation with 5 repetitions was used, resulting in 25 runs and a more accurate estimation. The mean was 0.917 and the median 0.944, with the distribution skewed due to outliers. Hence, accuracy of HyDPD-MP for these 3 DPs using an 8 MPs ruleset is on par with the 0.91 accuracy of our previous HyDPD-GA system [8].

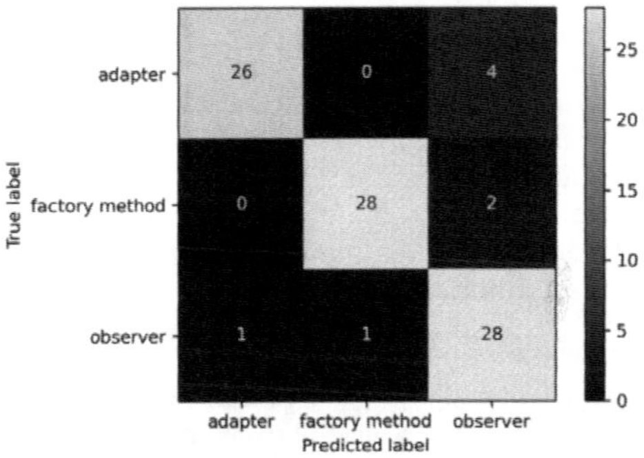

Figure 11. Confusion matrix for HyDPD-MP.

2) Confusion matrix: To determine if the results vary across different DPs, a confusion matrix was created using 5-fold cross-validation as shown in Figure 11. Adapter performed worse than the other patterns and was more frequently misclassified as Observer, an indication of some similarity between the DPs. Apparently, the ruleset does not properly distinguish Adapter from Observer. This result could likely be improved via better fitting Adapter rules, or via more restrictive Observer rules.

B. HyDPD-ML Performance

To evaluate HyDPD-ML, cross-validation was used, with the confusion matrix shown in Figure 12. Classification errors exist across all classes, yet no clear bias can be detected. Observer had the worst recall rate with 0.90, Adapter 0.93, and Factory Method with 0.97.

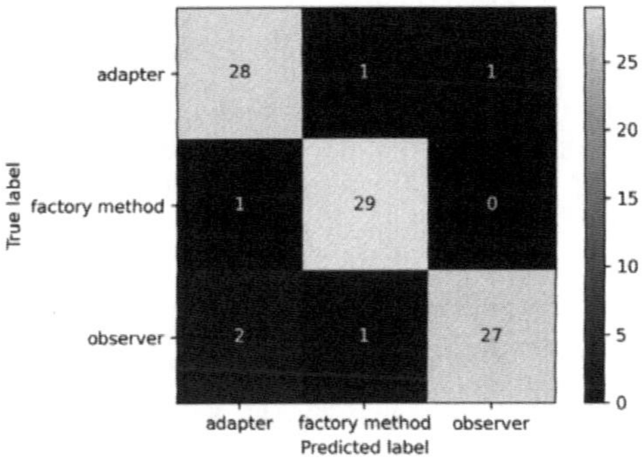

Figure 12. Confusion matrix for HyDPD-ML.

C. HyDPD-ML Variant detection

DP variant datasets are difficult to acquire since most example DP projects intend to exemplify the reference DP. To evaluate HyDPD-ML for unknown pattern variant detection, DP variations were removed from the training dataset and moved to a test set containing only variations.

TABLE I. DP VARIANT PREDICTIONS

DP Variant	Predicted DP
Adapter 2	Adapter
Adapter 4	Adapter
Adapter 7	Adapter
Factory Method 17cs	Adapter
Factory Method 2	Factory Method
Observer 12	Observer
Observer 13cs	Factory Method
Observer 18cs	Observer

As seen in Table I, 6 out of 8 variations were correctly classified. The recall rate for Adapter was 1.0, Observer was 0.66, and Factory Method was 0.5. On average, accuracy is 0.75. While worse than the estimated general accuracy of 0.95, it shows HyDPD-ML is somewhat capable of classifying unknown pattern variations.

D. Combined HyDPD-B

To evaluate the performance of the combined HyDPD-B, repeated cross-validation was performed. HyDBD-ML was trained on the same dataset as the Bayesian network. HyDBD-B (HyDPD-MP and HyDPD-ML combined) reached an accuracy of 0.944 as seen in Figure 13.

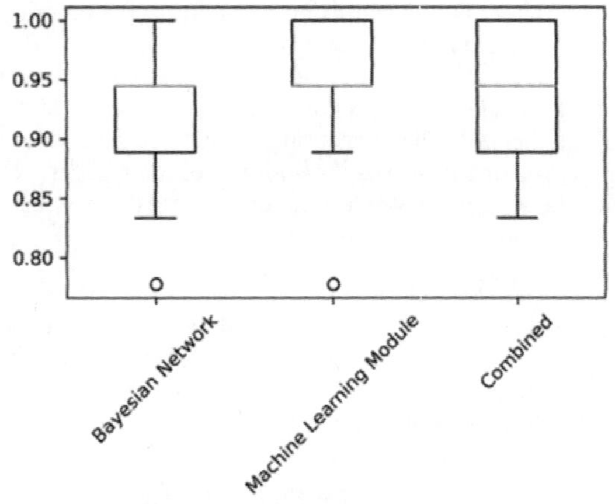

Figure 13. Performance comparison.

While the Bayesian network is quite performant, it outperforms HyDPD-GA only by a very small margin. HyDPD-ML performs better than the Bayesian network. The rule set could be improved, as there is lot of potential gain by introducing more fitting rules. This was not performed in the context of our current work as this could lead to a risk of manual overfitting of the available dataset. Combining the Bayesian network with the ML leads to a performance almost on the same level as ML itself. However, the new solution HyDPD-B is now more flexible for incorporating expert knowledge to continually improve and refine results.

VI. CONCLUSION

This paper described our hybrid DPD solution concept HyDPD-B, which uses a Bayesian network to integrate a graph-based expert rule system using micropattern detection (HyDPD-MP) with a ML system (HyDPD-ML) using graph embeddings. Via a Bayesian network, inexact DP matching via probabilistic reasoning is supported with a finer rule definition granularity via micropatterns. The Bayesian network provides a flexible framework for probabilistic reasoning that is comprehensible and interpretable for humans. Our simple DP rule language (DPRL) was introduced to integrate developers as experts in defining DP and MP rules. Whereas HyDPD-MP can support DP localization and known variant detection via MPs, HyDPD-ML only indicates a DP is contained somewhere in the dataset. HyDPD-ML can detect unknown DP variations, yet with less accuracy than standard DPs.

This could be improved with larger DP training and variant test datasets, but these remain challenging to acquire. Since the Bayesian system is dependent on manual knowledge engineering, future work will investigate its viability and scalability regarding DP variant detection. Future work includes expansion across all GoF DPs, measurements against benchmark pattern repositories and open source projects, and a comprehensive empirical industrial case study.

ACKNOWLEDGMENT

The authors would like to thank Victor Gouromichos for his assistance with the implementation and data preparation.

REFERENCES

[1] R. Minelli, A.Mocci, and M. Lanza, "I know what you did last summer: an investigation of how developers spend their time," In: Proceedings of the 2015 IEEE 23rd International Conference on Program Comprehension, pp. 25-35. IEEE Press, 2015.

[2] M. J. Pacione, M. Roper, and M. Wood, "A novel software visualisation model to support software comprehension," In: Proc.. 11th Working Conference on Reverse Engineering, pp. 70-79. IEEE, 2004.

[3] E. Gamma, Design Patterns: Elements of Reusable Object-Oriented Software. Pearson Education India, 1995.

[4] F. Buschmann, R. Meunier, H. Rohnert, P. Sommerlad, and M. Stal, Pattern-Oriented Software Architecture: A System of Patterns, Vol. 1. John Wiley & Sons, 2008.

[5] M.G. Al-Obeidallah, M. Petridis, and S. Kapetanakis, "A survey on design pattern detection approaches," International Journal of Software Engineering (IJSE), 7(3), pp.41-59, 2016.

[6] H. Yarahmadi and S. M. H. Hasheminejad, "Design pattern detection approaches: A systematic review of the literature," Artificial Intelligence Review, 53, pp. 5789-5846, 2020.

[7] R. Oberhauser, "A Machine Learning Approach Towards Automatic Software Design Pattern Recognition Across Multiple Programming Languages," Proc. of the Fifteenth International Conference on Software Engineering Advances (ICSEA 2020), pp. 27-32, IARIA XPS Press, 2020.

[8] R. Oberhauser, "A Hybrid Graph Analysis and Machine Learning Approach Towards Automatic Software Design Pattern Recognition Across Multiple Programming Languages, " International Journal on Advances in Software, vol. 15, no. 1 & 2, year 2022, pp. 28-42. ISSN: 1942-2628.

[9] D. Yu, Y. Zhang, and Z. Chen, "A comprehensive approach to the recovery of design pattern instances based on sub-patterns

and method signatures," Journal of Systems and Software, vol. 103, pp. 1-16, 2015.

[10] B. Mayvan and A. Rasoolzadegan, "Design pattern detection based on the graph theory," Knowledge-Based Systems, vol. 120, pp. 211-225, 2017.

[11] M. L. Bernardi, M. Cimitile, and G. Di Lucca, "Design pattern detection using a DSL-driven graph matching approach," Journal of Software: Evolution and Process, 26(12), pp.1233-1266, 2014.

[12] M. Oruc, F. Akal, and H. Sever, "Detecting design patterns in object-oriented design models by using a graph mining approach," 4th International Conference in Software Engineering Research and Innovation (CONISOFT 2016), pp. 115-121, IEEE, 2016.

[13] A. Pande, M. Gupta, and A. K. Tripathi, "A new approach for detecting design patterns by graph decomposition and graph isomorphism," International Conference on Contemporary Computing, pp. 108-119, Springer, Berlin, Heidelberg, 2010.

[14] P. Pradhan, A. K. Dwivedi, and S. K. Rath, "Detection of design pattern using graph isomorphism and normalized cross correlation," Eighth International Conf. on Contemporary Computing (IC3 2015), pp. 208-213, IEEE, 2015.

[15] S. Alhusain, S. Coupland, R. John, and M. Kavanagh, "Design pattern recognition by using adaptive neuro fuzzy inference system," 2013 IEEE 25th International Conference on Tools with Artificial Intelligence, pp. 581-587, IEEE, 2013.

[16] M. Zanoni, F. A. Fontana, and F. Stella, "On applying machine learning techniques for design pattern detection," J. of Systems & Software, vol. 103, no. C, pp. 102-117, 2015.

[17] L. Galli, P. Lanzi, and D. Loiacono, "Applying data mining to extract design patterns from Unreal Tournament levels," Computational Intelligence and Games. pp. 1-8, IEEE, 2014.

[18] R. Ferenc, A. Beszedes, L. Fulop, and J. Lele, "Design pattern mining enhanced by machine learning," 21st IEEE In"l Conf. on Softw. Maintenance (ICS"05), IEEE, pp. 295-304, 2005.

[19] S. Uchiyama, A. Kubo, H. Washizaki, and Y. Fukazawa, "Detecting design patterns in object-oriented program source code by using metrics and machine learning," Journal of Software Engineering and Applications, 7(12), pp. 983-998, 2014.

[20] A. K., Dwivedi, A. Tirkey, and S. K. Rath, "Software design pattern mining using classification-based techniques," Frontiers of Computer Science, 12(5), pp. 908-922, 2018.

[21] H. Thaller, L. Linsbauer, and A. Egyed, "Feature maps: A comprehensible software representation for design pattern detection," IEEE 26th international conference on software analysis, evolution and reengineering (SANER 2019), pp. 207-217, IEEE, 2019.

[22] A. Chihada, S. Jalili, S. M. H. Hasheminejad, and M. H. Zangooei, "Source code and design conformance, design pattern detection from source code by classification approach," Applied Soft Computing, 26, pp. 357-367, 2015.

[23] Y. Wang, H. Guo, H. Liu, and A. Abraham, "A fuzzy matching approach for design pattern mining," J. Intelligent & Fuzzy Systems, vol. 23, nos. 2-3, pp. 53-60, 2012.

[24] A. Alnusair, T. Zhao, and G. Yan, "Rule-based detection of design patterns in program code," Int'l J. on Software Tools for Technology Transfer, vol. 16, no. 3, pp. 315-334, 2014.

[25] M. Lebon and V. Tzerpos, "Fine-grained design pattern detection," IEEE 36th Annual Computer Software and Applications Conference, IEEE, pp. 267-272, 2012.

[26] I. Issaoui, N. Bouassida, and H. Ben-Abdallah, "Using metric-based filtering to improve design pattern detection approaches," Innovations in Systems and Software Engineering, vol. 11, no. 1, pp. 39-53, 2015.

[27] A. K., Dwivedi, A. Tirkey, and S. K. Rath, "Software design pattern mining using classification-based techniques," Frontiers of Computer Science, 12(5), pp. 908-922, 2018.

[28] F. A. Fontana, S. Maggioni, and C. Raibulet, "Understanding the relevance of micro-structures for design patterns detection," Journal of Systems and Software, vol. 84, no. 12, pp. 2334-2347, 2011

[29] I. Issaoui, N. Bouassida, and H. Ben-Abdallah, "Using metric-based filtering to improve design pattern detection approaches. Innovations in Systems and Software Engineering," vol. 11, no. 1, pp. 39-53, 2015.

[30] J. Dong, Y. Zhao, and Y. Sun, "A matrix-based approach to recovering design patterns," IEEE Transactions on Systems, Man, and Cybernetics-Part A: Systems and Humans, vol. 39, no. 6, pp. 1271-1282, 2009.

[31] K. Tu, J. Li, D. Towsley, D. Braines, and L. D. Turner, "Gl2vec: Learning feature representation using graphlets for directed networks," in Proceedings of the 2019 IEEE/ACM international conference on advances in social networks analysis and mining, 2019, pp. 216–221.

[32] S. Sang et al., "Gredel: A knowledge graph embedding based method for drug discovery from biomedical literatures," IEEE Access, vol. 7, pp. 8404–8415, 2018.

[33] J. Singh, S. R. Chowdhuri, G. Bethany, and M. Gupta, "Detecting design patterns: a hybrid approach based on graph matching and static analysis," Information Technology and Management, 23(3), pp. 139-150, 2022.

[34] R. Barbudo, A. Ramírez, F. Servant, and J. R. Romero, "GEML: A grammar-based evolutionary machine learning approach for design-pattern detection," Journal of Systems and Software, 175, p. 110919, 2021.

[35] M. Kouli and A. Rasoolzadegan, "A Feature-Based Method for Detecting Design Patterns in Source Code," Symmetry, 14(7), p. 1491, 2022.

[36] M. Collard, M. Decker, and J. Maletic, "Lightweight transformation and fact extraction with the srcML toolkit," IEEE 11th international working conference on source code analysis and manipulation, IEEE, 2011, pp. 173-184.

[37] N. Francis et al., "Cypher: An evolving query language for property graphs," Proc. 2018 International Conference on Management of Data, pp. 1433-1445, 2018.

[38] S. Khwaja and M. Alshayeb, "Survey on software design-pattern specification languages," ACM Computing Surveys (CSUR), vol. 49, no. 1, pp. 1–35, 2016.

[39] J. Smith and D. Stotts, "An elemental design pattern catalog," Technical Report TR-02–040, 2002.

[40] A. Dempster, F. Petitjean, and G. I. Webb, "Rocket: Exceptionally fast and accurate time series classification using random convolutional kernels," Data Mining and Knowledge Discovery, vol. 34, no. 5, pp. 1454–1495, 2020.

[41] K. P. Murphy, Machine Learning: A Probabilistic Perspective. MIT press, 2012.

International Academy, Research,
and Industry Association (IARIA)
412 Derby Way
Wilmington, DE 19810

ISBN 978-1-7138-8120-9

CURRAN ASSOCIATES INC.
proceedings.com

International Conference on Modern Systems Engineering Solutions (MODERN SYSTEMS 2022)

Held at SocSys 2022

Nice, France
24-28 July 2022